Breakthrough Swimming

Cecil Colwin

Human Kinetics

Library of Congress Cataloging-in-Publication Data

Colwin, Cecil.
    Breakthrough swimming / Cecil M. Colwin.
        p. cm.
    Includes bibliographical references and index.
    ISBN 0-7360-3777-2
    1. Swimming--History. I. Title.

    GV836.4 .C65 2002
    797.2'1'09--dc21

                                                                                2001039994

ISBN-10: 0-7360-3777-2
ISBN-13: 978-0-7360-3777-8

Portions of this work are based on the book *Swimming Into the 21st Century* (1992), authored by Cecil M. Colwin and published by Human Kinetics.

Developmental Editor: Cynthia McEntire; **Assistant Editor:** Scott Hawkins; **Copyeditor:** John Wentworth; **Proofreader:** Erin Cler; **Indexer:** Margaret Colwin; **Permission Manager:** Toni Harte; **Graphic Designer:** Nancy Rasmus; **Graphic Artist:** Francine Hamerski; **Photo Manager:** Clark Brooks; **Cover Designer:** Robert Reuther; **Photographer (cover):** Darren England/ALLSPORT; **Photographers (interior):** See credit notices on page ix; **Art Manager:** Craig Newsom; **Line Drawings:** Cecil M. Colwin; figure 6.1 by Robert B. Colwin; **Mac Illustrations:** Interactive Composition Corporation; **Printer:** Versa Press

Human Kinetics books are available at special discounts for bulk purchase. Special editions or book excerpts can also be created to specification. For details, contact the Special Sales Manager at Human Kinetics.

Printed in the United States of America   10   9   8

Human Kinetics
Web site: www.HumanKinetics.com

United States: Human Kinetics
P.O. Box 5076
Champaign, IL 61825-5076
800-747-4457
e-mail: humank@hkusa.com

Canada: Human Kinetics
475 Devonshire Road, Unit 100
Windsor, ON N8Y 2L5
800-465-7301 (in Canada only)
e-mail: info@hkcanada.com

Europe: Human Kinetics
107 Bradford Road
Stanningley
Leeds LS28 6AT, United Kingdom
+44 (0)113 255 5665
e-mail: hk@hkeurope.com

Australia: Human Kinetics
57A Price Avenue
Lower Mitcham, South Australia 5062
08 8372 0999
e-mail: info@hkaustralia.com

New Zealand: Human Kinetics
Division of Sports Distributors NZ Ltd.
P.O. Box 300 226 Albany
North Shore City, Auckland
0064 9 448 1207
e-mail: info@humankinetics.co.nz

To Margaret, my wife and best friend these many years

Contents

Acknowledgments

This book was made possible through the direct and indirect help of a great number of people. I wish to express my most sincere thanks to all of them, although their number precludes my naming more than a few.

Colleagues and Contributors

Edward Atraghji, formerly of the Canadian Aeronautical Establishment, taught me about flow visualization and provided helpful suggestions on the treatment of the fluid dynamic content of this text.

Dr. David Pyne, Physiologist, Australian Institute of Sport, contributed chapter 9 on the physiology of swimming training and shared his unique experience in day-to-day practical work with some of the world's greatest swimmers.

William "Buck" Dawson wrote on the history of American swimming in chapter 11.

Nort Thornton, head swimming coach of the University of California at Berkeley, gave permission to use material from his excellent article, "A Few Thoughts on Training," from the ASCA magazine.

Thomas Kirk Cureton gave permission to use materials from chapter 4 of *How to Teach Swimming and Diving* (1934), published by Association Press, New York, and to use the chapter footnotes as a framework in compiling my chronological bibliography of the history of the swimming strokes.

Resource Specialists

I am particularly grateful to those who guided me to valuable sources of information that I otherwise would have missed.

Liana Van der Bellen, chief of the Rare Books Division, National Library of Canada, gave me invaluable assistance in researching the works of Thevenot (1620–1692) and Olaus Magnus (1490–1557) and even placed before me original books by the two, both in pristine condition.

Dave Kelly of the Library of Congress in Washington, D.C. and Harry McKown, reference associate of the North Carolina Collection, Wilson Library, the University of North Carolina at Chapel Hill, went to great lengths to provide references on the early development of American swimming. I express my deepest appreciation to both for their courtesy and cooperation.

Sasha Orivi of the State Library of Victoria in Melbourne conducted a search for, and provided the first detailed account of, the first swimming race in Australia.

Mardyth Hewitt of the National Library of Canada and Michelle Robichaud of the Library of Parliament provided expertise in locating William Byrd's diary.

Robert Schleihauf granted permission to prepare and publish drawings adapted from illustrations in "Swimming Propulsion: A Hydrodynamic Analysis" (1977).

Cornell University Press, Ithaca, New York, gave permission to use the extract from 1st century Roman poet, Manilius, as contained in *Sport in Greece and Rome*.

Dr. Kare I. Birkeland and Dr. Peter Hemmersbach, both of the Hormone Laboratory, Aker Hospital, Oslo, Norway, and the publishers of *Sports Medicine*, Adle International, gave permission to use information from their article "The Future of Doping Control in Athletes."

Dr. Brent Rushall gave permission to reprint the list of positive drug tests by swimmer by country as it appeared in *Swimming's Hall of Shame* published by Sports Science Associates.

Karin Helmstaedt gave permission to reprint from her coverage of the German drug trials as reported in *Swimnews*, July 2000, and also to *Swimnews* for permission to reprint this article.

Professor Steven Vogel gave permission to reprint from his book *Cat's Paws and Catapults.*

John Leonard, executive director of the American Swimming Coaches Association, gave permission to adapt from his articles on coaching certification and his report on the FINA Conference on Doping Control, Hong Kong, March 2000.

Betty Armbruster gave permission to reprint from the work of her late father, David A. Armbruster, *Competitive Swimming and Diving* (1942), four sets of sequence drawings (namely of the freestyle stroke, backstroke, breaststroke-butterfly, and butterfly-breaststroke).

Dr. Phillip Whitten, editor in chief of Sports Publications, Inc., gave permission to reprint from "A Century of Change," an article written by the author that originally appeared in *Swimming World*, December 1999, as well as the ranking lists of the top male and female swimmers of the 20th century.

N. J. Thierry, editor and publisher of *Swimnews* magazine and secretary of the International Swimming Statisticians' Association, gave general permission to use extracts from *Swimnews* and prepared the graphs of progression of long-course and short-course world records on pages 195 and 196.

Fred Wilt, Olympic runner, Sullivan Award winner, and acknowledged authority on track training, kindly reviewed the information about the influence of track training on swimming and checked it for accuracy.

Gilmore Reproductions of 61 Queen Street, Ottawa, provided photocopying services and the use of advanced technologies in making copies of text and artwork. Their help and kindness in the preparation of three books over the years have been invaluable.

I am grateful to Colin Trewavas, Municipal Research and Merseyside Records Office, Liverpool, England, for his courtesy and kindness in providing access to records and photographs of milestones in the history of Liverpool's bath and washhouses, which were among the first pools built in England.

Whatever else a book may be, it is ultimately an offering to its potential readers, and it must be presented to them in a form that is accessible and attractive. A vast symbolic distance often separates the head of an author from the eyes of a reader, and those who seek to bridge that gulf, or at least to narrow it, bear a weighty responsibility. It can only succeed in the hands of men and women who revere books and their making. Of these there are greater and lesser, which is why an author published under the imprimatur and imprint of Human Kinetics must never forget his good fortune. In this regard, I express my deep appreciation to my publisher, Rainer Martens; acquisitions editor, Ted Miller; and developmental editor, Cynthia McEntire, whose advice and expertise were invaluable. I also appreciate very much the advice of art director Craig Newsom and the expert efforts of sales director Charles Walters and marketing manager Kelley Halliburton. Thanks are extended to assistant editor Scott Hawkins who ensured the book's smooth progress through the final production stages.

Last, but by no means least, I owe a special debt of gratitude to my wife, Margaret, for her hard work and assistance in preparing the final draft of this book. Her encouragement, wise counsel, patience, and untiring efforts eased the task.

Credits

Photos

Photo of Janet Evans on page 3 © Rob Tringali Jr./ SportsChrome USA.

Photo of Lenny Krayzelburg on page 33 © Bongarts/ SportsChrome USA.

Photo of Krisztina Egerszegi on page 49 © Bongarts/ SportsChrome USA.

Photo of Kristy Kowal on page 75 © Michael Zito/ SportsChrome USA.

Photo of Lenny Krayzelburg on page 91 © Michael Zito/SportsChrome USA.

Photo of Jenny Thompson on page 107 © Rob Tringali Jr./SportsChrome USA.

Photo of Ashley Chandler on page 123 © Rob Tringali Jr./SportsChrome USA.

Photo of Yana Klochkova on page 137 © Marco Chiesa.

Photo of Amy Van Dyken on page 151 © Rob Tringali Jr./SportsChrome USA.

Photo on page 156 © Cecil Colwin.

Photo of Alexander Popov on page 167 © Bongarts/ SportsChrome USA.

Photo of Mark Spitz on page 185 © Gjuljano Bevilacqua/SportsChrome USA.

Photo on page 207 © Tony Demin/International Stock.

Photo of Ian Thorpe on page 217 © Marco Chiesa.

Figures

Figure 9.1 Reprinted, by permission, from B.E. Counsilman and J.E. Counsilman, 1991, "The residual effects of training" *Journal of Swimming Research* 7:5-12.

Figure 10.2 from "Constructing workouts with energy system considerations" by E.W. Maglischo in *American Swimming Coaches Association World Clinic Yearbook 1985* (62) by T. Welsh (ed.), 1985, Fort Lauderdale, FL: American Swimming Coaches Association. Reprinted by permission of American Swimming Coaches Association and E.W. Maglischo.

Figure 10.3 Reprinted, by permission, from T.O. Bompa, 1985, *Theory and methodology of training* (Dubuque, IA: Kendall/Hunt).

Figure 10.4 Reprinted, by permission, from T.O. Bompa, 1985, *Theory and methodology of training* (Dubuque, IA: Kendall/Hunt).

Tables

Table 10.1 Reprinted, by permission, from J.E. Counsilman, 1975, "Hypoxic and other methods of training evaluated" *Swimming Technique* 12(1).

Table 10.2 Reprinted, by permission, from J.E. Counsilman, 1975, "Hypoxic and other methods of training evaluated" *Swimming Technique* 12(1).

Table 10.3 Adapted, by permission, from T. Absaliamov, 1984, "Controlling the training of top level swimmers" in *How to develop Olympic level swimmers* edited by J.L. Cramer (Finland: International Sports Media) **and** adapted, by permission, from D.B. Pyne and R.D. Telford, 1988, "Classification of training sessions" *Excel* 5(2).

Introduction

This book is about the evolution of competitive swimming in all its major disciplines, from its birth in early 19th-century England to the present era.

Almost every era of competitive swimming brought new ideas and breakthrough swimmers, who with scant regard for the record books, reached undreamed of heights. But never have there been such spectacular breakthroughs as those seen at the 2000 Sydney Olympic Games and the 2001 World Championships in Fukuoka.

Breakthrough Swimming focusses on the methods and the innovative thinking behind the success of these modern swimming giants who have literally destroyed seemingly unassailable marks, and brought the sport to a new high level of performance.

Portions of this book are based on my earlier work, *Swimming Into the 21st Century* which was published in 1992, after six years of preparation, but I could not have foreseen a need so soon for an expanded and almost completely re-written edition. The tumultuous events of the last decade of the 20th century dictated otherwise. Without doubt, no other period in the history of swimming has presented greater challenge or change.

The so-called velvet revolutions of the late 1980s that overturned Communism and eventually the Soviet Empire had an enormous impact on every aspect of modern life, including sport. The breakup of the Soviet Union saw several new independent states join the ranks of FINA (the international swimming federation), with a resultant increase in the number of swimmers competing in major international meets such as the Olympics and the World Championships.

With the reunification of Germany on October 2, 1990, literally thousands of East German sport administrators, coaches, and sport scientists suddenly became unemployed. It is unknown to what extent they became part of the new Germany, although some of their coaches found employment in other parts of the world. What they contributed to swimming in other countries is unknown, but at least one of their number spent some time in China, conducting clinics in that country. The appearance of performance-enhancing drugs in Chinese swimming seemed to have coincided with the fall of the East German regime.

It is rare that one is given the chance to tackle a job a second time, and this carefully researched new edition is but a modest attempt to bring past, present, and future into unison. However, we should not view the evolution of competitive swimming as a continuing linear process because the pioneers of the sport proceeded down many dead ends and also frequently failed to develop potentially valuable ideas. The gold was there but often thrown away to be retrieved by others years later.

The process of change consisted of long periods of normal development in which there were few deviations from the paradigms of existing ideas. Then would follow a shorter period of pronounced change, as rival ideas fought to take the place of a dominant framework that was beginning to decay through lack of progress.

The first part of the book introduces the reader to the ingenuity of the great coach-educators and how their restless inventiveness and persistence gradually built the technical foundations of a great sport. The evolution of the swimming strokes is described and illustrated in detail, from the start of formal competition in the early 1830s through the advanced techniques of today.

The 19th century saw experiments with different versions of the sidestroke, followed later by the trudgen stroke. Then, as if to celebrate the start of the 20th century, came an entirely new way of swimming, the surprisingly fast crawl stroke. But it took most of the 20th century for the crawl stroke to be improved and refined until it became the beautiful, smooth-flowing action exhibited by Pieter van den Hoogenband, Ian Thorpe, Alexander Popov, and Susie O'Neill at the 2000 Sydney Olympic Games, where they brought the understanding of crawl-stroke swimming into a new millenium and a new paradigm.

Over the years, during all the experimenting with new stroke mechanics, the question was often asked, "But what happens to the water when a swimmer exerts effort against it?" The answer is that we don't exactly know, but it seems obvious that if swimming and swimmers are to continue to improve we will need to become far more adept at manipulating the reacting flow with ever increasing efficiency. Then we ask other questions: How much effort should a swimmer exert against the water? Do we apply more effort than necessary? Here again, we don't rightly know. Suffice it to say that the text breaks new ground in describing how by studying the flow reactions created by the swimming stroke, certain fluid dynamic principles can be used to understand, analyze, and improve stroke mechanics.

The discussion on the evolution of training methods commences with the methods used by the 19th-century pioneers then progresses through the 20th century to the state-of-the-art scientific training methods used by the world's best swimmers in preparing for the 2000 Olympic Games.

The doughty champions of Victorian England pursued training methods characterized by ignorance and superstition. The old style regimen of reducing a man to a living skeleton by physicking, purgings, sweatings, and bleedings, to build him up afresh was stupid as well as cruel.

At the beginning of the 20th century, track athletes were already experimenting with interval training, but this form of training wasn't adapted to competitive swimming until 50 years later in the mid-1950s. Before this time, swimmers were too preoccupied with perfecting techniques and had no idea of how much stress

the human body could tolerate. The watch-word was "train but do not strain!"

The chapters on training describe how, in the 1950s, Yale and U.S. Olympic coach Robert Kiphuth introduced a method called wind-sprints, which consisted of 50-meter sprints interspersed with one-minute rest periods. Later interval training methods used on the running track were successfully adapted to swimming by the Australians who combined them with Kiphuth's earlier model. Not surprisingly, they went on to win the majority of the swimming medals in the 1956 Olympics. In the 1960s, Dr. James Counsilman developed the first clear outline of how different work-to-rest ratios used in swimming training produced specific physiological effects. As a direct result of his emphasis on empirical research and useful application, this era saw one of the greatest forward surges in swimming history.

Included in the discussion on training methods is a brilliant contributing chapter by Dr. David Pyne, physiologist to the Australian Institute of Sport and to the successful Australian National Swimming Team. Dr. Pyne covers the physiology of modern swimming training and the preparation of swimming teams for top-flight international competition. In this state-of-the-art presentation, Dr. Pyne presents insightful views on future directions for the successful application of scientific training.

The last part of this book traces the history of competitive swimming, examines the current problems facing the sport, and looks ahead to future innovations. The colorful story of the growth of organized competitive swimming is covered in depth. This chapter spans the entire panorama of competitive swimming, from its start in 1837 as a professional sport to its reign as an amateur sport for the next 100 years and then its insidious return to professionalism in the late 20th century. The text describes the growth of international swimming and the birth of FINA as the international governing body of swimming, a development largely brought about by prominent British officials who based the FINA constitution on that of the Amateur Swimming Association of Great Britain.

The development of the great Australian tradition in swimming is covered in depth, beginning with the construction of the first swimming pool in the 1870s and continuing to the reorganization of their national swimming program in the late 20th century, which led to the notable successes of Australian swimmers at the Sydney Olympics. Following the Australians is an account of the outstanding record and great contribution to world swimming by the United States, the giant of world swimming in terms of technical knowledge, coaching experience, excellence, and a long roster of brilliant Olympic champions that continued to increase at the Sydney Olympics. The growth of the national program concept and the sudden and remarkable rise to supremacy by the Japanese swimmers in the 1930s is also covered.

The chapter on the doping plague in swimming discusses the so-called success of the former state-sponsored East German program, which was based on the illegal administration of performance-enhancing drugs to athletes under the charge of state officials, and the subsequent trials of the officials involved. There is also a detailed account of the current doping problem in Chinese swimming, whose athletes have tested positive far more frequently than those of other countries. In the past 30 years, the scourge of doping has gradually reached a crisis point where the survival of competitive swimming now lies in the balance. The most astute minds of our sport, almost without exception, agree on this point.

The last 10 years have seen the abandonment of the once holy grail of amateurism and the growing influence of large corporate sponsors, warmly welcomed by officialdom as partners in the sport. The availability of prize money and large endorsement fees tempt the use of performance-enhancing drugs, a problem that shows no sign of diminishing, despite attempts to fight it.

With these changes has come a growing disregard, in some quarters, for the integrity of the sport and the educational values inherent in hard work and honest effort, not to mention the thrill and challenge of fair competition. As swimming moves into the new millennium, it is clear to keen observers that the sport is in danger of losing its connection to the traditions and values on which it was built. Unfortunately, people who abhor these trends often feel powerless, inadequate, and drained in the face of the attendant subterfuge and dissimulation.

In many countries, faceless bureaucratic systems control all levels of sport, and politics has become almost a vocation within their national offices, a job for professional administrators and pragmatists rather than the idealists and innovators of the past. The centralization of power in national headquarters and national sport centers, to a large extent, leads to a denial of individuality.

Swimming needs enlightened and courageous leadership to help meet these internal transformations. Instead, the love of power and personal prestige has become a preoccupation for many, and the old boys' network remains a constituent part of the so-called Olympic family.

There exists also the anomaly of an ostensible amateur body conducting a professional sport. Many are convinced of the need for a revised FINA constitution that would reflect the changed nature of the sport, as well as address the need for a more equitable voting system that recognizes the contribution of FINA's founding nations and the generations of outstanding coaches whose knowledge and experience have led to so much progress.

By giving special attention to the connective tissue that binds each phase of the sport's development, it may still be possible to take the best from the past and add it to the present to make a better future. With renewed pride in the traditions of our sport, we may yet be able to tackle the future with confidence, purpose, and resolve.

PART I

Development of Stroke Fundamentals

Chapter 1

History of the Swimming Strokes

From the sparse descriptions on record, early attempts at swimming probably consisted of random arm and leg movements with no specific techniques; otherwise, we know little of the early history of human swimming. Before organized competitive swimming started in England, about 170 years ago, there was little need to develop methods beyond those that came naturally to each individual.

The technical development of swimming didn't start until the mid-19th century with the building of swimming pools, the invention of the stopwatch, and the beginning of competitive swimming as a formal sport.

The first competitive swimmers were more intent on developing good style rather than speed. Graceful and elegant movements, with a minimum of splashing, were considered the hallmarks of style by the early exponents of the sport. This was evident in 1844, when English swimmers saw the swimming methods of visiting North American Indians in London. Because the Indians' more advanced overarm strokes were characterized by wild splashing, their methods were dismissed by the English as unworthy of imitating.

Neither did the English know that across the broad expanses of the Pacific Ocean, the inhabitants of Polynesia and Melanesia had been swimming with overarm strokes for more than a thousand years. And along the coasts of South America, Africa, and India, versions of the trudgen stroke, another technique more advanced than those that existed in Western culture, had been swum naturally for time immemorial.

Swimming in the Ancient World

Archaeologists know that humans developed watercraft by 40,000 years ago, and so it's reasonable to assume people were swimming by that time (Nemecek 2000). Many of these early swimming activities seem to have been part of religious rituals, recreation, or military maneuvers.

Swimming is one of the oldest arts, if we are to form an opinion from the fact that no trace of its origin, discovery, invention or improvement is to be found in any of the ancient writings.

—William Wilson (1883)

The first human swimmers most likely lived by the sea or near warm rivers. Five thousand years ago humans learned to divert rivers such as the Nile, the Euphrates, and the Indus, and it's likely that people living in these regions were at home in the water and swam frequently.

In the ancient world, diverting rivers to protect city–states led to swimming for military purposes. Bas-reliefs housed in the British Museum show a river crossing by Assurnasir-pal, King of Assyria, and his army. When these reliefs were found in the ruins of the royal palace at Nimroud, students of swimming techniques were excited because here, at last, they expected to find evidence of swimming skills used in ancient times. Nineteenth-century observers thought the reliefs showed soldiers swimming either sidestroke or the trudgen stroke, while 20th-century observers concluded that the Assyrians were actually swimming the crawl stroke! And so, as always, conclusions are drawn from one's own vantage point.

The Baths of Caracalla and other baths built by the Romans were enormous, but the swimming tanks set aside for actual swimming were very small. Those at Pompeii were only 13 feet

Descriptions in Ancient Literature

A nobleman of the Middle Kingdom of Egypt (2160–1780 B.C.) proudly recorded that his children took swimming lessons with the king's children, but no mention is made of skills being taught (Cureton 1934).

A few references to swimming are found in the Old Testament, but they, too, do not elaborate on swimming skills possessed by ancient peoples. The following Biblical excerpts must rank among the earliest references to swimming: ". . . he that swimmeth, spreadeth forth his hands to swim" Isaiah 25:11 (approximately 760 B.C.) and ". . . a river that I could not pass over: for the waters were risen, waters to swim in, a river that could not be passed over . . ." Ezekiel 47:5. (Ezekiel was exiled to Babylon in 597 B.C.)

Cursory references to swimming have been made over the centuries by the Egyptians, Israelites, Accadians, Sumerians, Babylonians, Hittites, Greeks, Romans, and other ancient nations. Much has been made of the fact that the Romans were said to have considered no branch of education more important than swimming, but like the other accounts from ancient times, they left few descriptions of methods they used.

Translations from Greece and Rome speak of swimmers using alternating overarm motions, and it's possible that a type of overarm stroke may have been in common use long ago. But this must remain pure conjecture because, as literate as the ancient Greeks and Romans were, their writings give few descriptions of actual swimming techniques.

However, one rare and beautifully written passage was left to us by Manilius, a 1st-century Roman poet, who waxes lyrical on the pleasures of swimming:

> For just as the dolphin glides through the water on swift fins,
> now rising above the surface and now sinking to the depths,
> and piles up waves and sends them off in circles, just so will
> each person born under the sign of the Dolphin fly through
> the waves, raising one arm and then the other in slow arcs.

(Marcus Manilius (circa 14 A.D.), from *Astronomica*, an unfinished poem on astronomy and astrology.)

One can envision the scene 2,000 years ago: a balmy day, a buoyant sea, and a skilled swimmer performing, yes, a type of overarm stroke. Across the centuries, a fellow enthusiast conveys with words his love of the water and his fascination with swimming propulsion. His reference to dolphin swimming was prophetic in the extreme, as imitating the dolphin action is the most successful adaptation humans have made from nature to their own swimming propulsion. And he must have had sharp eyes, for he describes not only technique but even the reacting vortex flows in the water, an unusual observation even today.

wide, and Cicero complained that he needed a wider pool to avoid hurting his hands against the wall. However, the baths of Mohenjo-Dario in the Indus valley (in today's West Pakistan) were somewhat larger. They measured 39 feet long and 23 feet wide and were said to have been the birthplace of a form of synchronized swimming that served a religious function (Cottrell 1960).

In the Middle Ages, swimming became unpopular throughout Europe because people believed water helped spread plague and other common epidemics. When people did swim, they preferred a form of breaststroke that kept their faces out of the water. Not until the second half of the 19th century was prejudice against swimming largely overcome.

Swimming in the Western World

In 16th- and 17th-century Europe, the breaststroke was performed with the head held high and completely out of the water (Thevenot 1699). Instead of using a frog kick, propulsion was applied with the insteps and not the soles of the feet (Muths 1798).

Early in the 19th century, breaststroke swimmers adopted a frog kick in which the ankles were dorsi-flexed and propulsion developed by pressing the soles of the feet against the

water (Counsilman 1968). As the stroke technique developed, so did the drills used by swimmers, although some of these drills were strange (figure 1.1). Debate followed on whether using the soles of the feet in the frog kick yielded more propulsion than spreading the legs and then straightening them before closing in a tight wedge, such as the kick shown in figure 1.2 (Thomas 1904).

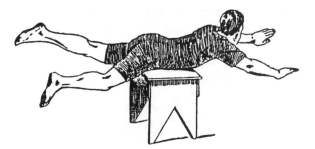

Figure 1.1 In the 19th century, breaststroke drills were weird and wonderful. From Dalton 1899.

Such discussions on the most efficient use of the legs in the breaststroke kick marked the beginning of technical thinking and a growing interest in improving propulsion. Understanding the positive effect that could be achieved by a slight change of technique was (and is) significant; this ability later was to prove an important characteristic of a capable coach.

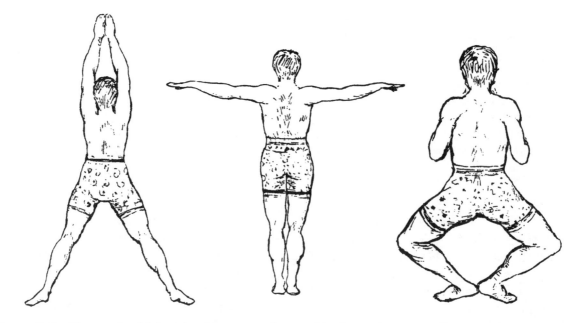

Figure 1.2 The wedge kick style of breaststroke used in the 19th century. From Wilson 1883.

Charles Steedman (1867) was probably the first to caution against drawing the knees forward under the body when swimming breaststroke (figure 1.3). He said that this negative or retarding action caused resistance and retarded the progress of the swimmer. He said that by "bending the knees laterally, rather than under the body the draught of the latter is decreased, or, in other words, the whole of the body remains nearer the surface of the water, and consequently the resistance to its progress is much less" (p. 93).

takes to a great extent account for the too often unsuccessful efforts made by those who wish to teach themselves." Wilson said that the major propulsion should be obtained from the leg kick because it is "easier to push the body forward than to pull it through or along. The legs are stronger than the arms, therefore it is economical to obtain all the power possible from the lower limbs" (p. 35). He added that learners tended to use the arms with all the power possible, and thus pulled the body along (figure 1.4).

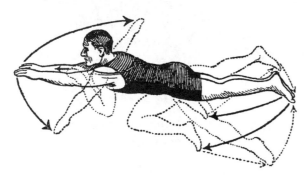

Figure 1.3 Breaststroke in the 19th century. Pulling with straight arms and drawing the knees under the body were common faults. From Sachs 1912.

William Wilson (1883) said that "another mistaken idea is that the propelling part of the kick is obtained from the soles of the feet; these mis-

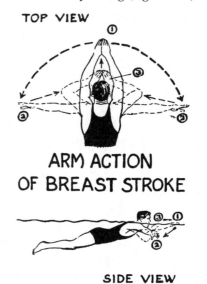

TOP VIEW

ARM ACTION
OF BREAST STROKE

SIDE VIEW

Figure 1.4 Breaststroke arm action in the 1920s. From Bachrach 1924.

Descriptions in Western Literature

Only in the last 400 years have references to swimming techniques appeared in books. Early examples say little, mainly because stroke analysis was still in its infancy and underwater observation nonexistent.

Although Nicolaus Wynman wrote the first book on swimming, *Colymbetes, sive de arte natandi et festivus et iucundus lectu* (published in 1538 by H. Steiner of the University of Ingolstadt, Augsburg, Swabia), an earlier book, *The boke named the governour* by Sir Thomas Elyot (published in 1531 by Thomas Berthelet in London), briefly discussed swimming as an important part of the education of gentlemen. (Copies of *The boke named the governour*, 258 folios, are housed in Cambridge University Library and the British Museum.)

But it was Wynman's book, *Colymbetes*, that first instructed Europeans that the human stroke was the stroke "which all must learn as the scientific stroke." *Colymbetes* is a little book in crabbed Latin, full of abbreviations and mistakes or misprints. Wynman, a German Swiss professor at Ingolstadt University, mentioned that the cogent reason for not learning to swim had been the mistaken belief that the souls who are confined to hell have to cross the river Styx by swimming. If they cannot swim, how would they cross?

Within the next 50 years, two more books of note followed. *Historia de gentibus septentrionalibus Romae* (*History of the Northern People*) by Olaus Magnus was published in Rome by Magno Gotho in 1555 and discussed swimming among the other leading customs of northern people. The other book was *De arte natandi* (*The Art of Swimming*) by Sir Everard Digby, published in England in 1587 but written in Latin because it was considered vulgar in certain quarters to write in English. Both books advocated breaststroke in preference to the more primitive forms of swimming that existed at the time (Cureton 1934).

Had Digby written in his own language, as Elyot did, his book would have sold better and also been too well known to have been so readily plagiarized or translated without permission. As it was, Digby's work was translated three times: twice into English and once into French. The French edition was translated into German, Spanish, and Italian. An abbreviated translation of Digby's work was published in 1595 by Middleton. Another, published in 1658, professing to be original, was an almost literal translation by Percey, who claimed it to be his own work.

Next, Melchisedec Thevenot translated Digby's original Latin work, *De arte natandi*, into French, and it was published by T. Moette in Paris under the title of *L'art de nager* in 1696, four years after Thevenot's death. In 1699, *The Art of Swimming*, translated back into English from *L'art de nager*, was published in London, the translator never suspecting that Thevenot was not the original author (Thomas 1904). Thus Digby's work was the only one known for centuries to French and English swimmers, but few, if any, could have known that Digby had been the original author because Thevenot was always given the credit for it. Even that great scholar Benjamin Franklin, who got to the root of most things he touched, quotes Thevenot without the slightest suspicion that the original author was English.

Thevenot described swimming "as an old sport which hitherto had not received the investigation necessary to improve in efficiency." During Thevenot's time, breaststroke was still considered the scientific stroke in Europe (Cureton 1934). Thevenot's book was regarded as the authoritative work on "scientific swimming," as it was called then, and was reprinted in 1764 and 1772.

In recognition of Thevenot's perceived preeminence among swimming authors during a century when swimming was considered a health hazard, Thevenot was inducted into the International Swimming Hall of Fame in 1990, nearly 300 years after his translation of Digby's

(continued)

(continued)

work had been published. Although Thevenot was a recognized scholar in many fields, a stronger case can be made for Digby's inclusion in the International Swimming Hall of Fame.

Although Ralph Thomas (1904) claimed that Thevenot in his famous book had plagiarized Digby's work, written a century before, the prestigious *British Library Catalogue* simply states that Thevenot's book was "adapted" from Digby's *De arte natandi*. Another point for consideration is that Thevenot's book was published four years after his death, and it is more than likely that Thevenot only translated Digby's work for his own scholarly satisfaction, without intent to publish it. The latter explanations would appear to be more plausible, particularly as Thevenot was a minor celebrity of his day, a highly respected and distinguished Oriental scholar, and a founder of the French Academy of Sciences. As librarian of the Royal Library (from 1684), he collected many valuable books and manuscripts. Nevertheless, he never went out of Europe, and he did not know how to swim.

The more recent evolution of swimming in Western culture is ably recorded by several outstanding authorities, and especially so in the classic descriptions by Steedman (1867), Wilson (1883), Sinclair and Henry (1903), Thomas (1904), Cureton (1934), and Carlile (1963).

From Breaststroke to Sidestroke

Although humans are not ideally endowed by nature to be highly proficient swimmers, they eventually discovered that improved technique could produce surprisingly facile and dexterous propulsion. This fact explains the almost obsessive fascination with stroke techniques in the early years of swimming development.

For many, the improvement of swimming skill became an interesting and fascinating intellectual exercise as well as a test of physical ability. More often than not, clues leading to improved methods were observed in the techniques of great natural athletes. The term *natural athlete* is worth proper understanding. Broadly stated, it means an athlete who does the right thing naturally, as part of his or her true nature. Yet the progress of many a natural athlete was stifled by the imposition of techniques that interfered with the swimmer's natural movement inclination. Of course, much was heard about their coaches' successes but little about their failures.

When organized competitive swimming started in the early 19th century, the sidestroke became the standard racing style. Both arms remained submerged throughout, and the legs performed a wide scissors kick with opening and closing movements that resembled walking. Swimmers eventually found they could reduce resistance by recovering one arm over the water instead of underwater as in the breaststroke. This stroke became known as the English overarm sidestroke, and descriptions by the experts of the day were belabored with numerous fastidious points of technique (figure 1.5).

Figure 1.5 Early chart showing the mechanics of the sidestroke. From Sinclair and Henry 1903, p. 81.

It's easy to imagine how the sidestroke evolved from the breaststroke. In effect, the early underarm sidestroke was really the breaststroke swum with the body turned on its side. Swimmers found that by turning onto their side they encountered less water resistance. Sachs (1912) says, "It is necessary to cleave the water with the head or shoulder in order to avoid undue resistance" (p. 133). At first, the sidestroke was swum with both arms in the water during both pull and recovery; this was known as the underarm sidestroke (figure 1.6).

Figure 1.6 "A figure swimming on the side, but it is intended for the sidestroke." From Reichel 1897.

With the start of widely organized swimming championships in England in 1871, the quest for speed encouraged even more swimmers to improve their stroke efficiency (Sinclair and Henry 1903). This desire for technical improvement was increased by the fact that until 1906, there were no separate events for different strokes. Except for the breaststroke, which was sometimes swum as a novelty item, swimmers competing in a single race used any stroke they liked (Counsilman 1968).

Realizing the superior speed of the English overarm sidestroke (figure 1.7), racers abandoned the underarm stroke and recovered one arm over the water (Cureton 1934). Sinclair and

Figure 1.7 The English overarm sidestroke. From Sachs 1912, p. 134.

Henry (1903) diagrammed overarm sidestroke technique and wrote that the great exponents of the art of swimming were the Englishmen Nuttall and Tyers, and no other nation had swimmers capable of extending them. The kick of the improved stroke that these swimmers used was a marvelous screw-like leg kick (scissors kick), which also gained J.A. Jarvis marked supremacy in England (figure 1.8).

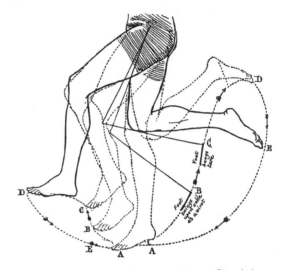

Figure 1.8 The Jarvis kick. From Sinclair and Henry 1903, p. 83.

J.A. Jarvis won many English championships with the use of what came to be known as the "Jarvis kick." Jarvis was the "first to discover that certain movements of the feet were of definite assistance in giving power to the English side-overarm stroke and of improving its speed" (Sachs 1912, pp. 139-140).

H.D. Faith of the Otter Club describes Jarvis's kick in a small brochure titled *The Over-Arm Side Stroke* (1912):

> The swinging forward of the top leg makes the water around the leg wash forward in the direction the leg is swinging. In the case of the under leg a back wash is created. As the legs are whipped together the top leg, coming back, meets and grips the water which is still being washed forward, and the under leg, coming forward, meets the wash going backward, the screw-like action of the legs giving a continuous grip of the water and making the stroke a continuation of screw and wedge (Sachs 1912, p. 140).

Faith's description indicates how advanced the skill of lucid stroke analysis had become. Of even greater interest is that Faith gives one of the few references to the flow reactions of the water that exist in the historical literature.

The adoption of the English overarm sidestroke showed a growing awareness of the importance of decreasing resistance in proportion to speed. The emphasis on the leg action was carried over from breaststroke swimming, and the indications are that at this stage, a full appreciation of the arms' potential for propulsion still did not exist. Nor did there appear to be much concern about developing a more continuous mode of progression, other than the fact that sidestroke swimmers were inclined to insert an extra tiny wedge (Jarvis) or flutter kick (Nuttall) into the closing phase of their leg actions.

In his classic work *The Swimming Instructor* (1883), William Wilson describes the method of the improved English overarm sidestroke. The stroke's popularity was apparent, and a number of swimmers laid claim to having been the first to use it. Harry Gurr—called the "Pocket Hercules" because of his short stature, healthy red skin, fair hair, and neat physique—and Harry Gardner of Woolwich were the first who won any races of importance by lifting one hand out of the water and carrying it in the air beyond the head.

The influence of the dominant leg kick of traditional breaststroke was hard to shake off. As a result, the pioneers were slow to appreciate the potential power of the arms. Sachs (1912) describes how the double overarm stroke was taught:

> In the double overarm stroke, the left arm is brought as far forward as it will go—the head being immersed and even turned slightly on to its left side in order to give the arm full stretch. As the left arm is pulled back towards the body, this tendency towards turning on the left side will be increased, and the right arm has thus the opportunity of coming clear of the water. The arm is then stretched ahead as far as possible, and the body rolls back on its right side again. It is necessary to observe here that this roll is very slight in-

deed, and is confined to the head and shoulders. It is mentioned only to assure those who try this stroke that they cannot do without it even to a modified extent (Sachs 1912, pp. 142-143).

History shows the double overarm sidestroke to have been a cul-de-sac in the development of swimming. Because of the constant change in body position and the consequent lack of continuity, the stroke was not very successful.

The Trudgen Stroke

John Trudgen was born at Poplar, London, on May 3, 1852, and went to Buenos Aires with his parents in 1863. While in Buenos Aires, he learned the South American Indian stroke from the natives, which was later named the trudgen stroke (figure 1.9) after his first appearance in a swimming race in England on August 11, 1873.

Figure 1.9 The trudgen stroke.

English spectators were startled when Trudgen won his first race, the English 160-yard handicap, with a most unusual stroke. The idea for a double overarm stroke came from observing his unusual technique, which later was to become the basic arm stroke of the crawl. (Keep in mind that the typical alternate, overarm windmill stroke of the Pacific Islanders had been swum for hundreds of years. Only when this action became part of Western swimming culture, after its rediscovery by the Australians, did it receive its present name of crawl stroke. See pp. 15 and 16 for more information.)

The difficulty with the trudgen stroke was that it lacked continuity; in fact, it was very jerky because it timed one breaststroke kick to every two arm strokes. An attempt was made to overcome this handicap by combining the scissors kick of the sidestroke with the trudgen arm action. The kick, originally performed with considerable knee-bend, was narrowed and the legs were held straighter, but the timing of the side scissors kick still prevented a perfectly continuous arm action (figure 1.10).

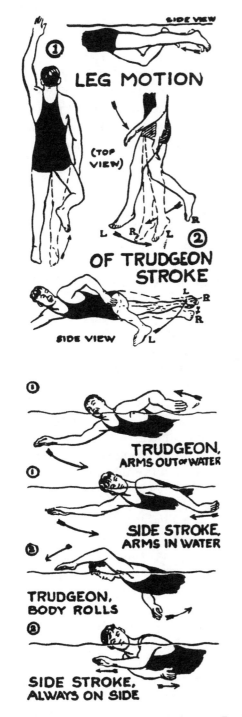

Figure 1.10 *(a)* Trudgen leg action. *(b)* Trudgen arm action and body roll. From Bachrach 1924.

According to Sinclair and Henry (1903, p. 87), Trudgen's championship swim was described in the *Swimming Record* (August 12, 1873) by the editor, R.P. Watson:

His time was very fast, particularly for one who appears to know but little of swimming, and should he become more finished in style, we shall expect to see him take a position almost second to none as a swimmer.

I question, indeed, if the swimming world ever saw a more peculiar stroke sustained throughout a 160 yards race. Here we had a man swimming apparently easy, turning very badly, and when finished, appearing as though he could have gone at least another 80 yards at the same pace. His action reminds an observer of a style peculiar to the Indians; both arms are thrown partly sideways, but very slovenly, and the head kept completely above water.

Sinclair and Henry (1903) agreed that Watson's opinion was well borne out, for Trudgen afterward became one of the speediest sprint swimmers of his time, and his peculiar action became known as the trudgen stroke. Trudgen swam high out of the water, thrusting both arms in front of him with his chest and head well raised but practically in the same position as a breaststroke swimmer.

As a result of Trudgen's influence, considerable experimentation followed with double overarm swimming. Many swimmers still wished to remain on their sides, however, because they feared that swimming in a flat position on the chest would cause too much frontal resistance, so they developed a stroke in which they turned from side to side to enable an alternate recovery of each arm.

There was no mention of a regular breathing method within the rhythm of the trudgen stroke. One can only guess how this important aspect of swimming technique evolved. Perhaps, as often happens, it was by chance; as a double overarm swimmer was turning from one side to the other, the swimmer may have noticed bubbles escaping from the mouth while the face was submerged. Of course, the next step would have been to learn to breathe in a regular rhythm with face-out-of-water inhalation followed by steady exhalation again as the face submerged.

Trudgen's hand-over-hand stroke was said to be common to the ancients and the aborigines of America and Africa. When the British first tried it, they could not continue it for any length of time. In the late 19th century many forms of the trudgen stroke came to be swum by sprint swimmers and water polo players. Because the stroke was so fatiguing, few swimmers could maintain it for over 200 yards, although in short races it won preference over the English side overarm stroke.

R. Thomas (1904) reported R.P. Watson as saying, "imitation of the trudgen or Indian stroke had completely demoralized Londoners as swimmers." The endeavor "to imitate Trudgen, together with short distance handicaps, ranging from 80 to 90 yards have degenerated Londoners to the level of mediocrity. However, the stroke or a modification of it has been taken up by water polo players with the most undoubted advantage. The swimmer appears to go much faster than with other strokes."

Swimming in the New World

Back in time, to the dawn of history, primitive peoples used the dog paddle, a stroke that naturally involves the principle of continuous propulsion. With the addition of a breathing technique, only one step is needed for the transition from dog paddle to an overarm stroke, but somehow making this slight change never occurred to these early swimmers. Today dog paddle is used only as a temporary expedient in teaching beginners to swim.

Around the 17th century, European swimmers started to copy the swimming movements of the frog, and from this came the stop-start action of the breaststroke, the first formal type of swimming in Western culture (see p. 5).

But recent research suggests a scattering effect that shows that the evolution of the swimming strokes did not follow a precise sequence of events, such as that contained in the literature of Western civilization. To say that the study of swimming was always an intellectual exercise would be incorrect because a veritable hodgepodge of swimming strokes, completely out of sync with the assumed traditional sequence, were swum in various parts of the world. In fact, the evolution of the swimming strokes provides a fine example of how history can take one body of evidence and turn it around.

Most accounts of the history of the swimming strokes have led us to believe that there had been but one pure line of ancestry—a sequence from dog paddle, also called the human stroke, to breaststroke, sidestroke, then trudgen, and finally to our greatest creation, the crawl stroke. In fact, this was not so because the principle of continuous propulsion, a derivative of the sport of ocean surfing, had already been observed for thousands of years in the overarm swimming strokes of the Polynesian peoples.

Long before Magellan, Balboa, da Gama, and Cook had broken out of the traditional confines of European waters to pursue their voyages of discovery, the peoples of Polynesia were naturally swimming the powerful overarm ocean stroke that later became known as the crawl. While Europeans pursued their laborious methods of swimming, the indigenous peoples of the South Seas had long been swimming the more facile overarm stroke that provided continuous propulsion instead of a stop-start progression through the water.

In 1849, Sidney Howard, an American, published *The Science of Swimming as Taught and Practiced in Civilized and Savage Countries*, in which he referred to de la Perouse's trip around the world in 1785. Captain de la Perouse said that the Indians, or natives, of Easter Island (one of the South Sea Islands) were remarkable swimmers using overhand strokes.

Not until the late 19th century did the self-termed sophisticated swimmers of Europe deign to dispense with their quiet, graceful, nonsplashing strokes and experiment with the newfangled, hand-over-hand action displayed to them with telling effect by visitors from overseas.

How would the Pacific Islanders have viewed the swimming of the 19th-century Europeans? A raised hand would politely have covered their smiles at the sight of the awkward stop-start movements of the breaststroke, sidestroke, and trudgen, and the theoretical explanations that accompanied their performance.

Let no one be mistaken: speed swimming started in the majestic, thundering surf of the Pacific Islands and not in the streams of the bucolic European countryside. In contrast, the 400-year literature of European swimming shows a more studied, tedious, and slower development of the sport than that which existed naturally for thousands of years among the Polynesians. (See "Descriptions in Western Literature," p. 7.)

The carefully preserved (by word of mouth) legends and mythology of the Polynesian peoples tell us that they swam their powerful oceanic overarm stroke long before it entered Western culture to become the racing crawl stroke, a masterpiece of human ingenuity and adaptation. Speed swimming found its origins hundreds of years ago on the warm-water surf beaches of the Pacific where surfing and swimming were the natural sports of the islanders. In the traditional surfing skill, known as the *huki*, they used a rapid overarm windmill stroke combined with a flutter kick to catch the gathering momentum of a cresting wave.

The huki was performed either on a surfboard or while lying prone on top of a wave as it began to break. This basic movement, designed to match the tremendous speed of a powerful incoming wave, was also the natural swimming method of the islanders when swimming in still water. In fact, there is distributional evidence to show that throughout Oceania, children were taught to swim with this method while lying on a short surfboard.

Many writers have described the thrill and excitement of speed as the essence of swimming in the surf. Jack London (1911) on his visit to Hawaii drew a vivid picture of how he paddled the windmill stroke to catch a big fast-moving wave. Born in the surf out of the sheer necessity to quickly generate speed, the huki, or the crawl, as it became known when it spread to Australia and other swimming nations, was

later to revolutionize the sport of speed swimming.

When Duke Kahanamoku, the great Hawaiian swimmer, gave an exhibition of surfboard riding at Long Beach, California, on July 30, 1922, he also unintentionally showed the estimated crowd of 5,000 spectators how the ancient Hawaiian huki technique of paddling and flutter kicking was used for mounting a cresting wave. On July 31, 1922, the *Long Beach Daily Telegram* described it this way:

> Duke Kahanamoku, Olympic champion and in his prime the world's greatest swimmer, gave an exhibition of surfboard riding in front of the Hotel Virginia yesterday. Lying face down on the board with the legs protruding into the water, the swimmer would begin a thrash with the legs such as is used in swimming the crawl stroke. At the same time, he would paddle with his hands furiously. This work was started just before the surf break. The rushing waters would lift the board and carry it along at a terrific pace. As soon as the board was going well, the surfer would pull himself up to a kneeling position and then gradually rise to his feet.

For more information and early descriptions, see King (1778), Ellis (1831), Thrum (1896), London (1911), Twain (1872), and Finney and Houston (1996).

The Advanced Styles of the North American Indians

There is every indication that for centuries Native Americans swam in great numbers with a superior overarm stroke, while the so-called civilized world persisted with breaststroke and sidestroke.

Unfortunately, early organized swimming in North America copied the European swimming style, particularly the methods brought to America by the colonial English. This was a pity because more advanced styles already existed in North America, as noted in 1739 in the diary of the English colonial William Byrd, founder of Richmond, Virginia, and a planter, satirist, and writer of diaries (Byrd 1928).

Writing on September 30, 1739, Byrd noted:

This being Sunday, we were glad to rest from our labors; and, to help restore our vigor, several of us plunged into the river, not withstanding it was a frosty morning. One of our Indians went in along with us, and taught us their way of swimming. They strike not out both hands together but alternately one after another, whereby they are able to swim both farther and faster than we do (Byrd 1928).

Even when the better American style was exported to England 100 years later in an 1844 London exhibition by two Native Americans from the Ojibbeway Nation—Flying Gull (We-nish-ka-wen-bee) and Tobacco (Sah-ma)—the English paid little attention and refused to change, despite the obvious superiority of the Native American swimming style. This fore-runner of the modern crawl stroke was de-scribed in *The London Times* (April 22, 1844) as being totally "un-European," declaring that the Indians thrashed the water violently with their arms like sails of a windmill and beat downward with their feet blowing with force and performing grotesque antics.

The Mandan Indians

In his *A Manual of Swimming* (1867), Charles Steedman quoted George Catlin's memoirs on the habits of the Mandan Indians. Catlin de-scribed a place half a mile or so from the village where the women and girls went every sum-mer morning to bathe in the river. All the people learned to swim well; even the worst swimmer would fearlessly enter the rushing current of the Missouri River, crossing the river with ease.

According to Catlin, all American Indians knew how to swim; they learned and taught it well. Many tribes spent their entire lives on the shores of lakes and rivers, paddling across them in fragile bark canoes that were prone to accidents, "which often throw the Indian upon his natural resources for the preservation of his life." Also in times of war, the Indians had to plunge into and swim across wild streams and rivers when they had no canoes or boats.

The mode of swimming the Mandans and most of the other tribes used was quite different from the swimming in other parts of the world that Catlin had visited. Catlin described the method:

The Indian, instead of parting his hands simultaneously, under the chin, and mak-ing the stroke outward, in a horizontal direction, causing thereby a serious strain upon the chest, throws his body alter-nately upon the left and the right side, raising one arm entirely above the water and reaching as far forward as he can, to dip it, whilst his whole weight and force are spent upon the one that is passing under him, and like a paddle propelling him along; whilst the arm is making a half-circle, and is being raised out of the water behind him, the opposite arm is describing a similar arch in the air over his head, to be dipped in the water as far as he can reach before him, with the hand turned under, forming a sort of bucket, to act most effectively as it passes in its turn underneath him.

Catlin called it a "bold and powerful mode of swimming" though lacking in grace. Still Catlin noted that the stroke used by the Mandan people helped them avoid much of the fatigue and strain inherent in other strokes, preserving their strength. (Adapted from Steedman 1867, pp. 192–193).

The Crawl Stroke

Because organized competitive swimming first started in England in the late 19th century, it was natural that English swimming methods, such as the overarm sidestroke and the trudgen stroke, would spread to the rest of Europe and be copied there, although more advanced double overarm methods actually existed in the Pacific Islands and other warm maritime countries. In fact, there can be no doubt that from time immemorial, overarm swimming strokes had existed in countries bordering on warm tropical seas. This was particularly true of the Pacific where the natives had swum a type of overarm stroke that was later to be known as the crawl stroke (figure 1.11). But, because no international governing body of swimming existed at that time, there were no visits with swimmers from countries outside of Europe.

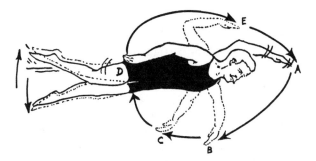

Figure 1.11   The crawl stroke. From Sachs 1912, p. 145.

However, the turning point in the development of the crawl stroke came when Dick Cavill, a member of the famous Australian swimming family that had originally emigrated to Australia from England, realized that the side scissors kick actually retarded continuous propulsion.

The probable sequence of events, as reconstructed by historians, was as follows: According to Carlile (1963), Fred Cavill, an Englishman, settled in Australia in 1879 and started a swimming bath at Lavender Bay in Sydney Harbor. Fred Cavill had six sons, three of whom—Syd, Arthur ("Tums"), and Dick—played an important part in the crawl's development.

In 1914, Syd Cavill wrote in the *Sydney Referee* that while on a visit to Apia in Samoa, he raced a woman swimmer who gave him the hardest race of his life. Syd noted with amazement that she swam an overarm stroke but did not kick at all. After watching her intently, Syd tied his legs and found that he could swim as quickly with his legs tied as he could with his legs free using any other stroke. Then he wrote home and told Tums about it. The rest is history (Carlile 1963, p. 133).

Sullivan (1928) relates how the original crawl stroke evolved in Australia, thus the name "Australian crawl stroke." Sullivan retells the story told by Louis de B. Handley, an American authority on swimming. Tums Cavill raced Syd Davis over 33 yards with his legs tied and

won. Then Cavill and Davis raced again, only this time Cavill's legs were untied. Davis won the second race.

Dick Cavill, Tums's brother, couldn't believe what he saw. After a few private time trials, Dick was convinced that his brother really could sprint faster without using his legs. Dick reasoned that when properly applied every ounce of power must increase speed; therefore, the scissors kick was radically wrong. The question was to find the right kick.

Then Dick remembered seeing Alick Wickham, a Rubiana sprinter, use an odd straight-legged kick, learned from the natives at Colombo, Ceylon. He experimented with it and was surprised by the results. The kick proved speedy from the very first trial.

Now he had the kick, but finding a harmonious arm action bothered him considerably. By the time Dick found it, the 100-yards championship was only a few days away. He entered the race anyway, anxious to publicly test his new stroke. Dick started at a terrific pace and reached the 50-yard mark five yards ahead of the nearest competitor. However, due to his imperfect mastery of the new stroke, he was passed by the speedy Bishop.

Even though Cavill was defeated, this race gave coaches an idea of the value of this new stroke. (The peculiar action of the stroke earned it the name "the crawl."). They immediately embraced the new stroke and formed classes to teach it. The success was marvelous. Men who had been indifferent swimmers gained in aptitude, good men improved, and soon the world was ringing with the news of the crawlers. At Rubiana, Al Wickham used the crawl to swim 50 yards in 24 seconds. Then Dick Cavill swam a phenomenal 100 yards in 58 seconds. Soon the stroke invaded Europe, eventually reaching America in 1904 (Sullivan 1928, pp. 37–38).

Duke Kahanamoku (see also p. 13), the first great Hawaiian Olympic swimmer, assured questioners in 1912 that the crawl stroke "had always been natural to the Hawaiians," while Alick Wickham, a Solomon Islander who lived in Sydney at the beginning of the 20th century, and who once held the world's 50-yard record for a fairly long period, said that all children in these islands swam a form of crawl stroke.

Wickham claimed that even before 1900 one of his brothers, who was being educated in Sydney, swam the crawl there on numerous occasions but, possibly because he was not a speedy or polished demonstrator, no particular notice was taken of him. Paradoxical as it may seem, Alick Wickham swam a perfect six-beat crawl stroke, but mainly because he was usually finished by 75 yards, his stroke was not copied in its entirety. However, a two-beat, heavy, muscular leg beat evolved, becoming known as the Australian crawl (Kiphuth 1942).

The Origin of the Term
Crawl Stroke

Carlile (1963) gives two versions on how the term *crawl stroke* may have originated:

1.   When Alick Wickham, a boy from the Solomon Islands, was first seen swimming his strange continuous overarm stroke in Australia in a 66 yards under-10 years handicap, George Farmer, a prominent Sydney coach, excitedly exclaimed, "Look at that kid crawling."

2.   The second version of the origin of the term is that 15-year-old Dick Cavill, the stroke's first great exponent, burrowed his head so deep below the water's surface while swimming the new stroke that he persistently swam over his rivals who complained that young Cavill was "crawling all over me."

However, in his benchmark book *A Manual of Swimming* (1867), Charles Steedman gives evidence of a much earlier origin of the term: "An easy method for a person to learn to swim without the aid of a teacher is first to acquire what is commonly termed the crawl or dog stroke" (p. 78).

Steedman then describes the action of the dog paddle, a stroke still in use today for teaching beginners. It is possible that the term *crawl stroke* may have long been in common use to describe the dog paddle and that George Farmer's use of the term *crawling* in reference to Wickham's spectacular method of swimming might have inferred that Wickham was crawling, or dog paddling, so fast that his arms were actually coming out of the water, instead of reaching forward underwater as in the conventional dog paddle action.

The Development of Fundamentals

It should not be thought that the crawl, the new wonder stroke, was accepted everywhere with acclaim. To the contrary, some thought it was inelegant and others regarded it as very tiring. Sinclair and Henry (1903) described the stroke like this:

> The swimmer appears to be crawling over the water instead of being in it, hence there is much splashing. It cannot be said that the action is graceful, but it certainly is particularly speedy, as Cavill has swum a 100 yards in a 44 yards' bath in the remarkable time of 58 3/5 seconds (p. 23).

The early crawl stroke was a difficult stroke to swim because it was born without a breathing technique. The first crawl swimmers swam as far as they could on one breath, before lifting the head forward out of the water to take another breath. A workable method of breathing came later.

The new method could be used only for short distances because it consumed energy rapidly. The first swimmers to use the crawl were mainly those who had grown up doing the trudgen stroke, and few could use it to complete the 100-yard racing distance. They swam trudgen for most of the distance before switching to the crawl to perform a spectacular grandstand finish.

The early crawl swimmers bore little resemblance to the polished technicians of modern swimming. They burrowed their heads in the water, mouths shut tight and lungs starved for air, and they let their arms fly round and round in a flurry of wild splashing, while the legs kicked once for each arm pull, using a deep knee-bend that caused each foot to hit the surface with a resounding whack.

Despite all the excitement about the new crawl stroke and its superior speed, closer examination would have revealed that crawl swimming, as it existed then, was no more than a rough concept that worked, but it was by no means a finely honed technique.

Two Influential Coaches

The son of American parents, **Louis de Breda Handley** (1874–1956) was born in Rome, where he was educated in the liberal arts and became adept in five different languages. He came to America at the age of 22 to work as an importer. He coached the New York Athletic Club and, with Charlotte Epstein, founded the Women's Swimming Association of New York (WSA), where he coached as a volunteer for 40 years and helped Charlotte Epstein put women's swimming on the map. Between them they produced a chain of great champions such as Charlotte Boyle, Helen Wainwright, Gertrude Ederle, Aileen Riggen, Alice Lord, Helen Meany, Eleanor Holm, and many others. He developed from novicehood 6 of the 12 girl stars who represented the United States in the Antwerp Olympic Games in 1920. One of the most innovative stroke technicians in the history of the sport (his innovations included developing the freestyle flutter kick), he became coach-educator to the world and swimming's first great communicator. When he died of a heart attack in New York at the age of 82, his lifetime contributions had transformed the sport of swimming (Colwin 1998).

William "Big Bill" Bachrach (1879–1959) weighed 350 pounds and was probably one of the most colorful coaches in the history of swimming. Together with Handley, Bachrach set American and world swimming on course into the 20th century. He was head coach of the Illinois Athletic Club in Chicago, as well as head coach of the 1924 and 1928 United States Olympic teams. His men and women swimmers captured 12 gold medals in Paris in 1924 and 10 gold medals at the 1928 Amsterdam Olympics. He was most famous as the mentor of Johnny Weissmuller, who was voted the greatest swimmer of the first 50 years of the 20th century and second-best swimmer (behind Mark Spitz) of the entire 20th century. His psychological handling of his swimmers was far in advance of his time, and he was also among the first with the ability to develop each swimmer's best individual style of swimming. His development of Weissmuller's crawl stroke established several fundamental principles—for example the pull-push arm action—that became part of the stroke in use for many years to come.

Bachrach developed four gold medalists at the 1924 Games: Johnny Weissmuller (100- and 200-meter freestyles and 800-meter relay), Bob Skelton (200-meter breaststroke), Ethel Lackie (100-meter freestyle and 400-meter relay), and Sybil Bauer (100-meter backstroke). Weissmuller also won two gold medals at the 1928 Olympics in the 100-meter freestyle and the 800-meter relay.

Nevertheless, the arrival of the crawl stroke in Western culture was an important technical development. It was the fastest stroke ever developed, and it highlighted the fact that a swimmer must produce continuous propulsion to maintain an even velocity.

In an age before underwater motion picture analysis and before the advent of underwater observation windows, the first crawl stroke pioneers learned the importance of streamlining, that we swim faster by reducing drag.

Keen observation resulted in the development of even more basic principles in the efficient performance of the crawl stroke. It quickly became apparent that coordination was most important, especially in reference to maintaining continuous propulsion.

As more people learned the crawl stroke, the various descriptions of the stroke needed to be more clearly defined. Research of the literature shows that the following were the main questions asked during the early development of the crawl as well as the other swimming strokes:

1. Where and how should the hand(s) enter the water?

2. Should the arm(s) be bent or straight during the pull?

3. What should be the path of the arm(s) during the pull?

4. Should the stroke be long and slow or short and fast?

5. How should the arm(s) be recovered to start the next stroke?

6. What should be the timing of one arm in relation to the other?

7. What should be the timing of the legs in relation to the arms?

8. When and how should inhalation and exhalation of air be timed into the rhythm of the stroke cycle?

Thanks to trial and error and research in biomechanics, we can now answer these questions with far greater certainty.

During the first 30 years of the 20th century, a synthesis of crawl stroke fundamentals gradually emerged, the process greatly aided by coaches Louis de B. Handley, William Bachrach, and Frank Sullivan, and swimmers such as Charles Daniels, Duke Kahanamoku, Johnny Weissmuller, and many others. They developed the first great exponents of the stroke, and their techniques became examples for others to follow. These coach-swimmer teams laid the foundations of modern American swimming, and as the 20th century progressed, their better understanding of fundamentals led to the invention of two new strokes, the back crawl and the butterfly, as well as the modernizing of the centuries-old breaststroke.

The Development of the American Crawl

Charles M. Daniels (1887–1973), the first of the great American swimmers, invented the American crawl. His career spanned the years 1903 to 1910, and when he retired he had almost completely rewritten the world-record book. Daniels stood 6 feet 3 inches and had the lithe, lean, symmetrical physique that was to become the prototype of nearly all the great crawl champions of the 20th century.

Although Daniels was a fine all-round athlete who excelled at many other sports, he decided to specialize in swimming. Only a year after starting his career as a member of the New York Athletic Club, Daniels had won two titles at the St. Louis Olympic Games and became the first American to win an Olympic swimming medal. He went on to win more Olympic titles in Athens in 1906 and in London in 1908.

Daniels started his career as a trudgen swimmer. But in 1905, after meeting the great Australian swimmer Barney Kieran during a tour of England, he decided to master the art of crawl swimming. Although Kieran was a trudgen swimmer, he was able to show Daniels how to swim the new crawl stroke. Daniels tried the two-beat rhythm of the Australian crawl (figure 1.12) but found that his legs tended to sink. Then it dawned on him that this was because the Australian style had been invented in buoyant sea water and that a faster kick was needed for freshwater swimming to prevent the feet from sinking.

Daniels added another two beats to his action with the result that he was now swimming what came to be known as a four-beat crawl. However, when swimming at top speed, Daniels found that he possessed the dexterity to slip two more beats into his leg action, and so was born the six-beat American crawl (figure 1.13).

Daniels did not consciously time his six-beat kick with his arm action but allowed the legs to work independently. This was in contrast with

Figure 1.12 Annette Kellermann demonstrates the Australian crawl. From Kellermann 1918.

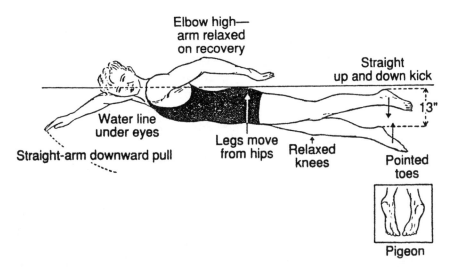

Figure 1.13 The American crawl, the beginning of stroke analysis. From Sullivan 1928, p. 42.

the rhythm of two major beats combined with four minor beats that was practiced by the other early exponents of the American crawl. (The tendency to prescribe a precise rhythm between the actions of the arms and legs was a carryover from the way breaststroke and sidestroke were swum in the old traditional styles.)

In Search of a Breathing Technique

Coaches realized the need to improve the efficiency of the crawl to enable its use for longer distances. The ability to breathe easily and regularly was the big problem. Cecil Healy, one of the great early Australian swimmers, developed the idea of turning the face sideways out of the water to inhale before returning it to the center position to exhale underwater. Some swimmers inhaled once every two strokes, while others breathed every three strokes, once to each side (also known as *bilateral breathing*). However, most of the short-distance swimmers breathed only when they needed a breath.

Healy said that a style of crawl swimming had long been indigenous to the South Seas and that he had seen this breathing method used naturally by all the native swimmers of Hawaii, who turned the head to inhale with every stroke of the right or left arm, according to which side suited them best. This was done by flicking the face sideways just as the forward hand entered the water (figure 1.14).

Figure 1.14 Crawl stroke breathing. From Bachrach 1924.

In stating the importance of correct breathing, Handley (1918) added that not only did body position, balance, and rhythm rely largely on efficient head-turning mechanics while breathing but that the ability to swim longer distances relied on a regular supply of oxygen to the working muscles.

Describing head-turning mechanics, Handley said, "The head is twisted toward the upper shoulder to facilitate the intake of air, but the swimmer should make sure it is a twist only, for if the head is raised the feet will unavoidably sink and break the balance of the body."

The addition of improved breathing techniques to the American crawl soon enabled swimmers to establish records over the longer distances. This was particularly true of swimmers who, as school children, learned the crawl as their first stroke.

Experiments With the Crawl Kick

The first crawl swimmers were quick to notice that the stroke was very flexible and open to many variations. To make the stroke more suitable for distance swimming, Frank Sullivan, one of Chicago's leading instructors, conceived the idea of combining the crawl with features of the trudgen stroke. Sullivan's trudgen-crawl was characterized by the insertion of a small straight-legged scissors kick with a narrow spread as the swimmer turned the head to breathe (Cureton 1934, p. 98).

Continuing Sullivan's idea of a more subdued leg action, H.J. Handy, also of Chicago, introduced a legless crawl, which as its name implies involved not kicking at all. Although Handy was successful using this method, this idea did not survive long.

Discussing the leg kick, Charles Daniels (1919) said, "The relative timing of the arms and legs in the American crawl can best be determined by the individual or his coach; one with strong arms and weak legs can adopt a rapid arm motion and a slow kick; one with strong legs can do the contrary. This is one of the stroke's best features, for it can be fitted to each person."

Handley (1918) said that the width of the leg action should not exceed 14 inches between the heels. A greater opening would cause the feet to rise above the surface, and energy would be wasted. Handley said that the most successful crawl swimmers used a very narrow leg action, seldom more than 8 or 10 inches in scope.

Handley described a leg action in which the legs were held straight but not rigid, whipping up and down alternately, while "closely imitating the movements one makes in walking on tip toe with mincing steps."

Handley believed that the speed of the kick should be adjusted to the individual. He said that most swimmers appeared to find the four- or six-beat action to be the most effective.

Some swimmers placed too strong an emphasis on synchronizing the kick with the arm stroke. In those early years, this forced timing must have limited the success of many talented swimmers. Modern swimmers allow their legs to work in a natural cadence, independent of their arms.

The Crawl Stroke Body Position

Handley said that in crawl swimming the body should be held as in standing upright on tiptoe, so that it formed a straight line, with the head erect, back slightly arched, legs together, and feet pointed. Resting on the water there should be a gentle downward slant from head to feet.

Handley (1918) added that when a swimmer's speed made it "possible to hydroplane more effectively, the slant of the body should be more pronounced, but it must lessen gradually as the pace is decreased to cover lengthening courses" (p. 28). Handley's idea that a swimmer could actually begin to hydroplane as speed increased was perhaps subconsciously inspired by the then-recent invention of the motorized hydroplane. However, hydroplaning becomes possible only when a craft is moving quickly enough to allow the bow wave to come under the boat. The enthusiasm for this misconception must have caused many talented swimmers to fall far short of their real potential.

It should be noted that it is generally believed that William Bachrach, in his coaching of the great Weissmuller, originated the incorrect concept of humans being able to hydroplane. However, it was Handley, not Bachrach, who was first to mention this topic, long before Bachrach ever saw Weissmuller. It was not until Bachrach had published *The Outline of Swimming* (1924) that he mentioned how he had taught Weissmuller "the hydroplane principle," as he called it (pp. 123–124). This account is a good example of how the pioneers of swimming often incorrectly rationalized the acceptance of new techniques.

Handley advocated a slight side-to-side roll "to facilitate inhaling and to permit a clean recovery of the arms. Excessive bending at the neck, waist, knees or ankles should be avoided."

The Crawl Stroke Arm Action

Handley (1918) said that the arms should work alternately, one propelling while the other recovered, each performing the same cycle of movement, although the arm opposite the breathing side dipped a little deeper due to the heavier roll of the body toward it (figure 1.15).

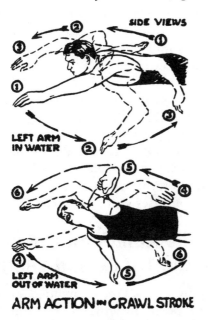

Figure 1.15 Weissmuller demonstrates the crawl stroke arm action. From Bachrach 1924.

He added that each arm should enter the water with the elbow slightly raised, forearm and hand aligned, palm down, fingers and thumb close together. The hand should cut the surface just before attaining full reach beyond the head, and dip down to its own side of an imaginary line drawn between the eyes and through the middle of the body. Then the arm pressed forward underwater, so that by the time it was comfortably extended it was slanted slightly downward at a sufficient angle to effectively apply power.

Handley said, "After catching smartly the arm sweeps backward, following a course parallel to the center line of progression and maintaining strong pressure on the water until the hand nears the thigh. Here the muscles are relaxed, the elbow is lifted and the arm drawn up and out. As the hand emerges from the water it is bent back from the wrist, palm up, to better clear the surface, then moved out and forward, simultaneously turning palm down, so that by the time it passes the shoulder line the whole arm is in the prescribed position for another entry" (pp. 28–29).

Bachrach (1924) said that, during the pull, the elbow should bend until it reaches an angle of 45 degrees. The arm is bent so that more surface area of the forearm is offered to the water. The pull ends at the hip where the muscles relax as the arm is brought out of the water. The forearm and wrist stay relaxed during recovery as the arm is carried out of the water to the forward position. The action of the right arm is similar. As the left arm comes out, the right arm starts its pull from the forward position, the hands at all times being equidistant. The motion is a continuous rotation; there is no break between one complete revolution of the arms and the one that follows.

Crawl Stroke Timing

Handley stressed that proper timing of arm and leg movements was essential to good swimming despite "the belief that seems rather prevalent that in the crawl the arms and legs may work independently. Whatever number of leg drives made per stroke, the wanted rhythm is attained by performing one of the beats of each leg at the end of the pull on that side of the body, and this establishes perfect coordination." This comment on the key to the timing of arms and legs was an astute observation, made long before the advent of underwater observation windows. (It was not until 1977, when Dr. James E. "Doc" Counsilman published photographs of this timing in his *Competitive Swimming Manual* (1977, p. 164) that this point was mentioned again in the literature. Counsilman said that all types of crawl stroke had this timing in common.) With great foresight, Handley commented that "speed and endurance could only be gained by accurate inter-timing of all movements." However, modern swimmers are not taught to time their leg kicks with the arm stroke, but rather to allow their legs to find their own natural counterbalancing action.

The Japanese Crawl in the 1930s

The victorious Japanese at the 1932 and 1936 Olympic Games introduced a method of crawl swimming eminently suited to their shorter stature, flexible bodies, short arms, and naturally strong leg drives. This new style was the result of filming in great detail the styles of Johnny Weissmuller, the 1928 Olympic 100-meter champion, and Arne Borg of Sweden, the 1928 Olympic 1,500-meter champion.

The Japanese freestyle stroke was an adaptation of the Weissmuller stroke and the Arne Borg stroke. Borg swam higher than Weissmuller and had a faster, shorter arm action. The Japanese stroke fell somewhere between the strokes of these two great international stars. The Japanese swam with their shoulders fairly high and their legs quite low in the water, using more knee-bend in the kick than Weissmuller.

The theory behind the Japanese arm stroke was that the middle arc of the 180-degrees from full reach in front of the body to the finish at the thighs was the most effective range in the pull. The idea was to get to the point 45 degrees short of the full reach as quickly as possible and to recover after a 90-degree pull, or 45 degrees short of the complete pull-through.

Basically, the Japanese stroke consisted of a rapid arm recovery that enabled the swimmer to overlap both arms submerged in front of the body. As each arm entered the water, it anchored there in a stationary position while the other arm, which had been waiting in front of the body for the entry of its opposite member, commenced the drive.

The stroke was successful for the Japanese but had the disadvantage of causing a dead spot in propulsion. This occurred while one arm was recovering in the air and the opposite arm was submerged and stationary in front of the body. This threw the burden of ensuring continuous propulsion onto the leg drive. Unless the swimmer had a powerful kick, this resulted in lack of continuity to the overall stroke. The Japanese style of crawl swimming, in modified form, was adopted by swimmers of other countries without much success.

The American Crawl in the 1940s and 1950s

Bob Kiphuth (1942) recommended a perfectly flat body position, with the head and chest fairly high, the water level just above the eyes, the shoulders level with the water surface, and the horizontal axis through the shoulders at right angles to the long axis of the body. He

Japanese Contributions

Swimming history holds many examples of the old adage, "Be right too soon and your word will be ignored; be right too late and everyone is bored." For example, rolling the body in crawl swimming was considered a fault for more than 50 years until it was given credit for part of the Australian 1956 world dominance. Actually, the victorious Japanese crawl swimmers at the 1932 Olympics had used considerable body roll. But Western swimmers attributed the Japanese ability to roll without setting up resistance to streamlined shoulders, which they claimed were a characteristic of the Japanese physique. They argued a Japanese swimmer could use body roll with impunity, but a Westerner who copied it would do so at peril.

Another classic example was the failure to heed another important principle discovered by the Japanese. Back in the 1930s, Japanese swimmers had realized that it was more efficient to swim with long strokes at a high tempo. Today, "distance per stroke" is considered to be an important index of swimming efficiency.

History abounds with stories of how people came close to discovering important new truths about swimming but were slow to follow up. For a long time, the pursuit of swimming knowledge followed this desultory approach before scientific methods were used to analyze stroke mechanics.

advocated not dipping the shoulders or rolling the body and said there should be no lunging or hunching of one shoulder before the other. Although the arms move in the shoulder joint, the shoulder should be fixed, with the body moving over the arms–literally crawling.

Kiphuth said that there should be decided pressure on the water at all times and that the arm stroke was a working phase of catch, press, pull, and push (figure 1.16). The catch was to be in a line forward of the shoulder, with the arm extended as far as a high elbow and wrist will permit. The elbow should be flexed enough to give a strong set to the arm so that when the

catch is made, strong pressure can immediately be exerted on the water. This means that there can be no stretching or overreaching of the arm. Kiphuth advocated that the direction of the arm be slightly toward the middle line of the body, and after passing the vertical there is a push straight through at the end of the stroke out past the thigh. There is no gliding of the arm on the catch, and a full stroke is taken with no attempt to finish short. The maximum amount of water must be engaged by the hand and forearm throughout the stroke with as little slide slip of the arm as possible. The broadest aspect of the hand and forearm should engage the water at all times. A working phase of press, pull, push indicates the necessity of such action (Kiphuth 1942).

The Australian Crawl in the 1950s

Circa 1954, the Australians, after their early introduction of the crawl at the turn of the 20th century, once more took to speculating on ways to improve swimming speed. They sought to eliminate the tiring effects of overkicking, particularly at middle and long distances, and to eliminate the stilting effect on the arm stroke caused by swimming too flat and trying to pull by merely rotating the arms in the shoulder joint.

In the new Australian technique, the hands obtained a longer purchase on the water by entering through the bow wave that precedes the swimmer. The shoulders were not held flat on the surface, as with Bob Kiphuth's American crawl, but were allowed to roll with the rhythm of the arm action. The resultant rotation of the torso brought the powerful large trunk muscles into action. As one arm finished stroking, the other was already propelling, and they likened their timing to the "split second coordination of a paddle-wheel steamer." The action of the legs was subdued but could be speeded up quite noticeably in sprinting.

Continuing the Australian trend, James Counsilman was one of the developers of the broken tempo style of crawl swimming with emphasis on the arm action and the relegation of the kick to that of stabilizing agent. Together with the Australian coaches, Sam Herford and

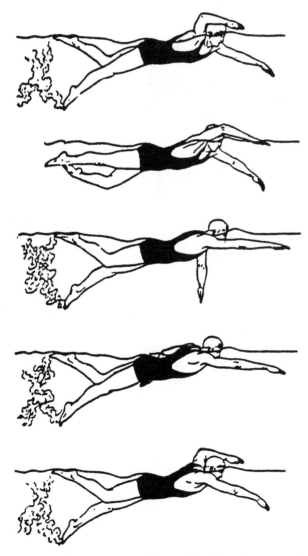

Figure 1.16   One version of the American crawl in the 1940s was characterized by an overlapping arm action and a wide kick like riding a bicycle. From Armbruster 1942.

Frank Guthrie, Counsilman experimented with dragging or resting the legs during the arm action without affecting the continuous action of the arms (Colwin 1969).

The Backstroke

In *Colymbetes*, Wynman (1538), author of the first book in the world on swimming, gives the first reference to swimming on the back:

> He adds a tale of a man on his back pretending to be a corpse: "but move your hands with swift movements as if shaking them like the birds do their wings, move them like the blade of a ploughshare when you sharpen it on a grindstone, or as if you were cutting smooth water. Keep as much breath as you can and blow through the nose (p. 45).

After this early description of swimming on the back, several centuries followed during which there were no significant developments in this form of swimming other than a backstroke developed by the Europeans that was really nothing more than an inverted breaststroke, consisting of a double-overarm recovery and an upside-down breaststroke kick, performed in the same rhythm as breaststroke.

Then in the early 20th century, H.J. Handy of Chicago introduced a trudgen backstroke, in which the arms stroked alternately. As the right arm reached forward behind the shoulder to the entry with the palm turned outward, the other arm was allowed to drift in the water next to the hip. The right arm then pulled outward and downward in a full sweep that ended at the hip. While the right arm was pulling, the swimmer recovered the left arm overhead with a relaxed elbow and wrist. Until this stage had been reached, the legs trailed close together, straight but relaxed. Then, as the left arm started its sweep, the legs opened and performed a scissors kick that ended just as the left arm completed its sweep. As in the trudgen stroke, there was a short glide before the next stroke started.

The Origin of the Backcrawl

Harry Hebner invented the crawl backstroke by converting crawl stroke principles to swimming on the back (figure 1.17). He rotated his arms continuously as in the prone crawl and did a straight up-and-down leg thrash, with the action starting from the hip. The knees were relaxed, partly bent, and the loose ankles permitted a whiplash kick. His face remained clear of the water while he inhaled through the mouth and out through the nose.

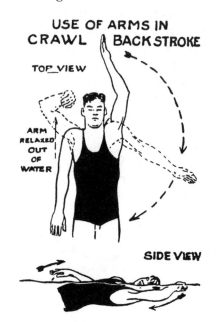

Figure 1.17 Backcrawl as swum by pioneer swimmer Harry Hebner. He used a bent-arm recovery and a straight-arm pull. From Bachrach 1924.

Hebner made his international debut in 1908 as a 17-year-old member of the 1908 Olympic team. Four years later, in Sweden, he won a gold medal in the 100-meter backstroke and a silver medal on the 800-meter freestyle relay team. A quaint comment on Hebner's backstroke appeared in the Swedish official report of the Games: "Hebner swam alternately with arm stroke and leg crawl."

The greatest female backstroke swimmer of the 1920s era was another Chicagoan, Sybil Bauer, also of the Illinois Athletic Club, and she brought the backstroke to a new level of development, her times at one stage being faster than the men's records. She swam with her head tilted forward and chin close to the chest. She flexed her knees slightly as she kicked, and the depth of her leg drive depended on whether she was sprinting or swimming at middle-distance pace. She rolled very little, using her arms independently of the body. Her body position was very low, with her shoulders seldom appearing on the surface. Each hand, palm turned outward, entered behind the head, just wide of the shoulder line. The hand then pressed downward and completed its pull at the thigh. Here the palm turned outward and the elbow led the recovery, almost like an upside-down crawl recovery. As the elbow passed the shoulder the forearm was raised above it, extending the arm for the next entry.

The Kiefer Style

In 1935, Adolph Kiefer, a Chicago school boy, swam the backstroke 100 yards in 57.6 seconds, and then went on to win the 1936 Olympic 100-meter backstroke title. His technique, described by Armbruster (1942), became known around the world as the "Kiefer style" (figure 1.18) and

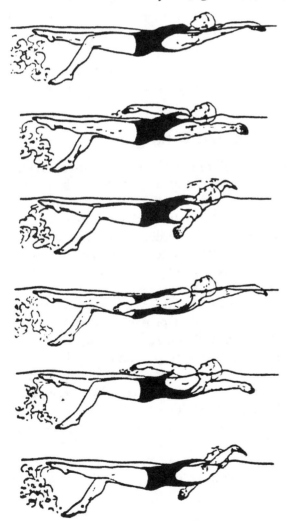

Figure 1.18 The Kiefer backstroke. From Armbruster 1942.

had three unique features: Kiefer recovered his arms, elbows held straight, with a low lateral swing over the water. He entered each arm wide of the shoulder and instead of using the customary deep pull, he pulled with a straight arm just below the surface. Kiefer's style was universally accepted for many years, although some swimmers recovered the arms with a bent elbow and introduced a slight bend at the elbow during the pull.

The Bent Arm Backstroke Pull

For the first time in the literature, Kiphuth and Burke (1951) described a bent arm pull in the backstroke. The swimmer appearing in the accompanying motion pictures was Allan Stack, the 1948 Olympic backstroke champion. Kiphuth and Burke described the backstroke as an alternate overarm action, synchronized with an alternate up-and-down beat of the legs, six kicks to a full cycle of the arms. The arm stroke started with the arm extended at full length behind the head and slightly outside the shoulder.

> The hand slices the water, with the little finger entering first. The catch is made with a straight arm, but as the arm approaches the side horizontal the elbow bends to enable the hand and broad surface of the forearm to drive as much water as possible backward to the finish of the stroke at the thighs. The recovery is made out of water with either a straight or bent arm (p. 101).

The Breaststroke

Frank Sachs (1912) advised beginners that "it is to the leg stroke that the swimmer must chiefly depend for success." However, although Steedman (1867) had advised against it nearly 50 years earlier, Sachs incorrectly spoke about drawing the legs up under the body. Sachs then continued as follows: "The legs are straightened and as wide apart as possible, before bringing them together very smartly and to as nearly as possible make them touch" (p. 20). This technique, known as the wedge kick, became extinct later in the century to be replaced by the whip kick, in which the swimmer propelled with the soles of the feet rather than by a closing of the legs.

William Bachrach (1924, p. 106) advocated learning the breaststroke first because if a person learned a faster stroke first, the chances were that there would be no interest in later learning this slower method of swimming.

Bachrach did not agree with the usual frog kick taught at that time. Bachrach said, "I don't know why it is called the frog kick because if we really kicked like a frog we would get nowhere. Recall the size of the frog's foot and the length of his leg in relation to the rest of his body. He gets almost as good a push against the water as you would get jumping on dry land. The human foot is a small thing in relation to the rest of the body, and compared to the relationship of the frog's foot to his body."

Bachrach's method of breaststroke kicking was to spread the legs to a wide straddle position, with the knees bent and turned out sideways, an action that required especially supple joints. From the full spread position, Bachrach advocated giving the legs a vigorous slap inward. Bachrach said, "It is really one motion, reaching the starting position and slapping back, like the snapping of a whip. Instead of resembling the frog's kick, it is like the flapping of two fishes tails." This was, in effect, yet another version of the now-obsolete wedge kick, which had the negative effect of merely washing the water sideways over the legs instead of directly backward.

Handley's Improved Style

Handley (1918) took the lead in coaching an improved form of breaststroke swimming, in which the arms were no longer swept back close to the surface until at right angles to the body, a method that had been incorrectly used for the best part of a century. Instead, Handley taught swimmers to take a shorter stroke and pull down as well as outward. Also, the arms and legs did not drive and recover together but alternately. The benefit derived from the alternate timing of arms and legs resulted in a more even distribution of effort, constant propulsion, and less stoppage between arm and leg movements.

The outward and downward pull lifted the upper body higher, enabling the swimmer to inhale freely and deeply. The shorter pull reduced the inward and forward movements of the arm recovery, thus minimizing resistance and providing a more powerful backward component to the stroke.

The legs were set in motion as the arms finished their pull. The knees were lowered and opened easily, without separating the heels; then the feet moved slowly apart until, finally, with a combined movement, the legs were kicked out vigorously and snapped strongly together.

For the stroke to be perfectly timed, the closing of the legs was timed to occur as the arms attained full reach ahead so that the body shot forward on the momentum imparted by the kick. Air was inhaled through the mouth during the drive of the arms and exhaled through the nostrils while the arms were recovering.

Tempo and Timing

Gilbert Collins (1934) advocated that tall swimmers with long legs should reduce the width of the kick, while short swimmers should use a wider kick. He compared the actions of the two leading male swimmers in the 1928 Olympics in Amsterdam, where Tsuruta (Japan) defeated Rademacher (Germany) by using a quicker stroke. The Japanese swimmer was 5 feet 4 inches tall, while Rademacher stood 6 feet. He said that the big German swimmer, with his long limbs and wide sweep, could not match the stroke speed of his smaller rival.

David Armbruster (1942) said that breaststroke swimming speed could be increased by shifting from a wide lateral arm movement to a more downward movement to get the arms under the body (figure 1.19). He said that "speed being the chief objective in competitive swimming, not only must the stroke be streamlined

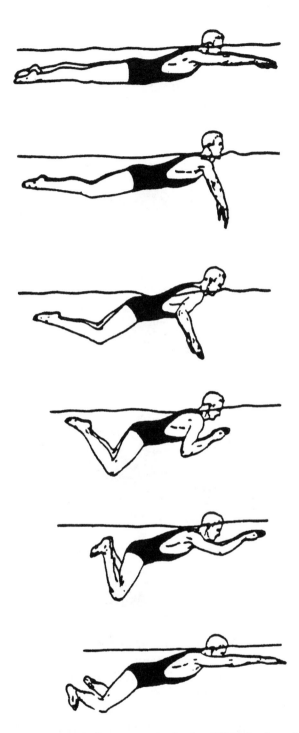

Figure 1.19 Breaststroke in the 1930s featured a more downward arm movement. Influenced by the way the breaststroke kick was used in the new butterfly-breaststroke, the kick also became narrower when swimming the orthodox breaststroke. From Armbruster 1942.

to overcome resistance but power must also be developed" (p. 176).

Armbruster discussed various types of arm and leg actions for individual body types. His text describes, for the first time in the literature, the differences in timing with the total stroke when using a wide knee-spread kick, as well as the timing to be used in the narrow knee-spread kick.

Mid-20th-Century European Style

Bela Rajki (1956) described a fully stretched body position that formed a slight angle with the water surface. The head controlled body position, and care was taken to avoid too low a head position, which would bring the feet up too high and spoil the effectiveness of the leg drive; conversely, if the feet sank too low the body angle would cause resistance.

Rajki advocated a wide arm action with the arms moving sideways, down, and back simultaneously. The wrists were bent slightly and the hands cupped to engage the water and pull the body forward. As the outward phase of the pull ended in line with the shoulders, a gradual bending of the elbows changed the action into a push or inward sculling motion at the end of which the hands, palms turned inward, came under the chest with forceful pressure applied to the water. The arms were thrust forward, level with the chin, and shoulders hunched to reduce water resistance and help the body slide forward.

In the leg action, the legs were drawn up, with the soles turned slightly inward facing each other, the knees spreading farther and farther apart as the movement progressed. When the knees reached maximum bend the feet, now quite close to the hips, were turned outward with extreme dorsi-flexion. The kick was performed "with an outward circular thrust moving quickly and forcefully backwards and downwards," finishing with a straightening of the knees and closing of the thighs. The feet were rotated inward, with the soles pressing the water with the greatest possible pressure.

The leg and arm actions followed one another, with the legs being drawn up as the hands reached the level of the shoulders and continued until the hands came under the chin, from which position the kick joined in the forward movement of the body, brought about by the arm action. Inhalation took place as the arm action ended. Rajki mentioned that the several variations of the breaststroke differed in style and coordination according to individual physique.

The Butterfly-Breaststroke

Breaststroke has undergone many changes as a competitive swimming style. During the 1930s the breaststroke had to withstand the onslaught of the butterfly-breaststroke swimmers. Butterfly-breaststroke was a hybrid stroke that combined the butterfly arm action with the breaststroke kick (figure 1.20), and it came about when swimmers found a loophole in the breaststroke rules as they existed at that time, namely in that the law made no stipulation about the need to recover the arms forward from the breast.

The butterfly-breaststroke (butterfly arm action with orthodox breaststroke kick) very quickly became the fastest method of competing in breaststroke races. The orthodox breaststroke swimmer, using the traditional action, became a rarity in competition because the International Olympic Committee (IOC) was not in favor of adding an extra event to the Olympic program to accommodate the two vastly different styles of swimming. In fact, at one stage, the breaststroke was almost in danger of becoming extinct as a racing stroke.

A saga of legalistic wrangling ensued for 20 years as swimming administrators attempted to sort out the muddle of their own making. It was not until the Melbourne Olympic Games in 1956 that reason prevailed and butterfly became a separate event and breaststroke was swum as breaststroke—not butterfly. (The hands had to be recovered forward from the breast, at least when swimming on the surface. While swimming underwater, the swimmer was permitted to use a full length pull through to the hips.)

Figure 1.20 The now-extinct hybrid butterfly-breaststroke in which the breaststroke kick was combined with the butterfly arm action. From Armbruster 1942.

The result of this ruling was a spectacle that the breaststroke traditionalists could not have imagined! A new trend rapidly developed in which swimmers, particularly the Japanese swimmers, took to swimming long distances underwater with a resultant long pull through to the hips. They would surface for a breath, then off they would go on their underwater journey.

In February 1957, in response to this development, the FINA International Swimming Technical Committee (ISTC) recommended to Congress that no underwater swimming be allowed in breaststroke and butterfly events. Breaststroke was then legislated to surface swimming with only one underwater pull and one kick allowed after the pushoff from the wall at the turn and an underwater glide allowed after the starting dive (Colwin 1998).

Apparently a big problem facing FINA's rule makers was the semantics—as well as translation difficulties between several languages—of describing when a swimmer's head was or was not submerged under the surface. First, it was ruled that part of the head should always break the surface of the water. This resulted not only in a stilted action but in the swimmers having to hold their heads too high thus reducing the body's streamlining. Some swimmers were even ridiculously disqualified when their heads disappeared under their own bow waves.

The result was a big debate as to when a swimmer's head was "above the general water level." This rather nebulous description was later changed to read that the head should always break the surface of the water. In 1980 the FINA Congress in Moscow thought it would be able to solve this problem by adopting the recommendation of the ISTC to read that part of the head should break the surface of the water during each complete stroke. Instead the Congress decided that part of the head shall break the surface of the water throughout the race, a decision that really was no different from the old rule (Colwin 1998).

Thierry (1981) was concerned with the wording of the new rule, writing that the swimming public had been led to believe that a "relaxed interpretation of the rule was to be made that allowed the head to submerge, provided the head broke the water level once on each arm cycle" (p. 2). This did not happen, and in Thierry's opinion, the new wording made the problems facing the stroke and turn judges worse than before.

Salvation came when Howard Hanson, an Australian coach, writing in *The International Swimmer*, said that the remedy suggested by FINA in Moscow "was worse than the original complaint." He offered the following solution: a part of the head or body shall be above the general surface of the water at least once during each arm stroke. This would effectively prevent underwater swimming and make judging possible. FINA finally got it right on February 15, 1987, when, using wording not much different than that suggested by Coach Hanson, they changed the breaststroke head rule to read: "During each complete cycle of one arm stroke and one leg kick, some part of the head of the swimmer shall break the surface of the water" (Colwin 1998).

Breaststroke Development in the 1960s

After breaststroke once more became a separate stroke, its evolution was characterized by an increased attention to streamlining the stroke, while also adapting it to different body types. In the process, variations in body build and stature, length of limb, muscularity, and individual buoyancy became important factors.

In the Australian and the American versions of the stroke, the aim was to try to avoid excessive up-and-down movement of the shoulders while trying to keep the entire body as flat and as high as possible. The heels were to be kept high enough so that they worked very close to the surface, both in recovery and during the kick.

On the other hand, the Europeans—particularly the Russians—permitted and even encouraged the shoulders and torso to rise and fall in the natural rhythm of the stroke. There was also a distinct difference between the leg actions advocated by the two schools of thought. While Westerners preferred an ultraflat and almost static body position in which the legs were drawn up prior to the kick with a deep knee-bend and hip flexion to preserve this position, the Russians in particular allowed the entire body to rise and fall while keeping an almost straight line down the front of the body to the knees, as the feet were recovered over the knees prior to delivering the kick.

During this period the emphasis on a downward and backward arm movement became more pronounced. At the same time, the width of the pull became narrower than it had been before. The aim in the shorter, narrower arm pull was not only to increase streamlining but also to achieve a more effective application of muscular strength and power while increasing the quickness of the movement. The same principle of quick movement was applied to the leg kick, which also became narrower and faster. It became apparent to coaches and swimmers alike that the narrower and quicker the pull and the kick, the faster the swimmer could go.

The Dolphin Butterfly Stroke

Henry Myers of the Brooklyn Dragon Swim Club is generally credited with developing the butterfly stroke. In 1933, while swimming breaststroke in practice, as a novelty diversion he tried pulling his arms through to his hips and recovering them over the water like a double freestyle arm recovery. He was amazed to find he could beat his club's best breaststroke swimmers in short practice swims by combining his new double overarm action with his usual breaststroke kick.

It seems unlikely that Myers had intended to invent a new stroke because only the kick resembled breaststroke. However, he and his coach W.W. Robertson looked up the rules and found to their surprise that the new stroke did not contradict the rules in any way. They decided that Myers should try out the stroke in the 150-yard medley event at the Brooklyn YMCA swim meet in December 1933 (Colwin 1998).

To everyone's surprise, Myers beat the favorite, Wallace Spence, the American medley champion. At first the odd-looking stroke took the officials by surprise, but after Robertson showed the rule book to the officials, Myers was not disqualified, and this set the precedent for future use of the stroke (figure 1.21).

Note: In 1927 the German swimmer Erich Rademacher, during a tour of the United States, gained considerable advantage by bringing his

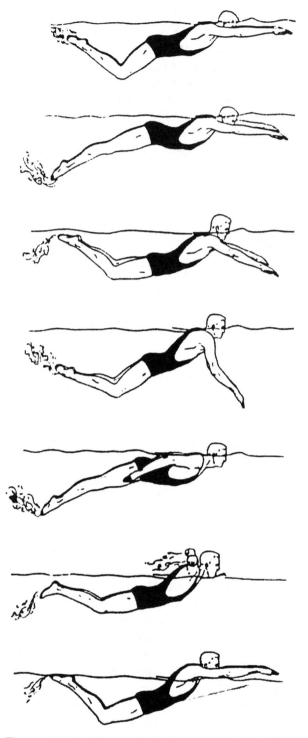

Figure 1.21 The early dolphin butterfly stroke, as performed by its pioneers, was swum with an almost straight arm action, an excessive undulation of the hips, and a very wide leg action. The legs kicked twice for every arm stroke cycle. The stroke was not permitted in competition until 1954. From Armbruster 1942.

arms over the water in a double overarm recovery as he approached the turn and also when he touched at the end of a race. Rademacher insisted, even at that early date, that this in no way infringed the rules of breaststroke swimming (Colwin 1998).

From here the butterfly rapidly grew in popularity in school, college, and national competition in the United States. People began to take it seriously and some even claimed to have originated it. The early outstanding exponents were Lester Kaplan and Paul Friesel.

In December 1954, the IOC finally agreed to the inclusion of separate butterfly events, starting with the 1956 Olympics in Melbourne, Australia. However, in June 1956, it was announced that entries for the breaststroke and butterfly events at the Olympics were to be limited by the IOC to only three competitors in breaststroke and butterfly together. This statement showed that even after 20 years, the IOC still did not understand that the butterfly and breaststroke were essentially different strokes that should have been separated long ago. The truth is that the IOC had been too concerned with its own priorities to consider, let alone understand, the developmental needs of one particular stroke (Colwin 1998).

Development of the Dolphin Kick

In 1935, Jack Sieg, a University of Iowa swimmer, developed the skill of swimming on his side while moving his legs in unison similar to the action of a fish's tail. He tried the same leg action while swimming face down on the surface and eventually developed a perfectly timed combination of arm and leg action using two leg beats to each arm pull. He showed the stroke's speed potential by swimming 100 yards in 60.2 seconds (Armbruster 1942, p. 24). However, the dolphin kick was ruled illegal because the legs moved in the vertical plane. Not until 1956 was the butterfly stroke allowed in Olympic competition, simply because the IOC refused to add new competitions to the Olympic program. Thus, for 21 years, the world of swimming had a new stroke with great potential but with no event in which it could be legally swum—a sad reflection on FINA and the IOC.

Use of the Dolphin Kick in Starting and Turning

FINA Rule SW 8.5 states: "At the start and at turns, a swimmer is permitted one or more leg kicks and one arm pull under the water, which must bring him to the surface. It shall be permissible for a swimmer to be completely submerged for a distance of not more than 15 meters after the start and after each turn. By that point, the head must have broken the surface. The swimmer must remain on the surface until the next turn or finish."

The dolphin kick is much faster when swum under the surface after the starting dive and when pushing off from the wall after the turn. This is because swimming below the disturbed surface water eliminates wave drag that constitutes about 80 percent of the overall drag acting on the body. (Friction drag, the result of the water being in contact with the body, is only about 20 to 30 percent of the total drag acting on the body when swimming.)

Chapter 2

Breakthroughs in Stroke Techniques

Biomechanics refers to the application of laws governing all forms of human motion. These laws deal with forces and their resultant motions. The laws concerned with the motion of bodies are commonly divided into two branches: kinematics and kinetics. *Kinematics* involves aspects of the *motions* of bodies, such as speed, velocity, and acceleration, without reference to what causes them. *Kinetics* is concerned with the *effects* that forces have on these motions.

During the second half of the 20th century, the biomechanical research conducted by James "Doc" Counsilman and Robert Schleihauf contributed to a better understanding of human swimming propulsion, particularly to the changing interactions between *lift* and *drag* forces, two terms they introduced into the swimming lexicon.

Counsilman showed why the pull in all swimming strokes does not follow a straight line (1969; 1971; Counsilman and Brown 1970). Before Counsilman began his experiments, many talented swimmers naturally changed the direction of the pull as the hand moved in a curved path across the line of the swimmer's forward movement. A detailed underwater photographic study of the familiar curvilinear pattern of the butterfly stroke prompted Counsilman to question

the validity of the prevailing concept (which Counsilman himself advocated at the time) of teaching swimmers to pull directly backward in a straight line in order to go directly forward. (This concept was in accordance with Newton's third law of motion: for every action there is a reaction, equal and opposite.)

Schleihauf, by accurate measurement of hand placements and use of vector analysis, showed the range of propulsive forces developed in the four swimming styles (1974; 1977; 1979).

The Lift Principle

Formulated by the Swiss mathematician Daniel Bernoulli (1700–1782), the law known as the Bernoulli principle states that as the velocity of a fluid increases, the pressure it exerts decreases.

When a stream of fluid passes around a foil—such as a swimmer's hand—the flow over the convex upper surface has a greater velocity and, following Bernoulli's principle, a lower pressure than that on the under surface; the difference in pressure between the two streams creates a force called *lift* (figure 2.1).

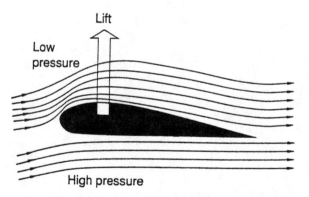

Figure 2.1 The difference in pressure between the low-pressure and high-pressure streams creates a lift force.

Lift, also known as side thrust, always acts in a direction perpendicular to the direction of motion. In the case of an airplane wing in level flight, lift is directed upward at a right angle to the direction of motion (figure 2.2).

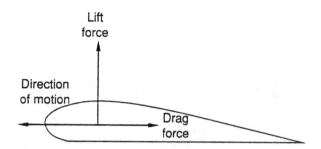

Figure 2.2 Lift always acts in a direction perpendicular to the direction of motion.

A propeller is like a wing in that it also generates lift, but the lift, acting at right angles to the blade's motion, is directed forward (figure 2.3).

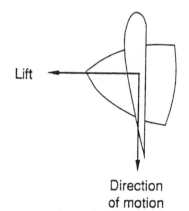

Figure 2.3 A propeller is like a wing and also generates lift.

Counsilman's presentation revealed that when a swimmer's hand moves in a curved-line path across the line of the body's forward motion, it at times produces forward lift (figure 2.4).

Basically, the swimmer uses the resistance caused by lift on the palm of the hand to apply thrust. The action can be likened to walking up a sandy slope, with every step up pushing the sand down. Both examples obey Newton's third law of motion.

The action-reaction principle mentioned earlier in the description of the straight-line pull still applies, but when lift propulsion predominates in a swimming stroke, the reaction is created by a different mechanism. Instead of

Figure 2.4 A swimmer's hand moves in a curvilinear path to produce forward lift: *(a)* front view and *(b)* side view.
Adapted from Counsilman 1977.

Figure 2.5 Lift propulsion is created by the hand moving in a curvilinear path (underneath view).
Adapted from Counsilman 1977.

pushing directly backward in a straight line with the palm of the hand, the hand moves in a curved path, splitting the water with the edge of the hand to create a pressure resistance on the palm of the hand against which thrust is applied (figure 2.5).

Counsilman's findings suggested a different approach to swimming efficiency in all the strokes. The hand should not always be pulled directly backward in a straight line (paddling) but, at times, and in certain strokes, should follow a curvilinear path (sculling), during which the angle of the hand (pitch) relative to the body's forward motion should be continuously adjusted to achieve the maximum lift propulsion (figure 2.6).

In recent years, freeze-frame underwater videography, taken with new robotic underwater cameras, has thrown an interesting light on the nature of a swimmer's supposedly self-

Figure 2.6 The pitch of the hand is continuously adjusted to achieve maximum lift propulsion.
Adapted from Counsilman 1977.

created sculling motions. These movement sequences were taken during actual racing conditions, when swimmers were traveling at speed and applying arm leverage to develop maximum force. Instead of deliberately attempting to use so-called sculling motions in a conscious attempt to scull in a curvilinear path, the sequences show that in the freestyle stroke, lateral deviations from the intended direct straight-back movements of the hands are caused naturally by the body's rotation on its long axis.

Interaction of Lift and Drag Forces

It is difficult to understand why biomechanists have divided into separate camps concerning the dominant use of either drag or lift force propulsion in swimming. Almost any elementary text on fluid dynamics will include within its first one or two pages a statement such as the following typical extract on the basic interaction between lift and drag forces:

> The force acting on a body moving through a fluid is usually resolved into two components: one called lift normal to the direction in the body, and the other called drag, in a direction opposed to that of motion (Karamcheti 1966).

Schleihauf, a swimming coach and also a trained engineer, pointed out that like any body moving through a fluid, human swimming propulsion results from neither lift nor drag forces acting in isolation but rather from a constant interaction between the two during the changing sequences of a swimming stroke (1974; 1977; 1979).

Schleihauf created an exact plastic resin replica of a hand, which he dipped into a flow channel through which fluid moved at a known speed. The hand was mounted on a rod that measured the total range of forces, both lift and drag, produced by the hand in varying flow conditions and at different angles of pitch (Schleihauf 1977).

Lift Coefficient

Schleihauf then compared the lifting characteristics of the hand with the characteristics of a commonly used airfoil of similar profile (NACA airfoil 0012) and found that the hand's maximum lift coefficient was 20 percent less than the wing's. He attributed this minor difference to the hand's slightly more irregular shape.

The term *lift coefficient* refers to the relationship between the amount of lift on an airfoil and its angle of pitch. The lift component, or amount of lift on an airfoil or human hand, increases or decreases relative to the size of the angle of pitch. According to Schleihauf, the lift coefficient on a swimmer's hand increases up to an angle of pitch (also known as angle of attack) of about 40 degrees and then decreases (figure 2.7; Schleihauf 1977).

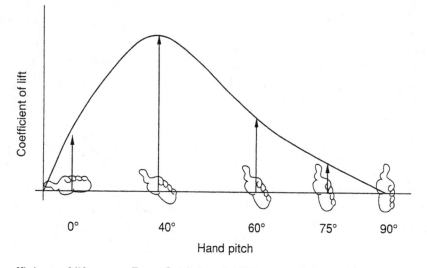

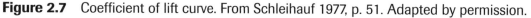

Figure 2.7 Coefficient of lift curve. From Schleihauf 1977, p. 51. Adapted by permission.

Drag Coefficient

Similarly, the term *drag coefficient* refers to the relationship between the drag component on an airfoil or hand and its angle of attack. The drag coefficient also increases or decreases in relation to the size of the angle of attack. Schleihauf's measurements show that the drag coefficient on a swimmer's hand increases as the angle of attack increases to 90 degrees (Schleihauf 1977). With a diminishing angle of attack, the drag coefficient decreases. There is an almost equal contribution of lift and drag forces at an angle of approximately 45 degrees, and drag forces predominate when the hand reaches angles greater than 45 degrees (figure 2.8).

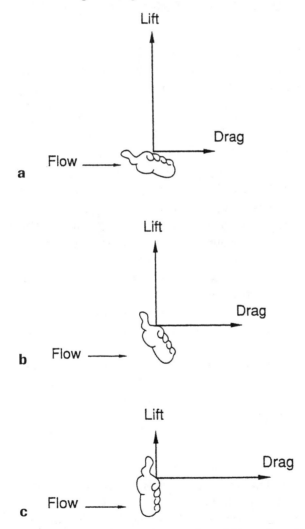

Figure 2.8 Lift-drag interaction: *(a)* less than 45 degrees; *(b)* 45 degrees; *(c)* greater than 45 degrees. From Schleihauf 1977, p. 53. Adapted by permission.

Resultant Propulsive Force

The next stage of Schleihauf's studies involved filming champion swimmers from directly below and at right angles to their forward direction. Before filming, Schleihauf placed four small lights on each swimmer's hands, which enabled Schleihauf to determine the hands' paths as well as their changing speeds and angles of attack in all four styles of swimming. Schleihauf then combined the data collected from his film studies of leading swimmers with the information obtained in the fluid laboratory (Schleihauf 1977).

By this method, Schleihauf determined the direction and magnitude of the lift and drag forces created by the hands at key points in the stroke. Using vector analysis of this information, he estimated the instantaneous direction and magnitude of the resultant propulsive force—that is, the net effect of the interaction between the lift and drag forces. Schleihauf then measured the resultant forces developed during the stroke at selected angles of hand pitch (figure 2.9). His work set the scene for the first comprehensive analysis of stroke mechanics and has since been followed by several other studies.

Angle of Attack

The angle at which a body meets the flowstream, or angle of attack, is a crucial factor. The angle of attack has nothing to do with the horizontal (parallel to the ground) angle but is instead the angle at which the object meets the flowstream. In the example of the thin plate (see figure 2.10), we know that there is minimum flow resistance when the plate is held with its edge to the stream and maximum drag when held at a right angle. But what happens when the leading edge is inclined at a slight angle?

The fluid pressure is now greater underneath the plate than on the top surface, a lifting force, or side thrust, acting at right angles to the oncoming flowstream. But whenever lift is generated, drag is also created. Drag acts in the direction opposite to the motion of the object. Whereas lift acts at right angles to the flowstream, drag acts parallel to the flowstream. The net result is that the total force on the plate is backward as well as upward (figure 2.11).

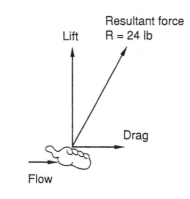

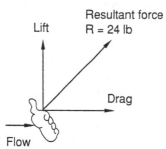

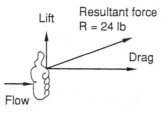

Figure 2.9 Resultant force production: *(a)* pitch equals 20 degrees, velocity equals 12.0 fps; *(b)* pitch equals 45 degrees, velocity equals 11.2 fps; *(c)* pitch equals 90 degrees, velocity equals 10.0 fps. From Schleihauf 1977, p. 53. Adapted by permission.

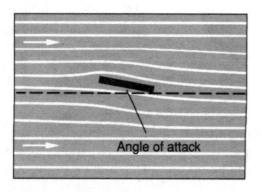

Figure 2.10 Thin plate inclined to the flowstream to form an angle of attack.

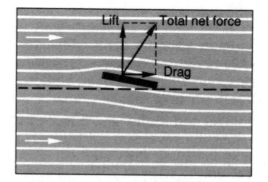

Figure 2.11 Lift and drag forces act on a thin plate inclined at an angle of attack.

Important Contributions of Biomechanic Research

Ernest Maglischo (1983) used three-dimensional motion picture photography and digitizing techniques to show distinct periods of acceleration and deceleration of forward speed during a stroke cycle. Maglischo posed the important question: "When are these periods of deceleration normal, and when do they indicate stroke defects?"

Following Maglischo's study, David Costill (1987) conceived a video-computer system that provided instant analysis of a swimmer's velocity at different points in the stroke. The system combines the use of a video camera with the swim meter invented by Albert Craig and David Pendergast (1979). (The mechanical parts of the swim meter were designed and built by Gerald F. Harris.) A computer synchronizes the video image with a velocity graph and superimposes the two on a video display. This information eventually may help swimmers time their strokes with greater accuracy, particularly when they know the relationship between the propulsive forces they develop and the fluctuating velocities within the stroke cycle. At present, we remain in comparative ignorance about this important practical aspect of swimming propulsion. The continuing challenge will be to reduce often complex scientific information to a simple, easily taught format.

Further complicating the new perspective was the realization that not only does the hand propel by moving in a curvilinear path but that this path is three-dimensional (figure 2.12). The hand moves simultaneously in three dimensions—the lateral, vertical, and horizontal planes.

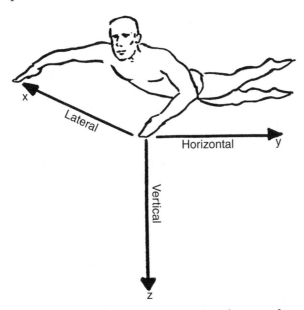

Figure 2.12 The three-dimensional aspect (x, y, z axes) of the pull. From Schleihauf 1977, p. 50. Adapted by permission.

Counsilman and Wasilak (1982), studying hand speed and hand-acceleration patterns in swimming strokes, found that the hand follows a velocity pattern in which the three-dimensional speed continuously increases except for a deceleration point in midstroke, a finding that confirms Schleihauf's study (1974).

The main impediments to a swimmer's forward motion are frontal resistance, form drag, and eddy resistance. Frontal resistance is caused by wave-making drag. The swimmer's forward momentum causes a buildup of moving pressure disturbances in the water in front of the body, which results in frontal resistance. Lifting the head and shoulders too far from the horizontal plane lowers the hips and legs to set up increased frontal resistance.

In freestyle and backstroke, the strokes in which the body rolls or rotates on its long axis, the use of gradually curved surfaces along the general paths followed by the water flow will minimize resistance. By rotating the body to each side within the natural rhythm of the stroke, smaller changes in the curvature of the flow lines result. In butterfly and breaststroke, the momentary submerging of the body beneath the surface greatly reduces surface wave drag.

Form drag (or skin friction) is caused by water resistance on the swimmer's skin, a resistance generally considered to have little negative effect on propulsion. However, the practice of shaving body hair ("shaving down") has been shown to enhance swimming speed (Sharp and Costill 1989).

Eddy resistance or separation (also known as tail suction) is caused by water pressure at a given region insufficient to force the water laterally inward and make it follow closely along the body, especially toward the body's tapering aft end. Water is dragged in from behind the swimmer to fill the gap left because the flow has not closed in from the sides. Resistance is generated by the forward acceleration of water that otherwise would flow backward and be left behind.

Prolonged Momentum

Some swimmers naturally prolong their momentum past the point where it would normally start to diminish. A stroke cycle well coordinated with each propulsive impulse occurring in ideal sequence can avoid extreme fluctuations of acceleration and deceleration. The more constant the momentum, the better the index of efficient technique (Colwin 1984b).

The ability to prolong momentum allows a swimmer to take fewer strokes to cover a set distance, an indication of proficiency. Measurement against a grid shows that a skilled crawl swimmer is able to complete a swimming stroke with the hand leaving the water ahead of the point at which it entered (Schleihauf 1977). At first, this phenomenon was thought to result from lift force causing the hand to move forward as it stroked. However, the real reason is that, as one hand enters the water, the body is propelled forward by the other hand. In figure 2.13, the right arm enters in a stream-lined posture that permits water to flow under the arm and torso, enabling the body to prolong the momentum developed by the left arm as it accelerates through its pull.

Other factors also result in prolonged momentum, such as having a streamlined and buoyant body and having the ability to accelerate the arm stroke to overcome resistance drag (Colwin 1984b).

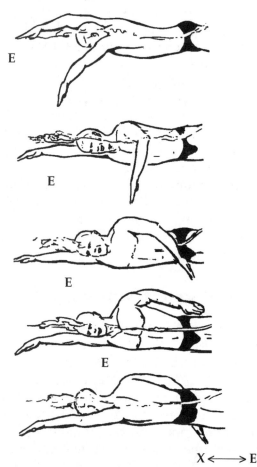

X ⟷ E

Figure 2.13 Skilled swimmers prolong momentum by accurately timing their arm strokes and streamlining their body alignments throughout stroke sequence. Observing the entry (E) and exit (X) points of a swimmer against a poolside grid creates a visual impression of the swimmer's stroking efficiency. If a swimmer's hand exits the water at the same point where it entered, it shows that there has been no "slip" in the stroke. As shown here, highly skilled swimmers exit their hands *ahead* of the entry point, the distance between "X" and "E" indicating the extent to which they are able to prolong momentum. This indicates their ability to swim with fewer strokes per lap.

Kinetic Streamlining

Kinetic streamlining refers to the synchronization of body and limb alignments aimed at reducing drag during the impulses of force and the resulting propulsion (Colwin 1984b). Most competent swimmers naturally assume stream-lined body alignments. However, the presence of bilateral body alignments in the crawl and backstroke, for example, will not necessarily result in prolonged momentum. The timing of the changing alignment sequences is the key factor.

When the body rotates on its long axis in freestyle and backstroke, the water flows smoothly around the body with reduced changes to the curvature of the flow lines. The rotation lowers resistance because the rotating action results in a smaller surface area of the body being presented to the water. To maximize this effect in crawl and backstroke, a skilled swimmer spends most of the stroke cycle with the body tipped equally to one side or the other rather than in the flat, central posture that produces increased resistance.

Transitional Phases of the Swimming Strokes

The body roll on its long axis in freestyle and backstroke results from the rotation of the arms as they alternately pull and recover over the water. The entire body—shoulders, hips, and legs—rotates at once. The total amount of roll varies from 70 to 90 degrees, or 35 to 45 degrees on each side of the body's long axis, in both the freestyle and backstroke.

The direction and speed of the body's rotation is controlled by the arms throughout the stroke cycle rather than by the swimmer consciously rotating the hips from side to side, using the so-called core muscles. (Core swimming was a popular catchphrase in the late 20th century, used mainly by purveyors of expensive exercise equipment designed to strengthen the large muscles of the trunk.) During each arm recovery, the shifting mass of the shoulder and upper arm causes the body to roll gradually to the other side. The directional change of the body roll is synchronized with the other arm as it starts its pull. This transition from the end of one stroke to the start of the next is critical to maintain momentum. It requires smooth streamlining of changing body alignments and split-second timing of one arm with the other to ensure the swimmer's prolonged momentum.

Some swimmers, because of their physical characteristics, are unable to roll quickly enough to synchronize the body rotation with the arm action. It is likely that each swimmer has an individual "rolling time," the time taken for the total of roll from one side to the other. This might be related to height, the average width of the body, buoyancy, and so on.

Usually, swimmers who are broad and stocky have a slow rolling time from one side to the other. Conversely, tall, light-boned, and buoyant female swimmers are able to roll quickly, thus avoiding excessive resistance by not staying too long in the central position.

Stroke Length and Stroke Frequency

Stroke length (distance per stroke) and stroke frequency (stroke rate) govern a swimmer's average speed. Should a swimmer use long, slow strokes or short, fast strokes? Actually, skilled swimmers tend to use long, fast strokes. When they increase their speed, better swimmers usually try to take even longer strokes and turn over the longer stroke more quickly.

Though the concept of taking long strokes is not a new idea, it took hold only gradually. Most competitors in the early years of the sport thought speed was to be achieved by fast and furious stroking. However, Louis de B. Handley (1928), one of the pioneers of women's competitive swimming and a prolific writer on aquatic subjects, observed that a swift stroke is not conducive to fast swimming.

Ron Johnson (1982) delivered an address on tempo awareness training at the American Swimming Coaches' Association's World Clinic, in which he outlined methods for timing stroke tempo with a 1/100-second stopwatch or a computer that depended on the stroke being swum.

For freestyle, Johnson timed the stroke from the right-hand entry through at least two stroke cycles to the next right-hand entry, obtaining the tempo by halving the time for two cycles. Johnson said that in freestyle a typical tempo for a middle-distance collegiate swimmer is around 1.30 to 1.35 seconds. For a good college male sprinter, a typical tempo is around .95 second, and female swimmers at the elite level are approximately .05 second faster than men per stroke cycle.

Backstroke tempo, on the other hand, is slower than freestyle by about .2 to .3 second per stroke revolution. Johnson said that backstrokers take about the same number of strokes per length as freestylers do, but because of the more limited mechanics of the stroke, backstrokers cannot stroke as quickly.

Johnson suggested two ways for measuring breaststroke tempo. First, measure from the time the feet close until they close again in one stroke cycle. Second, measure from when the chin breaks the surface as the swimmer breathes until the next time the chin breaks the water. He said that breaststroke swimmers on average stroke about .10 to .15 second faster than freestylers of similar expertise.

In butterfly, the stroke is measured from the time the hands enter the water until they enter again for the next stroke. Johnson said that the stroke revolutions in butterfly are similar to freestyle. A good collegiate male 100-yard butterfly swimmer is typically in the 1.05- to 1.15-second range, whereas females in the same category vary between 1.00 and 1.05 seconds.

With the exception of those swimming the butterfly stroke, skilled swimmers usually increase their stroke length as the distance of the race increases. However, probably because of the accumulative effects of fatigue, a swimmer's stroke frequency may decrease, and so will average speed (Pai, Hay, and Wilson 1984; Craig and Pendergast 1979; Craig et al. 1985).

Researchers report no consistent pattern regarding stroke frequency during a swimming race. Stroke frequency may often remain constant throughout a race, or it may either decrease or increase (Craig et al. 1985; Curry 1975; Hay, Guimaraes, and Grimston 1983; Pai, Hay, and Wilson 1984).

Researchers agree, however, that stroke length rather than stroke frequency is the determining factor in a swimmer's average speed. They also agree that in freestyle, butterfly, and breaststroke, stroke frequency is very similar. However, probably because of the mechanical disadvantage of the body in the dorsal position, backstroke usually has a much slower stroke frequency and greater stroke length than the other strokes.

Male swimmers attain greater speed than female swimmers because they swim with a greater stroke length. However, the two sexes have very similar stroke frequencies (Craig and Pendergast 1979; East 1970; Pai, Hay, and Wilson 1984).

Olympic Stars Break Through to a New Paradigm

At the 2000 Sydney Olympics, the advanced swimming styles of freestyle champions Pieter van den Hoogenband, Ian Thorpe, Gary Hall Jr., and Alexander Popov were seen as a breakthrough to a new paradigm of stroke mechanics.

Based on the skilled use of the principle of momentum, their easy gliding action drew much attention and comment. These four athletes showed the world of swimming that accurate timing and efficient streamlining produces momentum in the most efficient way to overcome resistance.

Accurate Timing and Momentum

The naturally accurate timing of the freestyle champions' arm movements and their constantly changing body alignments produced a continuous momentum and a steady, effortless application of power. The uncanny subtlety of their strokes was in marked contrast to most of the other swimmers, who often seemed to exert too much energy by powering their way through the water.

The techniques of the first Olympic champions of the new millennium were a complete breakout from the previously dominant framework of the specious lift versus drag arguments, pursued with pedantic obsession for 30 years.

How does the use of the principle of momentum influence the efficiency of the overall swimming stroke? Momentum affects the amount of power the swimmer must apply to keep moving forward with a minimum of body deceleration. For example, when a freestyle swimmer smacks the surface water with the arm at the entry, or starts the pull too powerfully before the other hand has finished the power phase of its stroke, the momentum created by the opposite arm is severely reduced. To overcome the inertia caused by poor timing of the arms, a greater amount of effort must be applied to maintain the swimmer's momentum.

Skill

Skill is that element of performance that enables the swimmer to accomplish a large amount of work with a relatively small amount of effort. Put the other way around, performance accomplished with the least waste of effort produces the highest standard of skill.

Visible effort is a sign of unproductive effort, and poor performance is usually characterized by the type of wasteful muscular activity described previously—using forceful motions when only light ones are required.

Swimming skill is acquired mainly through a refined coordination of the various major elements of the overall swimming action. The motor impulses from the central nervous system arrive at the muscles in such numbers and with such split-second timing as to result in a correct sequence of integrated propulsive and streamlining movements.

The principles involved include the following:

- Momentum should be employed to overcome resistance.

- Work arranged to permit an easy and natural rhythm—correct timing—is conducive to smooth and automatic performance.

- Hesitation or the temporary and often cessation of motion should be eliminated from the performance.

Subtle Differences Among Individuals

The tall, lean swimmer appears to have the advantage of being able to apply force against the resistance of the water through a greater range of movement. Today's top male swimmers are rarely under 6 feet 2 inches tall, while most of the top female swimmers stand 5 feet 8 inches or taller.

Swimmers vary in mechanical adaptability, including flexibility; the surface area of their propelling members; the entire body surface area related to resistance; the floating ability of the body; and the power of the propelling factors such as the leverage developed by the arms and the thrust or balance provided by the legs.

Similarly, body proportions; height; armspan relative to height; shoulder width; hip width; the length, shape, and girth of the torso; and even the shape of the head determine the type of surface wave a swimmer will make in the water, as well as the amount of skin-water friction presented below the surface line. Equally important are the relative dimensions of various parts of the swimmer's body—particularly limbs and extremities—to the whole physique, as these vary as widely as physical contours.

Theoretically, a strong, lean, tall swimmer with good buoyancy has the best body type for speed swimming. On the other hand, squarely built female swimmers of average height who do not glide well but are unusually buoyant are often able to develop great speed with a high-revving, continuous arm stroke, particularly over longer distances.

Hand Size and Surface Area

The importance of hand size and hand surface area has been overlooked in considering the efficiency of various types of stroke patterns. The wide range of hand sizes and surface areas in different swimmers also has not been considered. These differences can be easily measured by drawing the outline of each swimmer's hand on graph paper then measuring the total surface area by counting the number of squares within the outline of the hand.

These measurements can quickly highlight the differences among swimmers, particularly between average and elite swimmers. When biomechanists report studies said to measure the forces developed by the model of an elite swimmer's hand in a moving flow, no reference is made to the size and area of the hand of the swimmer or whose hand it is.

A large difference in propulsion can result from only a small increase in surface area. A good example of this is the difference measured when a swimmer uses a hand paddle versus when he does not. Sometimes a swimmer with a small hand finds it difficult to effectively use a direct backward pull and has to use a more transverse sculling action to propel. When the same swimmer wears a hand paddle, which applies a few more square inches against the resistance of the water, he finds the direct backward paddling action much easier.

Next time you see Thorpe or Hackett gripping the water at the start of the stroke with a hooked wrist and a hand planed directly backward, note the size of their hands. It will be clear why this technique is better suited to a swimmer blessed with super-sized hands that present at least 30 square inches of propelling surface to the water with each stroke.

Despite variations in individual strengths and weaknesses, unlike yachts of different design, differently designed swimmers compete in the same race and not in races designated for people of particular physical characteristics. In each of the eight lanes will be a swimmer with basically two arm propellers and two leg propellers. Each set of propellers varies in design regarding length, shape, and surface area; consequently, each swimmer will use slightly different propelling mechanisms.

Need for Descriptive Research

We will never be able to design more efficient swimmers (in the way that racing yachts are made to measure by naval architects), but it's reasonable to assume that better methods of talent selection that measure all the complex physical and mechanical attributes that contribute to speed will one day become possible. These measurements may include mathematically constructing a prototype of the ideal swimming physique—perhaps by measuring up swimmers such as Van Hoogenband, Thorpe, Hall, and Popov, for example—to develop a model of ideal composite factors.

Stroke Mechanics

Swimmers have the choice of using the hands and forearms predominantly as paddles or as foils. Different limb shapes and sizes affect the mechanics used by each swimmer in applying propulsive leverage on the water. In the water, swimmers often look different from each other even while employing the same basic fundamentals of propulsion.

Buoyancy and balance, the split-second timing between each arm, and the continuously changing body alignments throughout the stroke are contributing factors that enable a swimmer to produce continuing momentum throughout the stroke.

Wave-Making Resistance Applied to Human Swimming

In 1969, in a discussion of power-weight ratio and streamlining, it was said:

> The effects of a swimmer's shape and physical proportions on reducing resistance is largely governed by certain factors. The ratio of height to width is probably the most important single factor in reducing resistance. The more slender the swimmer, the less will be the underwater volume compared to his height or length in the water. If he has a gradually tapering physique, this will allow water to flow past more easily. (Colwin 1969, pp. 88–89)

Vast differences exist between human swimmers and ships specially designed to displace water efficiently, so comparisons of the two are not always applicable. For one thing, a ship's bow cleanly parts the waters and keeps the resulting wave closely encased around the hull, whereas a human swimmer diverts the flow sideways, both at the bow wave created by the head and with the transverse flow created at the hips. Some water does flow under the swimmer's body and is diverted sideways before it reaches the hip bones.

An important point is that water pressure wants to go from high-pressure areas to low-pressure areas and, as a result, can't suddenly change direction. This fact is not appreciated by some theorists who draw fanciful lines along a swimmer's contours to indicate that the flow strictly observes these particular shapes. To the contrary, a flow approaching a submerged shoulder, for example, will not go right along to the shoulder to follow its particular contour but will start changing its direction well before it arrives at the shoulder.

It can be seen that a surface ship faces a practical speed limit, called its hull speed. Once past its hull speed, the ship's drag increases suddenly and severely. Since hull speed depends on hull length, a larger ship can go faster before hitting that limit. (Generally, this is called the limiting Froude number.) Basically, the speed at which any boat can move is equal to the speed at which a wave, whose length is equal to the length of that boat, travels. This can be calculated as a function of water depth and wave length. For all displacement craft, this limit is hard to exceed. It can be exceeded slightly but not by much, as doing so would require a large increase in power.

Despite the stated disadvantages that face human swimmers, athletes such as Misty Hyman, David Berkoff, and Daichi Suzuki, with their dolphin-kicking, underwater techniques, have come closest to achieving some semblance of a perfect streamlining system for human swimmers. Olympic butterfly champion Misty Hyman in particular, using her novel fish-tail technique while lying on her side underwater with arms extended forward, creates pressure waves that increase in amplitude as they move aft, using her whole body as an integrated propulsive unit.

Problems in Human Swimming

The alternate kick of crawl and backstroke swimming prevents the flow of water from closing around the swimmer and leaving a smooth wake. The kick and recovery movement of the breaststroke leg action has the same effect. However, the butterfly leg action, in direct contrast to the other strokes, is the only leg action that permits the flow to close around the swimmer's aft end.

Rolling the body on its long axis in freestyle and backstroke causes transverse flows to form against a swimmer's line of forward progression. These transverse flows disturb the main flow trying to move aftward. However, the more buoyant female swimmer appears able to roll the body without disrupting rearward wave flow, probably because she displaces less water than her male counterpart does.

Biomechanists tend to be most concerned with measuring the resistance presented by a swimmer's surface area and sometimes ignore the important effect of shape in maintaining streamlining. But a principle of hydrodynamics is that gradually curved surfaces along the general paths followed by the water flow will minimize resistance.

Hydrodynamicists say that swimmers, especially when moving at speed, present more *form drag* than *friction drag*. Resistance presented against the surface water in wave making is approximately 70 percent, whereas the amount of skin friction against water accounts for about 30 percent of resistance. The rough surface presented is very much like a ship hindered by a bunch of protuberances (referring to the knees, ankle joints, hip bones, and changing muscle shapes) extending from its hull that set up numerous pressure waves radiating from it.

The motion of the body as the arms pull and recover, together with trunk rotation, creates lateral pressure disturbances, waves, vortices, and general turbulence. In addition, the breaking up of the flow caused by the leg actions in three of the racing styles prevents the flow from closing behind the swimmer.

In the freestyle and backstroke, a bow wave forms around the head. Contrary to descriptions in some of the swimming literature, flow is not deflected in two directions in a sharp V-shape, as around the bow of a ship. The first part of the body to meet the oncoming flow is the top of the head, not the shoulders, which are sometimes described as helping the body penetrate the water. The bow wave is rounded by the shape of the head and forms a divergent arc-shaped—not V-shaped—flow that spreads out wider than the shoulders.

Each entry of the arms in freestyle and butterfly causes a repetitive, abrupt splitting of the bow wave. We don't know what effect this has on keeping a smooth wave-flow encased around the body. In freestyle, this splitting or deformation of the bow wave occurs as the body rolls to the side of the entry arm. Not only is the bow wave broken with each arm entry, but water often is thrown vigorously forward as the arms come over to start each new stroke. This effect is more pronounced in male swimmers than in females.

The question is whether the speed of the entry arm should be faster or slower than the speed of the body to effect a more controlled entry and preserve the momentum of the body.

It is possible that even the shape of a swimmer's head may influence the shape of the bow wave produced. Some swimmers have round-shaped heads (bracycephalic), and others have long heads (dolicocephalic). A round head may cause a bow wave that is more rounded in front, while a swimmer with a head of narrower width may produce a bow wave with a sharper front.

Female swimmers because of generally smaller body size, greater buoyancy, and more rounded contours, produce narrower and smaller bow waves than their more angular male counterparts, but they still in no way split the water in the manner of a ship's bow.

Observation of the flow patterns developed in the various strokes indicates a smoother flow around the body in the backstroke, probably due to the more gradual curvature of the back compared with the more irregular shape of the front trunk. In addition, there appears to be less interference with the bow wave at each arm entry. This may be caused by the shallower entry of the arm and a more careful control of the arm as the hand enters the water.

Tall Swimmers and Wave Making

Most swimmers lengthen the bow wave as they increase their speed. This is particularly noticeable in tall swimmers such as Popov (6 feet 7 inches), Thorpe (6 feet 5 inches), Hall (6 feet 6 inches), and van den Hoogenband (6 feet 4 inches). Each swimmer creates one long, close-fitting wave along the length of his body.

Any object moving through surface water generates waves. At low speeds, the object generates very short waves, but with increasing speed the object creates a pair of waves separated by roughly its own waterline length—the so-called bow wave and stern wave. The waterline length (hull length) thus sets the distance between waves (wavelength). Waves always move, and their wave lengths set their speeds. The waves get longer and longer the faster the object goes, until eventually reaching the point where the wave equals the length of the object, more or less. It has a crest at the bow and another one near the stern.

Trouble arises because an ordinary floating ship finds it hard to go faster than its waves. As has been known for at least a century, wave speed increases with the square root of wavelength; double the wavelength, and you increase the wave speed about 1.4 times. By making waves of longer length, the bigger boat makes waves that travel faster. If the boat tries to go faster, a hill of water faces it, and the boat must either cut its way through or go perpetually uphill—up the down escalator as it were (Vogel 1998).

Videotaping swimmers of all levels of ability in all strokes and of different body types at varying rates of speed is a valuable, interesting, and thought-provoking exercise. These recordings should be made from all angles, including high above the swimmers from a diving tower or similar height, as well as at the waterline to determine wave height.

Exerting Natural Leverage

As stated earlier, much discussion has taken place over the years about whether swimmers should use predominant lift or predominant drag mechanisms in their arm strokes.

Biomechanists often present an idealized case analysis of the hand and the arm of an individual swimmer that does not consider the entire picture of a swimmer's limb being connected to a body. The limb's movement is not done in isolation. It is connected to the body's total movement, consisting of a complex set of continuous and interacting sequential actions. In the short term, an academic analysis of the forces acting on a single arm at a particular instant in which the hand is frozen in the water will not lead to real advances because the arm is never rigid but moves continuously.

The argument over whether swimmers should use predominant lift or predominant drag propulsion has become a drawn-out, specious, academic argument that long ago entered a cul-de-sac. Among practical and successful pool deck coaches, the lift-drag argument became a nonissue long ago, if in fact it ever existed. If biomechanists have had to perform scientific experiments to determine if swimmers use predominant lift or drag forces, how much more difficult is it for the coach practitioner to readily determine these factors from the pool deck?

Furthermore, how is the coach to teach the desired stroke pattern and know with certainty that it has been established? How will the coach know which mechanism is best suited to the individual swimmer? And, as Stix and Fischetti ask in *Scientific American* (2000), "Does it matter?" Surely it is enough for a swimmer to develop the most efficient propulsive leverage on the water based on what flows naturally from individual physical characteristics without considering whether lift or drag forces predominate. There is a difference between faulty technique and idiosyncrasy, and in this process the coach should not start out with any particular idea of what specific type of technique a swimmer should use, thereby trying to force all swimmers into a Procrustean bed of uniformity.

During a long experience in coaching, I have seen only one freestyle swimmer whose stroking pattern exactly duplicated that of another swimmer. Each swimmer is born with an individual neuromuscular pattern, and there is not much a coach can do to change it. Experienced coaches find that the most significant advances are made through intuition—either the natural feel of the swimmer or the intuition of a skilled coach, prompting each swimmer into his or her natural movement inclination.

Applying Effective Propulsive Leverage

Differences in individual physique affect the way each swimmer applies leverage against the water's resistance. So how should a coach instruct a swimmer on the ideal placement of the hand through the changing sequences of a swimming stroke?

The phrase "changing sequence" is used in contrast to a biomechanical analysis of a single arm position that will not help to establish the most effective moving stroke pattern for the individual swimmer.

As a coach, I discovered, quite by accident, that by wearing a weight belt most swimmers will automatically exert maximum leverage on the water and, in the process, find the stroke pattern best suited to his or her own body build or, to phrase it colloquially, his or her own individual set of levers.

Practicing the stroke while wearing a weight belt works well in all four styles of swimming. A breaststroke swimmer, for example, who pulls or kicks too wide will naturally groove both the arm stroke and leg kick into a narrower action, while noting at the same time that improved force application on the water has resulted.

Freestyle swimmers find that wearing a weight belt has a positive effect on their ability to place the stroke exactly where the strongest leverage results. The freestyle swimmer automatically adjusts the entry point of the hands to a position where he or she naturally feels the strongest resistance of the water during the pull, even after the weight belt is removed.

The coach should concentrate on teaching stroke mechanics based on the efficient use of the major muscle groups involved. In all the strokes except breaststroke, the swimmer pulls the body forward over the hands and then, in smooth transition, pushes the body forward past the hands. During the pull-push action, the arm is pulled down and back by three main muscle groups: pectoralis major, latissimus dorsi, and teres major.

Two key arm postures are common to all the strokes (figure 2.14):

1. the high elbow position during the initial pulling phase of the stroke; and

2. the adduction of the upper arm or arms during the second phase of the stroke.

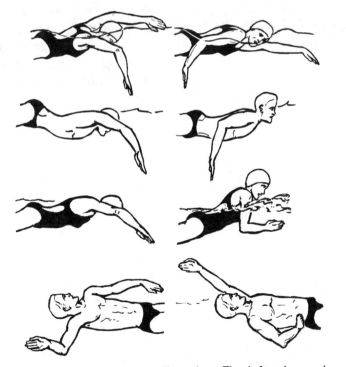

Figure 2.14 Two arm postures are common to all strokes. The left column shows the pull phase, and the right column shows the push phase.

In the pull phase of all the strokes (shown in the left column of figure 2.14), the upper arm is medially rotated, and the elbow is flexed so that the arm assumes an elbow-up position. This action also occurs in the backstroke, but upside-down. During the pull phase, the arm is kept elbow-up to provide the most efficient application of power. A simple way to achieve this high elbow position is to keep the armpit open and point the elbow out to the side. This action will increase the power the swimmer is able to exert during the pull.

In freestyle, butterfly, and breaststroke, the second phase of the stroke, the push phase, is marked by the powerful adduction of the upper arm (drawing the upper arm toward the side of the body; see the right column of figure 2.14). In breaststroke, however, once the arms are adducted they are moved forward to full extension in front of the body. Adduction, the act of moving the arm to the side, is one of the most powerful actions of the arm, involving some of the largest muscles of the trunk. The principle part is played by the latissimus dorsi and pectoralis major muscles (figure 2.15). From its wide attachment to the pelvis, spine, and ribs, the latissimus dorsi acts on all the joints concerned. The pectoralis major acts from the anterior chest wall while the movement of the scapular is assisted by the rhomboid and levator scapulae muscles.

Swimmers should pay particular attention to strengthening the muscle groups responsible for the movement of the arms in the shoul-

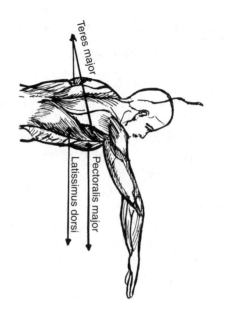

Figure 2.15   The three major muscle groups involved in the pull-push action of a swimming stroke.

der joint, specifically, the muscles that originate in the shoulder and insert into the upper arm, the muscles that originate on the trunk and insert on the shoulder blade, and the muscles that originate on the trunk and insert on the arms. A wide range of exercise routines exist for this purpose, for example, Nautilus and universal machine work, exercises that use stretch cords (either in or out of the water), weight training, free exercises, medicine ball training, rope climbing, chin-ups, or exercises on a swim bench.

Chapter 3

Strokes, Starts, and Turns

Long before the invention of underwater observation facilities, early attempts to view underwater action were made difficult by dirty or muddy water and the fact that the observer was usually standing next to a river, lake, or canal.

Starting with the earliest books on swimming until the mid-19th century, stroke descriptions in swimming books were accompanied by line drawings made without the aid of underwater observation. These drawings and descriptions purported to show how swimming techniques should be performed, but, in reality, they were almost always based on the writer's subjective opinion of what the stroke should look like. Sometimes, probably to impress the reader, the drawings were annotated with comments that said "drawn from life" or "taken from life."

In the late 19th century, these line drawings were replaced by photographs. *The Badminton Book of Swimming* (1885) by Sinclair and Henry

was the first swimming book to contain photographs, followed by *Swimming* by Ralph Thomas in 1904. *Swimming and Watermanship* (1918) by L. de B. Handley had still photographs showing swimmers demonstrating sequences of the swimming strokes while perched on rocky ledges or banked-up beach sand.

Motion picture sequences were used for the first time in *The Outline of Swimming* (1924) by William Bachrach. Bachrach's book contained abovewater motion picture sequences of his star pupil, the great Johnny Weissmuller, the first motion picture sequences to appear in a swimming book. *The Science of Swimming* (1928) by Frank J. Sullivan, swimming instructor at Princeton University, was the second book to contain motion film sequences (also of Weissmuller). *Swimming the American Crawl* (1930) by Johnny Weissmuller was the third book showing movie picture frames of swimming technique, with Weissmuller demonstrating the crawl.

A Quick Way to Better Swimming (1939) by Steve Forsyth, with photography by Moffat Studios and Mort Walton, marked the first time that underwater motion picture sequence frames of the swimming strokes appeared in a swimming book. *Competitive Swimming and Diving* (1942) by David A. Armbruster featured expert drawings by Lee Allen, a medical illustrator at the University of Iowa hospital, copied from underwater motion films by Lee W. Cochran, supervisor of visual instruction at the University of Iowa. This work records swimming techniques as they existed in the 1940s.

Basic Swimming (1951) by Yale University coach Robert J.H. Kiphuth and his longtime assistant Harry M. Burke includes strokes, starts, and turns filmed by Grantland Rice Sports Pictures Corporation. The book includes Jam Handy's historic 61-frame stroboscopic underwater sequence of the great Japanese swimmer, Hironoshin Furuhashi.

The Technique of Competitive Swimming (1956) by Bela Rajki of Hungary contains the first detailed underwater sequences of leading European swimmers. The sequences of the butterfly dolphin stroke are a valuable historical record of this stroke's early development. In 1963 Forbes Carlile published *Forbes Carlile on*

Swimming, which shows underwater still photographs of the techniques of mid-20th century world champions from Australia.

Over a 40-year period, James "Doc" Counsilman of Indiana University filmed the underwater techniques of most of the world's leading swimmers. Counsilman used flashing lights attached to the swimmer's hands to accurately measure the three-dimensional path of the swimming strokes, an important turning point in understanding swimming techniques. Counsilman designed a grid system on the wall of the pool as a reference for stroke analysis and invented a "roll-around" method for filming swimmers from directly below. He produced several instructional films of high artistic standard. In 1977 Counsilman privately published the *Competitive Swimming Manual*, which contained a section on stroke techniques that preserves the most complete and outstanding collection of photographic studies of champion swimmers ever published.

The Technique of the Crawl Stroke

The 20th century saw the invention of a completely new form of human locomotion in the development of the crawl stroke. The smooth, flowing action of the crawl is a far cry from the almost painful efforts of the pioneers and a tribute to human ingenuity. The style is characterized by split-second timing of the arms and smooth transitions from one phase of the stroke to the next. Throughout the changing sequences of the stroke, the body assumes streamlined alignments that reduce resistance and prolong the momentum developed by each successive stroke.

Side View

Split-second timing is shown during the transition phase of the arm stroke (figure 3.1a). The upper arms form an approximately 45-degree angle to each other as the left arm enters the water. The elbow-up position of the right arm places the hand at an efficient angle to push the water backward as the arm begins the power phase of the stroke.

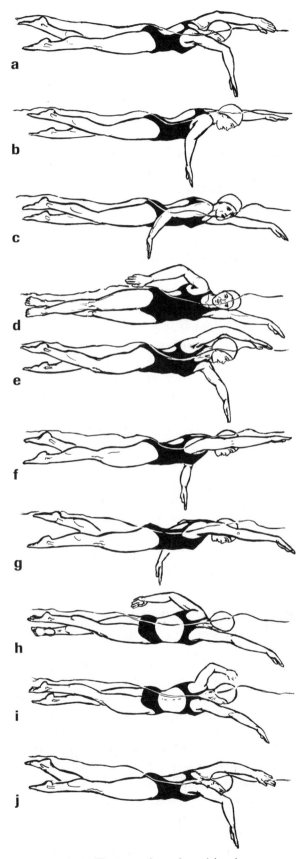

Figure 3.1 The crawl stroke, side view.

Note the marked acceleration of the right arm in comparison to the slower left arm, now completely entered into the water (figure 3.1b). The left arm's slower movement helps retain the body's momentum. The left arm and shoulder gradually extend forward in a movement that will eventually tip the body onto its left side. The right angle formed by the arms at this stage indicates accurate stroke timing of one arm with the other.

The swimmer's body weight starts to shift over the left arm as the arm starts to pull with the hand flexed at the wrist, applying pressure on the water (figure 3.1c). The right arm is drawn inward to the side of the body (adducted) as the right hand and forearm complete the thrust in what can best be described as a "duck foot" action. The face turns sideways in time with the backward thrust of the right arm.

The swimmer inhales as the entire body, from top of the head to tips of the toes, turns naturally on its long axis (figure 3.1d). The recovery of the right arm is made with the shoulder and elbow leading the action. Note that the swimmer has not lifted the head to inhale; the water level remains constant at the top of the head. The face will return to the water at a speed *slightly faster* than the recovery of the right arm, enabling the swimmer to see the right arm underwater as it enters.

The right hand and forearm move forward to the entry (figure 3.1e). As the right hand enters, the split-second timing of the arms is repeated, giving the stroke perfect symmetry (refer to figure 3.1a). The left arm, hand planed backward, is about to change its action from a pull to a strong backward thrust. The face is forward as the right hand enters the water, and the swimmer should see the hand as it enters.

The right arm has completely entered the water (figure 3.1f). The head remains centered in the long axis of the body. Note the right-angle timing of the arms in relation to each other. The swimmer's body position is streamlined and balanced—head down, buttocks at the surface, leg action inside the body line. Note also the left hand's marked acceleration in comparison to the slower movement of the right hand, which reaches slowly forward, ready to tilt the body over onto its right side (figure 3.1g).

As the left arm completes its stroke and recovers smoothly, the body moves onto its right side (figure 3.1h). In this transition phase, the weight of the recovery arm and shift in body balance provide powerful assistance to the start of the right arm pull. Note the posture of the right arm—elbow up, hand flexed at the wrist. The right hand grips the water as the swimmer feels strong water pressure on the palm of the hand. The left arm, elbow higher than the wrist, reaches forward to the entry as the right arm moves into the pull (figure 3.1i). The body retains perfect balance as the entire cycle is repeated in continuous rhythm. The right arm is now pulling powerfully and is well into the pull. A complete cycle of both arms is completed as the left arm enters and the right arm commences the power phase of its stroke (figure 3.1j).

Front View

The arm stroke is a working phase of pull then push. Throughout the stroke, the posture of the arm, elbow, and hand constantly changes (figure 3.2). These smoothly made adjustments give the swimmer leverage to apply muscular power.

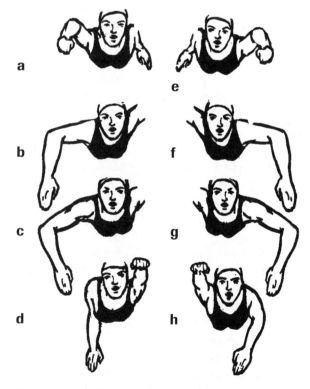

a

e

b

f

c

g

d

h

Figure 3.2 The crawl stroke, front view.

The hand enters the water fingertips first and the elbow set higher than the hand. The entry is on an imaginary line forward of the armpit. The arm slides forward until almost fully extended. The hand moves backward into the pull, and the elbow bends progressively until maximum flexion (approximately 90 degrees) is reached. Throughout the pull, the elbow is kept higher than the hand and pointed sideways (elbow-up position), which gives maximum leverage and reduces water slipping off the hand. The maximum elbow bend is reached halfway through the stroke. From here, a smooth transition is made into the push phase back to the hips. The stroke finishes with the arm not quite extended.

Although the swimmer tries to pull in a direct backward plane, the rotation of the body on its long axis causes the hand and forearm to move laterally inward and outward under the torso. This action produces a natural sculling effect as the hand pitches inward across the body and then outward to round out the stroke at the side of the body with the palm facing the body.

The arm is relaxed to enable the momentum created during the stroke to carry the arm into the recovery with minimal muscular effort. Although the arm stroke has been described as a series of part movements, the stroke is performed smoothly, with each movement flowing smoothly into the next. Complete fluency is achieved when a swimmer can repeat correct patterns continuously for stroke after stroke.

Key Points on the Crawl

• Body balance, correct timing, and momentum are important factors. Only when the body is balanced equally on both sides of its long axis during the swimming stroke can there be efficient timing between one arm and the other. When the body is balanced and each arm is timed with the other with split-second efficiency, the swimmer can maintain an overall momentum throughout each complete stroke cycle. The result is that the swimmer has an easy run through the water that produces a ghostlike glide. As one hand finishes stroking, the other is already propelling so that no time lag interrupts the continuous rhythmic flow of the arm stroke.

• The slow forward reach of the arm and shoulder at the entry performs three functions simultaneously:

1. Extending the entry arm forward slowly helps preserve the momentum being developed by the pull of the opposite arm.

2. The forward extension of each arm as it enters causes the body to roll onto its side, a motion that brings into play the large trunk muscles to aid the power phase of the stroke.

3. The forward extension also places the body in a streamlined alignment.

• Hand-wrist posture is important. Note how the posture of the hand on the wrist is constantly adjusted to keep the hand planed directly backward. Particularly at the end of the stroke, pulling upward would depress the hips and cause resistance. Relaxing the wrist keeps water pressure on the hand, which keeps the hand planing directly backward instead of upward.

• To avoid retarding momentum, a smooth recovery of each arm should be made at approximately the same speed as the body. Bring the hand forward in the recovery—don't snatch it forward as if you're swimming in glue! The face should be forward as each hand enters the water, and the swimmer should see each hand as it enters; this is a stroke fundamental.

• Be aware of head position as the hand enters. Many swimmers lose their timing by incorrectly turning their head to breathe before the forward hand has entered the water. Even top swimmers, try as they will, sometimes can't get the stroke into its normal rhythm. Often, the difficulty is caused by turning the head too soon to inhale. When a swimmer's stroke seems off balance or off timing, tell the swimmer to make sure to see the hand enter before turning the head to breathe.

• Head-turning mechanics and general posture of the head are important. The head stabilizes body balance and assists adequate respiration without interfering with propulsion. The head should remain in the long axis of the body. Moving the head out of the long axis will distort body alignment.

• Synchronize the movement of the head with the arm action. All movements of the head should be made slowly and smoothly, and the water level should remain constant. The head should be forward in line with the long axis of the body as each arm enters. The head turns smoothly to breathe a split-second after one arm enters. The turn of the head is made during the natural roll of the body. Inhalation is through the mouth. Exhalation commences immediately after the mouth returns to the water and continues through the mouth until the lips return to the surface for the next inhalation. The outward breath should *flow* out, *not be blown* out, except for a final puff of air through the mouth as it clears the surface. Lips should curl outward to prevent accidental inhalation of water. Should you gulp in water, shape your tongue as if you're pronouncing the letter K; this should prevent you from gagging.

• Special attention should be given to the changing postures of the elbow during the underwater stroke. Freestyle swimmers should attempt to keep the elbow in a high position during the initial stage of the pull. The high elbow posture is an important stroke fundamental and is easily achieved by pointing the elbow out to the side while keeping the armpit open. Although this is only a fleeting phase of the total action, a high elbow enables the swimmer to combine the strength of the arm rotators with that of the arm depressors as the body is levered forward using the shoulder as the fulcrum. The hand and forearm keep planing backward until they are almost perpendicular to the water surface. At this stage, the elbow and upper arm are drawn inward toward the torso in a powerful motion as the swimmer completes the stroke. Throughout the change in elbow posture, the swimmer must retain the pressure of the water on the palm of the hand by keeping it planed backward.

• Talented swimmers use several different kicking patterns, even during a single race. The principle involved in *broken-tempo* kicking, as it is called, is that the legs may follow any pattern, as long as rhythm and balance are not affected. Modern swimming greats are not as style regimented as those from previous swimming generations. They often shift naturally from one cadence to another without thinking about it. A swimmer may switch from a reduced, very light kick to a six-beat, depending on whether he or she is trying to conserve energy or sprint to meet a rival's challenge.

In distance swimming, one of history's greatest breakthrough swimmers, Australia's Grant Hackett, 2000 Olympic and 2001 World 1500 meter champion, (his world mark set in Fukuoka in 2001, is an amazing 14:34.56) reduces the tiring effects of overkicking by using a subdued kick when swimming the middle and long distances. A growing theory in modern swimming is that whether a two-beat or six-beat kick is used, as long as the kick is easy and at an aerobic level of intensity, it helps remove lactate.

• Loose ankles increase propulsion. The key to easy and efficient kicking is to keep the ankles and feet loose and flexible. Feeling the water passing between the toes of both feet is an indication that the ankles are loose and the feet are performing a supple, weaving action. At speed, this motion becomes a powerful whiplash that provides counterbalance and thrust directly inside the body line.

Swimmers should keep the ankles stretched by doing stretching exercises. One effective exercise is to sit on the floor, crossing the right leg over the left. With the left hand, grasp the toes of the right foot with the palm placed along the sole of the foot. With the right hand, grasp the leg above the ankle to steady the foot. The left hand now turns the right foot in a rotary motion. Pull the top of the toes down to fully extend the ankle and foot. Repeat the exercise on the left foot.

The Crawl Stroke Start

The grab start is shown in figure 3.3. In figure 3.3a, note that feet are positioned with toes gripping the front of the block. The hands lightly grasp the block with one hand on either side of the feet.

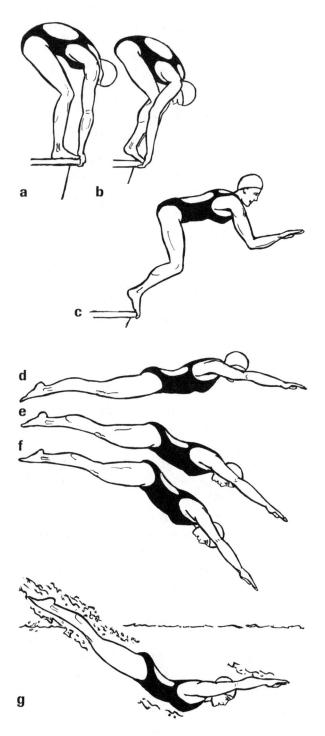

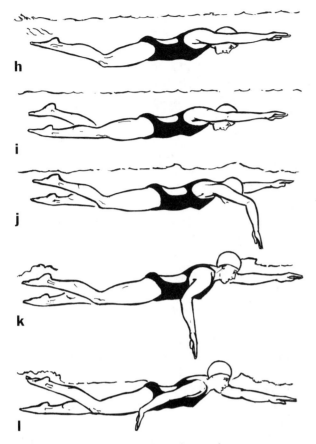

Figure 3.3 The crawl stroke grab start.

tance is being swum, the swimmer should not turn the head to breathe until he or she has taken about six strokes after surfacing and is well into the stroke rhythm.

The rules restrict the swimmer to 15 meters (16.4 yards) underwater after the start and turn. At this point, the head should appear above the surface.

The Crawl Stroke Turn

The crawl stroke turn is really a gymnastic event in which the swimmer performs a forward somersault with a half-twist. The swimmer's forward momentum is first arrested and then developed in the opposite direction. If the head stops at any stage of the turn, momentum is lost, and so is speed.

On the approach to the wall, the swimmer uses incoming forward momentum to provide the initial rotating movement of the turn (figure 3.4a). The head and forward arm dive below the surface. A quick dolphin kick adds momentum and lifts the hips.

At the starting signal, the swimmer pulls the body downward until the heels lift to tip the swimmer's center of balance forward over the front of the block (figure 3.3b). The arms are thrown forward as the legs extend vigorously (figure 3.3c). The swimmer's body is fully extended as it reaches the peak of its trajectory (figure 3.3d). As the head tucks down below the arms; the hips are piked to help the swimmer achieve an ideal angle of entry (figures 3.3e and 3.3f). The entire body enters through the same hole in the water. As soon as the body is completely submerged, the swimmer arches the back to bring the body horizontal to the surface (figure 3.3g).

Most swimmers perform the dolphin kick before starting the flutter kick prior to surfacing (figures 3.3h and 3.3i). The first arm stroke brings the swimmer to the surface, while the other arm remains extended forward (figures 3.3j and 3.3k). As soon as the head breaks the surface, both arms take up the rhythm of the full stroke (figure 3.3l). No matter what dis-

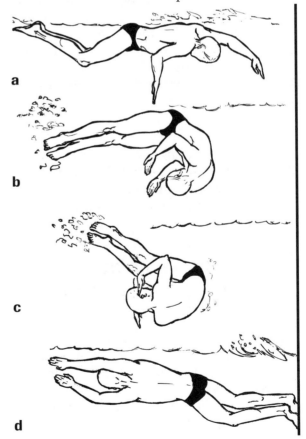

Figure 3.4 The crawl stroke turn.

The head continues through the turn without stopping (figure 3.4b). In fact, the whole body moves continuously. The swimmer's back is thrown toward the wall as the hips pike and the knees are brought into the chest. As the swimmer approaches the wall, the forward hand continues through without hesitation, while the pulling arm completes a half-stroke and flexes at the elbow to join in a backward sculling motion with the forward arm, which is also now bent.

In the continuing action of the turn the body performs a half-twist (figure 3.4c), almost like a jujitsu artist performing a break fall and landing on the point of the shoulder. As the hips pass over the head, the head continues through and the feet are placed on the wall. (Note that the rules do not require the hands to touch the wall at the turn but that some part of the body must touch the wall.) Without hesitation, the leg thrust commences, with the swimmer thrusting from the wall using the toes only and not a flat placement of the heels. Simultaneously, the arms extend forward as the swimmer's body once more assumes a prone position. At this point, the body should be deep enough to avoid pushing off into disturbed surface water. Note that as of March 6, 1998, a FINA rule limits the swimmer to an underwater pushoff no greater than 15 meters (16.4 yards), by which point the head must have broken the surface.

As the swimmer planes gradually to the surface before taking the first stroke (figure 3.4d), he or she may use either a dolphin kick or a flutter kick. Six strokes should be taken before the swimmer resumes a regular breathing pattern.

The Technique of the Butterfly Stroke

In the butterfly stroke, the swimmer's body moves through a rapidly changing range of different shapes, during which the hips, acting as a fulcrum, always ride high in the water. The complete stroke cycle is characterized by a teeter-totter motion of the body, which continues throughout the stroke cycle with the fulcrum centered just below the hips.

To achieve and maintain the desired high hip position, a butterfly swimmer depends on accurate timing of the head movement, arm stroke, and leg action. The face must come out of the water before the hands leave the water, then reenter the water a split second before the hands. The upper arms should be drawn toward the body (adducted) as the initial rounded phase of the arm stroke is completed. This action brings into play the powerful muscles of the trunk and the shoulder girdle for the final backward thrust of the stroke.

There are two downward leg beats for each arm stroke. The first beat occurs as the arms enter the water, and the second beat is timed as the hands push backward to end the stroke.

Side View

In figure 3.5a, the hips have reached their highest point in the stroke cycle as the preceding downward leg beat ends. (The preceding action is shown in figures 3.5h, 3.5i, and 3.5j.) The head is kept down between the arms, and the chest is pushed forward.

The hands are turned outward as the pull starts (figure 3.5b). The upper arms remain close and almost parallel to the surface. The elbows bend as the arms spread outward from the shoulder line. The spreading of the arms allows the body to continue its forward-sliding momentum as the torso is pressed downward between the outspread arms.

The hands and forearms are now angled directly backward, with the elbows still high and close to the surface (figure 3.5c). The rounded action of the arms gives the feet time to recover in preparation for the next downward beat. The swimmer remains below the surface as the hands and forearms round out to complete the first lateral phase of the pull. The head starts to lift to prevent the body from sinking too low. The high elbow position provides strong leverage and effective hydrodynamic shaping of the arms.

The pull remains shallow as the upper arms move back and in toward the sides of the body (figure 3.5d). The elbows remain high and in line. The hands come closer together under the shoulders while the forearms move to a posi-

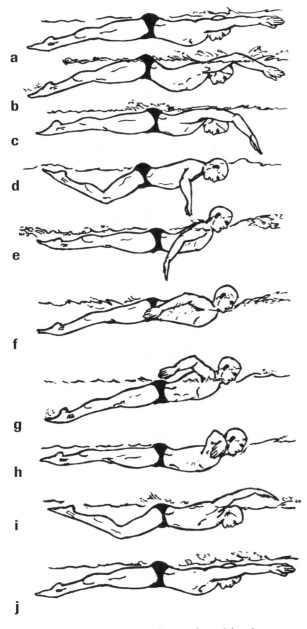

Figure 3.5 The butterfly stroke, side view.

3.5e). The pull rapidly accelerates as the hands and forearms thrust backward to complete the stroke. The combined forces developed by the final arm thrust and the second downward kick lift the head and shoulders above the surface. With face downward, the mouth clears the water just before the hands exit. The swimmer inhales a split second before the hands leave the water.

The hands, palms facing the body, continue through to clear the water's surface as the arms, rotating in the shoulder joints, recover laterally over the water (figure 3.5f). Note that the arms do not straighten completely at the end of the stroke.

The body is at its highest point in the stroke cycle. The arms recover with elbows slightly bent (figure 3.5g). The head will start to drop as the arms reach a line with the shoulders (figure 3.5h).

Figure 3.5i shows a key phase in the timing of the overall stroke. The head submerges quickly before the arms enter; the hands and forearms submerge last. The feet rise as they prepare to kick downward.

The legs complete their first downward kick and pause for a split-second to allow the body to continue its run before the next arm stroke (figure 3.5j). In this ultrastreamlined position, the body's momentum continues as it slips forward smoothly under the surface. The hands are bladed outward as they compress the on-coming flow of water along the palms before the start of the next stroke.

Front View

The head submerges *before* the arms enter (figure 3.6a). The arms are almost straight as they enter just wide of their respective shoulders. The arms, medially rotated, are almost straight and parallel to the surface. The arms are slightly wider than the shoulders, the hands turned outward at an approximately 45-degree angle.

An initial outward scull is performed as the elbows bend and the arms spread outward and downward (figure 3.6b). The hands blade outward as the rounded first part of the pull commences. The shoulders are submerged. Note the high position of the upper

tion vertical to the surface. The knees are flexed as the legs start the second downward beat. Unlike the first downward beat, which naturally results from the hips being pushed upward as the arms enter (see figures 3.5h, 3.5i, and 3.5j), the second downward beat is consciously directed by the swimmer.

The swimmer rapidly draws the upper arms inward toward the side of the body until the elbows face backward toward the feet (figure

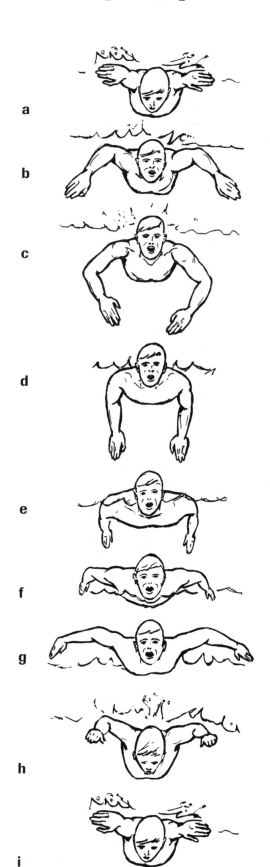

a

b

c

d

e

f

g

h

i

Figure 3.6   The butterfly stroke, front view.

arms and elbows. This position of the upper arms helps the swimmer develop powerful leverage and marks the difference between swimming efficiently and struggling with brute strength.

As the elbow bend increases, the hands cut inward in a rounded action that brings them close together under the body (figure 3.6c). The elbows reach their maximum bend (approximately 90 degrees) as the hands come closer together under the waist to complete the rounded first part of the stroke.

The action changes from a pull to a backward thrust as the upper arms move in toward the sides of the body and the forearms and hands push directly backward (figure 3.6d). Note how the chin is gradually eased forward as the stroke progresses until the mouth clears the surface for inhalation just as the hands complete their backward thrust.

The stroke finishes, and the hands turn palm-inward at the thighs (figure 3.6e). This action helps the swimmer recover the arms with bent elbows leading the action, as in the crawl stroke. The swimmer inhales just before the hands round out past the thighs to exit the water. As the shoulders clear the surface of the water, the arms start their recovery with elbows bent (figure 3.6f).

The body is in the high sailing position that results from correct timing (figure 3.6g). The elbow bend increases as the forearms swing loosely forward in preparation for the entry. The degree of elbow bend depends on the flexibility and strength of the swimmer. A bent-elbow recovery reduces the radius of the recovery action, thereby improving stroke accuracy and reducing strain on the upper arm and back muscles. The head and torso drop under the surface a split-second *before* the arms enter (figure 3.6h). Finally, as shown in figure 3.6i, the swimmer returns to the position shown in figure 3.6a.

Key Points on Butterfly

• Correct head-timing mechanics are vitally important to the rhythm of the total action. Remember two important points:

1. After the swimmer has inhaled, the face should return to the water a split-second before the hands enter.

2. The face should clear the water to inhale a split-second before the hands come out.

• Inhalation is through the mouth only. Exhalation is through the mouth only or through the mouth and nose simultaneously.

• Once the hands enter the water, the swimmer starts to exhale slowly. Throughout the arm stroke, exhalation gradually increases in intensity and finishes with a forceful puff of air a moment before the mouth clears the water. The inward breath is taken through the mouth in the final stage of the arm push.

• The swimmer should start easing the chin forward at the beginning of the stroke, then lifting the head gradually in time with the arm stroke. As the hands come close together in the middle of the stroke, the shoulders and head are rising in the water. From this position, the swimmer has strong leverage to clear the face from the water in time to inhale. As the push of the arms takes place, the swimmer should see the surface water beneath the face before inhaling. The lips are curled outward so that water does not enter the mouth.

• Inhalation should be completed as the arms pass the head during recovery. The face should return to the water a split-second before the hands enter. Novices may be taught to breathe once every arm cycle or once every two strokes, depending on which pattern results in the quickest learning process. In breathing once every two strokes, the breath is held throughout the first arm cycle. Exhalation and inhalation occur during the second arm cycle. The ideal breathing rhythm is a matter of individual preference and also

may depend on the length of the race. The swimmer may need to breathe more frequently the farther the distance covered.

• There are two downward beats of the legs to each arm stroke. The first downward beat occurs as the arms enter. The second downward beat occurs as the hands thrust backward into the push phase of the stroke.

• Timing the two downward beats has three important functions:

1. to ensure continuous propulsion,

2. to maintain body streamlining, and

3. to aid head mechanics.

• The first downward beat is made soon after the hands have entered the water. This timing is critical because the body has decelerated during the arm recovery. If the first beat did not take place at this point, speed would slacken more before the arms started the next stroke. Timing the first beat at this stage also keeps the hips high and the body streamlined as the arm stroke starts. The second downward beat counters the drop of the hips caused by the hands pushing up to the surface. When the second beat is correctly timed, the swimmer is more easily able to raise the head for inhalation.

The Butterfly Start

The grab start is shown in figure 3.7. In figure 3.7a, the feet are positioned with toes gripping the front of the block. The hands lightly grasp the block with one hand on either side of the feet.

At the starting signal, the swimmer pulls the body downward until heels lift to tip the swimmer's center of balance forward over the front of the block (figure 3.7b). The arms are thrown forward as the legs extend vigorously (figure 3.7c). The swimmer's body is fully extended as it reaches the peak of its trajectory (figure 3.7d).

As the head tucks down below the arms, the swimmer pikes at the hips to achieve a steep entry, with the entire body plunging through the same hole in the water (figures 3.7e and 3.7f). The lower back is arched to keep the body moving directly forward and parallel to the surface (figure 3.7g).

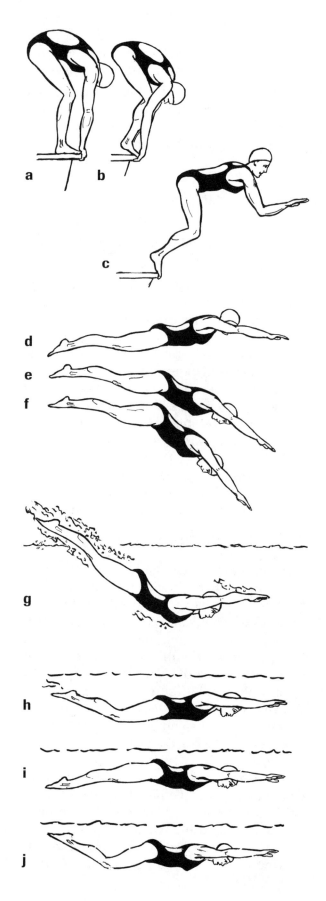

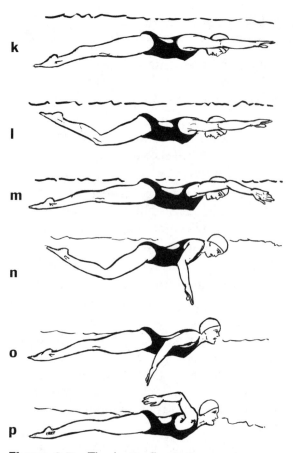

Figure 3.7 The butterfly start.

The rules permit swimmers to be completely submerged for 15 meters (16.4 yards) after the start and turn. By that point, the head must have broken the surface. While underwater, one or more kicks are permitted (figures 3.7h, 3.7i, 3.7j, 3.7k, and 3.7l), but only one pull is allowed, which must bring the swimmer to the surface (figures 3.7m, 3.7n, 3.7o, and 3.7p).

The Butterfly Turn

The swimmer uses the body's momentum to bring the body toward the wall. Then, by keeping head and shoulders moving out again, the swimmer redirects the momentum in the opposite direction.

The swimmer allows momentum to bring the body toward the wall, but the body should not come too close to the wall at the touch (figure 3.8a). The rules of butterfly swimming state that both hands must touch the wall simultaneously at, above, or below the water's surface.

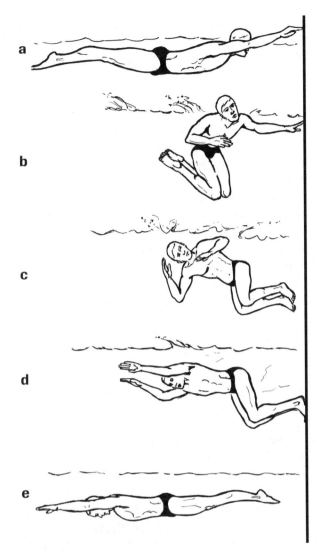

Figure 3.8 The butterfly turn.

After touching the wall, the arm on the side to which the body will turn is pulled back from the wall with the elbow bent (figure 3.8b). The opposite hand pushes against the wall to move the head and shoulders away from the wall (figure 3.8c). As this happens, the knees bend and tuck under the body. The touching hand is removed from the wall and joins with the free hand to prepare for the outward thrust from the wall. The feet are placed on the wall, and the swimmer thrusts out into the pushoff with body streamlined and arms and legs extended (figures 3.8d and 3.8e).

The rules restrict swimmers from being completely submerged for a distance greater than 15 meters (16.4 yards) after the start and after each turn. The swimmer is allowed one or more leg kicks and one arm pull under the water, which must bring him or her to the surface. By that point, the head must have broken the surface. The swimmer must remain on the surface until the next turn or finish.

The FINA rule on the butterfly turn is that at each turn the swimmer's body should be on the breast. The touch should be made with both hands simultaneously at, above, or below the water's surface. Once the touch has been made, the swimmer may turn in any manner desired. The shoulders must be at or past the vertical toward the breast when the swimmer leaves the wall.

The Technique of the Backstroke

The fundamentals of the back crawl stroke, or backstroke, are similar to those of the front crawl with two significant exceptions:

1. The face is not submerged in the back crawl, so there's no need for head-turning mechanics.
2. The back crawl stroke is performed with the arms out to the side of the body.

The lateral arm pull of the back crawl is less efficient than that of the crawl stroke because the arms are at a mechanical disadvantage when they cannot pull directly under the body and thus develop their full potential power. For all swimmers, except those highly talented, this limitation also inhibits ideal stroke frequency.

Side View

In figure 3.9a, the right arm has entered the water a split-second before the left arm has completed its stroke; this ensures continuous propulsion.

The right elbow bends as the arm starts to pull (figure 3.9b). The roll of the body toward the pulling arm brings the powerful large trunk muscles into the action. The left arm, with the shoulder leading, is about to leave the water.

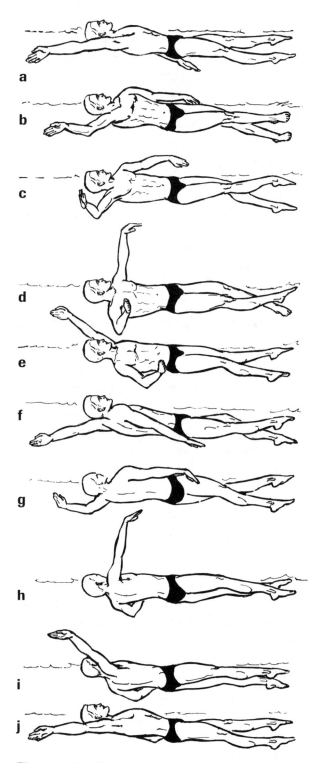

Figure 3.9 The backstroke, side view.

The right elbow bend increases as the left arm recovers in the vertical plane (figure 3.9c). The head is centered in the long axis of the body to ensure perfect balance and prevent excessive sideways movement of the body.

The right elbow reaches maximum bend, causing the right hand to come close to the surface (figure 3.9d); however, the roll of the body to that side prevents the hand from breaking out of the water. The right hand and forearm are at an approximately 90-degree angle to the surface. The left hand moves slightly faster than the right, ensuring the necessary slight overlap in the timing of the arms.

The recovery arm, still in the vertical plane, accelerates as it reaches forward to the entry (figure 3.9e). The hand will enter little finger first. The right hand and forearm, nearing the end of the push phase of the stroke, accelerate rapidly. The upper right arm is drawn toward the swimmer's side as the elbow extends, and the hand—relaxed at the wrist—thrusts directly backward.

The left arm enters the water (figure 3.9f), and the split-second timing of the arms is repeated, giving the stroke perfect symmetry (compare with figure 3.9a). The left arm enters deep below the surface in line with the back, an action that keeps the hips high and reduces resistance. The hand, palm-down, finishes the stroke by pressing down below the hip.

With the shoulder leading, the right arm moves smoothly into the recovery without waiting at the hips (figure 3.9g). The body roll brings the large trunk muscles into play and allows the swimmer to synchronize the pull of the left arm with the vertical recovery of the right arm (figure 3.9h). The right arm, still recovering vertically, moves to the entry slightly faster than the left hand, which is completing its stroke (figure 3.9i). Note the high position of the hips. Finally, the cycle is completed (figure 3.9j).

Front View

The arm enters the water behind the shoulder, elbow straight, little finger first (figure 3.10a). The opposite arm, palm down, completes its pull with a vigorous thrust below the hip. For a brief moment both arms are completely submerged, ensuring continuous propulsion.

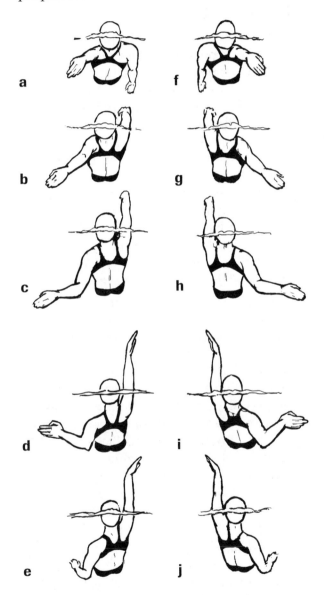

Figure 3.10   The backstroke, front view.

Without pausing, the entry arm presses down deep to a line with the back. Then the elbow starts to bend, and the body rolls toward the pulling arm (figure 3.10b). The opposite arm, with shoulder leading, leaves the water (figure 3.10c). The recovery arm, with elbow straight, recovers in the vertical plane in a trajectory aimed directly over the shoulder. The body roll starts to reverse direction. The elbow of the pulling arm continues to bend to a maximum of 90 degrees (figure 3.10d).

The recovery arm, without deviation from the vertical, accelerates slightly as it passes back over the shoulder (figure 3.10e). This acceleration will cause a slight overlap in the stroke as the arm enters the water. The pulling arm with the upper arm drawn to the side of the body is now set to thrust backward to the end of the stroke (figures 3.10f through 3.10j). The same sequence of pull and recovery is repeated on the other side of the body.

Key Points on Backstroke

• Ideal body position is essential if the stroke is to be made with maximum efficiency. All other phases of the complete stroke depend on this basic fundamental. The swimmer should imagine lying flat on the back without a pillow. The body should be balanced on the back of the shoulders with the front of the hip bones touching the water's surface. There is no break at the hips that would cause the broad surface of the back to set up resistance to the water, with the hand finishing the stroke too deep to exit easily. At speed, ideal body position can be checked by looking for the waterline at the waist.

• The arms are recovered from the water without any deviation from the vertical plane from the moment the arms leave the water until they enter again behind the shoulders. Any lateral motion of the arm in recovery will throw the body off balance and affect the propulsive action of the opposite arm. Permitting the arm to drop out of the vertical plane after it has passed over the shoulder will result in water resistance against the upper arm and shoulder. Furthermore, the hand will enter too wide of the shoulder and tend to slice the water instead of making a firm grip at the start of the pull.

• The entry is the most important phase of backstroke timing. Some swimmers crash the hand into the water or commence the pull when part of the hand and/or forearm is not completely submerged. These faults usually occur in swimmers who have poor shoulder flexibility or incorrect body position. At the arm entry, the arm should form an imaginary straight line from the fingertips to the lower aspect of the shoulder blade. This position is attained by keeping the shoulder blades slightly drawn together (adducted) to keep the back flat, enabling the entire arm to enter the water easily.

• As the hand approaches the entry, it should speed up slightly so that both arms overlap slightly, and for a split second both arms are submerged beneath the surface, thus preserving the momentum of the stroke. The hand should make a deft quickening movement as it enters the water—almost like a pickpocket in action—and feel the pressure of the water immediately. Without any preliminary riding action out front, the hand moves straight into the stroke.

• As the hand and forearm push backward, the upper arm is drawn strongly inward (adducted) toward the side of the body to bring into action the strong muscles of the chest and back. During this quick transition, the swimmer should retain strong pressure of the water on the palm of the hand.

• The recovery arm reaches up to the entry slightly faster than the hand completing the pull. As the recovery hand enters, the opposite hand completes a pronating (palm turned downward) action. At this stage, water pressure should be felt on the palm of the entry hand as well as the hand of the finishing arm. This is the swimmer's check

that the timing has been correctly handled. At no stage of the entire arm cycle do the hands pause in their continuous action and especially not when the hands reach the side of the body at the end of the pull. As the hands complete the stroke, the rhythm of the stroke is preserved by the swimmer thinking ahead of the movement and making the arm go around and out past the hips into the air, without stopping.

• The swimmer should find the fastest arm tempo possible without losing control of the movement, cutting or slicing the water open, or upsetting rhythm. The closer the swimmer can emulate the tempo of his or her crawl stroke arm action, the more efficient the backstroke rhythm will become. It is more common for backstrokers to stroke too slowly than too quickly. There is a balance between the amount of purchase the swimmer obtains and the tempo of the stroke. Too much purchase may cause the swimmer to bog down, while too little may cause useless rapid turnover and cavitation—like an automobile's wheels revolving in mud.

• Lenny Krayzelburg of the United States, the backstroke champion at the 2000 Sydney Olympic Games, is a rarity among backstrokers in that his backstroke turnover is faster than his freestyle turnover. He once told me that he works a great deal on his tempo. Using stretch cords, he practices swimming out to the middle of the pool and tries to hold a certain tempo for 30 seconds and 50 seconds. As a result, he is able to maintain a tempo of over 50 strokes per minute over the 100-meter distance in competition; over the 200-meter distance, his tempo is more than 40 strokes per minute (Colwin 2000).

• For many reasons, it is important to keep the kick inside the body line. This keeps the power source from the kick directly behind the swimmer's body and permits the water to flow smoothly along the legs to preserve streamlining. Dropping the lower legs will cause resistance by increasing the tendency to pull the hips down to a sitting position in the water which, in turn, will interfere with obtaining a clean arm entry. Too wide a kick will slow down the desired high tempo of the arms. Swimmers should try to make the kick start from the hips, then flex the knees slightly as the movement passes down the legs in a wavelike motion, finishing in a whiplash action of the ankles and feet. If the swimmer feels the water passing between the toes throughout the kick, the swimmer's leg action is working well inside the body line.

• A point often overlooked by novice backstrokers is the importance of correct breathing technique. Inhalation and exhalation should take place through the mouth. A point to remember is that if the swimmer breathes too slowly and leisurely, the tempo of the arm action may also become too slow. The swimmer should experiment to find a breathing rhythm that is neither too slow nor too fast.

The Backstroke Start

Prior to the starting signal, the swimmer holds steady by gripping the handles and placing one foot below the other against the wall to avoid slipping (figure 3.11a). A spring is created by exerting pressure on the fingers and toes. The eyes are directed forward, and the head is held erect.

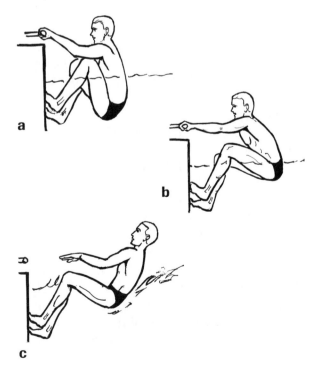

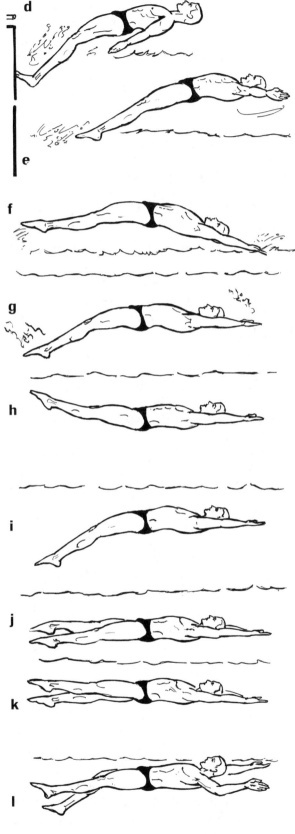

Figure 3.11 The backstroke start.

At the starting signal, the swimmer pulls strongly on the handles and pushes hard with the legs in a movement that will start to lift the body clear of the water (figure 3.11b). The hands release the handles, and the legs thrust powerfully against the wall (figure 3.11c). The hips lift, and the swimmer starts to move out over the water.

The swimmer drops the hands toward the water surface (figure 3.11d), which lifts the hips clear of the water. The head is aligned with the spine. Further momentum is added as feet and ankles extend to give a final powerful thrust against the wall. The arms are thrown vigorously out sideways and forward as the body launches into a shallow dive over the water (figure 3.11e). The swimmer enters the water in a shallow trajectory without landing flat on the back, which would cause tremendous resistance (figure 3.11f).

Before starting to kick, the swimmer takes a short glide. The arms are fully extended with head kept well back between the arms to ensure good streamlining. Most modern backstroke swimmers will do several underwater dolphin kicks. Some, such as Olympic champion Lenny Krayzelberg, manage to do as many as 13 dolphin kicks before surfacing. A swimmer may do either a dolphin kick (figures 3.11g, 3.11h, and 3.11i) or a flutter kick (figures 3.11j, 3.11k, and 3.11l), depending on individual aptitude.

Why is the underwater dolphin kick faster than the full stroke on the surface? Because there is no wave drag underwater. Wave drag is a considerable component of the overall drag in surface swimming.

Note that the rules limit the swimmer to 15 meters (16.4 yards) underwater after the start and turn. By that point, the head must have broken the surface. The swimmer commences the stroking action by pulling with the strongest arm first. (In this particular case, the swimmer is lefthanded.) The swimmer must take care to keep the opposite arm submerged and well behind the head as the first stroke is taken, or he or she may either come out from under the surface too suddenly or swim across the lane at a tangent.

The first arm stroke should be close to the body. This action, combined with the streamlined position of the submerged forward arm, will keep the swimmer moving straight ahead during the breakout into the surface. Once on the surface, the swimmer should not inhale for the first six strokes, which allows him or her to immediately work into a fast tempo instead of a gradual buildup to speed with each successive stroke.

The Backstroke Turn

At the approach to the wall, the swimmer looks toward the forward arm and starts to roll the entire body in the same direction (figure 3.12a).

The head keeps turning until the swimmer is facing the bottom of the pool (figure 3.12b). At the same time, the forward arm does a reverse sculling motion, which causes the shoulders and hips to roll over. The left arm and left leg cross over the body's long axis to assist the body's continuing roll to the prone position.

The head keeps moving as it leads the body into a forward somersault aided by a dolphin kick that lifts the hips as the body pikes, and the back is thrown over toward the wall. Both hands assist in pulling the body forward and over (figures 3.12c and 3.12d). Now the hands join together as they quickly reverse direction to help the body maintain its continuing roll (figure 3.12e). The legs swing over the head, and the feet are placed lightly on the wall without the heels touching the wall (figure 3.12f).

Once again on the back, the swimmer pushes off with arms and legs extended and the entire body in a streamlined posture (figure 3.12g). The swimmer will use either a dolphin kick or flutter kick before starting the arm stroke. The rules restrict the swimmer to 15 meters (16.4 yards) underwater after the start and turn. By that point, the head must have broken the surface.

The FINA rule on the backstroke turn says, "Upon completion of each length, some part of the swimmer must touch the wall. During the turn, shoulders may turn past the vertical toward the breast. If the swimmer turns past the vertical, such motion must be part of a

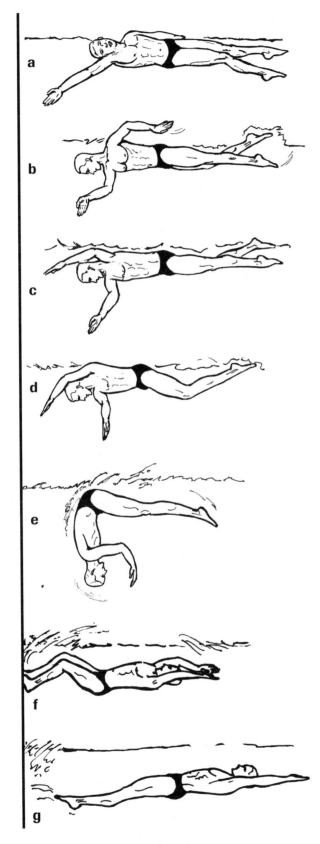

Figure 3.12 The backstroke turn.

continuous turning action and the swimmer must return to a position on the back before the feet leave the wall."

The Technique of the Wave Action Breaststroke

Unlike the conventional breaststroke in which the shoulders remain submerged throughout the stroke, the technique of the wave action breaststroke is designed to reduce water resistance by making the shoulders follow the line of an imaginary wave that rises and falls in perfect symmetry.

Side View

The body is in a streamlined posture with abdominal muscles drawn in, lower back flattened. The arms and legs are fully extended, and feet are pointed. The head is between the arms, and the swimmer looks straight down at the bottom of the pool (figure 3.13a). This is the basic position at the start of the stroke and will be repeated (figure 3.13i) when the stroke cycle ends.

As the pull starts, the entire body posture remains as in figure 3.13a, except that palms turn outward as the hands plane slightly upward to meet the oncoming flow of water (figure 3.13b).

With elbows up and in line with the shoulders, the swimmer completes an initial circular motion, at the end of which the hands are planed directly backward (figure 3.13c). Now, the hands and forearms are ready to change direction inward. The swimmer focuses on pulling the body forward, not upward. The front thighs remain lined up with the body. The swimmer begins to hollow the back, thus preserving the planing action of the body. Streamlining is maintained as the heels lift gently and the knees spread slightly sideways.

The head, shoulders, and front chest clear the surface (figure 3.13d). This phase is where the wave breaststroke differs fundamentally from the conventional breaststroke, in which the shoulders, the widest part of the body, are kept submerged. With the upper body still

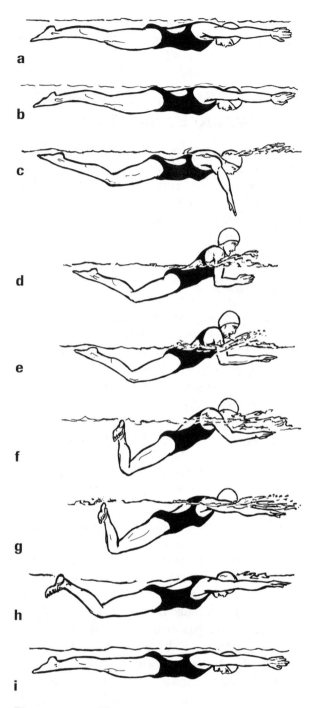

a

b

c

d

e

f

g

h

i

Figure 3.13 The wave action breaststroke, side view.

clear of the surface, the swimmer concentrates on moving forward, not upward. The swimmer inhales as the mouth clears the surface. The hands sweep down under the shoulders and continue forward with the forearms following. The feet do not hang down to cause resistance; both feet are kept in line with the shins.

The swimmer performs "the lunge," the unique feature of the wave breaststroke that enables the swimmer to follow the wave (figure 3.13e). In a radical break from the traditional pull-kick rhythm of the conventional breaststroke, the lunge phase takes place *between* the pull and the kick so that the rhythm becomes pull-lunge-kick. In this action, the hands and forearms are thrust forward on and parallel to the surface of the water; the swimmer literally throws the body forward over the water. The body continues to slide forward with the back still hollowed. The front thighs are kept in line with the torso to permit a smooth passage of water under the body. The heels rise in preparation for the kick, which will start when the lunge is about three quarters through. The kick does not start the lunge but rather serves to maintain the lunge and keep the swimmer on the surface.

The upper arms do not come close to the side of the chest but follow the hands in front of the chest to reduce frontal resistance (figure 3.13f). The posture of the back quickly changes from its arched shape (concave) to an exactly opposite rounded (or convex) shape. As the kick starts, the degree of hip-joint flexion is approximately 35 degrees, with the lower leg at almost 90 degrees to the surface. The feet, close below the surface, are dorsi-flexed (everted, or turned outward) at approximately 90 degrees to the shin to catch the water efficiently. Lowering the hips slightly helps the swimmer accommodate this changing posture of the legs, thighs, and torso.

The humped dolphin-like posture of the back and a powerful, directly backward kick help the swimmer keep moving over the water with shoulders and arms at the surface (figure 3.13g). The feet remain turned outward (everted) until just before the kick closes, at which point the ankles and feet extend to provide a final snap to the kick that thrusts the water directly backward (figure 3.13h). The swimmer maintains streamlining by looking at the bottom of the pool during this powerful phase of the overall action.

The swimmer slides forward under the surface with body in streamlined alignment (figure 3.13i). The swimmer must not let the legs drop, as a judge may consider this a dolphin kick, for which the swimmer could be disqualified.

Front View

The body glides forward with shoulders and hips aligned and arms, legs, and feet extended (figure 3.14a). The shoulders reach forward as far as possible, and the upper arms press against the ears to further streamline the oncoming flow of water along the body. As shown in figures 3.14b and 3.14c, the first stage of the arm pull closely resembles the start of the butterfly pull.

The elbow bend continues as the hands sweep down and inward (figure 3.14d). The elbows are kept away from the side trunk as the hands join. The head, shoulders, and front chest emerge from the water as the swimmer inhales (figure 3.14e). Two important points in streamlining: the shoulders are clear of the surface, and arms are in front of the chest. The swimmer starts the forward "lunge" of the arms (figure 3.14f).

The kick is directly backward and occurs three quarters into the lunge (figure 3.14g), thus helping the swimmer maintain the momentum of the lunge. The head is down as the legs close to complete their powerful backward thrust. The arms and shoulders reach forward as far as possible (figure 3.14h). With arms and legs outstretched, the body, once more submerged in streamlined alignment, slides forward parallel to the surface (figure 3.14i).

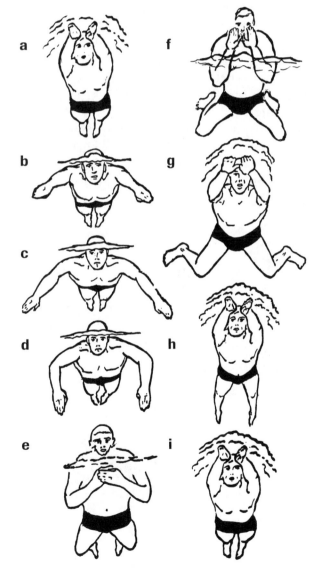

Figure 3.14 The wave action breaststroke, front view.

Key Points on Wave Action Breaststroke

• As stated earlier, the technique of the wave action breaststroke is designed to reduce water resistance by making the shoulders follow the line of an imaginary wave that rises and falls in perfect symmetry.

• Get the shoulders up. In marked contrast to the conventional breaststroke, during the wave action breaststroke the shoulders clear the surface as the swimmer continues to slide forward. To further improve streamlining, the shoulders hunch until they almost touch the ears.

• In raising the head and upper body, the change in the posture of the back is important. First the swimmer arches the back, and *at the same time*, sweeps the arms in quickly and powerfully to bring the head and torso high out of the water. The arching of the back brings the whole resistant part of the body out of the water and leaves almost only the swimsuit and legs below the surface. Important: The swimmer waits until the last moment to lift the head. The head is kept down until the hands have finished the insweep and are about to lunge forward.

• The lunge is the unique feature of the wave breaststroke, occurring between the end of the pull and the start of the kick; the hands and forearms are thrust forward on and parallel to the surface of the water. According to Mike Barrowman, the leading exponent of the wave breaststroke, the swimmer literally throws the body forward and over into the lunge (Colwin 1999, p. 54).

• Unlike the pull-kick rhythm of the conventional breaststroke, the wave stroke rhythm is pull-lunge-kick. The timing of the kick is critical—it should start only when the lunge is about three quarters through. If the kick comes too late, the shoulders will drop abruptly, creating a sudden trough in the imaginary symmetrical line. The kick should come in at the right time to maintain the upper body's forward surge over the water. This is the big difference between the conventional breaststroke and the wave action breaststroke. At this point, the posture of the back will rapidly change from arched or concave to humped or convex. The convex back posture further improves streamlining and when properly coordinated with the kick, enables the swimmer to apply great force during the lunge. The kick should be made directly backward, with no downward component at all.

• It's important to minimize up and down movements of the hips during the stroke; if the hips move too much, the center of gravity moves, thus creating extra work to overcome drag.

The Breaststroke Start

The grab start is shown in figure 3.15. The feet are positioned with toes gripping the front of the block. The hands lightly grasp the block with one hand on either side of the feet (figure 3.15a).

At the starting signal, the swimmer pulls the body downward until the heels lift to tip the swimmer's center of balance forward over the front of the block (figure 3.15b). The arms are thrown forward as legs extend vigorously (figure 3.15c). The swimmer's body is fully extended as it reaches the peak of its trajectory (figure 3.15d).

As the head tucks down below the arms, the swimmer pikes at the hips to achieve a steep entry with the entire body plunging through the same hole in the water (figures 3.15e and 3.15f). The lower back is arched to keep the body moving directly forward and parallel to the surface (figure 3.15g).

The underwater swimming phase, after start or turn, begins with a short preliminary glide with the body outstretched and streamlined (figure 3.15h). Then follows a long pull through to the hips with another short glide with the arms close to the body (figures 3.15i and 3.15j).

The hands are turned palms-up as the arms, with the elbows and forearms kept close to the body in streamlined fashion, are extended forward (figure 3.15k). As the legs kick, the back of the head is tucked down in line with the upper surface of the arms to ensure good streamlining (figure 3.15l). The head breaks the surface as the swimmer starts the arm stroke (figure 3.15m). (The swimmer shown here has lifted the head from the surface well before the arms have separated to start the stroke and so is safely within the confines of the rule.)

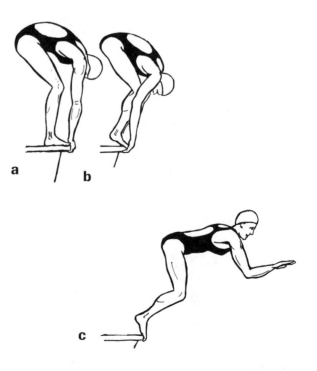

a   b

c

After a start or turn, the rules permit a swimmer to take one stroke completely back to the legs and one kick while wholly submerged. The head must break the surface of the water before the hands turn inward at the widest part of the second stroke.

The full sequence of entry-glide, pull-glide, kick-glide, breakout, is shown here. Note that some controversy exists about the ideal timing for each sequence of the underwater swim. A final decision is usually based on what produces the best results for the individual swimmer. The approach described here still appears to be sound coaching practice for every phase of swimming.

The Breaststroke Turn

The FINA rules of breaststroke swimming are that both hands must touch simultaneously at, above, or below the water's surface (see figure 3.16). Once the touch is made, the swimmer may turn in any manner desired. The shoulders must be at or past the vertical toward the breast when the swimmer leaves the wall.

The swimmer uses the body's momentum to bring the body in toward the wall. Then, by keeping head and shoulders moving out again, redirects the momentum in the opposite direction.

The swimmer allows momentum to bring the body in toward the wall. At the touch, the swimmer should not allow the body to come too close to the wall (figure 3.16a).

After touching the wall, the arm, on the side to which the body will turn, is pulled back from the wall with elbow bent (figure 3.16b). The opposite hand pushes against the wall to move the swimmer's head and shoulders away from the wall (figure 3.16c). As this happens, the knees are bent and tucked under the body. During this motion, the swimmer inhales in preparation for the pushoff and ensuing underwater swim. The touching hand is removed from the wall and joins with the free hand to prepare for the outward thrust from the wall. Note the sculling motion of the right hand,

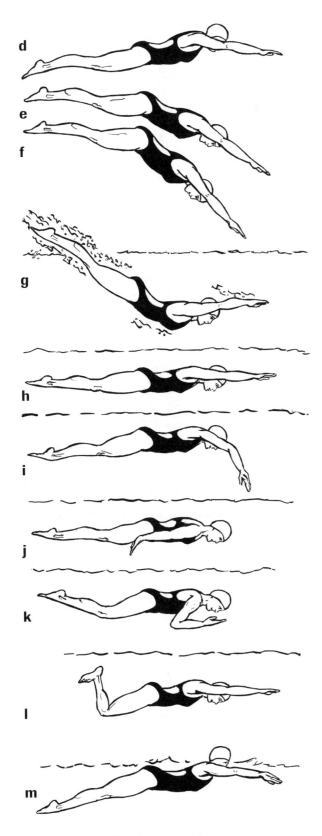

Figure 3.15 The breaststroke start.

which increases the speed of the body's rotation and helps set the swimmer at an ideal depth below the surface.

The feet are placed on the wall, and the swimmer thrusts out into the pushoff with body streamlined and arms and legs extended (figure 3.16d). In the pushoff from the wall, the body remains streamlined, with arms and legs extended and head beneath the arms and balanced evenly on the breast (figure 3.16e).

The FINA rule states, "After the start and each turn the swimmer may take one arm stroke completely back to the legs and one leg kick while wholly submerged. The head must break the surface of the water before the hands turn inward at the widest part of the second stroke."

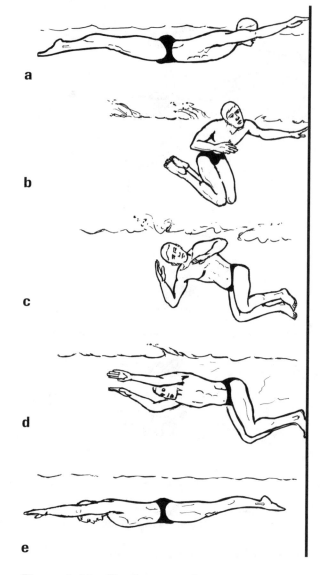

Figure 3.16   The breaststroke turn.

Part II

Movement Through Water

Chapter 4

Understanding Hydrodynamics

A moving fluid has very different properties from a static fluid, for as soon as a swimmer's hand and the water start moving in relation to each other, another force begins to exert its influence. This force is so familiar that we accept it without second thought, yet all propulsion through a fluid, whether mechanical or natural, depends on it. The force in question is *resistance*, or more precisely, the fluid's resistance to motion.

It's curious that swimming propulsion has rarely been analyzed in reference to the resistance of the water and its resulting flow reactions. Most biomechanical studies have been based on the convenient assumption of essentially still water, but this treatment is incomplete because it assumes that swimmers perform their strokes in negative space or dry water. Because water moves under the action of forces, however, we need to understand the relative velocities of the hand and water during swimming. Ideally, the effectiveness of swimming strokes should be analyzed from both the biomechanical and fluid dynamic perspectives.

I have conducted several studies aimed at explaining what happens to the water during the swimming action. In the course of these studies, I have observed the flow reactions produced by the stroke mechanics of world-class swimmers and applied fluid dynamic principles to a methodical analysis of underwater movies, videos, and still photographs. The flow reactions in the water produced remarkably similar patterns, and it was soon evident that fluid dynamic principles could provide a new basis for analyzing stroke efficiency (Colwin 1984a).

Understanding fluid dynamics as applied to swimming yields three practical benefits:

1. Understanding propulsion: learning how water reacts to the forces developed by different propulsive mechanisms—for example, pulling straight backward versus pulling in a curved-line path. Each mechanism produces its own distinctive pattern of flow reactions in the water (Colwin 1985b).

2. Analyzing propulsion: learning to observe and analyze the flow reactions caused by the swimming stroke. An observer can relate flow reactions to the efficiency of the actual stroke mechanics by assessing the size, shape, and placement of the vortex patterns (rotating flows) left in the flow field; when the flow reactions are clearly visible, the trained observer can analyze the net effect of an entire stroke almost at a glance (Colwin 1985a). It is not yet possible, however, to provide detailed and accurate measurements of the flow reactions to the swimming stroke—as fluid dynamicists do when analyzing the flows around ships and airplanes—because we lack a safe and reliable method of making the flow visible.

3. Improving propulsion: learning to recognize through the sense of touch the ideal flow reactions necessary to produce efficient propulsion. This involves a new and unique method of coaching stroke mechanics by having a swimmer associate the feel of the moving water with key phases of the swimming stroke (Colwin 1987). This method is described in depth in chapter 6.

Understanding Basic Concepts

The preliminary explanations in this chapter are essential to an understanding of the propulsive mechanisms used in swimming. They outline in simple terms the ideas that lie behind the mathematical theory of fluid dynamics, the branch of science dealing with the application of propulsive forces in fluids. Indeed, a first requirement for the following account is familiarity with the basic concepts and terms used in fluid dynamics.

It will be necessary, for example, for the reader to know how streamlines are used to form the patterns that show the direction, velocity, and pressure differences in the flow. These three factors always have an important effect on propulsion. In particular, a flow pattern reveals whether propulsion is taking place in steady or unsteady flow, a distinction I'll explain later. I'll also explain why airfoil-type lift propulsion cannot occur in unsteady flow.

Science and Swimming

Even at the end of the 20th century, many coaches had not yet realized that to obtain the full benefit of the new scientific concepts, an entirely different approach to the teaching of stroke mechanics was required. This is especially true of the interaction between the swimming stroke and the water.

If we are to develop more effective propulsive mechanisms than those based on present concepts, we must eventually employ fluid dynamic principles. We have only just begun to toy with the beginnings of this science as it applies to human swimming. A strong foundation for future progress will be laid only when biomechanical and fluid dynamic research proceed in tandem.

When we combine this knowledge with the fact that human swimming propulsion takes place mostly in unsteady flow, it becomes apparent that top exponents must use a propulsive mechanism other than the airfoil-type method previously thought to predominate.

Flow patterns show us that skilled human swimmers can develop propulsive forces in unsteady flow conditions via a comparatively unorthodox mechanism that does not require the hand to be presented at all times at an ideal angle of attack. In fact, propulsion in an unsteady flow is a common aspect of fluid dynamic propulsion in nature and is dependent on establishing a flow circulation around a propelling surface. Later I'll explain in detail this important principle of circulation as it applies under various sets of circumstances.

It is necessary, then, to proceed step by step through a sequence of simple explanations of important fluid dynamic principles, whose significance to human swimming, especially in developing new teaching and coaching methods, will gradually become apparent. (Refer also to chapter 6.)

Using Streamlines to Judge How Water Reacts Under the Action of Forces

Like all fluids, water changes shape under the action of forces. These changes are known as *deformation* and appear as *flow* and *elasticity* (caused by *viscosity*). Flow increases continuously without limit under the action of forces, however small. A given force produces elasticity, which vanishes if the force is removed. Flow and elasticity are the two characteristic qualities of moving water a skilled swimmer feels and recognizes.

Direction and Velocity of the Flow

Streamlines indicate the direction and velocity of the flow. Fluid dynamics makes considerable use of the concept of streamlines, or lines imagined drawn in the fluid to indicate the direction of flow at any point. A streamline is defined as a curve that is always tangential to the flow so that fluid cannot cross a streamline but only flow along it. We can thus imagine adjacent streamlines to form a series of tubes through which the flow is passing.

The picture of flow given by the pattern of streamlines is, however, much more than a chart of flow direction. It is at the same time a map of the velocity field, one that is quite easily read because of the simple rule that fluid velocity is high where streamlines are close together and low where they are widely separated. This is exactly what would be expected if the streamlines indicated the position of real tubes because in a fluid of constant density, wherever a tube narrows, the velocity must increase if the same mass of fluid is to pass in a given time.

Steady and Nonsteady Flow

When streamlines retain the same shape at all times, the flow is said to be steady. It is far simpler to analyze a pattern of steady flow than unsteady flow because the appearance and velocity of an unsteady flow at any fixed point vary from instant to instant.

Flow Patterns

The pattern of flow around a submerged object can be represented on a diagram by means of a selection of streamlines. When the fluid velocity at a given point depends on the position of the point *and* on the time, the streamlines alter from instant to instant. The aggregate of all the streamlines at a given instant constitutes the flow pattern at that instant.

A flow pattern can be indicated by selecting streamlines that show the direction of flow at various points in the pattern. Of the infinite number of possible streamlines, a few are chosen, usually from 5 to 10, in such a way as to divide the flow into a number of channels, all carrying the same quantity of water per second. Given that a reduction in width corresponds to an increase in velocity, a flow pattern can be used to give not only the direction of flow but, from the spacing of the streamlines, the velocity of flow at any point (figure 4.1). With a knowledge of the velocities, fluid

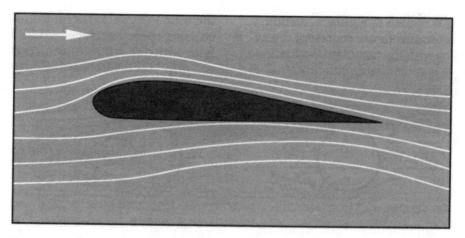

Figure 4.1 Flow pattern around an airfoil showing the direction and velocity of the flow. Smaller spaces between streamlines show where velocity of the flow is highest.

dynamicists are able to use a flow pattern to estimate the pressure forces on the boundaries of the flow.

Viscosity

Water does not accelerate to infinite speed because of its viscosity, or more simply, a stickiness or elasticity. If water had no viscosity, the world's rivers, moving down valleys under the action of gravity, would flow with ever-increasing speed, reaching hundreds of miles per hour with disastrous results. A swimmer is able to grip the water only because viscosity produces separation of the flow. Flow separation causes a difference in the pattern of pressure around the hand. Under certain conditions, this pressure differential provides the resistance against which propulsion can be applied.

Paradoxically, although it helps a swimmer propel, viscosity also results in the form drag that resists the body's forward motion. Because of viscosity, when a body moves through a fluid the elements of that fluid in contact with the solid boundary stick to it. They do not slide along it as one might expect. The elements close to the boundary move past their clinging neighbors. This relative movement brings into play viscous drag forces that oppose motion and cause friction or shearing. The reader can easily detect this viscous drag force by pulling a spoon out of a jar of honey. Part of the honey clings to

the side of the jar, and the intermediate honey suffers a distorting motion to which it objects and so resists. The faster the motion, the greater the resistance.

When a piece of rubber is bent or compressed it exerts a resisting force that disappears only when the rubber is allowed to return to its undistorted shape. In the case of honey, however, the resistance is to the distorting motion, not to the distortion itself, for when the motion ceases, the viscous drag force disappears—the spoon is not pulled back into the jar, as it would be if the honey behaved like rubber. In this sense, viscous resistance is different from elastic resistance.

Viscous drag effects are always present in the movement of air or water past solid boundaries, though they are less pronounced than those produced by thicker, stickier honey. Again, you can readily detect viscous drag effects by holding your hand out the window of a moving automobile or trailing it in the water over the side of a speedboat.

Viscosity plays a leading role in any state of fluid motion and is of particular importance in the process of fluid deformation. Fluids do not simply slip over solid surfaces, whether they are rough or smooth or, in the case of a swimmer, shaven or unshaven. In fact, right at the solid's surface, velocity is zero.

The major part of a viscous deformation is confined to what is known as the *boundary layer,*

What Happens to the Water?

James "Doc" Counsilman pioneered the use of the motion camera as a scientific instrument in the search for a better understanding of the swimming strokes. Counsilman's studies, and later those of Robert Schleihauf, brought the knowledge of stroke mechanics to a new and far more advanced level.

But one question remained: What happens to the water when a swimmer applies force to it? This was a question that had puzzled me for many years, and I wasn't helped by the fact that there was almost nothing in the literature on the subject. It was almost as though propulsion occurred in negative space.

Observing swimmers underwater, all I could see were air bubbles entrapped either by the arms as they entered the water at speed or by the feet whenever they broke the air-water boundary at the surface of the water. It took me some time to realize that these air bubbles left definite patterns in the water, and it took me even longer to finally realize what these patterns meant.

The thought occurred to me that by trying to relate these flow patterns to the swimming strokes, some light could be thrown on the topic. From the start, it was clear that the answer, if any, could be hidden somewhere in the flow field, the surrounding water affected by the movements of the swimmer's stroke mechanics.

Then, one day, quite by chance, I was studying some photo slides given to me by Ernie Maglischo that showed the underwater action of Dave Bottom, a top Californian backstroker when, among the usual trails of air bubbles, I noted interesting patterns of rotating flows. Did these flow reactions reveal anything about swimming propulsion? Then I remembered having seen similar patterns in photographs in Bela Rajki's book *The Technique of Competitive Swimming*. They were among some of the first-ever underwater movie shots of world-class swimmers and showed a leading Hungarian swimmer, Laslo Magyar, taken 30 years before. It was amazing to note that the flow reactions to the stroke mechanics of the two swimmers were almost identical, even though the Hungarian was filmed before Bottom was born.

The similarity between these two sets of flow reactions prompted me to seek further evidence of common flow reactions in the techniques of world-class swimmers. I also realized that air entrapment in a swimming stroke is a bonus for the observer because it often enables flow reactions to be seen. In fact, aeration of the flow field is an accepted visualization technique used by hydrodynamicists in experimental observation.

The circular patterns in the flow field showed a rotating flow or, in other words, a vortex circulation. The presence of these definite patterns of rotating flow seemed to show, once and for all, that air bubbles are not merely haphazard indications of the path taken by the swimming stroke, as most coaches appear to think.

I now started to look for specific patterns not only in still photos but also in underwater movies. Rotating flows or vortex effects consistently appeared in the flow field. Gradually, it became clear that the vortex patterns were definitely a reaction to the propulsive impulses made by the swimming stroke and, moreover, were not necessarily indicating the path taken by the stroke.

It was also significant that skilled swimmers uniformly produced symmetrical vortices, beautiful well-rounded rings that could be described as artistic patterns in the water, while less competent swimmers tended to have flow reactions in which the vortex rings were irregularly spaced and distorted.

(continued)

(continued)

What I observed was so simple that initially I found it difficult to believe the evidence. So, for a while I had my doubts, but despite myself, I remained fascinated by the regular and often beautiful vortex patterns I noticed while observing swimmers underwater. I studied many leading swimmers underwater, especially in the midst of competition when rapid stroking usually entrapped enough air to make flow reactions more easily visible. It was soon clear that vortex patterns were not a transient phenomenon because they were too consistently similar for that to be the case. Gradually it was possible to form a synthesis of the flow reactions that could be anticipated during key phases of propulsion (Colwin 1984a).

a relatively thin zone immediately adjoining the surface of a body moving through a fluid, such as air or water. The German mathematician Ludwig Prandtl gave to the world the term *boundary layer* (Grenzschicht) and thereby introduced a concept now so familiar that it would be difficult to find many papers on fluid dynamics in which the term does not occur.

The boundary layer, which is actually composed of a number of very thin layers, always holds a velocity gradient; this means that each successive layer moves at a greater speed than the previous one. At the surface, velocity is zero because the first layer sticks to the skin and each successive layer flows a little more

easily until free flow results (figures 4.2a and 4.2b).

Whenever a fluid flows past a stationary obstacle or a solid body moves through a fluid, molecular attraction prevents any relative motion between the fluid and the body at the surface itself. Thus, no matter how rapidly a fluid is forced through a pipe or a flow channel, its speed is exactly zero at the wall. When an aircraft or an artillery shell rushes through the atmosphere, the velocity of the air immediately adjacent to the surface of the body is, at any instant, exactly equal to that of the moving body, although a fraction of an inch away, outside the boundary layer, it is quite different.

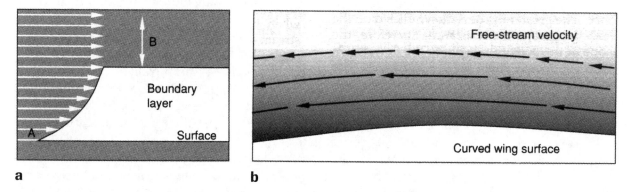

a   b

Figure 4.2 Velocity gradient at the boundary layer. *(a)* Viscosity at the boundary layer causes a velocity gradient in the passing flow. Flow decreases speed toward the surface. At A the flow is static and at B it is moving at full speed. *(b)* The nature of flow over a foil is the result of viscosity (or stickiness) of the fluid. The first layer actually sticks to the foil surface, not moving at all, but each successive tier of the flow moves a little faster and gradually builds up to free-stream velocity.

The Role of Airfoils in Creating Lift

Heavier-than-air flight is a frequently cited example of lift. *Lift,* or the force that pushes a wing upward, results from a difference in pressure between the wing's top and bottom surfaces. Although it is possible for a flat object to function as a simple wing—for example, the thin, balsa wood wings of toy gliders—shaping and streamlining a wing in a certain way can dramatically improve its aerodynamic and lifting qualities.

An airfoil is a body (in this case, a wing) designed to present a surface rounded and angled to the flowstream, creating maximum downwash and lift with minimum turbulence and drag. The gradual curvature of the airfoil produces a faster flow over its more rounded upper surface that does not break away and form eddies.

The wing's shape—slightly cambered, with a blunt leading edge and a sharp trailing edge—causes faster air flow over the top than across the bottom. This creates a lower average air pressure on top, producing enough lift to keep an airplane aloft or, for that matter, a bird. This is how the airfoil scores over a flatter wing. Unlike a flat plate, an airfoil, with its humped upper surface, produces lift even when the angle of attack is zero degrees. Further lift is gained by increasing the angle of attack so that the air meets the under surface at a steeper angle. A propeller works exactly as a wing does by making use of the lift-producing property of an airfoil but with this exception: an airfoil used as a wing should produce the maximum force at right angles to the direction of motion, but one used as a propeller should deliver a maximum force in the direction of motion.

The thrust of the propeller is obtained by giving a backward velocity to the fluid with which it comes in contact; to do this effectively, the propeller blades are given first an airfoil shape and then a twist. The airfoil contour combined with a twist is a shape common in nature, and in fact, these shapes originally were borrowed from nature. Unlike the mechanical propeller, however, birds and fish can change the shapes of their propelling surfaces according to the needs of propulsion: high-speed bursts, cruising, soaring, and so on.

The motion of an airplane propeller through a fluid is composed of a rotation about its axis together with the forward motion of the aircraft so that the blades move forward on spirals. This spiral, or helicoidal, path is common in locomotion in nature. The spiral-like action has a distinct application to human swimming propulsion, especially in butterfly and breaststroke swimming during transitional phases when the hands change direction.

Reference has been made to the unique qualities of the airfoil, a version of which is the propeller, but what is its application to swimming? James Counsilman (1971) cites the Bernoulli principle to show that during certain phases of the stroke, swimmers propel by using their hands and feet as foils to produce predominant lift. Counsilman's landmark presentation was followed by numerous papers by other observers contending that lift is produced by using hands and feet like propellers.

Fluid dynamic principles suggest, however, that although human swimmers sometimes use foil-like actions to propel, it is unlikely that the mechanism used is exactly like that of a mechanical propeller or any other form of conventional airfoil. Studies of the flow reactions produced by skilled swimmers indicate instead the use of unconventional mechanisms that albeit to a limited and modest extent, are basically similar in principle to those observed in nature. Before I develop this argument, however, the reader must understand the role of flow circulation and why circulation is necessary to produce propulsion.

The Role of Flow Circulation in Lift Propulsion

When a stream of fluid passes around a foil, the flow over the convex upper surface has a greater velocity and, following the Bernoulli principle, a lower pressure than that on the under surface; the difference in pressure between the two creates lift (figure 4.3).

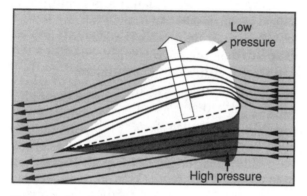

Figure 4.3 Differences in flow pressure around a foil create a lift force.

The Bernoulli principle can be demonstrated simply by lightly dangling a tablespoon between finger and thumb and directing a jet of tap water along its convex surface. Instead of pushing the spoon away, the water draws it into the jet. This experiment illustrates the drop in pressure that occurs when the speed of water increases. The shape of the spoon shows a marked similarity to the wing of a bird or airplane, and in fact, all three behave like foils.

Understanding Circulation

Circulation is a fundamental concept in fluid dynamics. Even a stone thrown through the air has a circulation associated with it. Circulation in the form of a bound vortex around a propelling member must exist before lift propulsion can take place. The principle of circulation is not only the basis of airfoil design, but is valid for bodies other than airfoils and applies to fish propulsion, bird flight, and human swimming. In the case of a human swimmer, a bound vortex appears as a rotating flow in circulation around a hand, foot, or limb (Colwin 1984a).

The Magnus Effect

The Magnus effect is the example commonly used in fluid dynamics to explain how lift is created when circulation exists around a rotating body in a uniform flowstream. If we could see a stream of fluid (air or water) flowing past a lifting foil, it would appear as if the fluid were actually circulating around it. Consider, for example, a horizontal revolving cylinder. When the cylinder is immersed in a fluid and spun counterclockwise around its axis, the surrounding fluid is set in motion and rotates with the cylinder. This is called a bound vortex (figure 4.4).

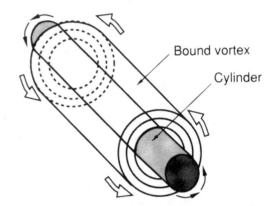

Figure 4.4 Bound vortex forms around a rotating cylinder in a still fluid.

If a horizontal flow were now to stream from right to left, the combination of the counterclockwise rotating fluid of the bound vortex and the horizontal flow would cause an increase in the speed of the fluid above and a decrease below. The net result would be a decrease in pressure above and an increase below—the usual Bernoulli effect—together with an upwash in front and a downwash behind. In effect, the spinning cylinder would be subjected to lift in the same way as an airfoil (figure 4.5). This phenomenon is known as the Magnus effect. The resulting pressure differential causes the cylinder to move upward. It is important to understand that without the rotational flow of fluid (bound vortex) and its superimposition on the flowstream there would be no lifting force. A difference in pressure transverse to the direction of motion always exists, as we have seen, when a cylinder or sphere rotates in a flow and so introduces circulation into a uniform stream. The Magnus effect also explains the flight of a cut tennis ball or the swerving flight of a golf ball.

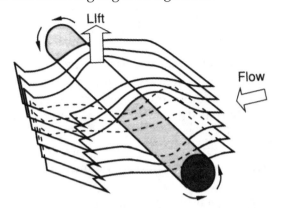

Figure 4.5 Lift generated by a rotating cylinder in horizontally moving flow.

Flow Circulation and the Human Swimmer

Although human limbs cannot develop lift propulsion in exactly the same manner as a revolving cylinder, this basic example of the Magnus effect shows that lift depends on the presence of a bound vortex around a propelling member that is superimposed on a flow.

Later in this chapter, I'll show how human swimmers often generate lift during certain phases of the swimming stroke by using this mechanism. The necessary flow circulation is developed mainly by directional changes of the foil-shaped hand aided by a significant degree of hand-forearm rotation particularly in the arm actions of the butterfly and breaststroke. However, we first need to enlarge on the subject of circulation with specific reference to the profile of the propelling member.

Lanchester's Theory of Circulation

In the case of an airfoil, there is no source of mechanical rotation so it is not obvious at first sight how it develops lift by creating circulation. F.W. Lanchester (1907), with what proved to be amazing insight, took the bold step of assuming that an airfoil's lift is associated with circulation even though the airfoil does not rotate.

This assumption must have seemed very dubious at the time, but we now know that any kind of body must have circulation around it to develop lift in a flowstream. Unless the body is specially shaped, however, the circulation is very feeble, and there is no lift. As I mentioned earlier, an airfoil has a specially designed shape that when the airfoil is propelled through a fluid, generates a strong circulation without causing a large drag. It is just this property that enables propulsion without rotating surfaces to create lift.

How an Airfoil Creates Circulation

We can now study airfoils as specially designed devices that do not need to rotate but are still able to create and maintain circulation. If we could move with an undisturbed flowstream and watch the fluid moving over an airfoil, the fluid would seem to circulate. The fluid moving upward and over the top of the airfoil flows more quickly then the main flowstream, whereas the fluid underneath flows more slowly; relatively speaking, the flow appears to move in a circle.

The idea of relative flow around an airfoil is a different perception of circulation. In this case, the bound vortex is a mathematical concept represented by the surface of the airfoil itself and not actually visible. The bound vortex around an airfoil is usually denoted as shown in figure 4.6.

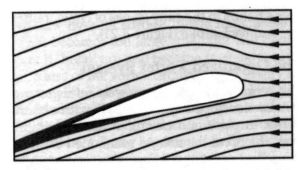

Figure 4.6 A bound vortex around an airfoil is a mathematical concept represented by the profile of the airfoil itself and is not actually visible.

How a Starting Vortex Creates Circulation in the Form of a Bound Vortex

To see what happens when a foil starts to move through a stationary fluid, hold a piece of inclined cardboard in smoke and move it from rest. You'll see an eddy shed from its trailing edge (figure 4.7). This is called a *starting vortex*, which is generated every time a foil starts its movement. A starting vortex is also generated when the hand or foot of a skilled swimmer starts a propulsive impulse in a particular direction.

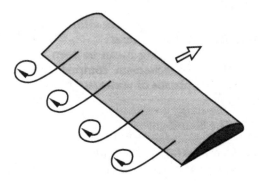

Figure 4.7 Eddies shed from the trailing edge of a moving foil.

One of the rules of fluid dynamics is that a vortex cannot be created without the production of a countervortex of equal strength circulating in the opposite direction (the principle of conservation of angular momentum). In the case of an airfoil, the countervortex is in fact the bound vortex, responsible for circulation and the production of lift, and it owes its continuing existence to the shearing forces over the surfaces of the foil (figure 4.8).

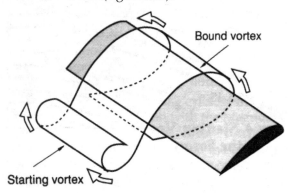

Bound vortex

Starting vortex

Figure 4.8 Starting vortex and the production of its countervortex, the bound vortex.

Experiments with a revolving cylinder in a flow channel show the reappearance of the starting vortex once the flow is switched off and circulation has ceased. Right at the end, the starting vortex appears, almost like a movie played in reverse. In the strict technical sense, however, this vortex is known as the finishing, or shed, vortex.

It is provable mathematically that because a flow does not contain a circulation at the start of a movement through it, it cannot contain a circulation at the end of the movement. This same principle applies to lift propulsion in human swimming. The shed vortex at the end of each propulsive impulse within a swimming stroke indicates that the propulsive effort in that particular direction has ended.

From the preceding it can be seen that any lift-producing mechanism comprises the following three phases of vortex action:

1. The starting vortex
2. The bound vortex
3. The finishing vortex (also termed the shed, or free, vortex)

Tip, or Trailing, Vortex

As well as providing lift, the difference in pressure between the lower and upper surfaces of a foil causes a related effect known as tip vortex, or trailing vortex. Explained simply, tip vortex results from the tendency of any fluid to flow from high to low pressure. As there is no barrier at the foil tips separating the high from the low pressure areas, the fluid leaks from underneath the foil to the top surface (figure 4.9). This flow, or leakage, deflects the fluid on the top surface slightly inward and that on the bottom surface outward, introducing a third dimension to the flow around the foil (figure 4.10).

The streams meeting at the foil's trailing edges cross one another to form a series of small trailing vortices that join into one large vortex at each foil tip. The energy used in the formation of the vortex trail appears as the induced drag. Obviously, to increase speed, extra thrust is needed to overcome the resistance caused by induced drag (figure 4.11). Even on a foil of finite span in steady motion, however, induced drag cannot be eliminated, for it is a necessary adjunct of lift. Similarly, a swimmer propelling with lift force predominating always produces induced drag. Accidental flow aeration (entrapment of air in the water) often produces visible evidence of trailing vortices on a swimmer's hands in the early stages of crawl, butterfly, and backstroke (figure 4.12). In these instances we know that lift is the predominant force acting on the swimmer's hand at the start of the stroke. However, if a swimmer's hand enters the water and immediately pulls directly backward, a predominant drag force is created, and instead of tip vortices, a typical loop (elongated) vortex is shed from the hand early in the stroke.

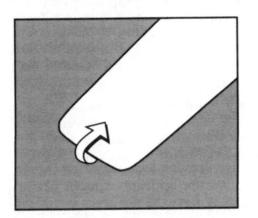

Figure 4.9 As there is no barrier at the foil tips, the fluid leaks from the high-pressure area beneath the foil to the low-pressure area on the top surface.

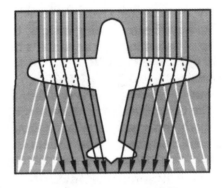

Low-pressure air = black

High-pressure air = white

Figure 4.10 Foil tip leakage introduces a third dimension to the flow around the foil.

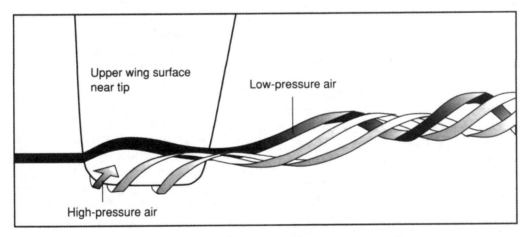

Upper wing surface near tip

Low-pressure air

High-pressure air

Figure 4.11 High- and low-pressure streams meet to form a vortex trail.

Figure 4.12 Trailing (tip) vortices are often shed from a swimmer's hands in the early stages of the crawl, butterfly, and backstroke pull.

The Organized Vortex System

The term *organized vortex system* refers to propulsion developed by foil-type lift with a bound vortex in place and trailing vortices springing from the tip of the foil. As mentioned earlier, a propeller is a rotating foil or wing. When lift is uniformly distributed along its blade span, an organized vortex system exists. Similarly, when swimmers use the hand like an airfoil, an organized vortex system will exist.

Foil-Type Propulsion in Steady Flow Conditions

The use of foil-type lift propulsion, in the strictest sense of the term, is limited to steady flow conditions in which the flow pattern does not change over time. Such is the case for a conventional airfoil lift-producing mechanism. This means that the foil must be positioned at an angle of attack that results in a steady circulating flow over its surface.

If the foil's angle of attack becomes too large, the flow detaches from it, breaks up, and becomes unsteady, causing a loss of the vortex circulation necessary for creating lift. This phenomenon is called *stall*.

Airfoils are designed to create the steady flow circulation that causes constant lift propulsion. Lift may be generated in any direction. A swimmer's arm can be used as a swimming foil, if angled properly (figure 4.13); for example, as a crawl swimmer's arm enters the water with the elbow set higher than the wrist, its cambered upper surface causes the oncoming flow to move more quickly over the upper surface of the arm and more slowly along the lower surface. The different flow velocities over the upper and lower arm produce the pressure

Figure 4.13 Different flow velocities over the upper and lower arm produce a pressure differential.

differential necessary for lift. In this case, the lift is upward, causing a high position of the upper body in the water but not contributing directly to propulsion.

As the hand moves further into the stroke it assumes an angle favorable to producing forward-inclined lift. This position lasts only a short while, however. Most skilled swimmers establish steady flow propulsion (with an organized vortex system) at the beginning of the stroke. But subsequent directional changes of hand and limb cause increased angles of attack that quickly lead to quasisteady, then nonsteady, flow. In crawl, butterfly, and backstroke, it soon becomes difficult to continue developing lift circulation by means of the conventional airfoil lift-producing mechanism because the changing postures of the hand cause too large an angle of attack.

The hand and forearm action in swimming propulsion has been likened to that of a propeller blade. But the 360-degree rotation around an axis of a mechanical propeller is anatomically impossible for a hand. An airfoil can maintain an angle of attack that produces continuous steady flow circulation. But photographs taken in a wind tunnel show what happens to the flow reaction around a cranked plate (a type of foil) as the angle of attack is changed. The flow changes from steady to quasisteady and then to unsteady. Under unsteady flow conditions, ideal foil-type lift becomes impossible.

The onset of unsteady flow conditions is marked by the tendency of the vortex trail to swell and start to burst. If the foil's angle of attack continues to increase, the vortex trail detaches from the foil, indicating that circulation has been lost and that an organized vortex system is no longer in place. Foil-type propulsion, in its accepted sense, has terminated. Similarly, when a swimmer's hand approaches too large an angle of attack, conventional foil-type propulsion is no longer possible.

The illustrations of an Olympic butterfly champion show reactions similar to those around a cranked plate in the wind tunnel (figure 4.14). This is not a unique observation, for the flow reactions produced by skilled swimmers consistently indicate that human swimming propulsion takes place in conditions of unsteady flow.

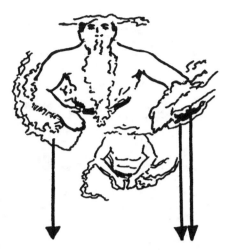

Right hand is pitched at too large an angle of attack, causing trailing vortex to swell and start to burst. Trailing vortex is about to detach from hand, indicating foil-type lift is ending (see inset figure).

Left hand is pitched at ideal angle of attack. Thin trailing vortices are characteristic of steady flow. Vortex sheet is seen as dark area between trailing vortices.

Figure 4.14 Butterfly stroke, quasisteady flow (right hand) and steady flow (left hand). Adapted from photos courtesy of James E. Counsilman.

Propulsion in Nonsteady Flow

The essential problem, hitherto ignored in analytical studies of human swimming, is that swimming propulsion occurs mainly in unsteady flow. There can be no doubt about this; the stroke mechanics of even the most skilled swimmers consistently produce unsteady flow reactions because a swimmer's hand, as it travels through a wide range of movement, quickly assumes too large an angle of attack for steady flow to continue. Although an airfoil, which is specifically designed for the purpose, can maintain the ideal angle of attack to produce the steady flow necessary for constant lift propulsion, a swimmer cannot use the hand like a conventional foil throughout a swimming stroke. The action of the hand in the swimming strokes simply cannot be compared with steady state aerodynamics.

Another important reason why the hand does not operate as a conventional airfoil is that at the start of an airfoil's movement (for example, an airplane at takeoff), the net lift around the airfoil

is very small. The smooth characteristics and lift of steady flow are established only after the airfoil has moved about ten chords (a chord is the width of the foil from leading edge to trailing edge) from its starting point. The interaction between opposing currents of air (or fluid) that delays the creation of steady lift is called the Wagner effect and contributes an unavoidable nonsteady phase in the action of normal airfoils. A swimmer's hand is not in the water at an ideal angle of attack long enough to obtain constant lift in the manner of an airfoil.

The question, then, is whether lift-force propulsion can be developed in unsteady flow conditions. It can, but the lift-producing mechanism is an unconventional one that does not require the propelling member to be placed at an ideal angle of attack.

The lift force generated by a foil is directly proportional to the foil's surface area and the density of the fluid in which it is moving. Given that the density of water is 800 times the density of air, the human hand moving in water generates a force equal to that generated by a surface 800 times its size moving in air at the same speed. Because the lift force generated by a foil is directly proportional to the square of its speed through the fluid, a 40 percent increase in the speed of the hand when employed as a foil can almost double the propulsive force generated.

In swimming, lift-force propulsion is developed in unsteady flow primarily by the directional changes of the foil-shaped hand as it moves through the stroke. The gradual rotation of the hand and forearm as a unit as the stroke progresses is an important part of this lift-producing mechanism. In all the styles of swimming, the stroke commences with the palm facing outward (to lesser or greater degrees, depending on the flexibility of the individual swimmer). As the arm reaches midstroke, the elbow reaches maximum flexion at plus or minus 90 degrees, thus indicating a considerable amount of hand-forearm rotation since the stroke commenced.

As stated, it is the rotating hand-forearm unit, moving laterally or transversely across the line of the body's forward movement, that generates lift. This action causes a pressure differential in the flow, which in turn sets up the flow circulation around the hand and forearm necessary for lift to occur. As the arm bends and the hand and forearm gradually rotate, the flow is swirled or wrapped around the hand and forearm. This swirling flow constitutes the bound vortex, or circulation, whose superimposition on the general flow is necessary for lift. As the arm extends again and the final propelling thrust of the stroke is applied, this circulating flow is gradually unswirled or unwrapped from the arm in the form of a shed vortex.

As already explained, directional changes of the hand combine with a significant range of hand-forearm rotation to set up the mechanism necessary for creating flow circulation. These flows are readily visible in shadowgram tests conducted at low speeds, when the flow is not too compressed to be easily seen.

You may conduct similar tests by simply moving a spoon or any other suitable foil-shaped object through the appropriate directions in a container of water. If you have a strong overhead light and the bottom of the tank is white, you'll see the shadow cast by the resulting vortex on the bottom of the tank and be able to note the different flow reactions produced by rectilinear and curvilinear movements. This simple test shows distinct differences between the flow reactions set up by drag propulsion (pulling directly backward), the conventional airfoil mechanism, and a curvilinear pulling pattern (figures 4.15a, 4.15b, and 4.15c).

Vortex Reactions in Producing Lift

Essentially, fluid dynamics as applied to lift-force propulsion in swimming comprises a three-fold sequence of events:

1. At the start of a propulsive impulse, a starting vortex produces a bound vortex around a hand, foot, or limb.

2. The bound vortex is then manipulated in such a way as to enable lift force to be applied.

3. When circulation (in the form of a bound vortex) can no longer be produced and maintained, a vortex is shed, indicating that the propulsive impulse has ended.

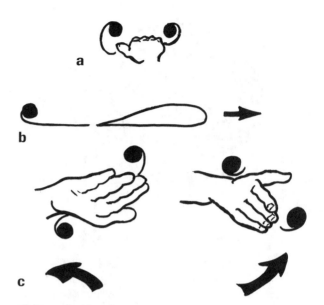

Figure 4.15 Typical flow reactions: *(a)* drag propulsion (pulling directly backward); *(b)* conventional airfoil method; and *(c)* outward and inward sculling (curvilinear pulling patterns, especially in butterfly and breaststroke). In the inward and outward scull, there are always leading edge and trailing edge vortices around the hand.

The Significance of the Shed Vortex

A vortex is shed whenever a propulsive impulse ends. The analysis of these vortex patterns produced by each swimming stroke provides a new perspective from which to view swimming efficiency. The pattern of shed vortices a swimmer leaves in the water provides an instant history of the swimming stroke, because each propulsive impulse within the overall stroke produces a distinctive type of vortex as its signature.

Recognizable patterns reveal how individual swimmers apply their power. By its size, shape, direction, velocity, and placement in the flow field in relation to the swimming stroke, the shed vortex reveals the type of propulsive mechanism the swimmer has used and the net effectiveness of the propulsive impulse just completed.

Kinetic Energy

A shed vortex represents a form of kinetic energy, or in other words, the energy of motion. We know that energy cannot be created or destroyed, but it can be transferred from one type to another. Energy is transferred from the swimmer to the water in the form of kinetic energy whenever a vortex is shed. (In fact, energy is being changed from one form into another whenever work is done or energy expended.) Vortices shed at random and not at the end of a propulsive impulse indicate wasted energy that a swimmer is not applying to the water in the most effective manner.

Studying Flow Reactions to the Swimming Stroke

I conducted a study that sought to identify flow reactions common to the stroke mechanics of world-class swimmers. A methodical analysis of underwater movies, slides, and photographs consistently revealed similar patterns of vorticity (Colwin 1984a).

By correlating commonly observed flow reactions with established fluid dynamic principles—particularly those concerning lift propulsion—I attempted to establish a basis for further study. The flow visibility was not always complete because observation depended largely on accidental air entrapment (aeration) in the swimming stroke; nevertheless, it was possible to form a synthesis of the flow reactions that could be anticipated during key phases of propulsion. More recently, I have noted the advantages of underwater video recordings of swimmers during actual competition. When swimming at speed, most swimmers accidentally entrap enough air into the water to make the flow reactions almost continuously visible.

I systematically compared these observations with fluid dynamic theory as well as with the theory that relates to lift propulsion in nature. I was especially interested in seeking reasons for what initially appeared to be unusual vortex formations that indicated propulsion was taking place in nonsteady flow.

Although airfoils are designed to develop steady flow, human swimming propulsion, because of anatomical restrictions, must employ directional changes of the limbs that cause nonsteady flow. I believe that skilled human swimmers, like birds, fish, and certain flying insects, are able to turn nonsteady flow to advantage by using dexterous movements that establish the necessary flow circulation through the rapid generation and shedding of vortices.

Chapter 5

Propulsive Mechanisms of Speed Swimming

The dynamics of all the swimming strokes cause fluctuating flow conditions because the continual directional changes of the hands are not conducive to maintaining steady flow. Although most skilled swimmers establish steady state propulsion with organized vortex systems at the beginning of a stroke, subsequent hand and limb directional changes quickly lead to a sequence of quasisteady to nonsteady periods. These changes are often difficult for some swimmers to accomplish without losing propulsion. However, underwater photography of skilled swimmers indicates that the shedding of large separate vortices occurs at approximately the same time as the hand's directional change.

In this chapter, we learn that propulsion in fluids is not limited to propellers and other purely mechanical means. To this end, we compare human swimming propulsion with the quick generating and shedding of vortices used by birds, flying insects, and marine animals in order to propel, and we find that human hands and feet function as

swim foils using mechanisms similar to those common in nature. This information is applied directly to coaching a swimmer to use the reacting pressure resistance in the flow to generate quick propulsion through the water.

The Hand as a Swim Foil

A shed vortex indicates that a propulsive impulse in a particular direction has ended. World-ranked swimmers are invariably observed to shed a large vortex during a change of hand direction; these great athletes may be showing the ideal way to propel. Acceleration to top swimming speed requires sharp directional changes of the hand instead of the smooth, rounded transitions seen at slower speeds. However, vortex shedding before a propulsive impulse has ended is often a sign of inefficient technique.

Common causes of prematurely shed vortices are holding the hand too rigidly on the wrist or too sudden a directional change combined with excessive acceleration and application of force. In high-speed swimming every stroke consists of distinct impulses that accelerate with each change of hand direction. After a vortex is shed at the end of an impulse, a new vortex is quickly generated around the hand as it changes direction. Proof of this can often be seen in the subse-

quent shedding of the new vortex—albeit a somewhat smaller one—at the end of the stroke.

An Alternative Lift-Generating Mechanism

The quick generating and shedding of vortices just described is a propulsive mechanism prevalent in nature. This alternative lift-generating mechanism, unlike that of the conventional airfoil, is independent of foil shape and the existence of an ideal angle of attack. Instead, lift is established when a circulation (bound vortex) around the propelling member is superimposed on the general flow. (The role of flow circulation in lift propulsion is discussed extensively in chapter 4.)

Careful study reveals different types of vortex patterns in the flow field (figure 5.1). The vortex pattern developed depends on the natural aptitude of the swimmer and the speed at which the swimmer is moving. Drawings adapted from films confirm that an organized vortex system is longer at slower swimming speeds (figure 5.2).

High-speed swimming may cause sharp changes in hand direction with shedding of ring vortices at the end of each propulsive impulse (figure 5.2a). A large ring vortex is

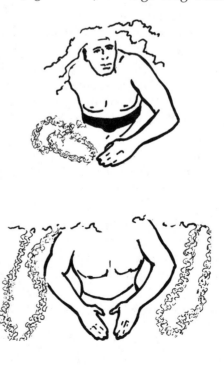

Figure 5.1   Different vortex patterns.

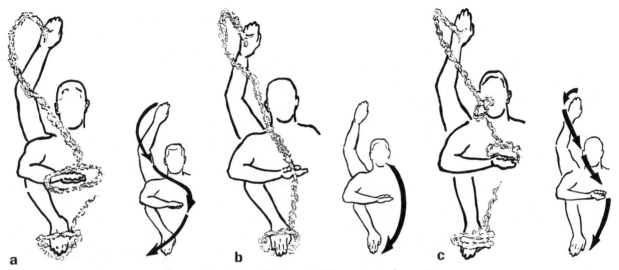

a   b   c

Figure 5.2   Vortex shedding reveals the effects of different stroke patterns.

shed as the hand changes direction in midstroke. The trailing vortices detach from the hand, indicating that the organized vortex system has ceased and that propulsion is no longer by foil-type lift. The remaining vorticity in circulation around the hand is shed at the end of the stroke by the fling-ring mechanism.

Smoother and rounder directional changes are achieved more easily at submaximal hand speed (figure 5.2b). Single-impulse propulsion and smooth hand acceleration help maintain an organized vortex system for most of the stroke. In the final stage of the stroke, the vortex trail becomes unsteady and starts to burst as a single vortex ring is shed by the fling-ring mechanism.

By applying excessive power or accelerating the hand too rapidly, even top swimmers may shed random vortices (figure 5.2c). Spasmodic vortex shedding represents kinetic energy lost to the water and is also characteristic of poor directional control of the hand. Excessive vortex shedding is common, which suggests that overapplying propulsive force and failing to accelerate the hand smoothly are more prevalent faults than generally recognized. These habits may account for subpar performance even when an athlete feels strong and powerful.

The Dual Function of the Hand

Although the literature contains frequent discussions of the elbow's changing posture during the swimming stroke, little reference is

made to the articulation of the hand on the wrist. A swimmer who possesses a natural feel of the water uses the hand to perform a dual function by directing and channeling the flow circulation while also applying propulsive thrust. In fact, the dexterous functioning of the entire arm in an undulating fashion, almost in the manner of an elongated flipper, is quite noticeable. Talented swimmers show unusual dexterity, particularly during transitional phases of the stroke, and create remarkably consistent vortex patterns in the flow field.

Comparing Swimming to Propulsion in Nature

Comparisons between human swimming and fluid dynamic propulsion in nature are appropriate because the two share similar difficulties in coping with nonsteady flow. In fact, the similarities observed among the most diverse phenomena of fluid motion are not accidental but constitute a universal law of nature. Thus, it makes sense to compare examples from nature with human swimming propulsion.

Comparisons With Bird Flight

Lift-force propulsion is based on aerodynamic principles that originated in Lilienthal's (1889) intensive observations of bird flight. Similarly, it's highly probable that skilled swimmers use methods of developing lift (in conjunction with drag) during nonsteady periods of propulsion similar to those that occur in nature.

Aircraft and the majority of flying creatures fly in what might be called a standard way, using well-understood aerodynamic principles. But small birds and flying insects fly in a manner that can't be explained in simple aerodynamic terms. We know that aircraft depend on airfoils that move through the air steadily. Nonsteady flows around aircraft wings must be minimized because they reduce flight efficiency. In contrast, nonsteady aerodynamics are an inherent feature of natural flapping flight.

The subtleties of oscillating, or flapping, wing movement are still not fully understood, but bird flight in its simplest form—gliding or soaring—does not require flapping or the consumption of muscle power. Simply by stretching out the wing, the outer part merges with the arm section to form a continuous plane so that the bird flies in a manner similar to a fixed-wing aircraft. This use of steady flow is similar to the way in which a swimmer spreads the arms sideways during the beginning phase of the butterfly and breaststroke arm actions.

The spreading of the arms is one of the most economical movements in swimming, particularly in the butterfly stroke. It's also a remarkable simulation of natural flight. In fact, I like to instruct young swimmers to imagine they are giant condors with wings outstretched, launching themselves from a high cliff into an oncoming sea breeze. When the start of the butterfly arm stroke is properly timed, this form of *subaqueous flying* (a term sometimes used to describe sea-lion propulsion) develops high body velocity and is aided by the momentum developed a split-second earlier from the downward thrust of the dolphin kick, another derivation from nature.

This steady flow phase of the arm action is present at the beginning of all four swimming styles. During this phase, an organized vortex system is in place, as shown by the presence of tip vortices coming off the hands. As the stroke changes direction, however, it becomes difficult to maintain steady flow and to continue to use the hand in an airfoil fashion. This is also true of the flapping (oscillating) wing. Because of anatomical structure, birds and insects are unable to maintain a constant production of lift.

Until recently, standard aerodynamics had failed to explain how birds and insects overcome these handicaps. But, with the help of high-speed photography, the mystery is now near a solution.

The Rapid Generating and Shedding of Vortices

Birds and insects apparently employ mechanisms that swiftly establish air circulation around their wings, entailing the rapid generating and shedding of vortices. By so doing, they are able to generate lift more quickly than would be possible in steady airflow. This discovery cast an entirely new light on the problems that had long perplexed observers of bird and insect flight. The examples of aerodynamic propulsion in nature provide valid comparisons with human swimming propulsion, which also has to cope with the problem of propelling in nonsteady flow.

Unsteady Flow in Nature

Most of our present knowledge of the flying characteristics of birds and flying insects has been gained by direct observation, aided by slow-motion photography. Their motion bears an interesting comparison to some phases of human swimming propulsion, most notably the butterfly arm action, which uses directional changes of the hands in a path transverse to the swimmer's forward direction. When this type of arm action is accompanied by a marked degree of hand-forearm rotation, it is probable that the necessary flow circulation is produced for predominant lift-force propulsion to occur. When observing propulsion in unsteady flow in nature, it is important to note that the necessary bound vortex is created by mechanisms that operate intermittently in timing with the directions of the oscillating wing. As each propulsive impulse ends, a vortex is shed.

An expert swimmer propels by means of directional changes of the hands, which cause the rapid generating and shedding of vortices. In butterfly and breaststroke, this mechanism is probably similar in principle to the oscillating wing but only to the extent that the quick changes of hand direction generate the flow circulation necessary to produce lift-force propulsion. But, there the similarity to bird flight ends. Apart from possessing a basically similar skeletal structure, the human arm bears not even a remote resemblance to a bird's wing, nor does it flap while it propels.

Comparisons With Propulsion of Marine Animals

Marine animals, fish, and birds are highly specialized for propulsion in their respective fluid mediums. At the outset, we may find it difficult to imagine how the human swimmer could possibly adopt any examples at all from nature, but consider the dolphin kick used in the butterfly stroke, developed in 1935 by Jack Sieg and his coach David Armbruster. Based on the movement of the dolphin's tail, the dolphin kick represents the most effective attempt so far by humans to adopt a swimming technique from nature. Yet, despite the natural ease with which the dolphin kick fits in with the butterfly arm action, certain limitations in the human physique prevent the butterfly swimmer from completely emulating the harmonious locomotion displayed by the dolphin.

The main difference between the natural action of the dolphin and the acquired dolphin kick of the human swimmer is that the dolphin can perform the upbeat of its fluke, or tail, more quickly than the downbeat. The upbeat of the dolphin fluke is also faster than the upbeat of a swimmer's feet at equal movement frequencies. This is because the dolphin's musculature is more suited to producing a stronger movement on the upstroke of its fluke. The traces of the dolphin's fluke appear to be more symmetrical than those of human swimmers (Ungerechts 1983).

Comparisons With the Flight of Flying Insects

The most fascinating aerodynamic discovery of recent times has a counterpart in nonsteady swimming propulsion. It concerns the novel lift-generating mechanism used by some flying insects (Lighthill 1973). Aerodynamic calculations have shown that some insects are unable to generate enough foil-type lift to remain air-

borne. Their unique lift-generating mechanisms instead depend on means different from those of ordinary foils; the actual shape of the foil is of little importance. What is needed is an elongated body that carries a bound vortex and is moved relative to the stationary fluid. It does not involve refined adjustments of the angle of attack but does require rapid control of the flow over the tip of the foil.

The Clap-Fling-Ring Mechanism

Some flying insects use a clap-fling-ring action of their wings, which circulates air to form a vortex on each wing tip (figure 5.3). At the end of the downstroke these two vortices are shed

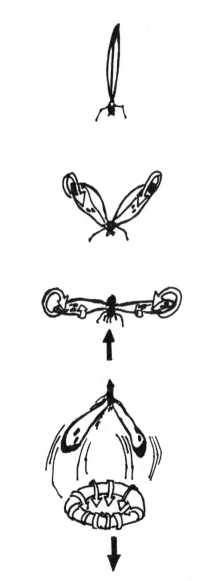

Figure 5.3 Clap-fling-ring mechanism of butterfly flight.

in a flinging action and combine to form one large vortex ring directly beneath the insect. The force needed to create the ring sustains the insect's weight.

The difference between a normal airfoil and the nonsteady fling-ring mechanism is that the vortex patterns leading to circulation are created prior to and independent of the movement of the foil through the fluid (Weis-Fogh 1973).

The Fling-Ring Mechanism in the Dolphin Kick

Obviously it is impossible for human swimmers to perform the clap phase that precedes the fling-ring mechanism. However, they may use similar mechanisms during nonsteady swimming propulsion. A typical example can be seen in the power dolphin kick when used at maximum effort. (The kick in the following description should not be confused with the gentler action of the soft dolphin kick, often used in the 200-meter event, which is more like a foil operating in steady flow.)

The power dolphin kick requires a rapidly established vortex circulation, in this case around the feet, prior to commencing the propulsive impulse. This is accomplished in a manner slightly different from the clap-fling-ring mechanism used by some flying insects.

In the absence of the preliminary clap phase of the mechanism, the soles of the feet set up the necessary preliminary circulation as they touch the surface of the water prior to the feet starting downward. The contact by the soles with the surface water sets up a surface tension caused by molecular attraction between the two fluids, water and air. As the feet thrust downward, a bound vortex forms around each foot. These vortices combine to form one large vortex ring that is shed in the vertical plane as the feet complete a powerful downward thrust (figure 5.4). The large size of the ring indicates that a large mass of water has been acted on, whereas the velocity of the water has remained relatively low. One indication of the dolphin kick's effectiveness is the distance between the regularly spaced vortices: The greater the distance between each shed vortex ring, the more effec-

tive the kick. I have often asked butterfly swimmers to swim a few strokes and then stop and look back underwater at their still-visible vortex trails. They were fascinated that they could actually see the result of their propulsion.

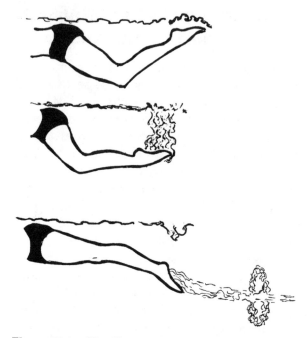

Figure 5.4 The fling-ring propulsive mechanism in the power dolphin kick.

Sometimes, when a swimmer's feet have spread too far apart during the downward thrust, two smaller vortices, one from each foot, will be shed. The effectiveness of this action is not as great as when a large single vortex is shed.

The use of the fling-ring lift effect in the power dolphin kick depends largely on a swimmer's ability to hyperextend the ankles and feet quickly to establish surface tension. Circulation results from the impulsive force created by the feet as they separate the air-water boundary.

The Fling-Ring Mechanism in the Two-Beat Crawl Kick and the Breaststroke Kick

Crawl swimmers using a power-producing two-beat kick also employ the fling-ring mechanism. Shed vortices of a smaller size can often be observed in the vertical plane behind each foot as it completes its downward thrust. For instance, this effect can be seen in the women's 1,500-meter event, in which the use of the two-beat kick usually predominates. Each swimmer in the race often leaves a ladder of small separate vortices trailing in the lane behind her.

Underwater movies of breaststroke swimmers show that the essential preliminary flow circulation is set up by the dorsi-flexion of the feet, combined with their change of direction, as they move from recovery into the propulsive phase. That the breaststroke kick uses the fling-ring lift mechanism can be seen when a breaststroke swimmer misjudges the depth of a push off from a turn and inadvertently introduces air into the kick. The resultant aeration of the flow reveals vortex rings behind each foot as the first kick off the wall is completed, a clear demonstration that the kick uses the fling-ring mechanism.

Practical Application of Flow Analysis as a Coaching Tool

The following discussion is couched in question and answer format. I am frequently asked these questions in conversation and correspondence.

What is a vortex?

A vortex is a mass of fluid that rotates about an axis. The axis of the vortex may be in almost any plane from vertical to horizontal.

What causes a vortex to be shed at the end of a propulsive impulse?

The presence of a bound vortex is essential for lift to occur. When a starting vortex is formed, it causes a bound vortex to be closed around a foil. Because a flow does not contain any circulation at the beginning of a stroke, it must not contain any circulation at the end of a stroke.

For example, experiments with a rotating cylinder in a flow channel show the reappearance of the starting vortex, now rotating in the opposite direction, once the flow is switched

off and circulation has ceased. Right at the end, the starting vortex reappears, almost like a movie film played in reverse.

Similarly, it can be seen that a vortex must be shed if the hand is brought to a complete stop with respect to the local flow because there is no longer a mechanism producing and maintaining circulation. So, during a swimming stroke, when the hand stops or completes a propulsive impulse in a certain direction, whatever circulation is bound on it is shed to form a vortex ring.

The reader can easily demonstrate these phenomena. Stand in shallow water, dip your hand into the water, and move your hand; the rapidly formed starting vortex appears. Now end the movement by stopping the hand suddenly, which causes a shed vortex visibly whirling away rapidly from the hand.

What is the ideal shape of a shed vortex?

A shed vortex should be circular rather than elongated because a circular vortex acts on a larger area or mass of fluid. Its velocity is slower than that of an elongated vortex, which acts on a smaller area and a smaller mass. Although an elongated vortex (long loop) produces a flow causing forward thrust, this is not the most efficient mode of propulsion, for the reason just stated. The elongated vortex usually results from predominant drag propulsion when the hand is pulled straight backward like a paddle instead of in a curved path like a foil (figure 5.5). The vortex is shed from both sides of the hand and arm and appears early in the stroke.

What should be the ideal plane of a shed vortex?

Refer to the example of the circular vortex and assume, for the time being, that we have a swimmer who can produce this perfectly shaped circular vortex. Again, a vortex is a mass of fluid rotating about an axis that may be in almost any plane. Let us orient the plane of this circular vortex at different angles, from vertical to horizontal.

When the plane of this circular vortex is vertical and its axis is horizontal, all the fluid

particles the vortex acts on will be moved in the stream direction (the horizontal direction), which results in ideal direct forward propulsion. When the plane of the vortex is horizontal, or lying parallel to the surface of the water, all the fluid particles that this vortex acts on will be directed downward, meaning that the net force created by the swimmer is upward rather than forward.

The conclusion is that if a swimmer's stroke is efficient, the plane of the shed vortex tends to be vertical or nearly vertical. The more vertical the vortex plane, the more likely the propulsive impulse has generated near maximum forward thrust.

What do different size vortices in the flow field tell us?

Counsilman (1971) states that it's better to move a large mass of water a short distance than to move a small mass of water a long way. In terms of propeller theory, this idea could be expressed as "it's better to move a large mass of water slowly than to move a small mass quickly." Stated thus, the principles of propeller theory apply directly to swimming propulsion.

In another of his prominent studies, Counsilman (1980) showed that skilled swimmers produce marked hand acceleration in the latter phase of the crawl, a finding borne out by analysis of the flow reaction. A smaller vortex appears after the end of the stroke, whereas a larger vortex appears during the stroke, when the first propulsive impulse of the stroke is completed (as the elbow reaches maximum flexion). The smaller vortex at the end of the stroke shows an increase in the flow velocity caused by the hand's acceleration.

It may be that the first, larger vortex creates a new flow direction and the hand may have to move faster to make maximum use of the new flow velocity. The skilled swimmer may be aware of this—albeit subconsciously—and adjust the hand accordingly.

Figure 5.5 Predominant drag propulsion: flow reactions. *(a)* The flow reaction shows drag force propulsion resulting from pulling directly backward. All organized vorticity is shed very early in the stroke. *(b)* The typical lasso-type vortex consists of a short vortex trail attached to a large ring. The stroke is completed with wake turbulence behind the hand. Sometimes this action is shown by early detachment of the trailing vortex without the presence of a ring.

What does the presence of excessive vorticity mean?

A coach can learn a great deal from a swimmer's subjective comments, especially immediately after a race. Sometimes, when a swimmer has turned in a particularly fine performance, the swimmer may say, "I felt so good that I could have gone faster," or, conversely, a swimmer may express disappointment at a recorded time by saying, "I felt so strong and powerful—I can't understand why my time wasn't faster."

As has been observed underwater, very powerful swimmers often shed vortices in the middle of a propulsive impulse, which shows they are exerting more power than necessary. In contrast, the swimmer who finishes with power in reserve, feeling it was possible to go faster, perhaps instinctively has not overapplied power.

There could be another reason for excessive vortex shedding, however. As the hand exceeds the ideal angle of attack (in terms of the conventional airfoil mechanism), the flow separates, destroying the circulation. At this stage a swimmer will start to use unconventional propulsive mechanisms to propel in the resulting unsteady flow. One reason for excessive vortex activity, then, could be that the swimmer can no longer adjust the hand incidence so as to maintain airfoil-type propulsion and thus has to shed the existing flow circulation to establish a new flow around the hand.

Why is it not always possible to see the swimmer's flow reactions in the water?

The presence of visible flow reactions depends on accidental air entrapment. Aeration is a recognized visualization technique used by fluid dynamicists. Although most swimmers produce a visible flow reaction when swimming at speed, no procedure ensures regular visualization of the surrounding flow field. Several flow visualization methods are used to analyze the flow around models in flow channels and wind tunnels, but the use of dyes, lasers, smoke, and so on could pose a safety hazard for swimmers. Up to now, photography, especially shadow photography, has provided promising results.

The flow patterns of great swimmers at key phases of propulsion are remarkably predictable. When observing these top performers, it's not difficult to form a synthesis of the flow patterns that can be anticipated. Nevertheless, we lack a sophisticated method of flow visualization that enables vortex reactions to be measured accurately against a grid. Ideally, such a method would require front- and side-view photography of swimmers at racing speed. The side views should be photographed by an underwater camera moving on a track and kept constantly abreast of the swimmer; where access to a swimming flume is available, the swimmer could be filmed while tethered in an oncoming flow. Comparing the results produced by the two approaches would add another dimension to flow analysis.

Should swimmers entrap air into their strokes to make the flow reactions visible?

Intentional aeration is not a good idea because under certain conditions, air entrapment can cause bursting bubbles that may increase drag. Although air entrapment should not be encouraged, the introduction of a bubble can improve efficiency sometimes, when a bubble attaches to the upper surface of a foil, causing a modified contour that prevents massive separation of the flow.

Shaping the Flow

Little is known about the effects of body shape on a swimmer's efficiency. The bulky, squat body type has not been as prevalent in competitive swimming as it once was. Most of the leading swimmers, irrespective of their events, are tall and lithe, with a lean physique like a basketball player's. Their muscles tend to be long rather than short and heavy like a weightlifter's.

The effects of a swimmer's shape and physical proportions on speed and efficiency are governed by the ratio of height to bulk, among other important factors. The more slender the swimmer, the less the underwater volume compared to the swimmer's height, or length, in the water. If a swimmer has a gradually tapering physique, water will flow past more easily. Other variables include buoyancy, body composition, flexibility, neuromuscular patterns, and individual aptitude.

However, the shapes of certain human body types (somatotypes) are at a distinct disadvantage in speed swimming. Observation of the water's flow reactions around individual swimmers confirms this.

Some swimmers have extreme difficulty controlling the oncoming flow of water along the entering arm(s) with sufficient continuity to obtain the best timing of the stroke. The more successful swimmers appear to be favorably endowed by nature with streamlined body profiles and functional limb shapes that enable them to continuously control the oncoming flow between one stroke and the next.

In all four styles of swimming, the arms at the start of the stroke should act much like the bow of a ship, channeling the oncoming flow along each arm and around the body.

The crawl permits a skilled swimmer to smoothly control the oncoming flow as one stroke ends and the next one commences. The overlapping arm action of the crawl stroke allows a swimmer to feel the oncoming flow of water advance along the entry arm at the same time as the opposite arm is unswirling the flow from the hand and forearm at the finish of its stroke. The expert crawl swimmer is thus able to control simultaneously two separate flow reactions during this fleeting but critical timing phase of the arm stroke.

Compared to the crawl, the other three swimming styles—backstroke, butterfly, and breaststroke—produce oncoming flows a swimmer cannot so easily intercept and translate into smooth continuous propulsion.

In the back crawl, the arms remain almost the same distance from each other during the complete stroke cycle and do not overlap as much as in the crawl stroke. So, unless a backstroke swimmer has a tall, lean body and an arm reach long enough to control the oncoming flow efficiently at entry, accurate timing between the entry arm and the finishing arm is more difficult than in the crawl.

In efficient crawl and backstroke swimming, the alternating action of the arms ensures that at nearly every stage of the stroke cycle one arm extends forward at entry to intercept and smoothly channel the oncoming flow while the other arm completes its stroke. In butterfly and breaststroke, however, because the arms move simultaneously, such nearly constant interception of the oncoming flow at entry is not possible. Moreover, some butterfly and breaststroke swimmers have difficulty controlling the oncoming flow around the arms at the beginning of each stroke because the momentum necessary to produce this oncoming flow depends on accurate timing between the arm and leg actions.

Exploiting Examples From Nature

I have described how humans developed their admittedly limited swimming ability. Through considerable invention and the gradual acquisition of increasing skill, we learned to adapt our comparatively awkward land-living bodies for efficient use in water.

Earlier, I made a comparison between human swimming and similar propulsive mechanisms in nature. Is it possible to improve the efficiency of human swimming by seeking out and adopting further examples from nature? Can we learn to use propulsive mechanisms and postural shapes derived from nature to provide a more facile, dexterous, and efficient mode of swimming?

Although probably no further adaptation from nature will have the same dramatic effect on the sport as the development of the dolphin kick, we can learn much by studying fish and birds, their natural shapes, and the changing shapes they adopt during various phases of propulsion. Much of their efficiency can be attributed to their skill in making smooth transitions from the end of one propulsive impulse to the start of the next. Unfortunately, the subject of transitional phases of the stroke in human swimming has yet to studied.

Ideal Postures and Shapes

The literature contains little mention of the possibility of ideal postures or shapes of the hand in relation to the wrist as the arm moves through the changing phases of a swimming stroke.

A better understanding of how to shape the hand-wrist posture during the arm stroke could improve swimming efficiency. This applies to the postures assumed by the hand and wrist in relation to each other during the propulsive impulse, at the end of the propulsive impulse, and during the transitional phase between the end of one propulsive impulse and the start of another.

Birds and fish exhibit shapes adapted to their function, and they are able to change their body forms somewhat to alter the flow reactions around their bodies. A study of the shapes and changing forms adopted by fish and birds may have beneficial applications for human swimming.

Careful study of the arm posture of an expert butterfly swimmer during the inward sweep of the stroke (figure 5.6) indicates that the swimmer, probably without knowing it, has adopted two characteristic shapes common in nature:

1. The projecting thumbs each act like an alula, or small extra wing.

2. The hand and forearm, from the tip of the little finger to the point of the elbow, assume a lunate, or crescent-shaped, configuration.

Both shapes are concerned with lift enhancement in that they help keep the flow attached to the hands and forearms. Some butterfly swimmers who keep their thumbs pressed in and their hands in a straight line with their forearms encounter flow separation very early in the stroke. The vortex patterns set up by the swimmer in figure 5.6 show that she has kept the flow attached to her hands and forearms even though her hands have already changed direction from their initial outward sweep and are well into the inward phase of the stroke. The only visible signs of pending flow separation are slight swellings in the vortex trails near the fingertips.

The Alula Effect in Smoothing Out the Flow

In bird flight, the alula, sometimes referred to as the bastard wing, is an interesting refinement that acts as a subsidiary airfoil in front of the leading edge of the main wing. Under normal flight conditions, the alula is folded back out of the way. As the bird approaches stalling speed, however, and the airflow over the upper wing surface becomes turbulent, the

Figure 5.6 Arm posture of expert butterfly swimmer.

alula is spread forward to form a slot through which air rushes, restoring a smooth, fast airstream and curtailing stall (figure 5.7). In similar fashion, when a swimmer's hand is inclined at too large an angle of attack to keep the flow attached to the hand, the thumb, when held away from the hand, produces a throttle effect through which the speed of the flow increases, creating a low-pressure area on the knuckle side of the hand that produces more lift and a smoother flow around the hand.

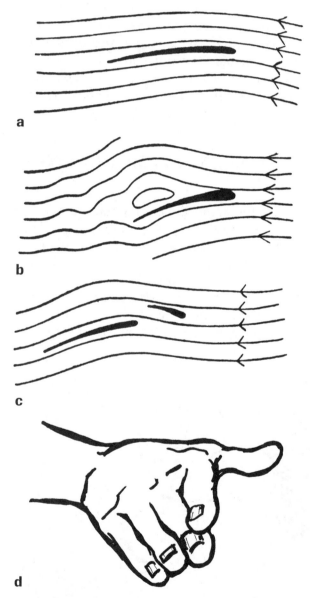

Figure 5.7 Use of alula mechanism to create steady flow. *(a)* Foil in steady flow. *(b)* Steep angle of attack produces unsteady flow. *(c)* Alula restores steady flow. *(d)* The thumb used as an alula.

The Efficiency of Lunate, or Crescent-Shaped, Contours

The wings of seagoing birds such as shearwaters and albatrosses, which spend an enormous amount of time in the air, are swept backward. Even the limbs of species adapted to propulsion through water (a fluid, just as air is, and thus subject to many of the same physical laws) show the same crescent shape, particularly the tail fins of fish such as marlin and tuna and marine mammals such as dolphins and whales (van Dam 1988; figure 5.8).

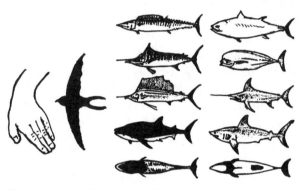

Figure 5.8 The ulnar-flexion of the wrist in the human swimmer resembles various lunate shapes in nature.

Does the crescent shape bestow some special advantage? Only recently, with the development of computerized modeling techniques that faithfully represent the dynamics of vortex wakes, was it discovered that the most aerodynamically efficient shape is not the conventional flattened ellipse. A half-moon planform, like that of a whale's tail, with a curved leading edge and a straight trailing edge is superior, and a crescent planform, in which both edges curve backward like a swift's wing, is more effective still.

These shapes enhance performance because the vortices that form at the trailing edge of the inboard section of a curved wing or fin wash downward (sideways for a fin) ahead of those further along the limb, producing updrafts and sidedrafts that like miniature hurricanes, agitate nearby fluid particles.

The tip of a wing or fin acts in turn like a sail, converting some of the kinetic energy of these spiraling streams into forward thrust. In this manner, a crescent planform generates at least 10 percent less induced drag than an elliptical one, a reduction that grows in significance as the time an animal spends flying or swimming increases.

In the human swimmer, the ulnar-flexion of the wrist in relation to the forearm creates a crescent-shaped contour that keeps the flow attached around the hand and forearm. This is important because if the flow were to separate from forearm and hand, drag would increase. In fact, some swimmers who changed to an ulnar-flexion of the wrist during the inward sweep of the arm reported increased ease in this phase of the stroke without experiencing loss of propulsion (figure 5.9).

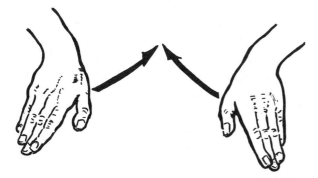

Figure 5.9 Ulnar wrist flexion on inward sweep of the hand.

The discussion so far has centered on the effect of ulnar wrist flexion during the inward sweep of a swimming stroke, but what are we to make of the ulnar wrist flexion sometimes seen during the outward sweep of a swimming stroke? In addition to assuming the crescent-shaped contour of the lower arm, some swimmers also incline the hand slightly upward during the outward sweep so that the fingertips appear to be the highest part of the entire arm.

The outward arm sweep of champion butterfly swimmer Mary T. Meagher is a good example of this action (figure 5.10). The slight upward tilt of her hands is not unlike that of a large soaring bird turning up its wingtip primary feathers to reduce drag induction. In other swimmers, the elbows are pronouncedly higher than the hands, which in turn are set at a sharp angle from the wrists to shape the whole arm remarkably like a cantilevered hydrofoil. By making models of the functional arm shapes of talented swimmers and testing

them in flow channels, it should be possible to analyze the exact effects these shaping techniques have on the surrounding flow field. It would also be possible to measure at what angles of attack flow separation (and consequent vortex shedding) takes place.

Figure 5.10 Outward arm sweep of champion butterfly swimmer Mary T. Meagher. The fingertips appear to be the highest point of the entire arm. Adapted from instructional film by Maglischo and Gambril, produced by First Essex Productions.

Midstroke Transitions

Even at topflight swim meets it's common to see swimmers whose techniques are based too much on tugging, pulling, and pushing, which are essentially land-type concepts. Many swimmers try to pull directly through the hard part of the stroke instead of adopting transitional postures of the hand that would enable them to more easily control the oncoming flow.

We might possibly learn something from observing the transitional shapes adopted by certain reef fish when maneuvering. Their fins move through a very flat angle as they fan around to a new posture in a helicoidal path. Fish do not waste energy by trying to overcome a developing or increasing resistance such as that encountered by a human swimmer as the elbow reaches maximum bend in midstroke and the hand reaches an angle almost perpendicular to the line of forward progression. The spiraling fin of the reef fish simply goes around the obstacle of increased resistance.

Perhaps the human swimmer could copy this action, when swimming crawl, for example. In midstroke the forearm is medially rotated so that the hand is turned slightly, as shown in figure 5.11. The transition is made with a quick, deft movement. The palm of the hand is turned to face slightly forward, almost like turning a vertical slat in a venetian blind. The motion quickly presents the hand at a more acute angle with less drag as the hand and forearm round out to finish the stroke with a fanlike action (figure 5.12). A biomechanical study of this suggested midstroke transitional maneuver, performed by a skilled swimmer, could prove interesting and enlightening.

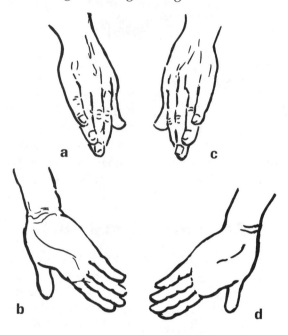

Figure 5.11 Midstroke transition showing four views of medially rotated hands in the crawl stroke: *(a)* top right view, *(b)* bottom right view, *(c)* top left view, and *(d)* bottom left view.

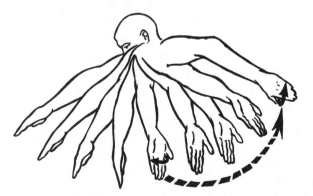

Figure 5.12 Fanning to avoid drag in midstroke transition, side view.

Functional Shaping as a New Approach to Stroke Technique

The purpose of this chapter has not been to recommend dramatic new changes in technique but rather to show how efficient propulsion depends on adroit manipulation of the reacting flow.

Underwater photography shows that talented swimmers use a variety of hand, finger, and thumb configurations during the changing phases of a swimming stroke (figure 5.13). It is highly unlikely that any one swimmer could incorporate all these principles within an individual stroke pattern, nor is it recommended that a swimmer attempt to do so. How should a coach approach teaching the various shaping techniques such as the alula effect, the ulnar wrist flexion, hand cupping, and so on? Each person should experiment to find which of these techniques can be comfortably used within his or her personal swimming style. For example, whereas one swimmer may feel an advantage is gained by assuming a lunate shape between hand and forearm, another swimmer may feel more comfortable keeping the hand aligned with the forearm. The coach's role will not be to enforce these finer embellishments on a swimmer but to recognize their value and not intervene when a swimmer uses them naturally.

Traditional coaching methods have focused on establishing desired stroke patterns but have neglected to provide the swimmer with adequate feedback on the efficiency of performance. Children should be taught flow recognition and manipulation from an early age. They should be made aware of functional shaping of the hand and arm as important aspects of technique. Learning to create, feel, and recognize the ideal reacting flow of the water gives swimmers instant feedback on the efficiency of their swimming strokes.

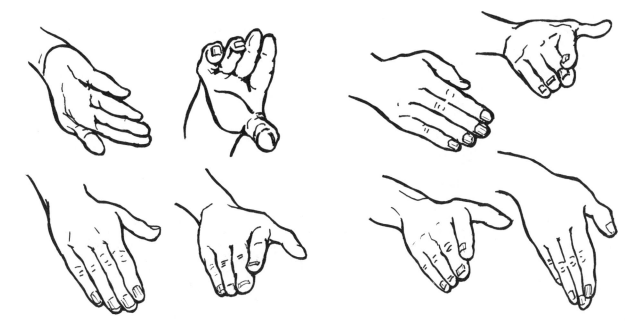

Figure 5.13   Various hand-digit postures used by talented swimmers.

Chapter 6

Coaching the Feel of the Water

The *feel of the water* refers to a swimmer's intuitive ability to feel and effectively handle the water. It is generally believed that feel of the water is an elusive quality unique to the talented athlete; swimmers of only average ability cannot hope to emulate the acute sensory perception of the talented motor genius. Nevertheless, I intend to show that by heightening the sense of touch and learning how to interpret sensations of moving pressure, swimmers of average ability can acquire the subtleties of advanced stroke technique. Talented swimmers coached in this method will likewise achieve greater expertise.

A more apt title to this chapter may well be "Coaching the Feel of the Flow." Water flows when a force acts on it; a swimmer's hand always propels against the pressure of moving water. The force exerted by a skilled swimming stroke causes the water to flow in a distinct pattern (Colwin 1984a). The method in this chapter shows swimmers how to feel for the ideal flow reaction to their stroke mechanics and thus receive instant feedback on their efficiency.

This new approach teaches swimmers to anticipate, control, and manipulate the flow of the water. They learn that the arm functions not only as a propelling instrument but also as a skilled and sensitive shaper of the flow.

Ideal Flow Reactions

The first step is to explain how the flow behaves during each phase of an efficient swimming stroke. The flow directions that can be anticipated in the different swimming strokes can be described simply. The oncoming flow—which in the crawl-stroke hand entry moves from the fingertips to the wrist and along the arm—is known as *distal* in its direction. A flow that moves toward the radial bone (or from thumb to little finger) is termed *radial,* for example, the flow produced when the elbows bend to bring the hands under the body in the crawl, butterfly, and breaststroke. An *ulnar* flow moves toward the ulnar bone or from little finger to thumb, for example, the flow produced as the arms extend and the stroke rounds out to the hips in the crawl and butterfly. A flow is *proximal* when it moves from the wrist toward the fingertips, as happens in the backstroke as the arm straightens at the end of the stroke (Schleihauf 1979).

The Importance of Hand-Forearm Rotation

Swimmers are shown how flow behavior is related to an important aspect of stroke mechanics: emphasizing hand-forearm rotation within comfortable limits for each individual swimmer. This is the mechanism that sets up the ideal flow around the hand and forearm in all the strokes. The practical application of this mechanism for swimmers of all strokes is simple: Start the stroke with the palm(s) facing outward and gradually rotate your hand-forearm unit throughout the stroke, with particular emphasis on achieving the maximum amount of elbow bend in midstroke that is comfortable. Find the amount of hand-forearm rotation and elbow bend that develops the strongest pressure on the moving flow but still feels comfortable.

New Terminology Related to Feedback on Flow Reactions

Introduce a new terminology. Short descriptive phrases such as "trap, wrap, unwrap" tell a swimmer how to handle the flow correctly during the split-second action of a swimming stroke. This differs from previous methods that describe only the mechanics of the stroke. In addition, the new terminology relates to obtaining feedback by feeling the flow on the hand and forearm. These verbal cues are important to the effectiveness of the method and are valuable as rehearsal techniques to enhance subsequent performance. Later in this chapter, I will discuss appropriate descriptions of what pressure sensations a swimmer should feel.

Flow-Shaping Skills

The swimmers are taught flow-shaping skills by which they create and detect specific flows in the water. These *flow shapers,* as they are called, have a beneficial two-way effect, in that a swimmer's efforts to shape the flow cause a reciprocal shaping effect on the limb itself. The feedback received from the flow reaction causes the proprioceptors in the muscles to respond by adjusting the posture and attitude of the propelling arm. Flow shapers produce positive and even exciting results because they instantly groove the hand and arm in accurate stroke patterns. Even the skeptics become convinced that this is a unique and effective way to teach efficient stroke mechanics. The essence of the method is: the feel of the flow shows a swimmer exactly where to place each moving sequence of the swimming stroke.

Sensitizing Procedures

Special sensitizing procedures are introduced to sensitize the sensory nerve endings to the moving pressure of the water (or, more precisely, transient pressure induced by motion). The propelling surfaces of the hands and forearms are also sensitized to simulate specific flow reactions. The method is simple. Sensitivity to the flow increases at once. Swimmers of average ability learn to regulate a smooth and efficient stroke.

Although these techniques quickly stimulate the sensory nerve endings, this is of little value unless the swimmer makes an association between the feel of the moving water and the particular phase of the swimming stroke.

Only then can meaning be given to the sense of touch and an intelligent concept formed of the desired stroke mechanics.

Connecting Sensory Information With Stroke Effectiveness

The method short circuits the motor-learning process and renders the complex more simple. The deliberate intention is to cause an immediate connection between sensory information and stroke effectiveness. By giving instant meaning to the sense of touch, the procedure adds a new perspective to traditional methods, so it is used even in the early stages of learning. Young swimmers rapidly improve their ability to seek out and recognize ideal flow reactions.

It is unnecessary to burden a swimmer with academic considerations—valid though they may be—such as lift, drag, ideal angles of attack, and which movement planes to emphasize. Talented swimmers, when exposed to the method, develop unusual dexterity in directing and channeling the flow efficiently. Even accomplished swimmers improve their techniques when made aware of the exact flow reactions they can anticipate; in fact, they become enthusiastic and keen to learn more about the process.

The Goal of the Method

The goal of this method is to coach the feel of the water by showing swimmers how to use their sense of touch to interpret and improve stroke effectiveness. The method encompasses the following tasks:

1. Describe and explain the flow reactions that can be anticipated during each phase of a skilled swimming stroke.

2. Demonstrate and explain hand-forearm rotation and elbow bending and how these mechanisms set up the ideal flow around the hand and forearm in all the swimming strokes.

3. Demonstrate flow-shaper skills and explain how they shape ideal stroke patterns for the individual swimmer.

4. Demonstrate sensitizing procedures and explain how they can be used to simulate specific flow reactions.

5. Emphasize the importance of regular practice. Ensure constant repetition by swimmers of all the procedures outlined in the preceding tasks.

Using Appropriate Descriptions

What sensations of touch should a swimmer experience when manipulating water efficiently? How should they be described? Little thought has been given to this aspect of coaching, which is not surprising when even acknowledged stroke technicians have used such descriptions of water as "fickle substance." We have all been guilty of inadequately describing how the water should feel to a correctly stroking swimmer.

For years, one of my favorite descriptions was "Enter your hand and feel the pressure of the water on your palm. Try to make the pressure progressively harder as you drive through." Although this may have been as good a description as possible at the time, it does not describe the desired feel accurately enough in the context of existing knowledge.

A once popular and comparatively apt description of the feel of the water likened it to the feeling of pulling through soft mud. More recently, however, a "fixed point of resistance" description has become popular. (This probably resulted from biomechanical studies based on the convenient assumption of essentially still water.) To convey the concept of a force acting on a mass of water, the act of propulsion has been variously described as feeling for undisturbed water, anchoring the hand on a fixed spot in the water and pulling the body past it, pulling along an imaginary knotted rope, and other similar descriptions.

These descriptions, strictly speaking, are inappropriate because the propulsive force is not applied against a solid or rigid resistance. Coaches should use carefully chosen words when instructing a swimmer. Many of our well-worn coaching terms may not produce the reactions we desire.

Understanding the Concept of Relative Flow

A good example of a potentially misleading term is the word "catch," which has been used since the early days of swimming to describe how a swimming stroke should begin. The old idea of feeling for the catch point is incorrect, however. Fluid dynamic principles contradict the popular notion that the hand attaches to a fixed point in the water and levers the body past it. Instead, one should feel the oncoming, or relative, flow advance over the palm of the hand and along the forearm. The hand always encounters an oncoming flow of water.

The instant the fingertips enter the water there is a reacting flow that continues throughout the stroke. Like all fluids, water responds immediately to any movement through it; like all fluids, water changes shape under the action of forces. These changes are known as deformation and appear as elasticity and flow. When a swimmer propels efficiently, the flow and the elasticity of the water will be felt as a stretching effect.

Correct Manipulation of the Hand

Swimming skill is dramatically increased by learning the simple act of splitting the flow with the fingers and hand throughout the stroke. Flow separation causes different patterns of pressure to form around the hand. There is always flow from an area of high pressure to one of lower pressure in a correctly performed stroke. This causes a bound circulation of water around the hand that generates the propulsive force. All one needs to do is to continue splitting the flow to maintain this propulsive force.

The contour of the hand and the angle at which it is held while splitting the flow will affect the amount of propulsive pressure produced. This is based on sound principles of fluid dynamics. It is more efficient to split the flow with the edges (either the fingertips or sides) of the hand than to use the hand like a paddle and pull with the palm of the hand flat against the pressure resistance of the water.

When the edges of the hand are used to split or separate the flow, the hand is used as a foil, causing a fine, thin, shearing separation at the trailing edge rather than the broad, blunt, excessively turbulent separation that results from the straight backward paddle action.

To avoid pulling straight backward, the hand is moved in a slightly curved path across the line of forward progress (Counsilman 1971). Another way of describing this action is to say that the hand is moved in the lateral, or transverse, plane. (Of course, the path of the hand actually moves in three planes simultaneously, namely, the lateral, vertical, and horizontal.) By moving the hand along a curved path a swimmer will be able to tilt its leading edge slightly upward, thus creating a foil-like effect that will increase the pressure resistance on the palm of the hand. In this manner, a swimmer can feel the pressure of the flow on the palm of the hand without pulling directly backward.

Pressure Sensations Caused by Different Propulsive Mechanisms

The obvious question at this point is what the differences are in the feel of the water between using the hand as a foil and using it as a paddle. When the hand is used as a foil, pressure resistance is felt on the palm of the hand and the flow is felt on the backs of the hands and fingers, particularly on the skin over the knuckles. The water is also flowing over the palm of the hand, but its presence is felt as pressure resistance, not flow, because the water flows more slowly over the palm of the hand than over the knuckle side, thus creating an area of higher pressure. The swimmer feels this pressure instead of the flow.

When the hand is used as a paddle, the pressure resistance is also felt on the palm of the hand, but there is no sensation at all on the knuckle side because the flow separates around both edges of the hand, not one edge only (the trailing edge) as in the foil-type method. Pulling the hand like a paddle causes excessive drag turbulence on the hand and results in wasted energy when compared with the more efficient foil-type method. Obviously, the previously cited descriptions are inadequate to convey the tactile sensations ("feel") of modern stroke mechanics.

Describing Flow Manipulation

Assuming a swimmer has been taught the function of hand-forearm rotation and elbow bending in manipulating the flow, the swimming stroke should be taught as a working sequence of "trap, wrap, and unwrap the flow." This helps relate each important phase of the stroke with the relative flow reaction. In the crawl stroke this sequence works as follows:

1. The *trap* occurs as the arm enters the water with elbow up and hand pitched diagonally outward. The swimmer feels an oncoming flow of water advance along the entire undersurface of the arm from the palm of the hand to the armpit. At this point the flow is considered to be trapped under the arm.

2. The *wrap* occurs as the flow is wrapped around the hand and forearm as they rotate inward after a short downward press. The wrap is completed when the elbow reaches maximum bend (approximately 90 degrees) and the hand has moved across under the body.

3. The *unwrap* occurs as the elbow extends and the arm straightens. At the end of the stroke the flow is finally unwrapped from the forearm and hand as the stroke rounds out past the hip joint.

The entire sequence of trap, wrap, and unwrap occurs within a fraction of a second. The swimmer is taught to think of the sequence as a very quick passage of events. Each successive phase happens with increasing speed to produce the desired stroke acceleration (Counsilman and Wasilak 1982). The precise application of the trap, wrap, unwrap concept of flow manipulation varies with each swimming stroke.

Manipulating the Flow at the Hand Entry

The way a swimmer controls the hand at entry is usually a first indication of talent. The hand entry of a talented swimmer often seems almost leisurely. The swimmer feels for the moving pressure of the oncoming flow and gradually starts to apply force against it. The hand of the talented swimmer possesses a complex sensitivity (or, more accurately, a sensibility) that almost seems to give it sight.

The talented swimmer appears to possess an innate awareness of not only the exact speed at which to enter the hand but also how to time the start of the stroke effectively. The hand neither slows to a stop out in front of the swimmer nor starts the stroke too soon, before the oncoming flow has been accepted and trapped under the arm.

The hand's first contact with the water at entry is critically important. Coaches often correct the middle part of a stroke before checking to see if the entry has been made efficiently. If the oncoming flow has not been engaged initially, there is no sense in correcting a subsequent phase of the stroke.

Anticipating the Oncoming Flow

Most faulty handling of the flow originates from incorrect technique at entry. The entry hand's forward motion into the water produces an oncoming flow. If this flow is broken up or disturbed at entry, the swimmer will have difficulty manipulating the water during the later phases of the stroke. A swimmer should know in advance the nature of the pressure sensation that will be experienced when the hand enters. In this way a swimmer can anticipate the oncoming flow and handle it effectively. The aim is to insert the hand smoothly into the oncoming flow and immediately feel the flow move along the palm and under the forearm and upper arm.

As mentioned earlier, the arm enters the water with elbow up and hand pitched diagonally outward. It is easy to imagine the hand and arm in this position as being shaped similarly to the side of a ship, which gradually slopes backward from the bow and bulges at the waist. By imagining this portion of a ship moving forward under the water, cutting the water sharply at the bow and channeling it backward around and slightly under the hull, a swimmer will form a good concept of the function of the hand at entry: The hand, pitched diagonally outward as it enters, performs much the same function as the bow of a ship.

As stated before, the entry is the preliminary phase of the stroke—the trap phase—during which the flow is allowed to advance along the undersurface of the arm as the swimmer maneuvers it into position for the wrap phase.

Entry Errors

Unfortunately, a swimmer can easily commit several errors at the hand entry that diminish the efficiency of the stroke and cause the swimmer to muscle through the water in a futile attempt to gain purchase on it. Probably the most harmful error is to crash the hand into the entry, attempting to start the stroke before subtly accepting the oncoming flow.

The effect of this error can be understood by imagining a fast naval destroyer equipped with a guillotine-like device fixed to the bow at a right angle to the oncoming flow. At intervals, this guillotine suddenly drops into the water and disturbs the flow. The effect is to continually interrupt the vessel's forward momentum.

A similar effect, surprisingly enough, can frequently be seen in competitive swimmers—even talented world-class ones—particularly distance swimmers using an inertial type of stroke. As the stroke starts with what used to be called a *dig-pull* or *chop-catch*, the bow wave drops, or splutters, indicating sudden interference with the body's momentum.

The rationale behind the inertial type of hand entry may be based on a technique used in athletics and rowing. At the start of a stride, a runner's foot is already moving backward to maintain the runner's momentum and prevent jarring the foot on the ground. Similarly, a rower's blade travels backward before it enters the water.

If the dig-pull is based on this principle, it cannot be applied successfully to swimming. The body is not favorably positioned in the water to perform such a technique; moreover, a swimmer cannot generate sufficient speed to achieve this effect.

Detecting the Stretching Effect in the Oncoming Flow

Great emphasis and attention should be given to adequate coaching of the entry phase of the stroke. Engaging the water correctly at entry is crucial to an effective stroke. The ship drill, which will be explained presently, is designed specifically to simulate the posture of the hand and arm at entry and to teach a swimmer to feel the moving pressure sensation of the oncoming flow.

The ship drill is perhaps the most valuable drill I've ever used in coaching. It is extremely effective in helping a swimmer form a concept of the entry phase of the stroke. As proficiency in discerning the sensation of moving pressure increases, it becomes possible for a swimmer to detect the stretching effect in the oncoming flow. A swimmer learns to relate the amount of stretch in the flow with swimming speed and correct timing of the arms.

The Role of Touch in Motor Learning

Skilled swimmers create a fast output of high-quality movements. Yet even when swimming at high speed, they frequently give the impression of being unhurried. The expert seems to have all the time in the world when compared with the novice, whose forward progress is more like a series of emergencies.

In skilled performance no surprises occur. The swimmer is always ready for each changing sequence of the stroke. Exact timing is an obvious element of skill, which largely involves the predictable repetition of many successive movements in accurate and precise patterns.

How are the components of each sequence coordinated and organized? We tend to think of skill mainly in terms of movement. In describing a swimming stroke, we focus on what is done. The analysis usually breaks the action down into detailed units of movement. This represents the swimmer's output, but we tend to ignore the input, partly because it is taken for granted and partly because it is difficult or impossible to observe directly.

I have often witnessed over an hour of stroke instruction without hearing any reference to the water or what a swimmer should feel. Many otherwise excellent technical articles make little or no reference to the water. Most descriptions of swimming technique neglect to mention the role played by the water, the very medium in which the activity takes place.

Many highly skilled swimmers cannot explain why they perform as they do. They may be unaware of the particular sensory input that controls their activity, which may be why a skilled swimmer is not always a particularly good teacher. Usually, a skill is taught by demonstrating how the desired movement should look rather than by explaining how it should feel.

The more purposeful or skilled the movement, the more it depends on sensory impulses, which in swimming are primarily those associated with vision and touch. In learning the more precise movements of swimming, visual information is essential while the degree of muscle tension and amount of muscle contraction are being delicately adjusted to the task, a point we easily appreciate if we try to learn any precise movement with eyes shut.

Voluntary movements are modified by sensory stimuli received from the skin, muscles, and joints. Sensory impulses act at all times to guide muscular contractions. The muscles are under the direct and perfect control of the motor neurons; these neurons never stimulate the muscles to action except when influenced to do so by other neurons.

Water pressure on the sensory nerve endings, the sense of balance, and the relationship of the limbs help to produce a smoothly coordinated stroke. Attention may be divided between different kinds of sensory messages. Confronted with a mass of available information, a swimmer learns to notice only some of it and ignore much that is irrelevant to the immediate task. Via the process of facilitation at the synapses, repetition causes special pathways to be slowly laid down so that the skilled movements become more accurate.

Muscular movements are driven by a servomechanism similar in many respects to the automated feedback systems used in modern aircraft to control various mechanisms. All these mechanisms have devices (sensors, we may call them) that measure some physical variable and use this feedback information to control the mechanisms that assist the pilot.

Modern aircraft controls are linked by servomechanisms to either electric or hydraulic actuators that automatically maintain the aircraft at the chosen altitude and speed. Servomechanisms sense an error (e.g., departure from the intended course) and apply a correction to the relevant control. Signals from the sensor, called the misalignment detector, activate a small servomotor (from the Latin *servus*, meaning slave), which turns the control surface in the direction necessary to correct the misalignment. Thus, the procedures are performed without the pilot's intervention.

The point is that these devices function automatically to help the pilot. Similarly, in coaching the feel of the water, the aim is to allow a swimmer to rely on only a minimum number of consciously perceived cues and let automatic feedback systems control other functions of the stroke without too much conscious effort.

The Use of Simultaneous Visual and Tactile Impressions

The traditional emphasis when teaching a stroke pattern to a novice has been on the visual. I, too, long believed that the sense of touch was usually too imprecise to be the source of form and shape in the early stages of learning. Furthermore, though some people learn more by means of tactile feedback whereas others receive more beneficial information visually, it is difficult to know whether this difference in perceptual capacity among individuals is significant.

Over a period of about six years, I experimented with developing a method of coaching stroke technique that would involve using simultaneous visual and tactile impressions. I had long before become uncomfortable with merely explaining the shape, form, and pattern of a desired movement without being able to relate its effect on the water. The aim of my method is to teach a swimmer to relate each phase of a swimming stroke with the feel of the flow and thus obtain instant feedback on stroke efficiency.

This method allows a certain amount of individuality. At first, the learner is shown a few sample flow-shaper skills and left alone to play around with them in the water.

After a week or so, some instruction is begun, usually individual. Not everyone is given the same instruction because each learner is directed to a particular phase of the stroke that appears to need attention. This is generally how the method is applied—not so much on items of technique but on particular movement phases of the stroke.

Using visual and tactile impressions simultaneously from the start in a definite teaching format causes noted changes in the sensitivity of the learner to particular features of the swimming stroke and its effect on the water.

Tactile perception can be developed to where a swimmer can receive continuous feedback on propulsive effectiveness. This information helps the swimmer to keep adjusting and refining the stroke at the delivery end to maintain efficiency. For example, the link between seeing the hand entering the water and bringing the hand into contact with it is somehow obvious. The hand just seems to move in the right way. If the swimmer's hand is alive and sensitive to the feel of the water, it acts as a sensing device that transforms the incoming signal into appropriate action. Equally important is that the swimmer has been taught not only to anticipate the oncoming relative flow but also to handle it in the most effective way.

The following sections contain descriptions of the flow-shaping skills and sensitizing techniques used in this conceptualizing process.

Flow Shapers

A flow shaper is an exercise that teaches swimmers to create and detect specific flows in the water. It operates in much the same way as the aircraft servomechanisms already described.

Flow shapers are remarkably effective in helping a swimmer automatically find the most effective path, posture, and attitude of the hand and arm during a swimming stroke; for ex-

ample, they help the swimmer position the arm correctly at entry, correct a dropped elbow, or, for a butterfly swimmer, know whether to pull wider or narrower. Most important, the flow shaper helps a swimmer find the stroke pattern that accords naturally with the characteristics of individual physique. Some examples of flow shapers follow.

The Ship Drill

This important exercise teaches swimmers how to insert their hands into the oncoming flow prior to starting the swimming stroke. The swimmer pushes off from the wall with body outstretched and hands back to back and touching, forming a shape akin to the prow of a ship. The swimmer will feel the oncoming flow produced by the pushoff as it advances along the palms of the hands and under the forearms and upper arms to the armpits. The pressure sensation of the oncoming flow can be prolonged by continuing momentum with the dolphin kick or by using fins (figure 6.1).

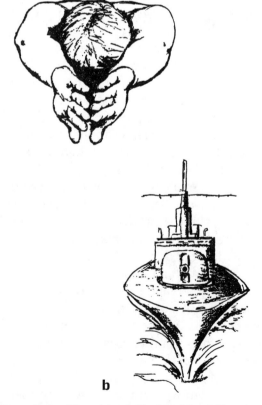

a

b

Figure 6.1 The ship drill: *(a)* ship drill posture and *(b)* action of the ship's prow.

The ship drill should be performed daily. It is more valuable than any other procedure in teaching a swimmer to feel and recognize the oncoming flow.

Beginning in the ship-drill position, the freestyle stroke should be started with elbow up, palm turned outward and pressing downward in a curved, diagonal motion. The palm gradually rotates inward as the hand moves inward in the lateral plane toward the center line of the body. During this motion the hand and forearm rotate as a unit. This motion changes the direction of the oncoming flow as it is wrapped around the hand and forearm in a strong swirl.

The swimmer should concentrate on bending the elbow to approximately 90 degrees or as much as feels comfortable. As the elbow bend increases, some swimmers may turn the palm of the hand slightly upward toward the chest to obtain maximum forearm rotation, but such extreme rotation may feel comfortable only to tall, lean swimmers.

Destroyer–Ocean Liner–Barge Drill

Practice ship drills with hands in the three different positions shown in figure 6.2. These drills show swimmers how the changing postures of the hands and arms cause a transition from streamlined flow to turbulent (resistive) flow. In figure 6.2a there is a free movement of the oncoming flow felt on the palms of the out-turned hands and along the forearms. In figures 6.2b and 6.2c, the flow gradually becomes more resistive as the hand and forearm posture changes.

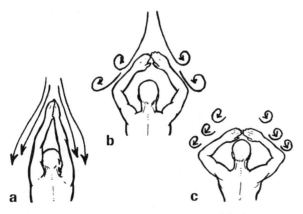

Figure 6.2 Ship drill variations: *(a)* destroyer; *(b)* ocean liner; *(c)* barge.

Half-Ship Drill

Use this drill to enhance feel of the flow at hand entry, especially for swimmers who experience difficulty in feeling the flow. The swimmer kicks while wearing fins and holding one arm out front simulating the entry posture. The hand should be pitched diagonally outward and the elbow up; the other arm is held at the side. The swimmer should feel for the oncoming flow.

Tunnel Flow, or A-OK

Press the thumb against the forefinger to form a tunnel through which the flow is channeled as the hand changes direction in the stroke (figure 6.3). This exercise effectively teaches flow recognition and how to angle the hands efficiently; in fact, it often will groove a stroke pattern automatically. If a butterfly swimmer's pull is too wide or narrow, for example, this exercise will direct the swimmer accordingly.

Figure 6.3 Tunnel flow, or A-OK.

This exercise also indicates if a crawl swimmer is allowing the elbow to drop during the pull because, if so, the flow will not pass through the tunnel. In fact, this drill should be used in all strokes. Swimmers may try forming the tunnel with one hand while keeping the other hand closed. When both hands are opened and used in the normal fashion, however, the hand that was closed will be found also to have improved its feel.

Piano Playing

In this exercise the swimmer pretends to play the piano by using individual finger movements while swimming. This helps the swimmer feel how separate finger movements influence flow channeling (figure 6.4).

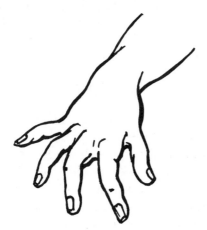

Figure 6.4 Piano playing.

Sensitizing the Sensory Nerve Endings

In developing this method I soon realized that there's no difficulty in increasing the sensibility of the nerve endings. There are many methods to achieve this, including the rehabilitative techniques used after hand surgery, the touch method for learning to type, and the methods used to learn to read Braille. The heightened tactile sensibility must be related to the various sequences of the swimming stroke, however. The swimmer should be able to recognize and interpret the feel of moving pressure against the hand and forearm during every phase of the swimming stroke.

A vast literature exists on the complex neurological functions of the human hand, which, as we know, is a truly remarkable instrument. Because of the complexity of the subject, I decided to concentrate on a few aspects that I thought most germane to my purpose. I found the experiments of A. Lee Dellon (Dellon, Curtis, and Edgerton 1974) particularly valuable. As late as 1972, Dellon showed that the sense of touch could be divided into two main areas: moving (transient) touch and constant (or static) touch.

Using this distinction, I experimented with sensitizing techniques for swimming that alternate the application of transient and static pressures. I found that such techniques as applying different pressures (including static and transient pressures), rubbing the hands and forearms in the desired flow directions, using a loofah as a sensitizing device, and several other procedures quickly stimulated the sensory nerve endings.

Interestingly, sensitivity to the water appears to decrease as a workout progresses, even for talented swimmers. There also appear to be day-to-day variations. I can only guess at the reason for this—perhaps fatigue or overstimulation of the sensory nerve endings.

Although swimmers have little or no difficulty in learning to recognize the oncoming (distal) flow at hand entry, some encounter difficulty in recognizing the subsequent flows (radial, ulnar, and proximal) set up by the hand and forearm as they move through the swimming stroke. This can be overcome by teaching swimmers to rub the hand and forearm in the direction of the appropriate flow.

I borrowed from the biomechanists another very effective procedure. Instead of videotaping swimmers underwater *after* they have learned their stroke mechanics, I videotape them *while* they are learning. Instead of the old method of practicing on land in front of a mirror, they practice—still on land—in front of video monitors while they are being videotaped simultaneously from front and side. Three large electric fans (kept well away from the water for safety) are placed around the swimmer to simulate the reacting flows of the water that occur during the various stages of the swimming stroke. Should a swimmer have difficulty in sensing the flow, the palm of the hand and forearm are wiped with a damp cloth to heighten the sense of touch.

A swimmer can thus simultaneously see front and side views of the stroke on the monitors and feel a simulation of the reacting flow. In addition, the swimmer can receive instruction while this is happening. The three stages of visualize, verbalize, and feel (Counsilman 1968) can occur almost simultaneously.

Sensitizing procedures dramatically enhance a swimmer's feel of the water and should be an everyday feature of the workout. Great emphasis should be placed on sensitizing the hands to the feel of the water, and the hands should remain sensitized throughout the workout. When questioned, even talented swimmers admit that their feel of the water tends to diminish as they progress through a workout, however. Whenever sensitivity to the water seems to lessen, a swimmer should resensitize the hands so that the sense of touch becomes more acute as the workout continues.

Fist Clenching

The nerve endings on the palms quickly become highly sensitized when subjected to contrasts between static and transient pressures. Thus, if a swimmer clenches the fists tightly for two or three minutes before starting a swim, the sensory nerve endings overcompensate in reaction to the static pressure. When the hands are opened again, they are particularly sensitive to the pressure of the moving flow.

Swimmers should sensitize the hands at the beginning of every workout by swimming the first 200 meters with their fists tightly clenched. Because they will feel that they are slipping the water, they should pull a little more slowly while doing this exercise, concentrating on keeping tightly clenched fists. The swimmer should start the stroke with wrist turned outward, thumb down, and emphasize hand-forearm rotation throughout the stroke while bending the elbow to approximately 90 degrees in midstroke.

Fist swimming was named by the great stroke technician Howard Firby. Firby recommended fist swimming to develop "the feel of pulling not only with the hands but with the forearms as well" and to correct dropped elbows and induce the "over the barrel" feeling of the pull (Firby 1975, page 15).

My rediscovery of fist swimming resulted from reading Dellon's reports and from my desire to develop as a sensitizing procedure a method of applying contrasting static and transient pressures on the sensory nerve endings of the hand. Clenching and then opening the hand was a natural choice. I also use fist swimming to show how hand-forearm rotation develops flow circulation. My personal belief, however, is that the greatest value of fist swimming is as a sensitizing procedure for stimulating the sensory nerve endings of the palms of the hands.

An effective exercise for sensitizing the hands and feet is to swim a set distance by alternating fist swimming and overkicking (kicking with more force than necessary) on successive laps of the pool. This can also be a demanding workout. Another variation is to swim with one hand clenched while keeping the other hand open. This contrasts the static pressure on the closed hand with the transient pressure on the open hand, increasing the swimmer's awareness of the water's flow reactions.

The breaststroke and butterfly should frequently be swum with fists clenched. While pulling in the breaststroke, the swimmer should use a slight dolphin kick for counterbalance. Emphasis should be on hand-forearm rotation and elbow bending because this action develops the flow circulation necessary for propulsion. This drill highlights the surprising amount of propulsion this mechanism can develop even when the hands are not open to provide as much propulsion as possible. Although the forearms do not provide a great amount of propulsion, their rotation is necessary and significant in setting up the desired flow circulation. When the hand is open, the hand and forearm work as a unit. The hand is capable of developing more efficient circulation than the forearm because it has a more favorable shape and can be manipulated on the wrist with more dexterity and through a larger range of movement. When the hand and forearm are used as a unit, they form a most effective mechanism for setting up flow circulation.

Fingertip Pressing

These exercises sensitize the fingertips to the oncoming flow as the hands enter the water.

1. Press each fingertip in turn against the thumb (figure 6.5).

2. Now use both hands. Press the fingertips of one hand against those of the other. Press hard and repeat frequently.

3. Now press each fingertip of one hand separately against its counterpart on the other hand. This develops dexterity.

4. Press the fingertips hard against the pool deck while waiting for the start of next training set.

Simultaneous Sensitization to Static and Transient Pressure

The hand can be held in a variety of postures during swimming to sensitize fingers, individually or in groups, to the sensation of moving pressure. Keeping the palm closed sensitizes it via static pressure. These exercises greatly sensitize the hands to the feeling of moving pressure once normal swimming is resumed (figure 6.6).

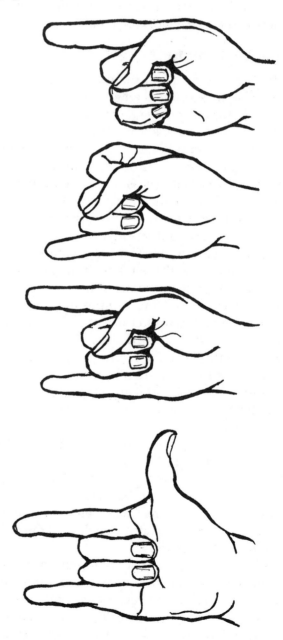

Figure 6.6 Simultaneous sensitization to static and transient pressure.

Figure 6.5 Fingertip pressing.

Hand-Rubbing Exercises

Swimmers find hand-rubbing exercises very effective in sensitizing the hands to recognize precise flow reactions. Rubbing one hand against the other can simulate a desired flow direction, which helps make each phase of the stroke consistently efficient.

1. Rub one hand against the other from the fingertips along the palm to the wrist and forearm. This teaches the feel of the oncoming flow as the hand enters the water and is inserted into the oncoming flow at the start of the stroke.

2. Rub one hand across the other hand in the desired direction to simulate transverse (lateral) flows as they occur in either an inward or outward pitch of the hands.

3. Rub one hand along the other down the palm to the fingertips to simulate the finish of the stroke.

The Use of a Loofah as a Sensitizing Device

A highly effective method of sensitizing the entire body to the flow of the water is to scrub the skin lightly with a dry loofah immediately before every practice or competition. (A loofah, or luffa, resembles an elongated sponge and is coarse and fibrous. It is the fruit of a herbaceous plant, *luffa cylindrica*.) The swimmer should scrub the entire body and, in particular, perform a routine in which one arm is held overhead while the loofah is rubbed from the fingertips down the palm of the hand, along the undersurface of the arm, and down the side of the trunk to the hips; the procedure should be repeated on the other side of the body. This exercise will sensitize the hand, arm, and trunk side to the oncoming flow of the water. After several days of using a loofah this way, most swimmers experience a noted improvement in their sensitivity to the flow of the water.

Daily Application of the Method

In applying the method to daily practice, focus on three areas: flow manipulation, stroke timing, and flow-shaper drills and sensitization.

For flow manipulation, swimmers should be taught always to feel they are inserting the hands into the oncoming flow instead of attacking the water and trying to push it directly backward. After feeling the oncoming flow, swimmers should be told to wrap, or swirl, the flow around the arm by gradually rotating the hand and forearm. The elbow at maximum bend should reach approximately 90 degrees and be comfortable to the swimmer; if it is not comfortable, adjust the amount of elbow bend to suit the swimmer.

After some practice, swimmers will improve in stroke efficiency and be able to recognize weak spots in the stroke through tactile feedback from the flow reaction. They can eliminate weak spots by experimenting with the amount of hand-forearm rotation and the degree of elbow bend they perform.

The timing of the stroke depends greatly on the desired speed. Swimmers should be told that the entry hand, palm turned outward, acts as a sensor, or radar, as it accepts the oncoming relative flow and helps them know exactly when to start applying force at the beginning of the stroke. The amount of oncoming flow to accept before starting the stroke depends on the pace and stroke length each swimmer wishes to establish.

Feeling the differences in pressure on the entry hand at various speeds helps the swimmers learn pacing. Feeling the oncoming flow is an important element in learning split-second timing. The swimmers should be taught to think momentum. By feeling the amount of stretch in the flow, each swimmer learns to judge the body's momentum and know when to start the stroke. For example, in a short race, the stroke may be started after allowing the flow to move along only as far as the wrist. Over a longer distance and at a slower speed, a swimmer may let the oncoming flow move along the forearm before starting into the stroke.

Swimmers should do flow-shaper drills and sensitizing procedures every day as part of the regular workout. Fist swimming should be done in all strokes at slow and fast speeds. Swimmers should always start the stroke with the hand turned outward. The fists should be tightly clenched throughout. Fist swimming in the breaststroke and butterfly is particularly effective for coaching effective hand-forearm rotation and elbow flexion and also has a positive transfer to the other strokes.

Swimmers should be aware that sensitivity to flow will vary from day to day. Every workout should start with skin sensitization—hand rubbing, the use of a loofah, fist swimming, tunnel flow (A-OK), and fingertip-pressing exercises. Every now and then during the work-out, swimmers should push off from the pool side using the ship-drill posture instead of the conventional locked hands. These occasional ship pushoffs enable swimmers to test hand sensitivity to the pressure of the oncoming flow.

Swimmers should resensitize their hands during the workout, especially during the middle stages of the workout or at the onset of fatigue. If this is done, swimmers will complete the workout with a greater feel for the water. The coach should not permit swimmers to re-gard these procedures as a passing fad because over the weeks and months, most swimmers will experience a pronounced improvement in technique resulting from their enhanced ability to feel and manipulate the flow of the water.

Part III

Advances in Training

Chapter 7

Progression of Training Methods

Even talented swimmers need years of training under well-integrated controls to produce superior performance. The outstanding feats of great swimmers attest to the prodigious internal adjustments the human body can make. Their achievements are the result of programs designed to progressively train the body's energy systems so that eventually a swimmer can cover racing distances at maximum capacity.

Although organized competition in track and swimming started about 150 years ago, training methods advanced more rapidly in track than in swimming, probably because swimmers found they could swim faster merely by improving their stroke mechanics. This approach proved so rewarding to swimmers that they either did very little training or none at all. In addition, the opinion prevailed in many quarters that training too hard would cause burnout.

In this chapter, we will examine how training evolved from the primitive methods of Charles Steedman to the scientific programs of today. Developments in track training gradually influenced swimming coaches, and land-based training supplemented swimming laps, creating athletes with superior muscle tone and aerobic and anaerobic adaptation.

Training in the 19th Century

The first detailed account of training methods in the swimming literature was contained in Charles Steedman's *A Manual of Swimming*, published in 1867, 13 years after Steedman emigrated from England to the Australian colony of Victoria. Steedman was the professional swimming champion of England, then the world's leading swimming nation, when he left for Australia, where he became champion of Victoria. Steedman's book, colloquially known as "the manual," contained vivid accounts of tough training methods used by great professionals of the day and raised considerable interest in England and Australia.

Steedman described how it was customary to commence training with "a course of medicine." To "free the stomach and bowels from any injurious accumulation that may be obstructing those organs," it was sometimes necessary to take two, or even three, purges at intervals from four to six days. The athlete began by taking an emetic, consisting of 20 grains of ipecacuanha in a wineglass of water. That was followed in a couple of days by "a mild purge," induced by taking a pill containing two grains of calomel and five grains of compound extract colocynth. Steedman mentioned that some athletes preferred to purge themselves by taking Glauber's salts, "an ounce generally sufficing for a dose."

The Effects of Judicious Training

Steedman said that the effects of judicious training were "beneficial, and evident from the following changes that take place in the person who submits to the necessary discipline:"

The appetite becomes keener, the process of digestion is easier, the sleep is sounder, less disturbed, and more refreshing. The condition of the lungs is improved; he is enabled to draw a deeper inspiration, to retain his breath longer, and recover it sooner after it is lost; in other words, his "wind" is improved. He feels light and cheerful; technically, "corky." His stomach is reduced in size, yet the skin, owing to its newly-acquired elasticity, does not hang loosely over the diminished surface. Fat is lost, and muscle is gained; his head becomes clearer, his bones larger, harder, and tougher, his sinews stronger. The whole contour of his body is improved. In short, the change for the better in his strength and appearance will both surprise and delight him who has just completed his first course of close training (pp. 223–224).

A Daily Training Schedule

In his *A Manual of Swimming*, Steedman (1867) emphasized the role of the trainer to the athlete: "A cheerful, yet firm, companion in the trainer is indispensable." Steedman provided the following daily schedule for a swimmer in training:

5:00 A.M.	Rise. Either plunge at once into cold water or have a sponge bath; be well rubbed down with a dry, coarse towel; dress quickly and eat a hard biscuit or small piece of stale bread.
5:30	Walk a mile briskly then run uphill for half-a-mile as rapidly as possible; afterward walk for four miles at a moderate pace.
7:00	Breakfast. Rump steak or mutton chop, underdone, without fat, and stale bread. Note: rest, or take very gentle exercise with dumbbells for the remainder of two hours.
9:00	Walk two miles at a moderate pace; swim sharply for a quarter-of-an-hour or 20 minutes; quickly and thoroughly dry with a coarse towel; dress and walk three or four miles at a moderate speed.
12:00 P.M.	Undress and lie down in bed for half-an-hour. On rising, take a glass of old ale or sound sherry and eat a hard biscuit.
1:00	Walk four miles.
2:00	For one hour and a half occupy oneself with athletic exercises calculated to develop the muscles of the arms and the trunk.
3:30	Rest for half-an-hour.

4:00	Dinner. Rump steak or mutton chop or a slice or two from a joint of beef or mutton, underdone, free from fat; stale bread, one or two mealy potatoes, and a little greens; no pastry or cheese.
4:30	Rest till five.
5:00	Walk a mile sharply; run half-a-mile at top speed; walk four miles at a moderate rate.
7:00	A half-pint of old ale or wineglass of sherry and hard biscuit. Gymnastics for the arms and chest till eight.
8:00	Rest and amusing conversation or light reading till nine.
9:00	Body to be well rubbed down with coarse towels, then bed till five next morning.

This schedule, according to Steedman, was "based in all essential particulars on the system so successfully pursued by the celebrated Captain Barclay" and would "if so modified as to suit age, locality, and previous mode of life, fairly indicate the method to be adopted by one who wishes to attain for any specific purpose a maximum condition of health and strength." Steedman recommended following the schedule for no more than four months. He made further claims for his program: "Slightly altered, so as not to interfere with one's business avocations, and persisted in with regularity throughout the year, it would ensure a good state of health, and, except in special circumstances, materially aid in prolonging a man's life."

Steedman's nutritional advice was strange based on current knowledge but at the time was state of the art. He insisted that swimmers eat ordinary, well-baked water biscuits and drink a little cold water if thirsty. However, "All the liquids . . . taken in any one day should not together exceed three pints." Tobacco and "spirits" were absolutely prohibited.

As a variation to the usual morning schedule, Steedman advocated what he called "the sweating process," which had grown in favor with trainers and their athletes. Steedman's plan called for swimmers to run four miles "well clothed in flannel at full speed." After finishing the run, swimmers drank what Steedman called "the sweating liquor." This precursor to sports drinks included "one ounce of caraway seed, half-an-ounce of coriander seed, one ounce of root liquorice, and half-an-ounce of sugar candy, mixed with two quarts of cider, and boiled down to one quart. To this some add one drachm of sweet spirits of nitre."

After drinking the "sweating liquor," the athlete was to be "put to bed in fresh flannels" and "covered up with half-a-dozen pairs of blankets; sometimes even a feather bed in addition is placed over him." After spending about half-an-hour in bed, the athlete was to be "taken out and rubbed perfectly dry." Then, after being dressed in a great coat, the athlete gently walked two miles, then returned to a breakfast of roast fowl instead of beef. The rest of the day he followed the usual schedule. Although some trainers in his day had their athletes use the sweating process once a week until seven or eight days before the contest, Steedman and other trainers felt it weakened the athlete, and therefore rarely used it, "except to jockeys, with whom reduction of weight is of greater importance than increase of strength."

Training in the Early 20th Century

Andrew "Boy" Charlton, the great Australian swimmer of the 1920s, is known to have trained for only four weeks before a big race, averaging a half mile a day. Another famous Australian, Noel Ryan, Empire Champion and 1932 Olympic finalist, told me that the most he ever swam in a day was 1,000 yards—this was when he was preparing for the 1932 Olympic Games in Los Angeles. When he arrived at the Olympic venue, he reduced his training distance to 440 yards for fear of burning out.

Ryan said that he used to sit back at the Olympic pool and watch the Japanese team cover up to five miles daily. According to Ryan, the Japanese dominance in 1932 and again at the Berlin Olympics in 1936 prompted several theories: that the Japanese had the ideal build for swimming; that they had developed a new stroke; and that they were using drugs. The main reason for the Japanese dominance, however, was that they trained harder than any other team. Few people showed a desire to copy the Japanese methods; in fact, the Japanese effort was dismissed by many as fanaticism. Either through laziness, jealousy, or genuine belief, people asked, "Who wants to go to such lengths to succeed?" The truth was that the Japanese idea of strenuous training was too far ahead of its time.

Shortly thereafter, World War II produced a brief hiatus in competitive swimming. As interest in competitive swimming revived in the immediate postwar period, swimmers began to realize the importance of improved conditioning. Kiphuth had pioneered supplementary land training for swimmers back in 1917, but a few swimmers now tentatively began to experiment with weight training. At Ohio State University, champion swimmer Dick Cleveland practiced weight training five days a week under the guidance of Fraysher Ferguson at his gymnasium in Columbus. Al Wiggins was another Ohio State swimmer who achieved good results under Ferguson's tutelage, setting world butterfly and medley records. In 1952 Walter Schlueter pioneered weight training for women swimmers with his world-record relay team at the Town Club of Chicago (Murray and Karpovich 1956).

Some swimmers now trained as far as three miles daily. But others, attempting to relieve some of the inevitable boredom of swimming long stretches at a comparatively easy pace, introduced periods of intermittent faster activity, which can best be described as a form of interval training. However, by no stretch of imagination can these procedures be construed as the first structured and formal application of interval training. Nevertheless, during this period there were isolated accounts of noted coaches and swimmers inadvertently using what can be termed a form of rudimentary interval training.

John Marshall, in his letters home to Australia, described the form of interval training used at Yale University. Some accounts credit Marshall's letters with giving Australian coaches the idea from which they developed interval training. In 1956 one of the leading Australian coaches, Frank Guthrie, who spearheaded the Australian revival and coached Lorraine Crapp to become the first woman to beat the then magic five-minute mark for 400 meters, said that the Australians had received the idea from the Americans.

Guthrie's statement may have been partially correct. Sydney University professor Frank Cotton and his understudy Forbes Carlile had read about interval training in track magazines and research papers. It is also likely that they had discussed the method with world-class Australian track athletes, who were already using the method.

In 1954, British track athlete Roger Bannister ran the first sub four-minute mile under the guidance of Franz Stampfl, who advocated a combination of fartlek (speed play), interval, and repetition training. Bannister's feat captured the imagination of followers of many sports, causing great interest in Stampfl's training concepts.

Stampfl's book *Franz Stampfl on Running* (1955) and Bannister's *First Four Minutes* (1955) were instant bestsellers and were intently studied by forward-thinking coaches in swimming as well as track. Bannister described the process through which he had attacked the four-minute barrier for the mile run. In December 1953, he had started an intensive training program in which he ran a series of 10 consecutive quarter miles, each in 66 seconds, with two-minute rest intervals between them. Gradually, through January and February, he stepped up the pace until by April he could manage the series in an average time of 60 seconds while keeping to the two-minute rest intervals.

Information on interval training thus probably reached Australian swimming coaches from several sources. Nevertheless, the Australians were the first to establish a protocol for using interval training as an accepted and regular method of training competitive swimmers.

In the 1950s, Australian swimming coaches, in conjunction with physiologist Frank Cotton, began a methodical study of the interval training method used in running since the late 1930s and applied the method to swimming. In a manner similar to Woldemar Gerschler's early research on interval training for track, the Australians attempted to relate heart rate to recorded swimming times at different work-to-rest ratios. Some coaches used heart rate checks in establishing interval training as a formal conditioning method for swimmers.

Coincidental or not, with the use of interval training, swimming took one of its rare quantum leaps forward. Within a matter of months in 1956, the Australians almost completely rewrote the world-record books for both men and women. The Australian swimmers, training under six highly innovative coaches—Forbes Carlile, Arthur Cusack, Gus Frohlich, Harry Gallagher, Frank Guthrie, and Sam Herford—made an almost complete sweep of the 1956 Olympic swimming events.

In the first 10 years or so that interval training was used in swimming, several phases occurred during which the concept, still incompletely understood, was misapplied. The total training load was often too great, mainly because in an attempt to strive for even more speed, coaches tended to demand too great a pace for the repeat swims. The result, recognized by only a few at the time, was often an inability by swimmers to recover from what Carlile termed "failing adaptation," a condition that requires either a marked reduction in the intensity of the workload or complete rest.

Although training methods in swimming developed later than in track, the development, when it came, followed a similar evolutionary pattern. In both sports, continued debate marked the search for the ideal balance between the volume and intensity of the workload. The issue remains alive in swimming as we enter the 21st century.

The Influence of Track Training

The training methods of swimming share an origin with those used on the running track. The basic training principles used by modern competitive swimmers were first developed by great track athletes working with renowned coaches and physiologists such as Holmer, van Aaken, and Gerschler.

Obvious differences exist in the physiological effects of running and swimming, but by looking at problems that beset early develop-

ment of track methods, we gain insight into similar difficulties encountered in swimming. There may be some as yet overlooked aspects of track training that can be beneficially adapted to swimming.

Competitive running started with competitions between England's Oxford and Cambridge universities. For most of the first 100 years, training emphasized developing endurance, but as time passed, it became evident that speed was also important.

Gosta Holmer and the Fartlek Method

Gosta Holmer (1893–1972), the famous Swedish track coach, developed a naturalistic method of training he called fartlek (speed play), which consists of running both quickly and slowly. To some extent, fartlek is an informal type of training in which the athlete jogs, walks, runs, or sprints as he or she wishes. This was particularly true of its use in early-season training, for which the method established informal fast and slow cross-country running as a fundamental form of endurance training.

Possibly because the term means "speed play," many people in swimming had the mistaken impression that fartlek was nothing more than an informal and almost inconsequential type of training serving little purpose other than to produce some basic early-season fitness. On the track, however, fartlek became a more strenuous and demanding form of training as the season progressed.

The application of fartlek to swimming appears to have been neither properly understood nor taken seriously enough. Perhaps the method has been mistakenly interpreted by some as a subterfuge for relieving boredom while accumulating early-season mileage. In fact, this kind of training is often termed *bulk mileage* or *garbage*, implying a certain mindless approach to the essential task of establishing an extensive aerobic endurance foundation to seasonal activity.

Variation of Pace

The main feature of the fartlek method of training is that the pace varies frequently from short, sharp sprints to long, easy jog-trots, with occasional fast quarter miles and sustained efforts over distances from a half mile to a mile. The emphasis on pace variation served as an introduction to the more exacting interval training on the track that came later. In swimming in the 1960s, Don Gambril, one of America's all-time great coaches, laid much emphasis on the principle of varying the pace, notably in training such fine swimmers as Patti Carretto, Gunnar Larsen, and Hans Fassnacht.

The Importance of Individual Coaching

A defining characteristic of the fartlek method is that it emphasizes the importance of coaching the athlete as an individual. Although the method involves more structure as the season progresses, it provides some opportunity for self-knowledge, producing an athlete who may be better at judging the effects of exercise through subjective observation. I believe that we have tended to neglect this aspect in recent years when training competitive swimmers. The dictum, "Man, know thyself," is as pertinent to competitive swimming as to any other endeavor.

Lactate testing, whatever its value may be in some quarters, may have been overstressed to the exclusion of a more important coaching task—showing swimmers how to recognize, on their own, the intensity of effort at different set paces. Learning to know one's self is the most important thing a coach can teach an athlete who wishes to compete successfully.

Relating Stride to Running Speed

The early-season application of fartlek to swimming training has followed formats mostly concerned with developing basic conditioning, but swimming coaches may have neglected the additional pace and tempo teaching possibilities the method presents.

Gosta Holmer began to recognize the importance of always relating pace to the training effort between 1921 and 1925 when he lived in Finland, where he had ample opportunity to observe Paavo Nurmi, one of the greatest runners in track history.

Holmer correctly believed that a runner learned technique only by running long dis-

tances (also true of swimming technique). Holmer always stressed the importance of relating a runner's stride to the runner's speed. Properly adapted to swimming training, this approach can be used as a challenging and effective training tool. Coaches and swimmers should be aware of the need to relate stroke length and stroke frequency to swimming time and, as conditioning improves, to assess efficiency by relating these factors to heart rate.

The Development of the Will to Overcome Fatigue

Holmer recognized that the will to overcome fatigue is an additional important factor in athletic success. Athletes who use the fartlek method are allowed to determine how far and how fast they wish to run, which teaches them to tolerate fatigue under a variety of physiological stresses.

Similarly, Counsilman recognized the need to motivate swimmers to withstand fatigue. Therefore, he created his "hurt-pain-agony" scale to assist sensory perception of fatigue at different levels of work intensity—or, as his swimmers would say, "at different levels of suffering." Counsilman also devised a "hurt-pain-agony" chart (Counsilman 1968, p. 338) that showed the differences in effort expended by hard workers and comfort swimmers during practice. Comfort swimmers rarely ventured out of the comfort zone and into the pain zone. But the dedicated, hard workers typically swam straight through the hurt zone, into the pain zone, and finally into the agony zone.

Fartlek and the Concept of Tempo Training

Holmer (1972) believed that twice a week a runner should alternate between one-quarter and one-half racing tempo and during the last month of training use one-half to three-quarter tempo. Holmer estimated the various tempos as follows: suppose a runner's full tempo is an average speed of 20 seconds per 100 meters for one hour. Decreasing this tempo by 2.5 percent, 5 percent, and 7.5 percent produces one-fourth, one-half, and three-fourths tempos, respectively (see table 7.1).

Table 7.1 Training Tempos

Tempo	Distance				
	100 m	1,000 m	5,000 m	10,000 m	15,000 m
1/1	20.0	3:20.0	16:40.0	32:20.0	49:00.0
3/4	20.5	3:25.0	17:05.0	34:10.0	51:15.0
1/2	21.0	3:30.0	17:30.0	35:00.0	52:30.0
1/4	21.5	3:35.0	17:55.0	35:50.0	53:45.0

From Holmer 1972. Reprinted by permission.

The Use of Tempo Training in Swimming

In the early years of interval training in the pool, swimmers used a variation of Holmer's long-distance tempo method. To determine the speed and intensity of effort for an interval series, swimmers calculated a percentage of their fastest time for a particular distance—for example, 70 percent, 80 percent, or 90 percent. To assess fitness, swimmers often compared pulse rate with the recorded time. They also predicted performance by plotting recorded time against a total of the heart rates taken at 10-second intervals during the first half minute after exercise (Carlile 1956).

The late 1950s and early 1960s were marked by trial and error—mostly error—in the application of interval training to swimming. Because swimmers tended to do interval training at too high a percentage of maximum effort, many teams often had disappointing results. Coaches such as Peter Daland, Sherman Chavoor, Nort Thornton, Forbes Carlile, Don Gambril, George Haines, and "Doc" Counsilman gradually came to appreciate the need for varying the pace and intervals according to the physiological effects they wished their swimmers to achieve.

Ernst van Aaken's Speed Through Endurance Method

Ernst van Aaken was a general practitioner in the small German town of Waldniel. He developed the pure endurance method of training after seeing Paavo Nurmi break the world record in 1928 for the one-hour run, but he did not make his methods public until 1947, when he wrote an article for *Sport und Gymnastik* (reprinted in English in van Aaken and Berben 1971). The adherents of his methods were known as "The Waldniel School" after the town where he lived.

During the 1970s, Australian coach Forbes Carlile adapted van Aaken's endurance method with great success. Carlile showed that the concept of speed through endurance very much applied to his proteges Karen Moras, Shane Gould, and Jenny Turrell, world-record holders, at distances from 400 meters to 1,500 meters and for Gould at all distances from 100 meters upward (Carlile 1976).

The Concept of Training for Pure Endurance

According to van Aaken, Emil Zatopek, who ran long distances with rhythmical changes of speed, exemplified the Waldniel method or classical form of interval training. This method enabled Zatopek to win Olympic supremacy in 1948. The method introduced the important new concept of training for pure endurance, van Aaken said.

Zatopek covered distances at relatively slow speeds. He daily performed 400-meter runs broken by 200-meter jogs at sub-racing speed over distances between 36 and 50 kilometers. Occasionally, he would run 400 meters at increased speed.

According to van Aaken, critics of the Zatopek method claimed that it took too much time and did not sufficiently overload the body. Thus they increased the quality of work by introducing breaks and reducing the distances run under stress to 100 and 200 meters. This

Summary of Holmer's Fartlek Method

The gradual seasonal progression used in the Holmer method can be easily adapted to the training of competitive swimmers. Above all, the method is simple. All too often a swimming training program begins to look more like a detailed thesis or an exposé of a coach's knowledge of exercise physiology rather than a plan whose purpose is plain and can be easily followed. The importance of simplicity in program planning is often overlooked, which is particularly a problem when coaching the younger swimmer, who should be able to recognize at a glance the purpose of each phase of a program as well as the progress made.

Study of Holmer's plan for a training season shows an initial concentration on building a broad and well-planned endurance base by means of fartlek training. Later, precise paces and tempos are gradually introduced. At first, paced work is done at one-fourth tempo. Then, as the athlete's fitness increases, the speed increases to one-half tempo. Finally, speed work is done at three-fourths tempo over almost the full racing distance. Thus there is a subtle change in the specificity of the training program as it moves from the development of general aerobic conditioning to establishing the peak season's final race pace. The work is applied in cyclic phases, however, depending on each athlete's individual reactions from session to session, day to day, and week to week.

Holmer's program is all-embracing yet notable for the simplicity of its application; indeed, it would have been surprising had outstanding outcomes not resulted from a program so clearly modeled on everyday common sense. Most coaches who have produced top world athletes and swimmers will confirm that their most successful seasonal programs were those characterized by an essential simplicity that nevertheless took into account a few basic principles of exercise physiology.

work was done in a long series of repetitions. They believed this method would develop greater endurance, speed, and strength. They maintained that for middle- and long-distance racing, it ensured a very quick and effective increase in heart size and also improved so-called muscle endurance.

Criticism of Interval Training

In an article that was published in *Swimming Technique*, van Aaken said that the whole concept of interval training was based on becoming used to oxygen debt by doing mainly anaerobic work (van Aaken and Berben 1971). According to van Aaken, this "improved" interval work—developed, propagated, and made obligatory in Germany—only showed what acute stresses athletes were capable of bearing.

Marathon runners training with the interval method performed 200-meter runs 170 times in 33 seconds each, van Aaken reported. He claimed that the interval training method de-

veloped the capacity for recovery after heavy stress, but this capacity was not specific to performance. He added that it was incorrect to assume that increasing total intermittent stresses necessarily resulted in increased capacity to withstand the continuous and accumulative stress that occurred when covering full distance at racing speed.

Even Herbert Reindell, one of the developers of interval training, showed interval training over short and middle distances caused only moderate increases in heart size, van Aaken said. He pointed out that marathon runners, as well as long-distance cyclists and rowers, were found to have the largest hearts. He expressed doubt as to how a long series of short, fast runs could bring about the necessary long-lasting endurance effects.

Steady State Training

The pure endurance training developed by van Aaken involves daily training at a steady state with the most favorable respiratory conditions, without an increase of initial oxygen debt and formation of lactic acid and with an average pulse rate of 130 beats per minute. To achieve this, the athlete performs long runs, initially with short breaks, after the principle of interval training. Later, the athlete runs continuous distances of 6 to 50 miles. This training method was used for the marathon distance. At the end of the daily run, the method requires a fast run at not faster than race pace over part of the racing distance.

The Use of Part Distances for Tempo Training

The ratio set by van Aaken of long unbroken runs to shorter distances covered at pace (tempo) is 20:1. The mileage is shortened or extended according to an athlete's preferred racing distance. The pace is determined by the runner's best time.

A 5,000-meter runner capable of 15 minutes would frequently be asked to do five 1,000-meter runs in three minutes each. An 800-meter runner capable of 1:44.0 would be asked to do six 200-meter runs in 26 seconds, and so on. After some practice, the tempo for the part

distances will be set by instinct instead of a stopwatch. In addition, all athletes train for the next event above their racing distance (overdistance); an 800-meter runner is expected to be able to achieve a reasonable time over 1,500 meters.

The longest distance to be covered in training was many times longer than the racing distance. Runs over these distances were scheduled at either the beginning or the end of the week. The 800-meter specialist ran at least 12 to 15 miles; the marathoners, 36, 40, even 48 miles, to build the foundation to last through 26 miles at racing speed. During the first years of such training, the distances were covered in segments of two to three miles interspersed with walking recovery breaks.

Speed Through Endurance Training Applied to Swimming

Carlile (1971) believed that swimmers should also train over long distances and that if the distance is reduced and the quality element becomes too intense, a swimmer very easily will go into failing adaptation. In fact, almost all of Carlile's work in physiology was oriented to avoiding too much high-pressure training.

Summary of van Aaken's Speed Through Endurance Method

In the speed through endurance method, athletes learn running mainly by running. Track running is mainly learned by training on level ground.

The most important factor in training for middle and long distances is endurance, which is a function of maximum oxygen intake capacity, low body weight, and economical application of the laws of leverage. Endurance is mainly acquired by endurance exercises at medium speed. This speed is determined by personal endurance limit; during training the athlete should always perform below this limit. Only occasionally should the endurance capacity be tested at racing speed.

Continually practicing at speeds faster than race pace is uneconomical and leads to a decrease of reserves. Speed runs are best practiced at race pace but only over part of the racing distance. The number of repetitions and breaks and the length of the breaks are determined by the recovery period.

The interval principle in endurance training is used only to enable the athlete to cover more distance without fatigue.

All relatively severe anaerobic stresses (e.g., speed runs) should be preceded and followed by aerobic functions (e.g., light jogging). That is, the athlete should warm up before speed work and cool down after it.

Carlile believed there to be a limit to the amount of training that should be done at high speed. Carlile's methods were instead based largely on the simple concept of keeping a constant duration for the twice-daily training sessions (approximately two hours per session) and encouraging swimmers to gradually increase the distances they were capable of covering within that fixed time.

In the 1960s, Sherman Chavoor, one of the most highly successful coaches in the history of American swimming, was an early advocate of training swimmers along the lines van Aaken suggested for track athletes (Chavoor 1967). Chavoor trained all youngsters for distance swimming. He felt that once they could successfully cover long distances, they could work back to 400s, 200s, and 100s. Chavoor would point out to those youngsters who initially did not like doing 1,500-meter swims in training that swimmers such as Don Schollander, Mark Spitz, Carl Robie, and Roy Saari could swim fast at all distances from 100 to 1,500 meters. He added that there were very few swimmers who were just sprinters.

Woldemar Gerschler's Interval Training Method

Woldemar Gerschler (Gerschler, Rosskamm, and Reindell 1964) said that he developed interval training through trial and error. He claimed that interval training produced greater endurance than running long unbroken distances—and in a shorter time. When interval training was first introduced it was a radical departure from traditional endurance training, yet it often brought dramatic results. Gerschler attributed this to a greater control over the training overload.

Using interval training, Gerschler's protege Rudolf Harbig set world records before World War II for the 400-meter (46.0), 800-meter (1:46.6), and 1,000-meter events (2:21.5) that were far in advance of the existing standards. When Gerschler died in 1982, he was acknowledged as "Gerschler: The Innovator" (Horwill 1982), recognized as being 30 years ahead of his time when he pioneered his interval training methods in 1932.

Pulse Rate as a Guide to Training Intensity

Departing from the general trend of his time, Gerschler shortened the distance of the longer training runs. Simultaneously, he increased the speed for these reduced distances. His formula for interval training was to have the athlete run 100 or 200 meters at a pace three and six seconds slower, respectively, than the athlete's best time for the distance. This gives a pulse rate of 170, plus or minus 10. After the pulse drops to 120 beats per minute within a 1-1/2-minute rest period, the athlete runs again.

This routine continues until the heart rate fails to recover to 120 beats within 1-1/2 minutes. Gerschler, Rosskamm, and Reindell (1964) claimed the daily repetition of this routine for 21 days could increase the heart volume by one-fifth. Gerschler said that it was the recovery period that strengthened the heart, that is, while the pulse returns from 180 beats to 120.

Counsilman (1967) described how he talked to Gerschler, who told him that swimming coaches did not apply the interval training method properly because they did not make swimmers wait until the heart rate dropped from 180 to 120 beats per minute. Counsilman explained to Gerschler that swimmers working to develop endurance rested for 10 seconds, those working for both speed and endurance rested for 30 seconds, and those working for top speed rested from 1-1/2 to 2 minutes.

Gerschler adamantly maintained that the heart rate must return to 120. In reply to Gerschler, Counsilman posed hypothetical cases of two different athletes, one with a resting pulse rate of 50 and the other with a pulse rate of 70 and asked whether both should try to attain a 180 pulse rate and wait for it to return to 120. Gerschler replied that this was just a norm. Counsilman went on to point out to Gerschler that heart rate targets must always be specific to the individual and that pulse rates will vary according to the work-to-rest ratio and the conditioning effect the swimmer wishes to achieve.

The Merits of Different Types of Training

In the 1980s, the Russians Viru and Urgenstein confirmed Gerschler's findings, which were based on checking 3,000 athletes (Horwill 1982).

Over a three-month period, groups of athletes were given hill training, interval training, steady running, and sprinting. The hill runners improved most, followed by the interval trainers. Few runners today do only one type of training, but though they do not regard interval training as the only method to use, it remains an important part of their training schedules.

Gerschler's Views on the Benefits of Interval Training

Gerschler, Rosskamm, and Reindell (1964) stated that interval training was more advantageous than continuous training because it was more intensive and therefore more powerfully stimulated the musculature, and because it provided the opportunity to control more precisely the duration of the effort and the intensity of the stimulus.

Gerschler objected to long, slow, uninterrupted running because he felt the training required to obtain the necessary stimulus was excessively long. He believed that the monotony of running for hours on end, day after day, was more tiring than the running itself and that the stimulus provided by long, uninterrupted runs produced neither high enough oxygen debt levels nor a demand sufficient to improve the condition of the muscles. According to Gerschler, interval training provided a balance of both requirements.

Gerschler referred to Reindell's findings, saying that deep breathing during the interval caused venous blood to return to the heart in greater quantity; the tension diminished and the systolic volume increased, resulting in an active stimulus for increasing heart volume. (This is now generally known as *Reindell's heart expansion stimulus*.)

Basic Elements of Gerschler's Interval Training Method

According to Gerschler, the speed at which a distance should be covered depends on the recovery of the heartbeat. The character of interval training changes when training for sprints because longer rests are needed for higher speeds. As for the number of times a training run should be repeated, Gerschler said that there was no fixed answer because the number of repetitions increased with an athlete's adaptation to training.

Summary of Gerschler's Interval Training Method

Having conducted several studies on the heart rate recovery that occurs between interval training repetitions, Gerschler, Rosskamm, and Reindell (1964) claimed to have obtained positive fixed numbers that put "for the first time in the history of training, exact values at the disposal of the coach" (p. 31).

Gerschler timed the recovery interval, which he defined as the time necessary for the heart rate to fall from 180 to 140 to 120 beats per minute. Trained runners who jogged between efforts required 90 to 45 seconds recovery, whereas those who rested passively needed 70 to 30 seconds.

Gerschler felt that applying interval training to adolescents required considerable care because young persons in full development are subject to the inexorable demands of growth and maturation. Comparisons were needed between the postexercise resting heart rates of young people and those of well-trained adults.

According to Gerschler, interval training was superior to long-distance running for increasing endurance because interval training takes less time than any other method, interval training can be dosed precisely and measured accordingly, and interval training provides more stimulus than long-distance running by itself. Gerschler said these claims were substantiated by research on endurance and interval training conducted in the former East Germany (Schleusing, Rebentisch, and Schippel 1964).

Gerschler and his colleagues (1964) regarded the duration of the rest interval as an important factor. The recovery interval is based on the time the heart takes to recover. Using five-second pulse rate counts, he conducted a one-year study in which he tested the cardiac frequency of hundreds of specialist runners of all distances, ranging from world-class performers to relatively unknown athletes.

Gerschler concluded that the stimulus resulting from a correct combination of distance, speed, and rest interval produced pulse rates around 180 beats per minute. According to Gerschler, these findings compared favorably with the continuous clinical controls established by Reindell (Gerschler, Rosskamm, and Reindell 1964). He thus claims that the elements of interval training are effectively proportioned when the heart rate is around 180.

A Comparative Appraisal of Track Training Methods

Track authorities have conducted a long-lasting and sometimes even acrimonious debate concerning the most effective training methods, some promoting continuous long-distance running with occasional speed bursts—as advocated by Holmer, van Aaken, and Lydiard—and others favoring the classic interval training of the Gerschler method, also known as the Freiburg School.

In fact, a detailed look at the training methods used by the different schools of thought shows that they all used a mix of distance running and interval speed work. Although this speed training did not always include actual breaks between runs, the interval was marked by a period of easy jogging or walking also known as *active rest*.

Apparently, a tendency by popular writers to play up the more obvious characteristics of a particular method to the exclusion of other components left many with a less-than-complete understanding of the total programs. For example, the mention of Holmer instantly produced the notion of fartlek, or speed play, van Aaken's name became synonymous with mileage mania, and Arthur Lydiard's with mara-

thon training for middle-distance athletes. In spite of this, their programs were in fact much broader and heterogeneous than cursory study would first indicate.

The Search for an Ideal Training Format

Many authorities doubt that a selective method for applying the training program will ever be found. When interval training was first introduced, many advocates emphasized that it enabled more work to be done in much less time than did prolonged long-distance training. A survey of the writings and presentations at major international conferences by the originators of interval training leaves little doubt that by "more work" they meant a greater stimulation of the heart as well as a more immediate and intensive overload of the working muscles.

At the Duisberg Congress on Running, Gerschler, Rosskamm, and Reindell (1964) presented a paper titled "Das Interval Training" (Interval Training) setting out the principles of the Freiburg method. At this conference, Herbert Reindell, one of the founders of the interval training method, sounded a note of warning to those who would mercilessly and too liberally apply it.

Possible Adverse Effects of Interval Training

Reindell expressed concern that interval training, with its potential for producing severe anaerobic metabolism, could easily have results other than expected, if incorrectly applied. He said that although heart volume increases quickly through interval training, performances often remain static or even regress.

Many athletes trained in this method had quickly become expert at interval training but little more. They had developed a specific capacity for quick recovery between heavy workloads, but though this may have indicated superior physiological conditioning, there often was not a corresponding improvement when racing. Obviously, either something was wrong in the seasonal application of training methods, the workload was incorrectly applied in the actual interval training sessions, or both.

Learning From Practical Experience

As mentioned earlier, advocates of the fartlek and speed through endurance training methods were not slow to criticize interval training using the previous arguments.

Proponents of interval training returned the volley by saying that long-distance aerobic training makes for expert joggers *and* expert conversationalists because of the ease with which athletes can talk while running at such slow paces. They said that to run distances from 400 to 1,500 meters requires more than a daily training base of steady state running with no oxygen debt and an average pulse rate of 120 to 130 beats per minute.

Most of the popular systems in use on the track were improved by learning from practical experience, especially from the experiences of talented athletes. Knowledge probably advances best in this way because scientific explanation can hardly be expected to keep pace with the successful methods discovered in practice—it nearly always follows later. Track coaches nevertheless took caution in extolling the virtues of any particular approach to the exclusion of new ideas.

Chapter 8

Principles of Modern Training

In a trained athlete, the physiological mechanisms of exercise appear to function more effectively. Although the details of this process of adaptation are not fully understood, many specific effects are now well substantiated. Broadly stated, these include increased cardiac output and reduced pulse rates for any given workload, increased muscular capillarization and more effective oxygen utilization and energy expenditure mechanisms, increased local (skeletal) muscular strength and endurance, and improved neuromuscular coordination and greater mechanical efficiency for any given workload.

In this chapter, we look at some principles guiding modern training programs, such as the principle of overload, overdistance training, and periodization. Interval training (which includes sprint training, repetition training, fast interval training, and slow interval training) was a major breakthrough in preparing swimmers for competition, for it allowed a swimmer to train under heavier but controlled workloads. Tapering, the concept of planning rest periods during training, also revolutionized training by allowing swimmers to recover prior to important competitions.

The Overload Principle

The overload principle accounts for the general phenomenon of adaptation to stress. Overload refers to a workload greater than that to which the body is accustomed, or more precisely, one for which the oxygen intake is inadequate to supply the needs of the body. The overload principle states that increases in muscle size (hypertrophy), strength, and endurance result from an increase in work intensity within a given time unit (see page 154).

Hypertrophy occurs only when a muscle performs work at an intensity greater than usual. An increase in the work duration without a corresponding increase in intensity produces no effect. In general, training effects are specific to the workload. For example, an increased training effect cannot be obtained merely by prolonging the activity; the speed of the activity must also be increased to produce a training effect.

Progressive overload is the gradual and progressive increase in workload in accordance with the body's capacity to resist stress. To improve performance, training should aim at progression but always within the individual athlete's fund of adaptive energy.

Adaptation is the gradual process of the body overcompensating to overload stresses, during which the body undergoes functional and constitutional changes. In adjusting to increased stress, the body draws on its fund of adaptation energy.

Failing adaptation is the body's inability to cope with overload stress and can result from several causes, particularly a too-rapid increase in the training workload based on a seriously misjudged ideal balance between volume and intensity. But failing adaptation can also rise from such hidden stresses as inadequate rest or nutrition, emotional stress, or the inexorable demands of growth.

The body makes certain adjustments and changes in adapting itself to prolonged stress. Coaches must be able to recognize differences among individuals in this respect. Applying the proper volume and intensity of exercise stress will produce the optimal amount of specific adaptation for each person.

Failing adaptation may be countered by reducing the workload—by swimming at a slower pace, increasing the amount of rest, or reducing the distance swum in training. Excessive local stress should be diverted, but excessive total stress requires complete rest (Selye 1956). Diversion can consist of varying the format of the training schedule and the strokes swum in training. In extreme cases where diversion is inadequate to counter failing adaptation to stress, the athlete may require complete rest from training and unnecessary daily activities. Some swimmers have been shown to benefit from bed rest immediately before a big meet, but an intelligently planned training program will not require such extreme measures.

Specificity of training is a fundamental principle of training but was only vaguely understood in the early days of formal training programs. People realized that to be able to swim fast, athletes should practice swimming fast and that to have endurance, they should practice swimming long distances; but the principle of specificity is far more complex than merely following these two concepts.

Training effects are specific to the type of workload placed on the body. Brouha (1945) studied this concept of training and reports that athletes in one sport require time to adapt to and reach maximum efficiency in another sport, even when equally skilled in both activities. Indeed, specificity applies between sports *and* between events within sports; it applies both to learning the precise skills and paces of a sport and to conditioning the body to perform at maximum capacity in the different events within a sport.

According to Selye (1956), specificity refers to a few units within a system, implying that training should be planned according to a purpose, whether the purpose is to establish desired physiological effects through training the appropriate energy systems of the body, to form skills, to swim a race at a certain speed, or to use certain strategies and paces in competition. Within a single daily workout, appropriate time should be allocated for training specific aspects of the body. As the season progresses, emphasis given to specific physiological requirements should gradually change according to the swimmer's improving fitness and the event(s) to be swum in competition. Each event of the competitive swimming program requires a certain balance between speed and endurance, which naturally varies among individuals.

Specificity does not refer merely to preparing for a particular competitive event, nor is the establishment of general physiological fitness the only requirement; rather, specificity takes the form of the particular quality being emphasized during any phase of seasonal activity, whether it's endurance training or specialized training for the season's important competitions. Thus, a swimmer should first build a broad base of endurance. Once the endurance base is established, the program gradually changes in format to include a carefully planned balance of duration and intensity of effort. These considerations are vital, as training at too high a level of intensity can easily result in failing adaptation to the exercise stress; in fact, training at very high levels of intensity should form only a small percentage of the seasonal activity.

Different types of work produce different physiological effects. The different systems of the body do not adapt to training at the same speed. An increase in capillarization, for example, may occur within days, whereas heart muscle takes years to condition properly. The *establishment of effect* is a loose term used to describe specific adaptation resulting from training.

Training has a cumulative effect. The positive effects of training do not appear the very next day after a workload has been applied. Adaptation to the stress of training is a gradual process and requires time to produce the desired biological changes.

Interval Training

Interval training superseded the older type of training in which swimmers did long continuous distances at a comparatively slower pace. The originators of interval training found that by breaking up the training into comparatively shorter periods of activity, with intervening rest periods of varying duration, it was possible to place a greater training overload on the swimmer. Swimmers were found capable of withstanding much greater workloads than previously believed possible.

Interval training involves swimming fixed distances at a fixed pace with fixed rest intervals, thus providing control of the duration and intensity of effort. Increased quality of effort should result when a longer rest period is provided between swims. Generally speaking, the higher the quality of a set of interval swims, the fewer the repetitions that can be accomplished.

Conversely, it's possible to produce a greater quantity of work when shorter rest periods are set between longer sets of interval swims. The prolonged activity reduces the intensity of effort.

In summary, the two options are as follows:

1. *Quality swimming* involves long rest periods, which permit high-speed activity, the intensity of which limits the duration of the activity.

2. *Quantity swimming* involves short rest periods, which permits only submaximal speeds to be maintained. The reduced speed enables the activity to be prolonged, thereby enhancing development of endurance.

This is a sketch of the ideal criteria for producing specific training effects, but the human factor—the swimmer's level of motivation, drive, and dedication—will contribute to the success or failure of the activity.

Types of Interval Training

Various training effects can be achieved by applying different work-to-rest ratios. There are four basic types of interval training:

1. sprint training,
2. repetition training,
3. fast interval training, and
4. slow interval training.

Sprint Training

Sprint training consists of short distances swum at top speed. Although speed starts to slow after about 50 meters, distances up to 100 meters are commonly called sprints and are treated as such for the purpose of speed training. Sprint training is usually done in multiples of 25-, 50-, or 100-meter sets. The heart rate should be allowed to recover to 100 beats per minute or below after each swim.

Work-to-rest ratios from 1:5 to 1:10 should permit adequate rest to enable training to emphasize speed. The ratio chosen depends on what percentage of top speed the swimmer wishes to attain. In sprint training the swimmer on occasion may try to swim at 100 percent of best time, especially over 25s and 50s. Sprint training attempts to develop speed and muscular strength and power as well as the ability to tolerate oxygen debt.

Here are some basic examples of sprint training sets:

8 × 25 (2 minutes rest)
4 × 50 (5 minutes rest)
4 × 100 (10 minutes rest)

Repetition Training

Repetition training consists of simulating the race pace by swimming distances shorter than the racing distance at a pace faster than the pace of the total racing distance. However, any kind of training in which the heart rate is permitted to recover to approximately 110 to 100 before the next swim may be classified as repetition training.

When performed at high enough speeds, repetition training accustoms the swimmer to anaerobic exercise in that there is an increase of oxygen debt and an accumulation of higher levels of lactate in the working muscles. Repetition training also increases speed and muscular strength and power.

The work-to-rest ratio should be at least 1:3 to permit speeds approximately 90 to 95 percent of a swimmer's racing speed. To develop a high level of blood lactate, the swimmer needs to exert close to 100 percent effort. The heart rate also should reach maximum, somewhere in the range of 190 to 200.

So that the swimmer can maintain a high enough level of work intensity, the distances used in high-lactate repeat swimming ideally

should not exceed 250 to 300 meters. Because high-intensity repeat swimming can be very stressful and send a swimmer into failing adaptation, the training set should not exceed a total distance of 1,000 meters or be presented more than twice a week in the workout schedule.

Here are basic examples of repetition training sets:

15 × 50 (3 minutes rest)
10 × 100 (5 minutes rest)
6 × 150 (5 to 10 minutes rest; the last two 150-meter swims should be faster than the swimmer's 150 split recorded on the swimmer's fastest 200-meter swim)
4 × 250 (10 minutes rest; the last two 250 repeats should be faster than the swimmer's 250 split recorded on the swimmer's best time for 400 meters. The swimmer's time at the 200 mark will usually accord with the 200-meter pace recommended to the swimmer by physiologists for the purpose of high-lactate training.)

Note. Applying the last two sets twice weekly during the hard training season can be particularly effective in improving a swimmer's times for the 200- and 400-meter events, respectively, possibly because a swimmer becomes accustomed to tolerating the higher levels of lactate that probably start to accumulate around the 150 mark in the 200 and the 250 mark in the 400.

Fast Interval Training

Fast interval training consists of work-to-rest ratios of about 1:1, permitting the swimmer to develop speeds approximately 80 percent of best pace. At least theoretically, this ratio enables the equal development of speed and endurance.

Fast interval training introduces a significant element of speed to any prolonged activity. It simulates to a high degree the type of stress experienced in racing events, which makes great demands on aerobic and anaerobic endurance. In fast interval training, the heart rate after each swim will be around 160 to 190. The heart rate should be permitted to recover to approximately 120 to 130 before the next swim.

Although the rest period in fast interval training is shorter than that permitted in sprint and repetition training, it is much longer than in slow interval training. Fast interval training develops heart muscle and the ability of skeletal muscle to tolerate oxygen debt.

Here are basic examples of fast interval training sets:

30 × 50 (30 to 60 seconds rest)

15 × 100 (30 to 120 seconds rest)

8 × 200 (30 to 120 seconds rest)

8 × 400 (1 to 3 minutes rest)

4 × 800 (3 to 5 minutes rest)

Slow Interval Training

Slow interval training, which consists of relatively slow activity designed to improve aerobic endurance, is based on the endurance development principle of prolonging the activity and gradually trying to increase the speed of the prolonged activity as the season progresses. Slow interval training involves swimming at speeds of approximately 60 to 70 percent of best pace for the distance. Speed of the swims is limited by the short rest periods. Activity continues for at least 20 minutes to ensure that the intensity of effort is kept primarily at the aerobic level. Activity may continue for one to two hours when used to lay the early-season endurance foundation. The heart rate after each swim will be approximately 160 to 170, but the recovery rate will be in the range of 150 to 160.

Here are basic examples of slow interval training sets:

30 × 50 (10 to 15 seconds rest)

15 × 100 (10 to 15 seconds rest)

8 × 200 (10 to 20 seconds rest)

8 × 400 (15 to 30 seconds rest)

4 × 800 (15 to 30 seconds rest)

Various Applications of Interval Training

Interval training can be applied in many ways, including straight sets, descending sets, broken sets, pyramids, permutations, simulators, and negative splits.

Straight Sets

A straight set is a series of swims done at near constant speed—for example, 16 × 100 (each 100 in 62 seconds) with 30 seconds rest.

Descending Sets

A descending set is a series of repeat swims in which each subsequent swim is done progressively faster—for example, 20 × 50 (30 seconds rest) descending (first 50 in 35 seconds, twentieth 50 in 28 seconds).

A variation of this method is to post the workout item on the board as 20 × 50 (30 seconds rest), 1-4 descending. This means the swimmer will decrease the time over the first four 50s and repeat the process four more times until 20 swims have been completed.

Yet another variation of descending sets is to decrease the average time for each set of repeat swims by starting each subsequent set with a faster first 50 than in the preceding set and then continuing to decrease the second, third, and fourth 50 accordingly.

In this type of training, however, the first repeats in a set are sometimes swum too slowly to warrant intervening rest periods. In the previous example, namely, 20 × 50 for a total distance of 1,000 meters (or yards), it might be better to swim the first half of each set continuously without rest intervals and then complete the second half of the distance as a descending set of equal multiples.

For example, the athlete would perform a 250 continuous swim at a fast pace followed immediately by 5 × 50 descending (30 seconds rest), repeating the set for a total of 1,000 meters.

Broken Sets

A broken set is a series of swims in which the total distance is broken into sectors with short rest intervals between them, for example, 400 meters broken at each 100 with 10 seconds rest. At the end of the swim, deduct 30 seconds (the total amount of rest) from the gross time to obtain actual swimming time.

Broken swims are highly motivating and can be used to break up all training distances. Several broken swims can be used to form a training set by providing a long rest after each swim, thus combining repetition training and interval training. Another interesting variation is to perform a set of broken swims in a descending series, reducing the gross time for each subsequent swim.

Here are some further examples:

8 × 400 broken at the 50 with 10 seconds rest and 5 minutes rest after each 400

8 × 200 individual medley broken at the 50 with 10 seconds rest and 3 minutes rest after each 200 medley

2 × 150 going straight through into 2 × 50 (a broken 400 with 10 seconds rest between each sector) and 5 minutes rest after each 400

8 × 100 with 10 seconds rest after each 100, 5 minutes rest after each set, and sets 1 through 4 descending

Pyramids

The pyramid format is a set of swims divided into irregular distance sectors and rest periods. The swimmer may keep the same pace in each swim or vary the pace by going faster on the shorter sectors. Three examples follow.

Example 1

Swim 50, rest 10 seconds

Swim 100, rest 20 seconds

Swim 200, rest 40 seconds

Swim 400, rest 1 minute

Swim 200, rest 40 seconds

Swim 100, rest 20 seconds

Swim 50

Example 2

Swim 400, rest 3 minutes

Swim 2 × 200, rest 2 minutes

Swim 2 × 100, rest 1 minute

Swim 2 × 50, rest 30 seconds

Example 3

(Individual medley in 25-meter pool)

Swim 400 medley, rest 5 minutes

Swim 200 medley, rest 3 minutes

Swim 100 medley, rest 1 minute

Swim 200 medley, rest 3 minutes

Swim 400 medley

Permutations

Permutations are swims broken at irregular sectors of the total distance. The following are examples of permutations of 400 meters in a 50-meter pool (eight lengths of the pool to complete 400 meters). The workout items are posted on the board as 4 × 400 meters (perm) (5 minutes rest after each 400).

2-2-2-2 (10 seconds rest)

4-2-1-1 (10 seconds rest)

1-2-3-2 (10 seconds rest)

4-1-1-1-1 (10 seconds rest)

The pace is kept constant on three- or four-length segments but increased on one- and two-length segments.

I developed and used this method and found it effective for developing a swimmer's ability to change pace or accelerate tactically at any stage of a race; alternatively, the pace can be held constant for all sectors. The method can also be used for teaching negative splitting (see Negative Splits, p. 143). Whatever procedure is used, permutations ("perms") provide an opportunity to practice a variety of paces.

Simulators

The simulator is a method used to replicate the desired pace of a specific racing distance (Counsilman 1968). Basically, the procedure is to cover half the racing distance at the desired pace before stopping for a short rest that permits the heart rate only a slight recovery. The swimmer then covers half the amount of distance already covered before stopping for another short rest. The pattern continues until some arbitrarily small segment remains for the total to equal the racing distance.

For example, suppose the racing distance being practiced is 400 meters. The training schedule would look like this:

Swim 200 meters, rest 10 seconds

Swim 100 meters, rest 5 seconds

Swim 50 meters, rest 5 seconds

Swim 25 meters, rest 5 seconds

Swim 25 meters

Note. The rest interval is reduced in this example from 10 to 5 seconds before the shorter segments of the racing distance.

Negative Splits

Swimming the second half of a racing distance faster than the first half (usually two to three seconds faster) is known as a *negative split.* Its purposes are to delay the onset of oxygen debt and to teach evenly paced swimming. In a sense, the negative split also pays back the momentum of the starting dive in the first half of a racing distance.

Other Types of Training

Many of the following options provide unique training benefits and add variety to the training schedule.

Broadly stated, *overdistance swims* are twice as long as the distance for which a swimmer is training. For example, a swimmer whose specialty is the 100-meter event practices overdistance swimming by doing 200-meter swims. (A 1,500-meter swimmer would also be doing overdistance training when swimming 3,000 meters continuously, although there's no 3,000-meter event in the competitive program.)

Locomotives provide pace variations over different segments of a total nonstop swim. They are an excellent early-season conditioning exercise and a useful diversion during the stress of hard midseason training. Here is one example:

Swim 1 lap fast, 1 lap slow

Swim 2 laps fast, 2 laps slow

Swim 3 laps fast, 3 laps slow

Swim 4 laps fast, 4 laps slow

Swim 3 laps fast, 3 laps slow

Swim 2 laps fast, 2 laps slow

Swim 1 lap fast, 1 lap slow

Time swimming, an effective method of developing increased endurance, is basically increasing the distance a swimmer can cover within a prescribed time, which, after all, is what speed swimming is about.

Fartlek (see chapter 7) was adopted by swimmers as an informal early-season conditioning exercise. Used this way, most of the distance is covered at an easy pace, with intermittent bursts of speed using such devices as changing stroke and pace after a certain number of lengths. Chapter 7 describes how to use fartlek training to greater purpose and effect by setting more definite requirements.

Tethered Swimming, or Sprint-Resisted Training

Tethered swimming (also known as sprint-resisted training) was first used 50 years ago at the Chicago Towers Club when Stan Brauninger, coach to 1936 Olympic backstroke champion Adolph Kiefer, attached canvas belts with long elastic bands around the midriffs of his swimmers. In the 1940s, coach Harold Minto of the Firestone Country Club, Akron, Ohio, trained the first postwar Olympic 1,500-meter champion, James McLane, in a canvas harness connected to several yards of elastic aircraft shock absorber cord. In the 1940s, Robert Kiphuth suspended scores of elastic stretch bands from the balcony of the Yale University pool for his swimmers to use in the water below (Kiphuth 1942). In similar vein, Santa Clara's George Haines had his swimmers use latex surgical tubing (type 202) for stretch cord exercises on land.

In the late 1950s and the 1960s, the use of tethered swimming became sporadic, but it was revived in the mid-1970s by Randy Reese, the renowned University of Florida coach. Reese experimented with several new in-water drills using 1/8-inch thick surgical tubing that had a 3/32-inch inside diameter and was cut into sections of 18 to 22 feet. He repopularized the use of tethered swimming throughout the world (Colwin 1984c).

Tethered swimming was used originally to improve the muscular power necessary for sprint swimming, but research suggested that swimming against an increased resistance actually slowed muscle speed instead of increasing it (Maglischo 1982). In light of this, Counsilman (1986) used the method for aerobic training of distance swimmers only. He prescribed selected periods of activity such as three five-minute segments with one-minute rest intervals and cut rubber stretch cord to approximately one-third the length of the pool, with allowances for size and strength of the swimmer and elasticity of the cord.

Like so many other swimming training methods, the concept behind speed-assisted training came from track—in this case, the use of such methods as towing, downhill running, and treadmill running at accelerated speed. Ernest Maglischo (1982) referred to a variation of the use of tethered swimming for improving sprint swimming speed. He described how leading coaches Randy Reese and Nort Thornton used the method in their programs. The swimmer first swam down the pool, stretching the tubing, and then allowed it to snap back on the return, thus assisting the swimmer to swim at a faster speed than normally possible. Counsilman (1986) developed a system of anaerobic lactate training by having the swimmers use repeat swims such as 10×50 on two to three minutes or 5×100 on three to five minutes while attached to stretch cords. He instructed the swimmers to swim diagonally across the pool to avoid becoming entangled in the cords when returning down the pool. The method was not practical in a 50-meter pool because the cords would not stretch tightly enough, and the course was too long for sprinting.

Counsilman (1986) devised another variation of the method wherein sprinters pulled themselves along the lane markers to the other end of the pool and then rested before allowing the taut stretch cord to snap back and give them a speed-assisted sprint back to the starting point.

Periodization of the Training Program

Varying the intensity and duration of workouts from day to day and week to week results in a long-term cyclic application of the training program. The days of easy, moderate, and hard work should not be planned more than one week in advance; even then a coach may decide to change the intensity of a workout based on on-the-spot observation of a swimmer's reaction to a previous workload. Workouts are monitored by means of measuring blood lactate in only a few teams, and for most programs, this phase of coaching remains an art instead of a science. When a program is under the direction of an experienced coach, however, it's often remarkable how a well-balanced pattern of easy, moderate, and strenuous sessions appears consistently over a period of many weeks.

Several researchers, notably Kindermann (1978), Matveyev (1981), Harre (1982), and Berger (1982), have studied the periodization of the training program. As a result, it is common in Eastern Europe for training preparation to be viewed in the context of three distinct cycles—microcycles of one week duration, mesocycles of three to seven weeks duration, and macrocycles, one to four per year up to four years.

During the 1960s and 1970s several leading programs, mainly in Europe, adopted a new terminology to describe the various phases of seasonal training. For example, Igor Koshkin (1985), coach of the great Soviet 1,500-meter world-record holder Vladimir Salnikov, described a typical training year as being divided into five spirals, each having a duration of 8 to 12 weeks and ending with a one- to three-week competition period.

Each spiral comprises two-week development stages called mesocycles. Each mesocycle concentrates on developing specific qualities in the swimmer. During the last mesocycle—the preparation for major competition—the aim is to integrate all the specific qualities developed in the four or five preceding mesocycles.

Search for a Selective Method of Applying the Training Workload

The erstwhile East German sports regime developed a method of blood lactate analysis.

One method for determining the lactate/ ventilatory threshold* involves timing evenly paced swims at 200 or 300 meters, some of which are done at an easy pace. The pace is then slightly increased to a moderate intensity just above the lactate/ventilatory threshold. Finally, much faster swims at almost 100 percent of maximum effort are performed.

As few as two blood lactate concentrations are plotted against the velocities of the test swims, and the lines joining them are extrapolated to cut the 4 mmol/L blood lactate level. The estimated velocity at 4 mmol/L is read off to predict the exercise intensity for each individual swimmer's lactate/ventilatory threshold.

East German coaches regularly used the 10 × 200 anaerobic test on their swimmers. Studying the nature of the lactate velocity curve helped them assess at regular intervals the changing aerobic and anaerobic capacities of individual swimmers throughout the training season. In addition, they were able to determine a swimmer's ability to reach a high lactate level with a maximum-effort performance. The purpose of the procedure was to test a swimmer's mobilization capacity, or the highest level of blood lactate the swimmer is able to generate. The East Germans maintained that this scientific approach to training enabled them to make very accurate judgments concerning the training condition of a swimmer right through the season, up to and including the final precompetition tapering-off period.

Tapering for Competition

In the early years of competitive swimming, swimmers took little if any extra rest prior to a major competition other than retiring earlier on the previous night. It was not uncommon for training, such as it was, to be continued up to the day before a meet.

In the early 1950s, swimmers began to increase distances covered in training. As the quantity of work increased, they found they could swim faster. At this time, the tendency was to swim long, unbroken mileage with wind sprints—usually a series of 50s interspersed with rest periods—performed at the end of a workout to introduce an element of speed.

Some thought that if a lot of mileage gave good results, then more would give even better. Of course, this was not always true. What they found was that swimmers often carried considerable residual fatigue over long periods. They saw that they needed an adjustment to the training regimen that would enable swimmers to produce their best performances in important competitions.

The introduction of alternating easy and hard training days was an attempt to permit a measure of adaptation in the midst of strenuous training, but swimmers still did not obtain sufficient rest to perform at their best. Nevertheless, the idea of alternating days of easier and harder work was to lead to experiments with even longer rests.

Basic Concept of the Taper

Carlile's interest in Selye's concepts of stress (Selye 1956) combined with his own studies of failing adaptation to stress (Carlile 1963) prompted him to provide his swimmers with far more rest before competition than was previously thought necessary. This period of reduced activity became known as the taper. The beneficial effects of tapering on performance became clear to coaches once they learned to taper swimmers skillfully.

During the 1970s and 1980s, the tapering process grew more complex for several reasons, one of them being the increased frequency of top international competition. Often, radical changes had to be made to already busy regional and national schedules. Preparing swimmers to compete successfully in a series of topflight competitions became a fine art—and only partially a science. Many swimmers chose to swim through (either not taper or use a reduced taper) for some meets and then taper completely to swim at a higher level

---

* *Note.* Once again following the lead of track and field athletics, swimming scientists are beginning to replace the term *anaerobic threshold* with *lactate/ventilatory threshold*. The former term refers nonspecifically to the upper limits of aerobic work, whereas the latter refers to measurable levels of blood lactate and ventilatory capacity.

in others. In addition, many lower-ranked swimmers tapered in midseason, attempting to meet required qualifying times for entries to championship and major meets.

Principle Considerations in Tapering

Before a major competition, swimmers gradually reduce their heavy workload and increase their rest. This period is known as the taper (Carlile 1963) or tapering off. The transition to easier work causes the adaptive processes of the body to overcompensate as the swimmer prepares for maximum effort. The word *taper*—diminishing toward the end—aptly describes the process. Its use in training was coined by Frank Cotton, professor of physiology at the University of Sydney, Australia, and his understudy at the time, Forbes Carlile, now the dean of Australian swimming coaches.

These two pioneers discovered that for physiological adaptation to occur, arduous training must be tempered with adequate rest. The concept of tapering is based on this realization, and over a period of more than 30 years, it has proved to be one of the most significant contributions to the progress of competitive swimming. Tapering was first described in the literature—and in detail—by Carlile (1963). Both the concept and the term were quickly accepted and employed worldwide.

A successful taper results from good judgment and careful planning. The taper should be planned carefully for each swimmer. It's rare for a swimmer to taper in exactly the same way every time. Variations in the taper arise from different factors that have acted on the swimmer during the period preceding an important meet, several of which must be considered on every occasion. Planning an effective taper requires the coach to have technical skill and acute insight into the state of individual swimmers, particularly their reaction to precompetition anxiety.

The taper should be relevant to the work done in the preceding months. Its duration and the amount of rest it provides should allow complete recovery from accumulated fatigue.

The body then overcompensates in its adaptation to stress, enabling a superior performance.

During the taper, attention should be given to every aspect of preparation—mental as well as physical—including mental attitude, physical conditioning, stroke technique, pace, and strategy. Finally, the effects of rest on adaptation should be understood. Rest is a vital determinant of performance and just as important as an ideal balance among different levels of work intensity.

A note of caution: for young swimmers, excess energy levels that result from tapering often cause a tendency to indulge in horseplay. The coach should forewarn the team against wild or unruly behavior, calling it "excessive exuberance," that could cause injury and the consequent waste of a whole season of preparation.

The entire season should be mapped out in advance and major and minor meets decided. The program design should include the duration and emphasis of each training cycle with adequate time for the final taper.

Typical Questions on Tapering

Here are some typical questions a coach often encounters during the taper phase of the season:

How long should each swimmer taper?

Should all swimmers taper the same length of time?

Should all swimmers perform the same preparation items, irrespective of the events in which they will compete?

Should there be a difference between the taper for a swimmer who is competing only on the fourth day of a meet and, for example, one who is competing on the first day and probably on other days, too?

What is the swimmer's capacity for recovery from hard work?

What allowances should be made for individual temperament?

Has enough time been built into a tapering period to counter any possible errors of judgment?

None of these questions is purely hypothetical. On the contrary, they enter into nearly every planning of a taper period. They constitute only a few examples of possible circumstances that may arise. Experience teaches a coach that these circumstances appear to be unlimited.

General Guidelines on Tapering

What worked last season may not work as well—or at all—this season. Any number of changes in conditions can cause this, including alterations in the annual program of competitive events, the available time for workouts, absenteeism, conditioning emphasis, swimmers' levels of development, temperament, and many other factors. Although a coach may recognize recurring situations, it is wise to be alert for new sets of circumstances likely to influence tapering decisions.

Before I identify situations that need special attention in making tapering decisions, it may be helpful to provide a few general guidelines.

1. The shorter the race, the longer the taper; conversely, the longer the race, the shorter the taper. Distance swimmers and sprinters need different tapers.

2. The more races to be contested, the shorter the taper.

3. The younger the swimmer, the shorter the taper. Younger swimmers have a higher level of vital energy; moreover, they tend to lose the feel of the water quickly if they taper too soon. Conversely, an older swimmer may need a longer taper. Swimmers who have competed for many years appear to need a longer taper with each successive season.

4. Nervous athletes need a shorter taper.

5. Large, well-muscled athletes generally need a longer taper.

6. Swimmers with an adequate background of hard work usually obtain good results if tapered fairly early. Those who have been overstressed in training show dramatic adaptation and recovery from accumulative fatigue after a long, well-planned taper.

7. Swimmers who have done only a moderate amount of work through the season often will not show great improvement when tapered because they lack the background training.

8. Seasonal goals should be established at the start of the training program when the coach first meets the swimmers. At this time, the coach should identify and outline to the swimmers the type of work and the duration of each training cycle necessary to achieve these goals. Early on, the coach should decide which meets the swimmer will enter and the level of importance to be accorded each competition. More important meets require more complete tapers (major taper).

The importance of the meet and the stage of the season determines whether to use major, minor, or mini tapers. A meet may be used to check the progress of the team as a whole toward its established goals or to provide opportunities for individual members. In particular, the coach may decide to rest a swimmer who lacks confidence so that he or she can record a morale-boosting fast time. It is sometimes necessary for an up-and-coming youngster to record a fast swim to encourage continued dedication to a demanding program of hard work.

9. An ideal psychological climate should be nurtured and every effort made to foster a positive team spirit. Physiological and psychological preparation should keep pace with each other throughout the season and into the tapering period, resulting in a well-conditioned athlete with a strong, positive mental attitude.

10. An ideal taper, from the physiological standpoint, is when a swimmer has had just the right amount of rest. Sometimes a swimmer appears unaffected by the taper and shows no improvement in speed. There's not much to do in this situation but be patient and wait for the taper to take effect.

It is just as possible to have too much rest as to have too little. Usually, a swimmer who has had too much rest lacks the conditioning to finish a race strongly; conversely, the swimmer who has had too little rest may not have sharp speed initially but may still be able to finish a race strongly. If competing in a three- to four-day meet, for example, the underrested swimmer may improve over the subsequent days as a result of having more rest. The outlook for the overrested and underworked swimmer will not be as optimistic, however, as there obviously would be insufficient time to become conditioned.

Preparing a Basic Plan for the Taper

A basic plan for the tapering period should be mapped out at the beginning of the season when the number of training days and competitions leading to the major meets first become known. The plan should include an outline of each phase of the season together with the duration of each training cycle, as well as adequate time for the tapering period.

Nearly all coaches agree that tapering is a complex phase of the season—in fact, the word "complex" seems most readily to spring to mind in any frank discussion of the topic. The challenge, then, is for the coach to ensure clear communication on all the important aspects of the planned taper with individual swimmers and the team as a whole. Team meetings and clearly drawn charts help explain the tapering plan to swimmers at all levels. Not least of all, the coach should warn the swimmers about overeating and becoming overweight as a result of the reduced energy demands placed on the body. The importance of early bedtimes and adequate sleep should also be stressed.

Super-Adaptation

At some stages of the season, many swimmers work so hard that they are unable to approach their best times in training or competition before they taper for the season's most important meets. Counsilman (1968) calls this phase of training "the valley of fatigue" and considers it necessary for what he terms super-adaptation. The reasoning behind its use is that when the workload is finally reduced in the taper period, the body's adaptive mechanisms continue to overcompensate at the same high level even though the unusual stress of the hard training period has suddenly been removed. If the taper is well planned, a superior performance results.

The Warm-Up

Here is a list of the benefits of warming up:

- The resultant increase in body temperature and pulse rate, combined with dilation of blood vessels in the muscles, takes the body from its resting state to the physiological level needed for the competitive event.
- It loosens the muscles and increases flexibility.
- It familiarizes the swimmer with the pool conditions in which the competition takes place.
- The swimmer gets into stroke rhythm and feels out the required pace of the race.
- Muscle fatigue occurs later in the race after adequate warm-up.
- A muscle that is warmed and stretched prior to maximum exertion is less likely to sustain injury.
- The warm-up induces a sense of well-being.

During the workouts of the hard training season, a swimmer should cultivate a sense for how much swimming is sufficient for warm-up. This sense significantly aids a swimmer in tapering and warming up before meets.

In some teams, the amount of swimming needed to warm up in daily training sessions is the amount of swimming used in each session during the taper period. The swimmer does just enough work to be able to swim at pace. This is usually followed by some short, sharp work, a loosen-down swim, and practice in starts and turns.

Warm-up procedures vary according to a swimmer's racing events. Short-distance swimmers and sprinters include some short speed work—mostly 25-meter and 50-meter efforts—

whereas distance swimmers establish their race pace by covering a few 100-meter sections.

The warm-up should last 20 to 45 minutes, and the swimmer should be out of the water at least 20 minutes before the meet starts. A swimmer preparing for morning competition may need more warm-up time to wake up. In the evenings, before swimming in the finals, a shorter warm-up is usually enough because of the swimming done earlier in the day.

After warming up, a swimmer should don warm, dry clothing, gloves, socks, and shoes. The swimmer should stand up and become active just before the race starts by walking around and doing mild stretching exercises.

As the season progresses, each swimmer should determine his or her best basic warm-up. Every competitive session should be preceded by a warm-up and followed by a loosen-down; this helps eliminate stiff or sore shoulders, hips, knees, and ankles.

Effects of Massage

A benefit of massage is its effect on the circulation of the area treated. By improving the circulation of blood and lymph, it facilitates the removal of deleterious substances formed in excess by injury or liberated by movement.

Superficial light massage affects only the skin circulation, specifically, the skin capillaries, superficial veins, and lymphatics. The first two, however, hold so much blood that massage in the direction of their flow materially increases the return of blood to the heart and produces an effect rather like exercise without the more exhausting effects of fatigue. Because the superficial veins draw blood from the muscles as well as the skin, the muscles of the massaged area will drain somewhat. Massage of the lymphatics increases the flow of lymph and removal of tissue fluid, the accumulation of which causes pain and stiffness. In injury, this fluid contains an abnormally large amount of protein, and if it is allowed to remain stationary it may be converted into fibrous tissue and cause permanent stiffness. Merely rubbing the skin also sends a vast number of beneficial impulses into the nervous system.

Deeper massage hastens circulation through the muscles and the soft tissues because each compression tends to drive the blood toward the veins where the pressure is least. Similarly, deep massage facilitates the dispersal of accumulated lymph or blood in the deeper parts. It cannot be overemphasized, however, that loosening movements, either on land or in the water, best stimulate the circulation.

Chapter 9

Physiological Research and Applications

David Pyne, PhD

Sports Physiologist,
Australian Institute of Sport

In high-level competitive swimming, coaches and swimmers need to understand the energy demands involved in successful performance. The same requirements hold true in learning the neuromuscular patterns involved in performing efficient stroke mechanics. When properly mastered, muscles contract, extend, or remain static in length in perfect sequence, even when swimming at high speed.

These processes require the integration of neural signals from the cerebral motor cortex (nervous system) to the muscles. In turn, a chain of biochemical reactions within the muscle transforms potential chemical energy to mechanical energy for use in the working muscles. The improved level of fitness that training provides enhances the body's ability to perform more work with less fatigue.

About Dr. David Pyne

Dr. David Pyne holds a PhD in biochemistry and molecular biology from the Australian National University, Canberra, and was awarded the Australian Sports Medal in 2000 for his contribution to swimming in Australia. Since 1987, Dr. Pyne has worked as a sports physiologist at the Australian Institute of Sport (AIS), specializing in swimming. Dr. Pyne works with both the AIS swimming team and the Australian national team and was the physiologist to the 2000 Australian Olympic swimming team. Dr. Pyne travels extensively with the AIS and Australian teams to national- and international-level competitions and training camps. His research interests include the applied physiology of swimming; exercise, training, and immune system research; and environmental physiology. Dr. Pyne is the secretary to the Australian Swimming Sports Science Advisory Group and writes coaching/scientific articles for *Swimming in Australia*, other coaching publications, and scientific journals.

Energy Metabolism

Energy metabolism is based on the relation between fuel availability and its use. These fuel sources rely, in turn, on the contribution of different energy systems to the activities involved.

There are four basic energy compounds. The primary energy compound is adenosine triphosphate (ATP). The three secondary energy compounds are creatine phosphate (CP), glycogen (carbohydrate), and fat. ATP is the currency (energy) that powers all cellular functions, including muscular contraction. However, there is only sufficient ATP in muscle to sustain a short burst (a few seconds) of muscular effort. Even in the 50-meter freestyle, the shortest competitive swimming event, ATP must be constantly replenished from other sources within the muscle. The additional sources of energy are derived from the dietary intake of carbohydrate, fat, and protein.

A fundamental principle of energy metabolism is that all three energy systems are active throughout exercise. Their relative contribution in swimming is determined by the duration and intensity of the event. Short explosive sprints such as the 50-meter events are predominantly anaerobic in nature. Middle-distance events (100 to 400 meters) require a combination of anaerobic and aerobic energy. Long-distance events such as the 800 and 1,500 meters and open-water swimming are predominantly aerobic in nature.

Table 9.1 shows the relative contribution of the three energy systems to various swimming events. Modern swimming training should include a full range of training speeds. The need

Table 9.1	**Estimated Contribution of Energy Systems to Different Swimming Events**		
Event	**ATP-CP (%)**	**Anaerobic glycolysis (%)**	**Aerobic (%)**
50 m	55	40	5
100 m	15	50	35
200 m	10	30	60
400 m	5	25	70
1,500 m	0	15	85

to combine different speeds with the different strokes (freestyle, backstroke, butterfly, breaststroke) provides great opportunities for the innovative coach. The challenge for the coach and swimmer in the 100-meter, 200-meter, and 400-meter events is to blend endurance and speed in ideal proportions to produce a winning performance.

Endurance Training

Two questions are often posed:

1. If the majority of competitive swimming events are primarily power based, why is training largely endurance based?

2. Do swimmers need high-mileage training, and does this violate the principle of specificity of training?

Several factors support a traditional high-mileage training program. First, the duration of most events, from the 100 meter to the 1,500 meter (50 seconds to 16 minutes), has a substantial aerobic requirement. Low-volume, high-intensity training has its proponents, but most coaches recognize that endurance fitness is needed to maximize anaerobic and speed development.

A swimmer's buoyancy permits a greater training volume than weight-bearing exercise such as running. Endurance training facilitates stroke correction by constant repetition of a greater number of movements, whereas sprint swimming may serve merely to perpetuate faults. Stroke faults are often hidden at high speeds but are magnified at slower speeds, thus enabling earlier detection.

Basic Training Principles Applied to Swimming

Several basic training principles can be applied to the preparation of competitive swimmers. These have evolved over time from the hard-earned practical experience of coaches and swimmers alike, as well as from the results of scientific investigation. Careful application of these principles is a key step in preparing an effective training program. The details of training programs vary significantly according to the age, skill level, and training history of swimmers and the availability of facilities and equipment. Figure 9.1 shows a hierarchy of training adaptations.

Specificity

The principle of specificity states that the maximum benefit of training is obtained by replication of the movement patterns and energetic demands of swimming. Specificity of movement patterns is a key aspect of swimming, and training drills and sets should include each of the four major swimming strokes (freestyle, butterfly, backstroke, and breaststroke).

The development of efficient technique at different speeds is the foundation of all high-level training programs. In practice, freestyle and backstroke constitute the major proportion of training for swimmers of all strokes.

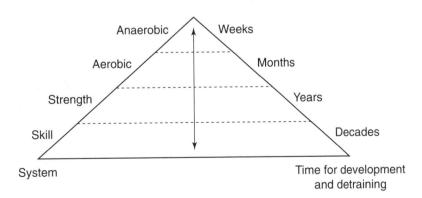

Figure 9.1 Hierarchy of training adaptations. From Counsilman and Counsilman 1991.

Butterfly swimmers in particular complete only a small proportion of training using their main stroke. Medley swimmers need to train all the different strokes, both in isolation and combination with IM switching sets.

Overload

The principle of progressive overload is based on a process of stimulus, response, and adaptation (Bompa 1983).

A combined pool and dry-land training program provides the stimulus to various physiological systems (i.e., cardiovascular, muscular, skeletal, nervous, and hormonal systems). A swimmer's short-term response to training is seen in the daily cycling of fatigue and recovery, but several weeks of a gradually increased training workload are required for significant adaptations to occur.

Adaptation to the judiciously applied stress of training is evident in improvements in cardiovascular fitness, lean muscle mass, muscle composition and function, and the hormonal and nervous systems. The extent of improvement is influenced by individual genetic limits, specificity of physiological responses, accumulated fatigue, and the nature of the training stimulus itself.

Periodization

Periodization involves division of the annual training plan into smaller, more manageable parts. A mesocycle normally covers the entire summer or winter season plan. A macrocycle refers to specific three- or four-week training phases or blocks with different emphases. Macrocycles can take the form of general or specific preparation, taper, competition, or recovery. A microcycle refers to the standard seven-day training week (Monday to Sunday) that forms the basis of most swimming programs.

In the 1970s and 1980s, training for international-level swimmers was generally based on single or two-peak annual cycles. Swimmers were prepared for their national championships and the major international competitions (e.g., Olympic Games, World Championships) in each calendar year. How-

ever, the increasing fragmentation of the international swimming calendar has resulted in a greater focus on shorter macro- and microcycles to prepare swimmers (especially sprint swimmers) for several long-course (50-meter) and short-course (25-meter) competitions each year.

Individuality

Swimmers and coaches should recognize that the principle of individuality is one of the most important aspects of training. Tolerance of training loads, the rate of recovery from high-intensity training and competition, preferences in pool and dry-land training, and the need for rest and recovery vary from swimmer to swimmer. Most coaches appreciate the need to organize their training squads by age, ability, and event and within those groups, to individualize training where appropriate. Training loads can be modified in terms of the number of sessions completed each week, the length (volume) of training sessions and sets, and the intensity of different intervals.

Reversibility

The principle of reversibility, or detraining, suggests that skill and strength require the longest time to develop (years) and aerobic and anaerobic fitness the shortest time to develop (weeks and months). The principle is elegantly illustrated in Counsilman's *Hierarchy of Training Adaptations* (Counsilman and Counsilman 1991; see figure 9.1). The rate of detraining largely mirrors the rate of training improvements, with fitness starting to decline within a few weeks of detraining (Coyle, Hemmert, and Coggan 1986).

The loss of competitive fitness relates to changes in cardiorespiratory, metabolic and biochemical parameters, and neuromuscular control. Studies of elite athletes show that fitness can be maintained on 30 to 50 percent of previous training levels for several weeks. This has implications for taper and when returning from illness and injury. Swimmers and coaches should be encouraged that short breaks in training do not necessarily cause a reduction in fitness, and in some cases the reduction in residual fatigue actually enhances performance.

Evolution of Interval Training Programs

What combination of training volume and intensity is necessary for competitive success? The evolution of modern swimming training methodology has been largely based on the periodization of training volume and intensity.

Despite general acceptance by coaches for an organized and systematic approach to training, no common training theory exists that describes the type, quantity, or pattern of a particular training program that guarantees a given result (Steinacker et al. 1998). There are as many training programs as there are swimming coaches.

In swimming, as in other endurance-based cyclic or repetitive sports (e.g., running, cycling, rowing), the consensus among most coaches is that training and performance are related by a dose-response relationship (Banister, Morton, and Clarke 1997). Improvements in swimming performance are achieved initially through a sequential increase in the volume and intensity of training.

A common trend in world swimming has been a gradual shift away from distance events and training to more sprint-based programs. This has been fueled by increasing commercialization of swimming with an upsurge in short-course swimming and in the number of competitive events in the calendar. These changes appear to have had a significant impact on the type of training programs at two levels.

The traditional one or two peaks per year has given way to a more fragmented and congested training plan with a greater number of macrocycles (short two- or three-week training blocks). Second, the design of individual training sessions also appears to be more fragmented, with combination-type workouts preferred over the older-style simple workouts.

These changes may partly explain the plateau and even decline in the standard of distance swimming, while times in sprint events and short-course swimming continue to improve. Although concerns for traditional training have been expressed for some time (Thornton 1987), it is inevitable that interval training programs will become further specialized in the coming decades. Greater recognition is also being given to the importance of race pace training (Anderson 1999).

Physiological and Biomechanical Testing of Swimmers

Testing of swimmers can be broken down into two primary categories: training analysis and competition analysis. Both kinds of evaluation are important in preparing, training, and strengthening swimmers.

Physiological testing is largely directed toward assessing the fitness of swimmers. Testing generally involves measuring physiological attributes of elite swimmers and the way training affects performance. There are several reasons to undertake fitness testing in highly trained swimmers. Testing helps to

- monitor progress in fitness levels (adaptation);
- develop training zones (prescription);
- assess training responses to different sets and drills (evaluation);
- identify individual strengths and weaknesses (evaluation); and
- predict performances (prediction).

Fitness tests should be relevant to swimming, valid and reliable, and easy to administer. A worldwide trend is to conduct more specific pool-based testing rather than general laboratory testing. Pool-based testing is more readily acceptable to coaches and swimmers and eliminates the difficulties in transferring results from the laboratory to the pool.

Competition Analysis

Comprehensive race analysis has been conducted at international meets for over a decade. Competition analysis involves overhead video filming and computer-based analysis of swimmers during each event. Dr. Bruce Mason, a biomechanist with the Australian swimming team, has been at the forefront of these developments. With his system, the camera is positioned so that all swimmers in a race are analyzed for split times, start, turn and finish times, and stroke characteristics such as rate, length, and efficiency (figure 9.2).

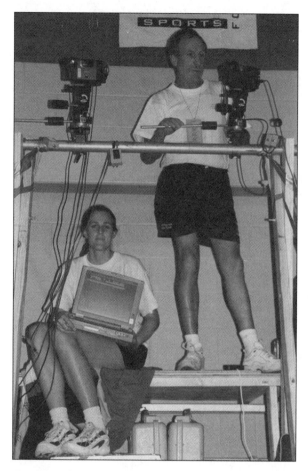

Figure 9.2 Camera setup for competition analysis.

This process provides a clear and concise summary of each swimmer's performance during the event. The spreadsheet output of the competition analysis permits a simple comparison between swimmers in a particular race. Analysis of results over a number of championships has revealed that starts, turns, and finishes are as important as free-swimming speed in determining the final results (Mason and Fowlie 1997). A typical set of competition analysis results is shown in table 9.2.

The measurements made are start time (time from the starting signal to 15 meters), turn time (time in and out from a distance of 7.5 meters off the wall), and finish time (time from 5 meters from the finishing wall until hand touch).

The other phases are denoted as free swimming. In the report sheet, these times are also reported as swimming velocity. The information provided for the free-swimming phases includes stroke length in meters, stroke frequency in strokes per minute, swim velocity in meters per second, and the derived efficiency index.

Multiplying the stroke frequency in strokes per second and the stroke length in meters per stroke provides the swim velocity in meters per second.

At the base of the spreadsheet, the average information and total time for each aspect of the race is provided. During the meet, the competition analysis results for a session are given to the coaches before the next session begins.

Stroke characteristics are also presented in graphic form to assist the coach. Access to a video monitor is often arranged, and a copy of the tape is given to the coach for subsequent analysis. Newer video systems overlay the digital analysis information on top of the video film of the race.

Monitoring Swimming Training Workloads in Practice

Modeling of swimming training in its simplest form defines training load as the product of training volume and intensity. Training volume in swimming is relatively easy to quantify. Multiples of 25-meter and 50-meter laps can be easily added to determine the total distance covered in a single set, session, or training week. Most coaches and swimmers are comfortable with the notion and terminology relating, for example, to a 2,000-meter set (e.g., 20 × 100 meters), a 6,000-meter session, or a 40-kilometer week.

High-level training involving planning for longer periods also necessitates the calculation of training volumes. For example, coaches can plan a two-week training camp (e.g., 160 kilometers in a 14-day camp), a complete preparation or training macrocycle (e.g., 500 kilometers for a 12-week cycle), or a full training year (e.g., 2,000 kilometers in 46 weeks). Although these calculations can be time consuming, they are

Table 9.2   Competition Race Analysis: Typical Results From a Men's 50-Meter Freestyle Race

	Swimmer A (1st)	Swimmer B (2nd)	Swimmer C (3rd)
First 25-m lap			
Start time 15 m (sec)	5.91	5.77	6.04
Stroke length (m)	2.14	2.14	1.88
Stroke frequency (strokes/m)	58.80	59.70	67.90
Velocity (m/sec)	2.34	2.34	2.33
Index (m × m/sec)	5.00	5.00	4.38
25-m split time (sec)	10.68	10.68	10.74
Second 25-m lap			
Stroke length (m)	2.14	2.09	1.81
Stroke frequency (strokes/m)	57.50	58.00	66.70
Velocity (m/sec)	2.08	2.02	2.03
Index (m × m/sec)	4.45	4.22	3.67
25-m split time (sec)	12.03	12.36	12.33
50-m lap time (sec)	22.71	23.04	23.07
Finish time (sec)	2.30	2.45	2.41
Results (sec)	22.71	23.04	23.07

very instructive during the planning and review processes.

A central issue in swimming relates to the relative potency (and paradoxically, the relative danger) of substantial increases in training volume and intensity. Although high-training volumes and periodic doses of high-intensity training are a fundamental part of training, the problems associated with excessive training are well known.

Coaching experience and the results of scientific research collectively suggest that excessive training volume and training intensity can induce fatigue, overtraining, injury, and illness. Distance swimmers generally require higher training volumes (approximately 20 to 25 percent higher) to develop the background necessary for success in events ranging from 400 to 1,500 meters.

Substantial increases in either training volume or intensity during early season to midseason place considerable physical demands and stress on the body. In the competitive phase, some swimmers exhibit fatigue and poor performance when required to race frequently over a short period.

Training Intensity

In contrast to training volume, training intensity is much more difficult to quantify. Coaches must employ a systematic approach for effective planning and monitoring of training intensity. The most common approach involves the use of a training classification system that gives rise to different training intensities.

In the past, most of these training systems have relied on relatively subjective descriptors of intensity, which gave rise to a wide range of terminology (e.g., moderate intensity aerobic, aerobic threshold, anaerobic threshold, lactate tolerance, onset of blood lactate accumulation, maximal alactic anaerobic, etc.) that is difficult to quantify and examine objectively (Counsilman and Counsilman 1993). To overcome this deficiency, various systems have been devised where different intensities of swimming are given a particular weighting or physiological stress coefficient. This process is based on blood lactate concentration, which is assumed to reflect the physiological demands of different exercise intensities.

The most important feature of these systems is that the degree of physiological stress experienced by the swimmer increases exponentially above the level of the anaerobic threshold. To account for this, greater weighting coefficients are given to the higher training intensity levels.

Table 9.3 shows a typical system where low- and moderate-intensity aerobic swimming have an intensity coefficient (IC) of 1, moderate intensity aerobic development an IC of 2, and anaerobic threshold training an IC of 3. Maximal oxygen uptake training is intensive and exhausting and consequently has an IC with the greater weighting of 5. Sprint training, which can be the most physiologically demanding, is given the highest IC of 8. Other training systems used in swimming employ a similar system of weighting coefficients (Mujika et al. 1996).

The total training load equals the number of kilometers swum at each training intensity multiplied by the appropriate training intensity coefficient. The resulting training load is reported in arbitrary units, but these are reproducible and comparable with repeated calculations.

Training Load, Monotony, and Strain

Training load cannot be fully described by training volume, training intensity, or a combination of the two. There are many subtleties in the prescription of training, and it is not just a simple process of preparing training sets with

Table 9.3 Training Weeks

In training week A, aerobic-based training was completed with a total training load of 98 units. Training week B had a total load of 103 units.

Zone	Intensity coefficient (IC)	Week A Volume (km)	Week A Load (IC × km)	Week B Volume (km)	Week B Load (IC × km)
A1	1	27	27	20	20
A2	1	15	15	5	5
A3	2	10	20	5	10
AT	3	5	15	8	24
MVO_2	5	1	5	4	20
SP	8	2	16	3	24
Training load		60 km	98 units	45 km	103 units

A1 = low-intensity aerobic swimming
A2 = moderate-intensity aerobic swimming
A3 = moderate-intensity aerobic development
AT = anaerobic threshold training
MVO_2 = maximal oxygen uptake training
SP = sprint training

differing volumes and intensities. Recent advancements in training (Foster 1998) have focused on additional descriptors of training stress, including training load (an average of the previous six weeks' training), training monotony (daily mean/standard deviation), and training strain (product of training load and training monotony). Inclusion of these training indices gives the coach up to five variables in the planning process: volume, intensity, load, monotony, and strain.

Training loads generally increase during a competitive preparation. Loads should be increased gradually and combined with sufficient rest and recovery. Short recovery periods of active or complete rest (24 to 48 hours) are unlikely to have a significant effect on long-term fitness.

Training monotony represents the degree of variation or fluctuation in training loads over time. Reducing training monotony is achieved by varying training volumes. For example, session volumes should range from 3.0 to 9.0 kilometers rather than repeating the same volume (e.g., 4.0 to 6.0 kilometers) session after session. Another strategy is to vary the pattern of the number of training sessions per day.

All three derived training indices (training load, monotony, and strain) can be plotted to show changes over time. Thresholds can be established for different swimmers, permitting the coach to tailor training programs to suit individual needs. Simple methods of monitoring the characteristics of training can help to minimize fatigue, injury, and illness.

Support Networks in Sport Science and Medicine

The national team programs of leading swimming nations are using a range of sport science and sports medicine personnel during training and competition. *Physiologists* administer a range of pool- and laboratory-based tests to monitor changes in fitness through a training season. They also assist the coach in planning and reviewing specific training sessions and programs. *Psychologists* work with individual coaches and athletes and contribute to overall team manage-

ment. *Physical and massage therapists* provide support in the areas of injury prevention, treatment and rehabilitation, and pre- and postrace massage during competition. *Dietitians* work with catering staff in the planning and scheduling of meals, conduct individual counseling and dietary reviews, and provide advice on nutritional supplements and ergogenic aids. *Biomechanists* conduct extensive filming of swimmer's skills and technique during training and provide full race analysis during major competition. The *team physician* coordinates medical care for team members involving medical screening and examination, treatment and management of illness and injury, and education, and also oversees compliance to drugs-in-sport regulations.

The increasing involvement of sports science and sports medicine support has been a feature of international swimming through the 1990s. Although experimental research in swimming is conducted in many countries, direct and extensive involvement of scientific staff with national team programs has been limited to a few of the leading swimming nations. Political and societal changes have seen a decline in the domination of swimming by two or three nations, and the emergence of many smaller and former middle-ranking nations from all parts of the world. In a fashion similar to the international coaching community, swimming scientists from many of the different countries engage in dialogue with their colleagues to share information and experiences.

Physiological Testing at the Australian Institute of Sport

The Australian Institute of Sport (AIS) is one of the major centers for swimming in Australia and provides approximately one-third of the swimmers for the Australian swimming team. Testing of swimmers at the AIS has evolved over 20 years on the basis of practical experience, empirical evidence, and applied research.

The AIS uses several testing protocols to assess various components of fitness in international-level swimmers. For reasons of specificity and practicality, their tests are usually done in the pool. Physiological testing is done throughout the year but is concentrated primarily during the preparation for the major championships in each calendar year. In normal circumstances, there are two competitive cycles each year for international-level Australian swimmers. Training through the Australian summer (November to March) prepares swimmers for the national championships held in March or April each year. The winter season (May to August) prepares swimmers for the major international swimming championships usually conducted in July and August (summer in the Northern Hemisphere). The testing dates are made in conjunction with the coaching staff and follow the competition schedule and training program.

Testing at the AIS has focused on three areas: pool-based assessment of aerobic and anaerobic fitness, measurement of body composition, and routine blood and saliva testing (Pyne 1999b). The 7 × 200-meter step test (Pyne, Maw, and Goldsmith 2000) is useful in monitoring changes in discrete aspects of endurance fitness during a season (figure 9.3).

Physiological details obtained during submaximal and maximal testing provide critical information for the coach to determine training loads and monitor performance improvements with training (Pyne, Maw, and Goldsmith 2000). Routine blood lactate and heart rate testing is conducted on demand to assess the responses to various training sets, particularly in the final few weeks of a preparation. Body composition measures include standing height, body mass, and sum of skinfolds, and a derived body mass to sum of skinfolds ratio (figure 9.4).

Blood testing is done during medical screening and to assess the impact of training and dietary interventions. Saliva testing is used to assess a swimmer's risk of upper respiratory illness during training (Gleeson et al. 1999).

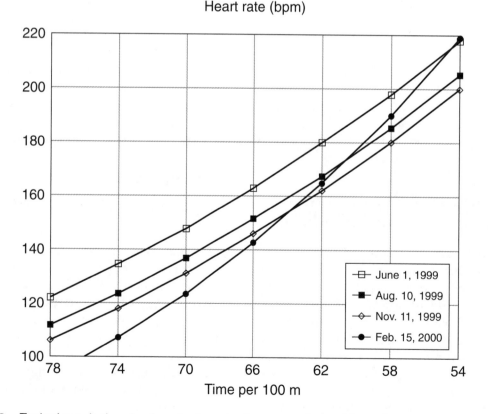

Figure 9.3 Typical result showing heart rate-velocity curves derived from the 7 × 200-meter step test.

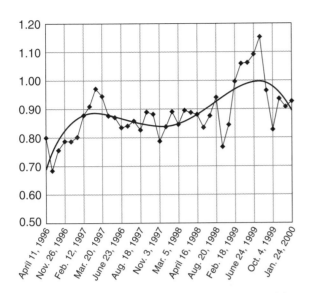

Figure 9.4 Coefficient of body composition (calculated as the ratio of body mass in kilograms/sum of skinfolds in millimeters) in a male swimmer over a four-year period. The trend line is a fitted polynomial curve showing the long-term trends in body composition.

Physiological Research in International Swimming

International physiological research regarding swimming focuses on many areas, but two of the most important are metabolism and overtraining and fatigue.

Metabolism

One of the enduring lines of research in swimming is determining the metabolic requirements of different swimming events and how this information can be used in training (Lavoie and Montpetit 1986). Metabolic measurements of oxygen uptake often prove difficult in swimming. The mouthpiece and ventilation mask worn by the swimmer can be uncomfortable and may affect the ability of the athlete to perform optimally and with maximal efficiency.

Several research groups in Europe and North America have conducted extensive research into the metabolism of highly trained swimmers (Lavoie and Montpetit 1986; Troup 1999). Estimates of aerobic capacity (maximal oxygen uptake or $\dot{V}O_2$max) and anaerobic capacity (maximal accumulated oxygen deficit or

MAOD) can be made. The results of testing generally show that elite swimmers have larger anaerobic and aerobic capacities than moderately trained swimmers.

A recent study of the energetics of swimming confirms the long-held belief that at competition speeds, freestyle is the most economic stroke, with the technical limitations of breaststroke and butterfly increasing the energy cost of those strokes (Capelli, Pendergast, and Termin 1998).

Overtraining and Fatigue

A prolonged state of fatigue that does not recede with rest and recovery can lead to overtraining, which is typically characterized by poor training and racing. A distinction needs to be made between overreaching and overtraining (Keast and Morton 1992).

Overreaching refers to the normal daily fatigue that is a fundamental part of high-level swimming training. Swimmers should be encouraged to see fatigue as a feature of training to be respected and not necessarily feared. *Overtraining* refers to poor training and racing over an extended period of time that doesn't, at least initially, respond to rest and recovery. Careful management of training loads and sufficient rest and recovery maximize the benefits obtained from training and minimize the risk of overtraining.

Indicators of overreaching and overtraining include poor performance, recurrent illness, injury, elevated heart rate, muscle soreness during recovery, acute localized fatigue during exercise, faster onset of fatigue, and higher ratings of perceived exertion (Rowbottom, Keast, and Morton 1998).

Physiological parameters that have been studied as possible markers of overtraining include resting and postexercise heart rate and blood pressure; resting and exercise oxygen consumption; and blood levels of proteins, enzymes, and hormones. Despite a large amount of research, the results of these tests have proved inconsistent. Self-reported ratings of well-being may provide a better means of monitoring overtraining and recovery in highly trained swimmers (Hooper et al. 1995). The system requires swimmers to record subjective ratings of quality of sleep, fatigue, stress, and muscle soreness on a scale of 1 to 7, from very, very low, or good (point 1) to very, very high, or bad (point 7).

Fatigue and recovery occur more quickly in simple tasks such as swimming. Drills and activities with higher skill levels tend to cause fatigue more slowly. The nature of the recovery activity influences its effectiveness, and this is best illustrated by the widespread practice of active recovery (low- to moderate-intensity swimming) during training sessions and after racing.

Other recovery strategies include rest; the use of flotation devices and equipment, such as the pull buoy and kickboard; fluid replacement and dietary considerations; remedial massage; and alternating hot and cold water treatments using a spa, shower, or bath. Training volume and intensity should be managed carefully.

Altitude Training

Should coaches use altitude training to prepare their swimmers for competition? Swimmers from many nations have trained at altitude (1,300 to 2,500 meters) for varying lengths of time to prepare for competition at altitude or, more commonly, to accelerate the normal rate of physiological adaptation that occurs at sea level.

Despite its relative popularity, the scientific community is still largely divided on whether significant physiological and performance benefits are obtained (Stray-Gundersen and Levine 1999). However, a number of coaches and swimmers report substantial improvements in performance after altitude training and continue to use this form of preparation.

High-altitude exposure imposes significant physiological stress on the human body, and care needs to be exercised when training at race pace. Much of the knowledge of altitude training was accumulated during the 1970s and 1980s after the Mexico City Olympic Games in 1968. Many of the leading swimming nations (including the United States, China, Germany, Australia, Great Britain, Italy, Canada, France, and Japan) have some swimmers using altitude training.

A typical 21-day altitude training program is normally divided into three phases: an initial acclimatization phase (days 1 through 3), the main training phases (days 4 through 18), and a final recovery phase (days 19 through 21). The main training phase can consist of up to four microcycles, each three to four days in duration (figure 9.5). Within each day, swimmers can train up to three times in the pool with supplementary dry-land training.

Training volumes can reach 16 kilometers per day, with a total of 140 to 210 kilometers over a three-week camp for sprint and distance swimmers. Training of this type elicited modest but significant improvements in Australian national team swimmers in their 200-meter maximal swimming time at altitude and on return to sea level (Pyne 1998).

The timing of competition after altitude training is widely debated. On return to sea level, most swimmers would compete within 10 to 28 days after altitude. Experienced coaches have a preferred altitude-competition schedule, although these are generally based on opinion rather than objective experimental data. Considerable individual variation exists among athletes in their response to altitude training; this is partly related to the adequacy of iron stores (Chapman, Stray-Gundersen, and Levine 1998).

Illness and Immunity in Swimmers

Many swimmers and coaches have expressed concern that high-level training leads to increased risk of illness and infection. Despite the interest in the area and many experimental studies, it remains unclear if the immune system and overall health are significantly compromised by high-level training.

Critical assessment of the relevant studies shows that the incidence of illness is only likely to be increased in two specific groups of athletes. Swimmers undertaking longer competitive events (distance and open-water swimmers) or those suffering from the consequences of excessive training volume and intensity coupled with inadequate recovery may be at risk (Pyne and Gleeson 1998).

	1	2	3	4	5	6	7	8	9	10	11	12	13	14	15	16	17	18	19	20	21
Day	Mon.	Tue.	Wed.	Thu.	Fri.	Sat.	Sun.	Mon.	Tue.	Wed.	Thu.	Fri.	Sat.	Sun.	Mon.	Tue.	Wed.	Thu.	Fri.	Sat.	Sun.
	Initial				Training I			Training II				Training III			Training IV				Final		
	Microcycle 1				Microcycle 2			Microcycle 3				Microcycle 4			Microcycle 5				Microcycle 6		
Sessions	2	2	2		3	3	2	3	3	2		3	3	2	3	3	2		2	2	2
A.M. Volume	3.0	Off	4.0		5.0	4.0	5.0	5.0	5.0	5.0		5.0	5.0	5.0	5.0	5.0	5.0		5.0	Off	Off
Noon Volume	Off	4.0	Off		5.0	5.0	5.0	6.0	7.0	6.0		6.0	7.0	6.0	5.0	5.0	4.0		Off	5.0	4.0
P.M. Volume	4.0	5.0	5.0		3.0	3.0	Off	3.0	3.0	Off		3.0	3.0	Off	3.0	3.0	Off		4.0	4.0	3.0
Total	7.0	9.0	9.0		13.0	12.0	10.0	14.0	15.0	11.0		14.0	15.0	11.0	13.0	13.0	9.0		9.0	9.0	7.0
	Microcycle 1	25.0			Microcycle 2	35.0		Microcycle 3	40.0			Microcycle 4	40.0		Microcycle 5	35.0			Microcycle 6	25.0	
Total (km)	25.0				60.0			100.0				140.0			175.0				200.0		

Figure 9.5 Schematic diagram showing the structure of a typical 21-day altitude training program undertaken by international-level swimmers. The program is divided into six 3-day microcycles, with three complete rest days. The total volume is 200 kilometers.

A recent study in Australia showed that highly trained swimmers have no more illness than sedentary or moderately trained age- and sex-matched individuals (table 9.4). The swimmers had an average of 2.9 upper respiratory tract illnesses (e.g., common cold), which compared favorably with the general population mean of 3.0 illnesses per year (Fricker et al. 2000).

Management of swimmers with a history of illness is based on maintaining a healthy immune system and minimizing exposure to infected individuals (Pyne et al. 2000). The immune system is influenced by a wide range of physical, environmental, psychological, and behavioral factors that collectively form the basis of the recommended intervention strategies (Pyne et al. 2000). Reducing the risk of illness requires the cooperation of athletes, coaches, and team staff (table 9.5). Swimmers suffering respiratory illness during the final few weeks before competition are likely to experience a decrement in performance (Pyne et al. 2001).

Coaches are responsible for training loads, which directly influence immune function. Moderate-intensity training can boost immunity, but high-intensity training can cause temporary suppression of immunity in some swimmers. Team management members are responsible for the provision of suitable accommodation, transportation, and training facilities. Medical staff are responsible for screening team members and providing medical care and medication to treat illness. Most important, the behavioral and self-management skills of swimmers play a significant role in reducing the risk of illness. Swimmers should be educated and reminded of the importance of hygiene, adequate sleep, diet, and other lifestyle factors.

Table 9.4 Incidence of Upper Respiratory and Gastrointestinal Illness in 97 Swimming Scholarship Holders at the Australian Institute of Sport (1988–1998)

Group	Average age (range)	% URI/year (range)	% of four or more URI/year	% GITI/year (range)
Male (n = 56)	19 (16–25)	2.5 (0–8)	15	0.4 (0–2)
Female (n = 41)	17 (14–33)	3.1 (0–10)	22	0.7 (0–3)

URI = upper respiratory illness
GITI = gastrointestinal tract illness

Table 9.5 Strategies to Limit the Risk of Illness in Highly Trained Swimmers

Strategy	Recommendations
Training	Carefully manage training volume and intensity, and make provision for adequate rest and recovery periods.
Environmental	Limit initial exposure when training or competing in adverse environmental conditions (heat, humidity, altitude, air pollution, etc.).
Psychological	Teach swimmers self-management and coping skills. Monitor swimmers' responses to individual and team stresses of high-level training and competition.
Behavioral	Adopt a well-balanced diet with adequate intake of macro- and micronutrients. Limit transmission of contagious illnesses by reducing exposure to common infections, airborne pathogens, and physical contact with infected individuals.
Clinical	Liaise with team or family doctor. Organize medical screening prior to travel or major competition. Check immunization and vaccination schedules.

Practical Guidelines and Recommendations

Application of training principles, experience, and the results of scientific investigation give rise to several practical suggestions to maximize the benefits from training (Pyne 1999a). Quality of training should be emphasized over sheer effort. While the need for swimmers to tough out their workouts cannot be discounted, it's preferable for swimmers to reach desired speeds.

One-pace training should be limited. Swimmers should be encouraged to become proficient through a full range of swimming speeds. Sprint swimmers should develop speed on a foundation of endurance fitness; middle-distance swimmers need to blend speed and endurance; distance swimmers should focus on developing the various aspects of endurance fitness. Muscular strength and endurance are important for all events and should be developed in both pool and dry-land training. Fitness should be maintained throughout the year rather than relying on a big preparation for major competitions.

Individual variability in recovery potential, exercise capacity, and tolerance to stress explains the range of vulnerability among swimmers under similar training regimes. Part of the reason for these differences is that most swimmers are able to train with very high loads, provided the program includes strategies devised to control the overall strain and stress. Swimmers should be encouraged to undertake intensive training programs in the knowledge that variations in performance and fatigue are to be expected and are not necessarily problems to overcome.

In accordance with these concepts, it is recommended that a swimmer should:

- start training with a program of low to moderate volume and intensity;
- employ a gradual periodized increase in training volumes and loads;
- use a variety of training volumes and intensities to avoid monotony and stress;
- avoid excessive mileage that could lead to exhaustion, illness, or injury;
- include some nonspecific cross training to offset staleness; and
- include sufficient rest and recovery.

Science and Swimming: Future Directions

Research in the sport and exercise sciences expands at an ever-increasing rate. In the period from 1950 to the early 1970s, the focus of most scientific work was primarily at the organ and whole-body level. Many studies showed the importance of cardiorespiratory fitness, body size, flexibility, muscle strength, and power, illustrating how these attributes could be improved through athletic training.

In the 1980s and 1990s, advancements in medical instrumentation and technology shifted focus to examining the effects of exercise and training at the cellular level (Baldwin 2000). This period saw a great deal of interest in using emerging medical technologies to study muscle and blood. This situation persists today, where highly trained swimmers are routinely tested for parameters such as heart rate and blood lactate.

The next few decades of the 21st century will see application of molecular biology tools in sports science research (Baldwin 2000). The new molecular tools center on gene cloning and sequencing technology and molecular probing to identify different cells and cellular structures.

At present, most attention is directed toward solving the medical complexities of heart disease, diabetes, obesity, aging, and cancer. Future work in the exercise and sport sciences will target such issues as identification of genetically gifted athletes, optimization of training programs, enhanced injury treatment, and improved detection of fatigue.

Advancements in the different scientific disciplines will continue to shape the evolution of swim training and performance. Ultimately, improvements will come from a deeper understanding of the primary factors contributing to swim performance. Scientists will continue to work with coaches and swimmers in their quest to improve training and competition performance.

Chapter 10

Development of a Training Program

Planning a successful season training program entails more than designing a series of workouts that bring a team to peak form at the championship season. A systematic approach should consider all the other factors that may influence performance.

These factors include the type of meets in which the team intends to compete, the particular league or conference and the specific events for which the swimmers need to prepare, the dates of major competitions, the amount of pool time available for training, and the training background of each swimmer on the team. To provide motivation for purposeful effort throughout the season, team as well as individual goals should be established soon after the team has gathered to begin training.

In this chapter, we examine the methods of developing an effective training program based on each swimmer's characteristics. Each training method produces specific effects so the coach must know which training format will provide the best results for each swimmer. For example, a swimmer in a college program will need to balance training with academic responsibilities. Therefore, the most effective training method that produces maximum

results within the confines of the athlete's schedule should be used.

The Individual Swimmer

Because there is no average person, you cannot uniformly apply a single method. What is good for one may not be good for another. Albert Einstein, just before he died, said that one of the few things that he felt sure about was that the individual is unique. And the individual changes with time—no person is the same person today as last year. We cannot successfully train swimmers with canned, cut-and-dried, overstandardized methods. A swimmer's development, or any human development for that matter, can never be an assembly-line or stamping-machine process.

The coach should know the training history of every swimmer. This knowledge lets the coach carefully plan workloads in accordance with each swimmer's capacity. To set a training program that is beyond a swimmer's ability invites failure, but a program that is too easy does not offer a realistic challenge.

Swimmers react differently to the same training workload, and they have different potentials for improvement. Genetic factors set limitations, physiological and psychological, on one's level of achievement. It also appears that not too much can be done to change temperament. A coach may encounter a wide range of temperaments among swimmers on a team, from unstable neuroticism to the spontaneous cheerfulness that is so often characteristic of the physiologically robust.

A coach can usually expect different responses from athletes at various levels of maturity, especially in their reactions to stress and their abilities to handle the training workload. The coach should recognize and respect these differences and avoid treating younger athletes as miniature adults.

The importance of good nutrition as a major factor in performance should not be overlooked. And for athletes to maintain improvement within a regimen of hard training, adequate rest is a prime essential. Many athletes, trying to keep pace in modern urban society, tend to neglect the importance of rest, at night and between twice-daily workouts. Quality rest allows for regeneration of the body and adaptation to stress. In fact, rest can be regarded as unseen training.

A coach should observe each swimmer's reactions to training, particularly during the most demanding phase of the season, to plan workouts compatible with the individual's ability to tolerate stress. The coach should assess the accumulative stress placed on the swimmer and use this knowledge to plan the tapering period as carefully as possible.

Individual Capacity for Training

It is not understood what makes a great athlete different from a mediocre one of similar physique; skill, economy of movement, and tenacity must all play a part. It is difficult enough to find out how any muscle works—subtle differences among individuals are still beyond our means. It is thus a mistake for swimmers to slavishly copy the training methods of champions. Many years of conditioning are necessary before a swimmer can hope to emulate their workloads.

The coach should understand the athlete's present state of training; the fitter the athlete, the less improvement that can be expected. Effective coaching requires that the training overload be applied carefully until the coach knows how an athlete reacts to stress. Another reason coaches should study and understand individual reactions is that athletes differ in their reactions to stress and to training formats.

The constitutional limitations of the individual constrain the rate of improvement and the amount of training that can be absorbed. A coach who knows the maximal capacity of an athlete can carefully plan the intensity and duration of the training effort. If the athlete does not appear to be adapting to the training workload after about two weeks, the coach should reassess the type of stress placed on the athlete. Although physiological monitoring—particularly blood lactate measurement—may indicate a swimmer's reaction to training, most teams lack ready access to facilities for it. Counsilman's three basic tests for assessing a swimmer's progress are easily applied, however, and provide an effective measure, especially in that the results can be readily compared with a swimmer's previous workouts using the same repeat sets (Counsilman 1968). Counsilman's three tests are the average time for a set of repeat swims; the pulse rate after exercise; and the swimmer's stroke rate counted on the last length of every second, third, or fourth repeat swim.

The Individual Swimmer in the Team Setting

Should practices be scheduled for the team or for its individual members? This simple question may elicit further questions that touch on the training policies of different teams and on important aspects of the philosophy of swimming. Non-state controlled programs have tended to skirt this important issue. The large size of many teams, often an economic necessity, and the consequent wide range of individual ability often present a formidable challenge to the coaching staff.

It is important to remember that competitive swimming is ultimately an individual sport. Particularly at the higher levels of competition where really talented athletes are involved, it has become absolutely necessary to know a great deal about the individual athlete to fully develop that person's potential. We need to know more about each swimmer and to schedule training along individual lines, yet this does not happen in most teams. Although many coaches think this is their approach, close scrutiny often reveals it is not.

In fact, most schedules take form either around the requirements of a few champion athletes or, at the other extreme, where a team has no outstanding swimmers, around the average needs of the group, which is at best a shotgun method.

During the development of the novice competitor, the shotgun method may produce improvement for a while. But regardless of a swimmer's level of maturity, it will not produce the best possible results; rather, it creates swimmers cast in the same mold with little regard for their individuality.

In this type of program, it is common to hear much about the success of a few outstanding swimmers but little about those who fail. The

pity is that youngsters seldom learn to enjoy and fully appreciate the subtle challenges of the sport. Many young swimmers do not flourish as they should because they are in a program with little if any instruction in stroke techniques or the whys and wherefores of training, paces, strategies, and so on.

The first pitfall for a coach is thus the standardized workout in which an entire group is subjected to the same schedule. The standardization of workouts has become traditional in many teams at all levels, from local to international. The coach walks on deck and writes the workout on the board for the whole team. Nevertheless, the idea that what is good for the champions is good for everyone is not necessarily true.

Training Formats

Although the formats of most top-level training programs often have a distinct similarity, differences in planning arise from the specific requirements of each team. Other modifications may occur as a coach tries out new ideas.

Many considerations affect the design of a training program. For example, when coaching college athletes an effort must be made to help them effectively balance their available time between academic obligations and the demands of training. Older athletes have no time to waste on training items of doubtful value. It is especially important that each of their workouts be as specific as possible with no extraneous items.

A well-planned conditioning program should enable a swimmer gradually to improve the physiological qualities necessary to produce peak performances in the season's major meets. Effective training consists of cycles of varied activity, each aimed at a specific purpose.

Weight Training

Weight training is done for a half hour every day for the first 8 to 12 weeks of the season. Later in the season the frequency is reduced to three days a week. Some type of weight training should continue to within 14 days of the national championships or whatever major meet the team may enter. It is important that strength work continue as late as possible into the season to retain strength gains.

Stretching exercises to keep the joints flexible should always be an integral part of any weight-training program. Nort Thornton (1979), one of the pioneers of weight training for swimming when coaching world-record breaker Steve Clarke in 1961, stresses that strength training and flexibility work should always be done together and that it is a big mistake to do one without the other.

Swimmers on Thornton's team at the University of California at Berkeley lift very heavy weights three days per week, on Monday, Wednesday, and Friday. The other days—Tuesday, Thursday, and Saturday—are devoted to work done on the biokinetic swim bench and geared toward developing speed and strength.

Ron Johnson (1978), another expert conditioner of swimmers and a renowned master swimmer, also insists that deck training must include exercises for the development of strength, endurance, and flexibility. He says that though not all teams can afford expensive and often elaborately equipped exercise machines, it is possible to do effective strength training with free weights. Johnson maintains that most strength programs for swimming do not provide enough sets or repetitions, and he points out that emphasis should be changed from one muscle group to another after a particular muscle group has been broken down through strenuous exercise.

Not all leading coaches have used weight training to the same extent, however. For example, Jochums (1982) expresses the view that weight training provides only psychological benefits and uses it with his sprint swimmers, who look at their arms in a mirror and believe they have become stronger and thus will swim faster.

Jochums believes weight training transfers only a very slight gain to swimming but probably enough to make a difference. He adds that women swimmers may need weight training, but his personal preference is for swimmers to do pulling drills with their feet immobilized in a tube or to use paddles and the pull buoy. He says that these methods are a form of resistance training and as such fit his definition of weight training.

The Biokinetic Swim Bench

Counsilman (1979) refers to biokinetics as the ultimate exercise, in that it permits a swimmer to accelerate the simulated swimming stroke while recruiting muscle fibers in the same sequence as actual swimming. The biokinetic machine is said to be the only exercise machine capable of measuring work done in terms of force, time, and distance.

Counsilman reports that swimmers at Indiana University were tested once a week to assess the total amount of work that they could create in 10 seconds, 30 seconds, and 90 seconds. He found that sprinters had the best scores for work done in 10 and 30 seconds, and the middle-distance swimmers performed best over 90 seconds. When tested over five-minute periods, the distance swimmers had the best results.

Efficient Stroke Mechanics

Much emphasis should be given to establishing efficient stroke mechanics in the early season. (See also chapters 3 and 6.) Neglecting stroke technique partially defeats the purpose of training. A foundation of effective technique should be laid during the early season. It is good policy to include practices aimed at improving a swimmer's ability to feel and control the flow of the water. This should be done during warm-up and throughout the workout.

Emphasis should be placed on taking fewer strokes per length of the pool at a given speed. In other words, keep the speed constant and reduce the number of strokes per length. As the season progresses, speed should increase while the number of strokes either remains the same or is reduced. Ability to reduce stroke frequency while increasing speed is a reliable indication of a swimmer's improving fitness and efficiency.

The Two Main Aspects of Training

Most descriptions of training routines refer to differences between duration and intensity of exercise. Nort Thornton, one of America's most consistently successful coaches over a 30-year period, brought these two terms into a more practical focus by referring to them as *base training* and *sharpening training*, adding that a correct combination of the two gives a swimmer an overall capacity to swim a race in the most effective way (Thornton 1987).

Thornton describes base training as the inner basic strength of the athlete that results from years of training and produces a performance without specific muscle adaptation for that event. Such a base is usually best built through long, slow-distance training at a pace well within one's capacity for a long period of time.

For sharpening work, Thornton recommended training techniques that produce efficient muscular coordination for a chosen event. He believed that pace work, such as broken swims or ideal pace rehearsal swims, condition the reflexes for peak efficiency at speed. Sharpening work is basically muscular and neurological in nature, whereas base training conditions primarily the circulatory system.

Thornton also said that a swimmer's future capacity to perform well in a given race depends on ideal proportions of base work and sharpening. Too many swimmers were constantly sharpening and devoting little time to developing the essential base conditioning. It was important that enough time be devoted to building the ideal base of aerobic endurance necessary for world-class performance.

Thornton added that any good engineer could gauge the approximate height and size of a new building by looking at the size (depth and width) of the new foundation. A skyscraper cannot be built without a large enough foundation; nor can you expect to achieve world-class performance without an adequate base.

Thornton pointed out that although base training and sharpening training are necessary for best results, they are in many ways opposite from each other. His experience was that the two types of training could not be combined for optimal results over a long period of time because improvement in base conditioning requires a large reserve of adaptation energy. (Adaptation energy permits the body to respond favorably to increased stress overload.) This reserve is quickly depleted by the fast swimming needed for sharpening work. Base training is like money in the bank, but sharpening, when done properly, is like taking out the accumulated interest. When done improperly, sharpening is like draining one's financial reserves. Thornton outlines the following characteristics of base training and sharpening training.

The swimmer's base conditioning can be measured by the performance he or she can produce without specific muscular adaptation for an event. This is best achieved through long, controlled swimming. The base has the following features:

- It can be improved continuously, even over many years.
- It can only be developed at a slow rate— in fact, much more slowly than the observed improvement from sharpening training.
- Its effects are long lasting and not easily destroyed. Swimmers who have taken the time to build a good base often observe that competitive performance remains essentially the same even after a considerable reduction in training.
- The slow pace used in its development and the requirement of freshness reduce the likelihood of injury or illness.

Sharpening adds muscular and neuromuscular efficiency to the circulatory efficiency gained from the swimmer's base training. Sharpening training involves numerous repetitions of a short distance at a racing pace or faster. The essential features of sharpening are as follows:

- Its effects are short-lived and at times appear volatile. The high performance level that results rarely lasts longer than three months.

- When done properly, astonishing improvement can be observed within just six weeks.

- Special care is necessary when attempting this type of conditioning, for if not done properly it can result in performances inferior to the athlete's base.

- The faster pace of this training more easily provokes injury and illness, which thus must be consciously avoided.

- Sharpening training can drive the athlete into a slump if continued too long. It must be terminated after about three months or when symptoms of energy depletion are first noticed.

In his classic presentation, Thornton (1987) outlines three hypothetical case histories in which swimmer A, swimmer B, and swimmer C use different combinations of base training and sharpening training while training for the same event.

Swimmer A trained only at race pace or faster using successive short-distance repetitions. Swimmer A's performances, which were erratic and sometimes totally unpredictable, showed little basic improvement from the freshman through senior year.

Swimmer B wisely used a combination of various forms of interval training throughout the year but did not swim as hard or as fast while training as swimmer A did. Swimmer B did not swim to depletion and maintained a wise balance of stress and recovery. Swimmer B also did not experience the extreme slumps swimmer A did. Swimmer B's base level improved significantly over four years and, when combined with sharpening, resulted in greatly improved performance in the senior year.

Swimmer C used the type of training that produces optimal results over many years because it most dramatically improves the base level of the swimmer. Swimmer C did sharpening training only before the most important races. The rest of the year, swimmer C trained at a slower pace to improve the base level. Although swimmer C spent much of the year training at base level, this swimmer performed better in the senior year than swimmer A or swimmer B because swimmer C's base level

was higher than either of the other two. When sharpening was added, optimal performance was attained.

Thornton summarizes his three hypothetical case histories by saying that the swimmer who conditioned first with long, slow-distance training is like a builder who lays a strong and deep foundation for a skyscraper. Swimmer A, who began with speed work, is like a builder who lays a weak foundation to get the first few stories of the structure up quickly. Swimmer A showed the fastest initial improvement. However, just as the weak foundation severely limits the height to which the builder can build, so too inadequate conditioning limits the hasty swimmer's future performances. Swimmer B, who combines base training and sharpening training throughout the year, eventually builds to greatly improved performance in the senior year. However, swimmer C, who did sharpening training only before the most important races, was more successful than swimmer A and swimmer B. Swimmer C started slowly and eventually surpassed the others because this swimmer's larger foundation provided the base from which higher and higher performances could be launched.

The Good and Bad Effects of Three Types of Training

No one form of training suits every situation. Knowing the pros and cons of each regimen helps coaches maximize the training effect.

Long, slow-distance training involves long swims at a steady pace, well within the capacity of the swimmer yet still requiring a real swimming effort (such as 1:00 to 1:15 per 100 yards). Usually, the swimmer stops long before becoming exhausted. Long, slow-distance training conditions the cardiovascular system, helps develop robust health, helps prevent injuries, produces continuous improvement (although at a very slow rate), develops a swimmer's base level, and has a desharpening effect, thus permitting the swimmer to conserve adaptation energy. Unfortunately, long, slow-distance training also has little effect on muscle strength and thus does not prepare a swimmer for fast racing, does not develop efficiency and coordination for swimming at race pace, and has a desharpening effect, resulting in slower racing times during midseason.

Distances covered in *race pace training* should be about three-fourths of the racing distance. This is perhaps the most taxing of all training techniques. Race pace training develops a keen sense of race pace and teaches the swimmer to relax at actual racing pace and to master efficiency of movement. On the bad side, it also is very taxing to the swimmer, will quickly break the swimmer down if done frequently, and increases the likelihood of illness and injury by producing greater fatigue than usual.

Interval speed training, also known as repetition training (see chapter 7), refers to frequent repetitions of a short distance at a speed faster than race pace. Interval speed training teaches the swimmer to relax when swimming at speed, helps the swimmer to learn efficient coordination when swimming at speed, develops muscle strength, has a fast sharpening effect, and often results in astonishingly rapid improvement. Two bad effects of interval speed training are that it robs the swimmer of adaptation energy and thus, if continued, could cause illness, injury, or poor performances, and that it places a great strain on the tendons because of its fast pace and can easily result in injury. It can draw a swimmer into a slump quickly if done improperly. Thus, great care must be exercised to see that interval speed training is effectively performed, as it can improve a swimmer who uses it well (Thornton 1987, p. 11).

The Energy Continuum

ATP (adenosine triphosphate) is a nucleotide compound found in all cells but chiefly in striated muscle. It is the energy source of the muscles and is supplied to them in three ways. In two of these ways, oxygen is not a prerequisite in producing ATP; these two methods are called *anaerobic*, meaning "without oxygen." In the third method, oxygen is a prime ingredient in manufacturing ATP; this method is called *aerobic*, meaning "with oxygen."

The body's three chemical systems for producing ATP are the ATP-CP system (anaerobic); the lactic acid, or LA, system (anaerobic);

and the oxygen system (aerobic). The duration of a swimming event determines which of these three methods comes into effect during the activity. Most swimming events engage at least two of the energy systems. Swimming events of approximately one minute involve all three systems. No matter what the duration, one system usually dominates the other systems during any one event. Thus, if the energy system predominant in an event is improved through specific training, the swimmer's performance in that event will also improve.

Let's first look at the ATP-CP system. Creatine phosphate (CP) and ATP are stored in the muscles in relatively small quantities. Energy can be supplied by this system for a short time only, for example, a 25-yard sprint. If all-out effort is continued for longer than approximately 10 seconds, energy is drawn increasingly from the LA system.

After ATP-CP has been depleted, the production of ATP depends on energy in the form of sugar (glucose) stored in the muscles. The focus shifts to the lactic acid (LA) system. When the supply of oxygen is inadequate, glucose is broken down to lactic acid, allowing ATP to be produced. The accumulation of lactic acid and oxygen debt become limiting factors to performance and are associated with painful fatigue. All-out swimming for periods of one to three minutes draws energy primarily from the LA system.

ATP is manufactured most efficiently and abundantly in the presence of oxygen (aerobic). Lactic acid and glycogen are resynthesized by the supply of oxygen. The aerobic system dominates in work over two minutes long.

Chemical Changes in Muscle

The primary chemical change in a contracting muscle is the oxidation (burning) of the carbon and hydrogen in the carbohydrate glycogen and the production of carbon dioxide and water as in any other engine. In the case of a muscle, however, energy is stored in advance of combustion in a readily available form, just as an automobile battery is charged so that electricity is immediately available for starting.

The substance stored in the muscle is adenosine triphosphate. Through its two molecules of high-energy phosphate, ATP liberates much more energy when split up than any other phosphate. Applying ATP to threads of actomyosin (the sliding filaments in muscle fiber) causes them to contract. ATP is made fairly rapidly from ADP (adenosine diphosphate) and from creatine phosphate, both of which have high-energy phosphorus.

Storing energy as organic compounds of phosphorus enables a muscle to continue contracting in the absence of oxygen for a long time—indeed, until all its creatine phosphate has been converted into creatine. It cannot, however, recover without oxygen, for this is necessary to recharge creatine and adenosine with high-energy phosphate. The muscle may therefore accumulate considerable oxygen debt. Although a swimmer may take in a large amount of oxygen during a race, it may not be nearly enough to recharge the chemical system. The swimmer must pay off the oxygen debt by taking in a large amount of oxygen after the race is over, which is often indicated by continued breathlessness, for example, after a 100-meter swim.

Anaerobic Metabolism

When the oxygen supply is insufficient to provide all the needed energy from aerobic metabolism, the balance of the energy requirement is derived from anaerobic metabolism. Contracting muscles produce lactic acid when their supply of oxygen is inadequate to meet energy requirements. Pyruvic acid is formed by glycolysis and converted to lactic acid. This action regenerates one of the factors (NAD+) required to maintain glycolysis. The rise in the concentration of lactic acid in the blood indicates the amount of anaerobic metabolism involved.

The disadvantages of anaerobic metabolism are the low yield of ATP (two molecules per molecule of glucose utilized) and the formation of lactic acid. A further disadvantage under some conditions is that only carbohydrate can be used in anaerobic metabolism. In spite of these drawbacks, anaerobic metabolism is indispensable in two circumstances. First, it is an immediate source of energy at the beginning of

exercise, before oxygen supply has been increased by circulatory and respiratory adjustments. Second, it is used during exercise intensity in which all the energy cannot be supplied by aerobic metabolism.

During oxygen deficiency, the body makes a little high-energy phosphate as a result of the anaerobic breakdown of carbohydrate to lactic acid, which accumulates in the blood as lactate. This waste of combustible lactate is uneconomical, but it makes the body more capable of withstanding a physical emergency. Figure 10.1 diagrams the chemical changes that take place.

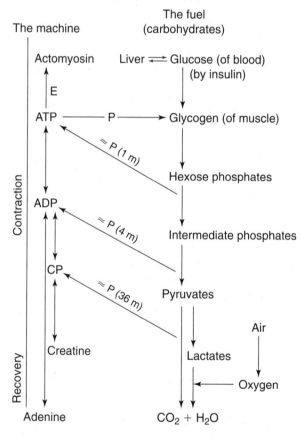

Figure 10.1   The chemistry of muscle contraction.

The Lactate/Ventilatory Threshold

The more arduous the exercise, the more lactic acid accumulates in the muscle cells and diffuses into the bloodstream. Performance declines once the amount of blood lactate reaches a certain level.

By measuring heart rate and blood lactate we can assess a swimmer's response to different workloads. Pyne and Telford (1989), who did continuing research work on the pool deck for eight years with Australia's leading international swimmers, confirmed that although lactate measurements have contributed to a better understanding of the physiology of swimming training, coaches without access to lactate testing find that simply measuring heart rate provides very useful information in training classifications.

The exercise rate at which an athlete's blood lactate level, although elevated, will not continue to rise is known as the lactate/ventilatory, or anaerobic, threshold. The average value is 3.5 to 4.0 millimoles per liter and up for all swimming distances, although Pyne and Telford mention that this threshold can vary from 3 to 6 millimoles in well-conditioned, middle-distance swimmers.

Some physiologists maintain that 80 to 90 percent of training should be done at this level. Improved speed over longer distance results from being able to swim faster while retaining a lactate level equal to or lower than that previously produced at lower speeds. Years ago, I coined a saying in this connection: "The anaerobic work of today is the aerobic work of tomorrow." A good example of this is that there was a time when beating 60 seconds for the 100-meter crawl was considered a notable feat for a male swimmer and also was one that put him into severe anaerobic distress. Top swimmers now regularly average well under 60 seconds for each 100 meters over 400 meters, and swimmers such as Kieren Perkins, Grant Hackett, Daniel Kowalski, Glen Houseman, Vladimir Salnikov, Chris Thompson, Alexi Filipets, Emiliano Brembilla, Graeme Smith, Erik Vendt, and Stefan Pfieffer have accomplished this feat over 1,500 meters.

The lactate/ventilatory threshold is not really a new concept but merely a new term for what physiologists used to call "maximum steady state work" (Morehouse and Miller 1971) and what some coaches still term "fastest comfortable pace." Morehouse and Miller (1971) say that a constant level of oxygen intake during exercise is not sufficient evidence of a steady state. The oxygen consumption may be constant simply because the athlete has reached the maximal level of oxygen intake, yet lactic acid may be accumulating.

According to Morehouse and Miller, the maximum rate of sustained work describes a person's ability to maintain steady state activity at high levels of exertion. The aim of such training is to improve the athlete's physical condition so that the organs can sustain a physiological equilibrium at increasingly higher levels of activity. In the process, a swimmer learns to recognize the maximum rate that can be maintained in a physiological steady state.

Pyne and Telford (1989) make the important observation that swimmers who swam so-called threshold sets often did not achieve their lactate and heart rate targets. They emphasize that swimmers need to swim very fast when doing threshold workouts, adding that well-conditioned swimmers should attain heart rates of 180 to 190 beats per minute because when swimmers improve their aerobic fitness, higher speeds and heart rates can be achieved before the lactate/ventilatory threshold is reached.

Work Time at Maximal Effort (Approximate Distance)

According to Counsilman (1975), work is mostly anaerobic in events less than two minutes long (approximately 200 meters). After two minutes, the swimmer's aerobic ability becomes more important. For a 1,500-meter swim, the oxygen system provides approximately 90 percent of the energy used. Therefore training to improve the transportation and utilization of oxygen at the cellular level should be the focus of a swimmer training for this event. Training examples include overdistance training and short-rest interval training (table 10.1).

Counsilman pointed out that most literature confirmed that up to a pulse rate of 150 beats per minute, the energy source was aerobic. At a higher pulse rate, the body's focus shifted to an anaerobic source of ATP. Counsilman stressed, however, that pulse rate depends on many factors. Thus factors such as emotion, age, individual differences, the time since eating, and the time since drinking coffee should be considered. For coaches and swimmers who wanted to use pulse rate to determine when the swimmer was performing aerobically and when the swimmer was performing anaerobically, Counsilman provided the data in table 10.2.

Table 10.1 Work Time at Maximal Effort (Approximate Distance)

	Anaerobic work (%)	Aerobic work (%)
10 sec/25 m	85	15
60 sec/100 m	60–70	30–35
2 min/200 m	50	50
4 min/400 m	30	70
20 min/1,500 m	10	90
120 min/6,000 m	1	99

From Counsilman 1975. Reprinted by permission.

Table 10.2 Pulse Rate Related to Aerobic/Anaerobic Work

Pulse rate (bpm)	Aerobic work (%)	Anaerobic work (%)
Under 120	Probably 100	* See note
120–150	90–95	5–10
150–165	65–85	15–35
165–180	50–65	35–50
Over 180	Depends on anaerobic	Over 50

* Little or no benefit will be derived for developing the anaerobic systems.
From Counsilman 1975. Adapted by permission.

Counsilman warned, "In short sprints, this table [table 10.2] has little validity. For example, in a sprint [25 yards] the work is almost completely anaerobic, but there is little increase in pulse rate."

Aerobic, Anaerobic, and Sprint Training

There are three main types of training, the effects of which combine in proportion to the specific energy demands of the different swimming events. These three types of training are aerobic, anaerobic, and sprint training. Aerobic training enables a swimmer to maintain a faster rate of speed through the middle stages of a race. Anaerobic training helps a swimmer better withstand the accumulative effects of fatigue. Sprint training assists a swimmer in developing faster initial speed.

Aerobic training is performed at submaximal levels of intensity. The primary aim of aerobic training is to build endurance—that is, to enable the athlete to swim farther and faster before lactate buildup in the muscles, with its consequent lowering of the pH level. The gradual improvement in aerobic fitness eventually enables a swimmer to achieve a higher percentage of race speed before reaching the lactate/ventilatory threshold, at which point the body begins to experience difficulty in supplying energy to the muscles by means of aerobic metabolism.

The modern theory of endurance training is based on the belief that much of the work should be performed at or slightly below the lactate/ventilatory threshold. This is commonly believed to occur when the blood lactate has reached approximately 4 millimoles per liter. This type of training is known as threshold training, and its aim is eventually to produce less lactate at higher rates of speed.

Training at the lactate/ventilatory threshold is intended to improve aerobic function and will not improve a swimmer's anaerobic capacity. An improvement in aerobic fitness is indicated by faster swimming times accompanied by lower blood lactate levels and heart rates. The development of improved aerobic capacity requires a carefully devised long-term plan based on gradual progression, year in and year out; by the same token, the resulting adaptation will be retained for a long time.

Whereas the aim of aerobic training is to produce less lactate, anaerobic training aims to produce more lactate by having the athlete perform work at greatly increased levels of intensity, with the deliberate purpose of building a high accumulation of lactic acid in the muscles. The goal is to enable the muscle to tolerate a high level of lactic acid and to improve its capacity to buffer the accumulating lactic acid effectively while also stemming to some extent a decrease in pH. Work performed at this higher level of intensity is often referred to as lactate training.

The chemical changes resulting from severe anaerobic training occur more quickly than the changes associated with aerobic training, but the effects are lost just as quickly, with a subsequent reduction in training. The intensity of the anaerobic workload should be carefully monitored. This type of training should be introduced in the training schedule at the appropriate stage of the season, and even then it should not be used in more than two workouts a week because of its highly stressful nature.

Sprint training is anaerobic and uses ATP and creatine phosphate, which are stored in the muscles in relatively small quantities. Only very short distances, for instance 12-1/2 to 25 meters, should be used in sprint training because energy is drawn increasingly from the lactic acid system if all-out effort continues for more than approximately 10 seconds, and the resulting fatigue disables the swimmer from maintaining top speed. For the same reason, the intervals between swims should be long enough to ensure that the swimmer is able to continue working at maximum speed.

Effects of Varying Training Intensities

Although the preceding sections outline differences among the three main forms of training, research has enabled further delineations among relative levels of training intensity (table 10.3).

Table 10.3 Effects of Varying Training Intensities

	Stage 1	Stage 2	Stage 3	Stage 4	Stage 5
Type of training	Low intensity	Aerobic endurance (maximal equilibrium)	Anaerobic endurance	Race pace simulation	Short sprints (10–25 m)
Energy source	Aerobic	Aerobic	Aerobic/ anaerobic	Anaerobic	Anerobic lactic
Heart rate (bpm)	120–150	160–170	160–190	190–200	160–180
Maximal blood lactate (mmol/L)	1–3	2–4	6–10	8–12	3–5
Effort (%)	80	85–95	90–95	100	100
Perceived exertion	Comfortable	Somewhat uncomfortable	Hard work	Hurtful	Fast but comfortable

Adapted from Absaliamov 1984 and Pyne and Telford 1988.

Low Intensity

Easy swimming—a comparatively relaxing activity—can be used as a warm-up, as active rest immediately after completing a race, or as partial recuperation between high-intensity lactate swims. The heart rate may vary from 120 to 150 during the activity.

Aerobic Endurance (Maximal Equilibrium)

Swimming at a high, steady pace provides a level of intensity just below or at the lactate/ventilatory threshold. The heart rate may vary from 160 to 170. The following sets are some examples:

30 × 50 (10 to 15 seconds rest)

20 × 100 (10 to 15 seconds rest)

8 × 200 (10 to 20 seconds rest)

8 × 400 (15 to 30 seconds rest; any stroke)

4 × 800 (15 to 30 seconds rest)

8 × 200 individual medley (20 seconds rest)

1,500 meters freestyle (after the first 250 meters, overkick and fist swim on alternate laps)

4 × 1,500 freestyle (30 seconds rest)

2 × 3,000 freestyle (2 minutes rest)

3,000 swim (first 1,400 meters freestyle, last 1,600 meters individual medley in reverse order with continuous 400 on each stroke)

10 × 100 kick (20 seconds rest; choice of specialty)

10 × 100 pull (20 seconds rest; choice of specialty)

To ensure that the muscle fibers used in the other strokes are also mobilized, aerobic training should not be done entirely in freestyle.

Anaerobic Endurance

Anaerobic endurance training consists of fast swimming, in which the energy demands are met aerobically and anaerobically. The heart rate will be between 160 and 190, depending on the individual and the level of fitness. This type of training may produce blood lactate concentrations of 6 to 10 millimoles per liter. The following sets are some examples:

30 × 50 (30 to 60 seconds rest)

15 × 100 (30 to 120 seconds rest)

8 × 200 (30 to 120 seconds rest)

8 × 400 (1 to 3 minutes rest)

4 × 800 (3 to 5 minutes rest)

5 × 300 (8 minutes rest; faster than 400 pace)

8 × 150 (7 minutes rest; 4 × 150 on specialty, 4 × 150 in freestyle)

8 × 200 specialty (last 50 of each 200 on butterfly; 2 minutes rest; 1 to 4 descend)

8 × 200 individual medley (1 minute rest; 1 to 4 descend)

4 × 500 freestyle (3 minutes rest; 1 to 2 descend)

8 × 200 (2 minutes rest; alternate 200 freestyle, 200 specialty)

Race Pace Simulation

Race pace simulation involves swimming sections nearly as long as the racing distances at race speed or faster. This type of work produces severe anaerobic metabolism. The heart rate, and probably the lactate concentration as well, reaches maximum. The heart rate will be in the range of 190 to 200, again depending on the individual and level of fitness. The lactate concentration reaches levels of 8 to 12 millimoles per liter.

All swims should start from a dive and be accurately timed for future comparison against other race pace simulations. A swimmer's average time per set indicates progress or lack thereof, so great importance should be placed on this type of training, which should be undertaken only when a coach feels reasonably sure that the swimmer is motivated to the task. The following sets are some examples.

For Sprinters

15 × 50 (3 minutes rest)

10 × 75 (3-1/2 minutes rest)

10×75 specialty with 25 freestyle easy swim-back after each swim as active rest (sets 1 to 5 descend; on each fifth repeat try to improve on the 75 split recorded on swimmer's best-ever 100 swim)

6×100 (5 minutes rest)

5×150 (5 to 10 minutes rest; last two 150 swims should be faster than the 150 split recorded on the swimmer's best 200 swim)

4×200 (5 to 10 minutes rest)

For Middle-Distance Swimmers

20×50 (2-1/2 to 3 minutes rest)

14×75 (3-1/2 minutes rest)

10×100 (5 minutes rest)

7×150 (4 to 5 minutes rest)

5×200 (5 to 6 minutes rest)

For Long-Distance Swimmers

10×200 (3 minutes rest)

8×250 (3-1/2 minutes rest)

7×300 (3-1/2 minutes rest)

5×400 (5 minutes rest)

4×500 (6 minutes rest)

Short Sprints

Short sprints are short bursts at maximum speed over distances of 10 to 25 meters but no farther. Depending on the swimmer and the stroke, a swim seldom lasts longer than 10 to 15 seconds. This type of work develops speed and is not exceptionally fatiguing unless carried out for a long time. All swims start from a dive. The following sets provide some examples:

$32 \times 12\text{-}1/2$ (2 minutes rest)

16×25 (2 to 3 minutes rest)

16×25 (3 minutes rest; alternate 25 freestyle with 25 specialty; start from a dive and finish each 25 with a turn and complete pushoff)

Shorter sprints, such as 12-1/2 meters and 25 meters, are more effective than 50s and 100s for developing pure speed and the ability to swim without a buildup of blood lactate. Because creatine phosphate in the muscles tends to last

for only 1/4 minute at most, the intervening rest intervals, even for these very short swims, should be about 2 to 3 minutes to permit CP replacement.

Proportions for the Training Season

The percentage of varying training intensities when averaged out in terms of a total seasonal training program is approximately as follows (see table 10.3, p. 177):

Stages 1 and 2 (aerobic training): 50 to 60 percent

Stage 3 (aerobic/anaerobic training): 20 to 25 percent

Stage 4 (anaerobic training): 3 to 5 percent only

Stage 5 (anaerobic lactic): 5 to 10 percent

Heart rate provides useful information when access to lactate testing is unavailable.

Outline of the Annual Training Program

The annual training program (macrocycle) is built on a series of microcycles (one-week periods), which in turn form mesocycles (blocks of several weeks) devoted to distinct phases of preparation. Each phase should exhibit an ideal balance between the volume and intensity of training specific to the development of desired physiological qualities. An excellent model of ideal daily, weekly, and seasonal planning designed by Ernest Maglischo (1985) is shown in figure 10.2.

Realize that figure 10.2 represents an ideal; much depends on a coach's skill, feel, and plain common sense in correctly proportioning the workload and controlling the subtle transitions from one phase of the season to the next. In addition, as the program enters its competitive phase, the requirements of preparing for specific events need to be considered. The transitions from one phase of preparation to the next are reflected in the size of the general workload, as well as the volume and intensity of work, and are shown in figure 10.3 (Bompa 1985).

Planning the Season

1. Adjustment phase—2 to 4 weeks
2. Endurance phase—8 to 10 weeks
   Transition to competitive phase—1 to 2 weeks
3. Competitive phase—4 to 6 weeks
4. Taper phase—1 to 3 weeks
   Transition to taper phase—1 to 2 weeks

Weekly Planning

Endurance phase

Mornings
Emphasis on aerobic endurance

1. Stroke drills
2. Aerobic training
3. Occasional short sprints
4. Occasional long sprints

Afternoons
Monday, Wednesday, Friday

1. Long aerobic sets at optimal pace—mix kicking, pulling, and swimming
2. Short sprint sets
3. Occasional long sprint sets

Afternoons
Tuesday, Thursday, Saturday

1. Stroke drills and aerobic endurance sets at a slower pace
2. Major sprint sets
3. Occasional long sprint sets

Competitive phase
Mornings—same as endurance phase

Afternoons
Monday and Wednesday

1. Major anaerobic sets
2. Aerobic sets at optimal pace
3. Some short sprints

Afternoons
Tuesday and Thursday

1. Stroke drills
2. Aerobic sets at slower pace
3. Pace work
4. Some short sprints

Afternoons
Friday or Saturday

1. Major sprint sets
2. Stroke drills
3. Aerobic sets at slower speed

Daily Planning

1. Warm-up
2. Short sprints
3. Major aerobic set or minor aerobic set
4. Recovery set—pulling, kicking, or stroke drill
5. Major aerobic, anaerobic, race pace, or sprint set
6. Recovery set
7. Sprints, relays, fun sets
8. Cool-down

Figure 10.2 Outline of an annual training program. From Maglischo 1985, p. 62. Reprinted by permission.

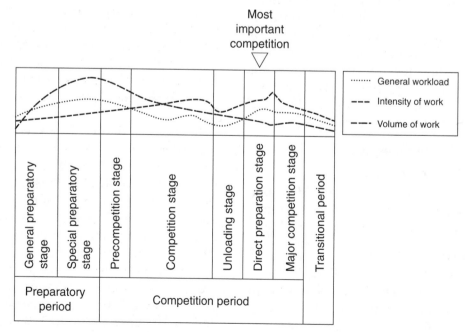

Figure 10.3 Major training cycle: basic year-round training plan. From Bompa 1985.

The Need for Interspersed Regenerative Periods

One of the problems with designing charts and ideal training configurations is that we cannot rely on swimmers to perform like clockwork machines. Consequently, we can neither synthesize training methods mechanically nor put them into neat pigeonholes to be used willy nilly, irrespective of situational needs. Most experienced coaches develop a natural feel for changing moods among the members of a team and may alter a planned workout simply as a result of this type of empathy. This approach is not witchcraft but merely the application of everyday common sense.

Paul Bergen (1985) says that some coaches fail to address the need for recovery and regeneration time within the training program. He suggests that microcycles be grouped in periods of three building weeks followed by one regeneration week. This method can be varied as a season progresses—for example, four weeks of building followed by one week of regeneration, then 3–1, 4–2, 2–2, and 1–1 as the major competition of the season approaches.

The Number of Training Sessions in a Week

Bergen (1985) draws attention to the work of Tudor Bompa (1985) in classifying frequencies of training sessions within a one-week microcycle (figure 10.4).

The first chart in the figure shows eight workouts in a microcycle with only one day

	Mon.	Tue.	Wed.	Thu.	Fri.	Sat.	Sun.
A.M.						T	T
P.M.	T	T	T	T	T	T	

	Mon.	Tue.	Wed.	Thu.	Fri.	Sat.	Sun.
A.M.	T	T	T	T	T	T	
P.M.	T		T		T		

	Mon.	Tue.	Wed.	Thu.	Fri.	Sat.	Sun.
A.M.	T	T	T	T	T	T	
P.M.	T	T		T	T		

Figure 10.4 The classification of microcycles, the number of training lessons: *(top)* microcycle with eight training lessons; *(middle)* microcycle with a 3 + 1 structure; *(bottom)* microcycle with a 5 + 1 structure. From Bompa 1985.

containing two sessions. Although there is no complete day off, the absence of morning sessions during the week enables the swimmers to sleep a little later before leaving for school. The second chart depicts three workouts and one off. This means that there is one day of two workouts followed by a day with only one workout. Then the swimmers have a complete day off at the end of the week. The third chart shows five training sessions followed by one off. This pattern is repeated and then followed by one day off. There are several other permutations for applying the number of workouts in a microcycle.

Part IV

Past, Present, and Future of the Sport

Chapter 11

Evolution of Competitive Swimming

The early 19th century saw a new type of sporting encounter in which two skilled swimmers would compete for money in a staged challenge match. These match races, usually swum in the sea, a canal, or a river, marked the beginning of the modern sport of competitive swimming.

In a manner similar to the prize-fighting ring, the swimmers competed for a champion's belt and a money purse collected by spectators who placed large bets and wagers on the outcome. Because the stopwatch had not been invented, there were no times to be beaten or used for comparison. The vagaries of wind and tide had to be taken into account, and a swimmer's knowledge of prevailing conditions could contribute to the outcome.

The people involved with these match races were colorful but not always the most savory members of society. Many of the swimmers, and those who bet on them, were well-known regulars at the horse-racing tracks and prize-fighting rings. It was not unknown for a match race to be fixed or roped in collaboration with accomplices who made large wagers on the race.

Early Races

Swimming in Japanese schools became an organized sport by Imperial edict as early as 1603, and Japanese interschool competitive swimming has continued to the present time (Oppenheim 1970). Probably because of the isolated nature of Japanese culture for many centuries, Japan's early start did not influence other countries to follow suit.

Although Japan held a giant three-day swim meet in 1810, competitive swimming was not organized on a regular basis until John Strachan, a London wine merchant, formed the National Swimming Society in 1837. He later changed the name to the British Swimming Society, in the belief that this would be more comprehensive than national.

Until the start of the National Swimming Society, newspapers hadn't mentioned swimming. Then a report of a swimming match in the Serpentine River appeared in *Bell's Life*, a sporting newspaper, on August 6, 1837. From that time, swimming was regularly reported in the press, and the sport grew in popularity.

While Strachan was said to have done an enormous amount for the advancement of swimming, like many officials in the history of the sport, he was a master of the art of self-aggrandizement. When the National Swimming Society issued a medal to commemorate its foundation, John Strachan was not above having his own portrait, with the words "John Strachan of Perthshire, born 7th of January 1806" appear on one side, while the obverse side said "National Swimming Society founded by John Strachan, 30th of June 1837" (Thomas 1904). Commenting on this, Thomas said,

> Though not on record, there can be little doubt that, like many a greater man, he paid for these things himself. It is impossible for the present generation, accustomed to orderly galas graced by the presence of ladies to imagine the degraded condition of swimming in those days, and for many years after. Any swimming entertainment was the resort of low class characters, who chiefly went to the bath for betting purposes (Thomas 1904, p. 249).

Nevertheless, the society's efforts resulted in many clubs being formed in London.

Organized Matches

On August 26, 1838, instead of merely staging the usual race between two swimmers, the National Swimming Society held the first annual grand match between 12 swimmers in the Serpentine River. The first prize was a silver medal of exquisite workmanship and one guinea in money. Second prize was a bronze medal from the same die and a half-guinea. Third prize was a metal medal. Much money was lost and won by gentlemen betting on the competitors.

On August 4, 1839, it was announced that a gold medal and chain, valued at 20 guineas, would be competed for in London by the 12 yearly champions, each from a different town or place. (This was the first time that the word *champion* was used in the sport of swimming.) The gold medal and chain were to become the property of the swimmer—the champion of champions—who won it for four successive seasons.

The Need for Public Swimming Pools

At the beginning of the 19th century, public swimming pools, as we know them today, did not exist. People swam in the sea or wherever there was a suitable and safe stretch of water such as a canal, a local pond, or a lake.

Many of the leading schools in England encouraged their pupils to learn to swim. Races in a nearby river or pond became part of the school sports curriculum. But, for the working classes, the industrial revolution had made the problems of urban life acute and pressing, and whole families, including children, were involved in industrial labor. People in large towns and cities had little access to places suitable for swimming. Indeed, their time was mainly occupied by coping with the harsh conditions in which they lived. Few of them had the chance to learn to swim, and drownings were almost a daily occurrence, as confirmed by newspapers of the period.

Fast-growing populations caused great congestion, and early-century epidemics of cholera with heavy mortality often swept through cities and towns. Control of disease depended on the development of a higher standard of living with clean water supplies and efficient and hygienic sewage disposal.

The Baths and Wash-Houses Act

In 1834, barrister Edwin Chadwick showed that expenditure on the poor and the prevention of disease were two sides of a single coin. Most people had no running water in their homes, and Chadwick's measures to reform the poor law included provision of increased water supplies and improved sanitation.

In August 1842, the British Swimming Society presented a petition signed by 322 persons in favor of extra bathing places. The petition stated that over 2,000 people drowned annually, 350 in London alone, mainly attributable to the neglect of the art of swimming (Thomas 1904).

The Baths and Wash-Houses Act, which received Royal Assent on August 26, 1846, enabled local authorities to provide swimming baths and wash houses. The Whitechapel Baths, then under construction, were regarded as a model to be copied. By 1852, seven more such establishments existed, estimated to have been used by 800,000 bathers.

The building of these first baths were events of immense social and political significance. Usually situated in areas of great deprivation, they improved the lives of many thousands of people. With the provision of copious hot water and steam, they also represented a triumph of early Victorian engineering.

Many people in the middle and upper classes contributed large sums of money to these bath-building projects not only because they had social consciences, but because they regarded the urban poor as sources of disease and potential troublemakers requiring moral improvement. As *The London Times* for May 12, 1847, put it in its report on the Whitechapel Baths, "there

will [now] be no excuse for bodily filth in the neighbourhood."

Engineering to the Rescue

The Act provided for indoor and outdoor swimming baths, warm or cold slipper baths, vapor and shower baths, and wash houses for laundry. The growing popularity of swimming, due mainly to the energy of swimming clubs, made the actual swimming pool a remunerative feature of the new public bath houses. In locations where population size warranted it, it was usual to construct three types of swimming pools: the first-class bath, 100 feet by 40 feet; the second-class bath, 120 feet by 40 feet; and the women's bath, 60 feet by 40 feet.

It was compulsory to provide a shower and soap-hole for laborers coming from dirty work to use before entering the swimming bath (Sinclair and Henry 1903). It became a novelty for people to have a good wash and scrub down before they entered the pool to try their skill at the new sport of swimming, often under the instruction of an ever-growing number of so-called swimming professors.

Before electricity was invented, the effective heating of water in the new swimming baths was a problem because of unnecessary waste of water and fuel. Water was expensive, costing from four-pence to one shilling per 1,000 gallons. A simple but noisy system of circulating warm water into the pool was to inject jets of live steam through a perforated pipe directly into the bottom of the deep end. The pipe had to be insulated to prevent bathers from being scalded.

The water was constantly circulated, warmed, aerated, and purified, then forcibly returned through patent spreaders placed at equal distances over the floor of the bath. This method was said to heat the water uniformly, thereby eliminating the cold patches of water frequently found in baths heated by other systems. The cost of heating was reduced to a minimum as cold water did not need to be introduced into the bath so frequently (Sinclair and Henry 1903).

The Need for Standardized Distances

There grew a need for standardized racing distances, but it was to be a long time before the authorities constructed pools of standard dimensions to ensure uniform racing conditions. Racing distances were regulated according to the size of the pool. Even when such facilities were built, architects often failed to consult with the potential users, resulting in the omission of features necessary for competitive swimming.

Most races held in inland towns were over short distances in measured swimming pools. Long-distance races were the exception; these were staged in canals, lakes, and reservoirs. At the coast, long-distance competitions were usually held in the sea between piers or breakwaters.

Officials would have preferred to see more long-distance racing in the open sea and in swimming pools. However, short-distance events were financially more successful. For a short race they could easily secure over 100 entries, while for a long race an entry list of 20 swimmers was considered good. In open water, 220 yards and 500 yards were the best racing distances; but for swimming pools any race over 100 yards would not be well supported.

Apart from irregular pool dimensions, other criticisms included impractical and inconvenient location of spectator and dressing room space, inadequate facilities for the growing number of female swimmers, uncomfortable water temperature, and lack of lane lines on the floor of the pool. An uninterrupted view could rarely be obtained "without fear of splashings and drenchings" (Sachs 1912, p. 242). Dirt and grit were carried into the baths by people wearing muddy boots. The entrance was often a large door, opening directly onto the pool deck, through which icy blasts caused swimmers extreme discomfort.

Competitive swimming in its present form resulted largely from the evolution of the artificial environment of the measured pool. The modern swimming complex is a far cry from the first public bath halls and washing houses or even the first public swimming baths, divided as they were according to social class and sex and built in a diversity of sizes. At the international level, it was to be a long time before competitions were held over standard distances. Some 28 years passed after the revival of the Olympic Games at Athens in 1896 before the Olympic swimming events were conducted in the 50-meter course we know today.

It is difficult to imagine competition without regulation-size pools, standardized distances, and precise time measurements, yet these challenges faced the organizers of the first swimming competitions. More often than not, the size of the course governed the length of the race. The first swimming races bore no resemblance to modern swim meets in which eight swimmers, each in an assigned lane, compete over a set distance in a measured course, at the end of which their times and placings, electronically recorded, are displayed on a large board at the end of the pool.

Variations in racing distances even affected the swimming events at the Olympics in Athens, Paris, and St. Louis, and made a uniform list of records impossible. One of the main objectives of the Amateur Swimming Association (ASA) was to stimulate public opinion in favor of building swimming pools. The ASA published a list of 800 bathing places in 460 towns. Of these, almost 600 contained swimming baths. According to Sachs (1912), although a number of baths were built, most were totally inadequate for the purpose of competitive swimming.

The Royal Life Saving Society

During the Victorian period, swimming was encouraged in most English public schools. Although a growing appreciation existed of the health benefits of the sport, the main consideration was safety. Death from drowning was common because most of the population could not swim.

The Royal Life Saving Society encouraged the teaching of swimming because it viewed swimming as a way to save life, which it held should be the main objective of the activity. It promoted competitive swimming because the speed and endurance developed by racing would enable a rescuer to reach a drowning person fast. The ability to swim quickly was encouraged by holding school swimming sports at set times of the year.

The first swimming promoters realized that the future of the sport depended on introducing swimming to school children. Reports of the time suggest a certain social tinge to the developing structure of the sport; "the records of the Public Schools gives assurance that the future at any rate of one class of Englishmen as swimmers is secure" (Sachs 1912, p. 39). Not all parents encouraged their children to swim; many withheld permission because of superstition concerning imagined ill effects of prolonged immersion and physical strain, and the risk of contracting disease from water. According to Brasch (1970), as late as 1880 a rhyme of unknown authorship was popularly quoted:

Mother, may I go out to swim?

Yes, my darling daughter;

Hang your clothes on a hickory limb,

But don't go near the water.

The common fear of swimming prompted the Southern Counties Branch of the ASA to publish a small pamphlet titled *Can You Swim?*, containing articles by eminent doctors on the benefits of swimming.

Professors of Swimming

Old-time coaches—*swimming masters* or *professors of swimming*, as they sometimes called themselves—often exuded an aura of secrecy. "Come and be coached by me and I'll teach you technique," they would say. "You see, swimming is really nothing more than pulling and kicking, but it's done in this certain way and that is . . . technique!" But eventually, intelligent swimmers expected to be told why they were being advised to use a particular method. They became tired of the clichés, the old hand-me-downs, the platitudes and folklore that had become part of the repertoire of many a so-called swimming professor.

Wilson (1883) said that it was a mistake to suppose that a man who was a good swimmer and a successful competitor would also be a good teacher. Many really good swimmers could not tell, and really did not know, why

they traveled so fast through the water, and they were ignorant of the peculiarity of action that gave them such power over their rivals. Many professional swimmers used movements that were

> . . . completely the reverse of being correct, or in accordance with any rule, or recognized law governing the swimming motions, but whose very ignorance accounted not only for their own egotism, but was the cause of oft-repeated mistakes and distorted ideas of swimming. To be a successful teacher of the art of swimming requires almost as much thought, application, hard work, and constant practice as almost any branch of education or science (Wilson 1883, pp. 24–25).

According to Thomas (1904), the system of teaching advocated by Professor Stevens, who claimed that he had taught upward of 12,000 to swim in 10 years, was "all humbug and his instruction is not good." For example, Thomas said that Stevens had given out such advice as the need to always keep ones eyes open when diving because so many people had drowned by keeping their eyes shut!

Wilson said that he hoped to see the day when the title of professor would mean something different. He also wanted to see would-be professors pass an examination to prove themselves qualified for the title. In similar vein, Sinclair and Henry (1903) said that a code of fixed principles should be laid down so that the profession could be built on a sound foundation, but that attempts to institute certificate examinations had been foiled by those who would chiefly benefit by them.

Thomas (1904) criticized the common practice of publishing a work under the name of a well-known professional swimmer to gain credibility, even if the swimmer was not a writer. Thomas pointed out the poor quality of the materials swimmers endorsed, probably for financial consideration. Thomas said that many swimming books were nothing more than miserable pieces of ignorant scissors-and-paste compilation.

In the late 19th century, a swimmer could not lay claim to being an expert unless he could do

Ralph Thomas, Swimming's First Historian

Ralph Thomas, a little-known man who seemed to have shunned the limelight, was swimming's first historian. With great dedication, he researched everything written or illustrated on swimming, from antiquity to the end of the 19th century. Thomas was born in 1840 and was a lawyer by profession. His book *Swimming* (1904) is recognized as the most important bibliography of swimming. Archibald Sinclair, a noted English authority on swimming, said in the *Swimming Magazine*, January 1915, "This book is a mine of wealth for it contains a record of every known book on the subject up to 1904 (Cureton 1934, p. 86)."

Thomas lists all the important works on swimming published in English, German, French, and other European languages. It is a remarkable biography, history, and annotated bibliography, with upwards of 100 illustrations. Thomas published a much shorter version of the book in 1868, but after 36 years (1904) the author, now in failing health and not satisfied with his first effort, published the second edition (488 pages), which over the years, has become the much-prized gem for the rare-book collector.

scientific and trick swimming. There were variations on this theme, such as fancy swimming and acrobatic swimming, which were probably the ancestors of modern synchronized swimming. These feats required much painstaking practice, and any swimmer who attempted them in public before attaining perfection risked appearing ludicrous and absurd. But the leading professionals were very popular attractions at swimming galas where they gave great entertainment and interest to their patrons and earned large purses in doing so (Sinclair and Henry 1903).

The Advent of the Stopwatch

The stopwatch was to competitive swimming what the wheel was to civilization. Greater emphasis was placed on speed and not only who placed first, second, or third. The efficiency of the evolving speed strokes—overarm sidestroke, trudgen, and crawl—could be tested more accurately and scientifically. An additional benefit was the possibility of comparing performances recorded in different towns and even countries, provided they were recorded over the same distances and in the same size pools.

Pocket watches were first used to discover how long it took to perform some action; a general term for these is stopwatches. Sometimes they are called chronographs, but since this implies a written record of the time, the term is not correct. The stopwatch was a cheaper version of the chronograph developed by E.D. Johnson in 1855, but it was not until 20 years later that an affordable stopwatch became generally available for timing sporting events. When horse racing became popular in the mid-1850s, a wide variety of timing devices were patented but none came into general use. In 1859, the American Watch Company of Waltham, Massachusetts, patented the chronodrometer for timing horses. However, the sweep hand was not the fly-back type we know today and had to be constantly reset.

The first stopwatches had a lever that literally stopped the watch by interfering with the train. This was obviously an unsatisfactory method for obtaining elapsed time since the starting time was arbitrary and the stopping caused the watch to be wrong as a timepiece. To overcome this problem, some watches used two trains: one for the conventional timepiece and one that could be stopped and started at will, which drove a separate second hand. The hand sometimes moved in one-second jumps.

This type of watch was an improvement but still lacked two vital ingredients of the modern concept of a stopwatch—the ability to count elapsed times of greater duration than a minute, which necessitated a minute counter to be successful, and the convenience of starting the counting hand from zero each time to avoid the need for arithmetic, which necessitated a reset device. These two functions were achieved in the mid-19th century. In 1842, Nicole patented a reset system for a second hand that could be independently stopped and started; and in 1862 the now-familiar three-press button system was patented (Cutmore 1985). In the 1860s, Swiss watchmakers successfully tackled the problem and succeeded in making cheaper watches.

According to records, the first timed swimming race was the English one-mile championship of 1869 swum in the River Thames, from Putney Aqueduct to Hammersmith Bridge. As far as can be ascertained, the winner of that event, T. Morris, was the first champion ever to be timed (27 minutes 18 seconds).

Official lists of records were soon published. The first official swimming record belonged to Winston Cole, who in 1871 swam 100 yards in 1 minute 15 seconds. His time was ratified by the recently formed Metropolitan Swimming Club Association.

Later, the building of swimming pools of measured length made handicap races popular in the 19th century. The idea behind handicap races was to even out the competition and give slower swimmers an opportunity to excel. The handicapping system also provided spectator excitement at a time when there were few fast swimmers. Handicapping probably also provided leeway for people wishing to covertly place bets or stakes on the outcome of a race.

The slowest swimmers started first, and then the handicapper walked behind each waiting swimmer, shouting out the time off the ticking stopwatch. As each swimmer's handicap time was called, that swimmer started and chased after the swimmers who had already taken off. There was an objection to accepting records set in handicap races because of the unfair advantage gained by having a pacemaker.

Swim Meets in the Late 19th Century

The London Swimming Club did much to promote swimming in its early days. There was still very little difference between professionals and amateurs. In those days, if the glove was thrown down, anyone could pick it up. At all the chief events, betting was widespread and of more importance than the swimming.

The general management of swimming meets, especially those held in what were called baths, improved vastly during the last 10 years of the 19th century. Organizers first had to obtain a permit from the Amateur Swimming Association (ASA) before holding a meet because amateurs put their amateur status in jeopardy if they competed in an unsanctioned meet (Sinclair and Henry 1903).

Where competitions were held in open water, the tides had to be considered before fixing a date for the competition. In addition, care had to be taken to avoid clashing with another meet in the same district, as otherwise both could be run at a loss.

The ASA advised organizers of swim meets to do everything possible for the comfort of the competitors; otherwise swimmers would abstain from entering the next season. They advised that it was bad policy to ask competitors to undress in a wretched, ill-ventilated room in order to accommodate more spectators. Arrangements made for competitors at some open-water meetings, particularly in the sea, were perhaps the worst. Sometimes competitors were required to undress in small cabins, the floors of which were often wet and filthy, so that their clothes could not be put down. Organizers didn't have to provide a drawing room, but a decent dressing room added greatly to the popularity of any club's annual gala (Sinclair and Henry 1903).

Accounts of three different swimming meets, two of them for amateurs and one for professional swimmers, described in *The London Times* of September 18, 1899, provide a good idea of what these late-19th-century competitions were like.

The first race described, the Ulph Annual Challenge Cup Competition for Amateurs, was held in the sea at Yarmouth. *The London Times* described the course:

> The course was, as usual, between the Britannia and the Wellington Piers, a distance of about 1,000 yards, with the tide, and, though a stiff breeze was blowing off the land, the sea was pleasantly calm and the conditions favourable, as was proved by the fact that the winner accomplished the record time of 9 min. 8 sec.

The winner, J.A. Jarvis, had the outside station at the beginning of the race but shifted his course seaward to take advantage of the faster tide. Jarvis's strategy was copied by two of his competitors, Sharp and Pugh. At the halfway mark, Jarvis led by about 20 yards, Sharp was second, and Arnold, another competitor, was third. The swimmers finished in that order; Jarvis finished about 50 yards ahead of Sharp with a winning time of 9 minutes, 8 seconds. Arnold was third. Pugh finished in fifth place.

The London Times went on to describe the 100 yards Amateur Championship of 1899. In this race, eight swimmers competed in three trial heats. The three trial winners competed against each other. J.H. Derbyshire of the Manchester Osborne Swimming Club, who won the same race in 1898, led throughout the race and finished two yards ahead of F.C.V. Lane of East Sydney, the Australian champion. Lane finished half a yard ahead of W.H. Lister of the Manchester Osborne Swimming Club. Derbyshire won with a time of 60-2/5 seconds, "one-fifth of a second slower than the record he established when he won last year."

The record referred to by *The London Times* was, in effect, the official world record. Thus, since this was Derbyshire's last championship appearance of the 19th century, he can justly be labeled the fastest swimmer of the 19th century.

Finally, *The London Times* recounted the County of London Long-Distance Professional Championship that had been held the day before on September 17, 1899. Swimmers competed for the 60-guinea challenge cup on a course 5 miles, 60 yards long, from Kew to Putney. Although six entries were received, only three swimmers—Titchener of Putney, Harrison of Raynes Park, and Charles Ball of Battersea—competed in the race. Tide and weather conditions delayed the start for over an hour. At about 5:00, the men dived into very cold water. Titchener and Harrison eventually withdrew from the competition, leaving Ball to finish the race alone. Ball's final time was 1 hour, 35 minutes, and 59 seconds, "which, although slow time, was a good performance under the bad conditions that prevailed."

Early Professional Swimmers

As the popularity of competitive swimming grew, professional swimmers began to emerge. One of the first notable professional swimmers was Charles Steedman. Steedman learned to swim in 1843 at the age of 13, and by the age of 15 was a professional swimmer who already had won the then princely sum of 10 pounds in a race over 400 yards, the longest distance swum in those days. At 19, he won the Championship of England from George Pewters, a master of the sidestroke, the new racing style of the day. In 1852 and 1853, Steedman beat Frederick Edward Beckwith, nine years his senior, for the Surrey Club Championship, the event commonly regarded as the Championship of England. Thomas (1904) said that after this defeat, Beckwith declined to swim against Steedman again. Steedman took the prize belt with him when he emigrated to Australia in 1854, where he kept it as a prized possession until the end of his life.

The champion of England in 1844 was George Pewters (then about 17), who swam against Samuel Hounslow (then about 38) of Oxford for 50 pounds on September 2 in the Serpentine at 7:00 in the morning. Pewters gained the beach 20 yards ahead of his competitor; never was there such a feat of dexterity. George Pewters is generally credited with introducing the sidestroke. Thomas (1904) gives further information about Pewters in his published correspondence with Charles Steedman who had emigrated to Australia.

On September 25, 1842, in winning the 1842 championship, Pewters swam across the Serpentine and back in 6-3/4 minutes. In 1839 and 1840 he joined other champions of the National Swimming Society—Kenworthy of London and Hounslow of Oxford—with Charles Lewis, the London champion, in the first great contests of the kind of swift, long, and fancy swimming for speed, distance, scientific swimming, and indeed tricks of all descriptions. In 1848 Pewters competed in a number of challenge races, one with Fred Edward Beckwith of the Lambeth Bath and others with Professor Stevens and Harold Kenworthy.

Samuel Hounslow was a shoemaker in Holywell Street, Oxford, as well as a teacher of swimming. He won the National Swimming Society medal for completing 400 yards in 7 minutes, 9 seconds, swimming in the Thames at Oxford. While teaching swimming, he could stay in the water for 5 or 6 hours a day.

Henry Gurr, known as the Pocket Hercules, was originally a shoeblack at Endell Street Baths, London. Occasionally in recognition for his assistance to the attendant, George Dunham, Gurr was allowed to swim in the pool, an opportunity he often used, staying in the water for hours at a time. On July 22, 1863, Gurr won the Fraser gold medal in the Serpentine. He was also a talented trapeze artist, and in 1870 he left England with the Hanlon Acrobats.

Professional versus Amateur

The Professional Swimming Association was formed on July 6, 1881, as a result of a decision of the Swimming Association of Great Britain. However, it collapsed within a few years (Sinclair and Henry 1903). The Professional Swimming Association became the wealthiest swimming institution in England or elsewhere, and it might have gone on prospering if its financial stability had not been wrecked, but ultimately the members killed it (Watson 1873).

What Is an Amateur?

Thomas Arnold's introduction of sports as regular extracurricular activity in English public schools spurred a great development of sports during the late Victorian age. This athletic revival of the 19th century led to the restoration of the ancient Olympic Games at Athens in 1896 and also revived what was said to be the classical ideal of amateurism.

For a long time the future of the ASA was in jeopardy because often for profitable reasons, not everyone wanted to be an amateur. Only after its membership spread sufficiently did the ASA finally have the power to enforce its amateur laws. This caused much friction between the amateur southern counties and the professional swimmers of the north of England, many of whom were the fastest in the world at all distances.

The northerners, who earned their living as professional swimmers, rose to combat the inroads—in the form of suspensions—made by the interfering southerners. Enforcing the amateur rules throughout the country became a difficult task, especially as many local corporations held out the temptations of money and value prizes at their regattas.

The ASA eventually won the day but not before such fine swimmers as T. Cairns, J. Nuttall, W. Evans, S.W. Greasely, J.H. Tyers, and D. Billington had been declared professionals. Among them they had shared most of the championships, from 100 yards to 1 mile.

Every year attempts were made to separate amateurs from professionals in all contests but without success, with the result that the strictly amateur clubs would not join the new Swimming Association of Great Britain.

Earlier in 1880 the Amateur Athletic Association (track and field) had adopted a definition of an amateur at their inaugural meeting. When the ASA was finally able to hold a meeting on June 28, 1880, Dr. Hunter Barron (Otter Club), Horace Davenport (Ilex Club), H. Benjamin (Cygnus Club), H.H. Griffen (London Athletic Club), and a number of other well-known supporters proposed the adoption of the Amateur Athletic Association's definition of an amateur.

By 1881 the ASA was receiving steady support, but the growing amount of office work became difficult to handle, and the government of amateur swimming became chaotic. A swimmer who had been declared a professional at one meeting would be declared an amateur at the next. On April 7, 1884, the Otter Club and eight or nine other clubs resigned their membership in the association over the lax administration of the new amateur laws and formed a new body named the Amateur Swimming Union (ASU). A feud commenced between the Swimming Association of Great Britain and the newly formed ASU.

For two years the struggle for supremacy continued until finally, in 1886, Mr. H. Benjamin of the Cygnus Club managed to bring the leaders together to sort out their differences and form a new body, the Amateur Swimming Association, with a revised set of rules.

Open Revolt Against Amateur Laws

In 1889 the enforcement of these rules and the consequent suspension of some Manchester swimmers led to an open revolt in the north. Representatives from the south went to Manchester to address a crowded meeting of swimmers who had been worked up to a spirit of antagonism by writers in the press.

After a long discussion it was resolved, on the casting vote of the chairman, that the scheme brought forward by the southerners be accepted as a basis of settlement. The ASA removed the suspensions that had created the difficulty and agreed to recognize the jurisdiction of the northern counties' ASA over all swimming matters north of 53 degrees latitude.

The first general meeting under the new constitution took place in London on April 12, 1890. The new association now consisted of 135 clubs from all over England. (A New Zealand Amateur Swimming Association was formed in 1890 by R. St. Clair of Auckland, with a constitution similar to that of the English association.)

The Question of Open Betting in Amateur Sport

The continuing problem of open betting at race meetings resulted in a gathering of the governing bodies of athletics, cycling, and swimming in London on March 29, 1889, to discuss the situation, which prevented the more respectable members of the community from taking part or interest in many competitions.

They decided to try to detect competitors in any way in league with bookmakers because they believed that this was the direct cause of roping and other malpractice. (A swimmer was said to "rope" when he did not exert himself to the utmost to hide his true ability, thereby drawing better odds for betting purposes (Sinclair and Henry 1903).)

The Growth of International Swimming and the Birth of FINA

After January 7, 1869, when competitive swimming was first placed on an organized basis at a meeting in the German Gymnasium in London, England, the sport spread gradually to other countries. Initially, the two big centers were England and Australia, and it is interesting to note the influence of the one on the other, even though separated by thousands of miles.

Each new country to adopt competitive swimming inevitably followed the constitutional formula designed by the officials of English swimming. They also applied the definition of amateurism, which was apparently based in large measure not on altruism but on the prevailing class consciousness in Great Britain. With the rebirth of the so-called Olympic movement, it became clear that universally accepted rules would be necessary if competition was to be conducted on a consistent basis.

In 1908, at the Olympic Games in London, George Hearn, president of the English Swimming Association, was asked to establish an Olympic swimming code. He was assisted in his deliberations by Englishman William Henry, Max Ritter of the United States, and Hjalmar Johnson of Sweden. Hearn realized that a more farsighted policy would be to establish rules that could be applied on a permanent basis and not only for the Olympic Games.

To achieve this aim, George Hearn decided to use the opportunity of the Olympic meeting in London to form an international swimming association. Because representatives from 10 nations (England, Germany, Denmark, Sweden, France, Ireland, Finland, Hungary, Belgium, and Wales) were participating in the London Olympic Games, Hearn called a meeting to set up an international governing body of swimming with a set body of laws. On July 19, 1908, at the Manchester Hotel in London, the Federation Internationale de Natation Amateur (FINA) was formed. The swimming code of FINA was based on the model of the English ASA.

In addition to its swimmers competing in the Olympic Games, FINA introduced the World Long-Course Swimming Championships in 1972. The inaugural meet was held in Belgrade in 1973. In 1992, FINA introduced the World Short-Course Swimming Championships. The inaugural championships were held in Majorca in 1993. Figures 11.1 and 11.2 show the total number of long-course and short-course records set per year.

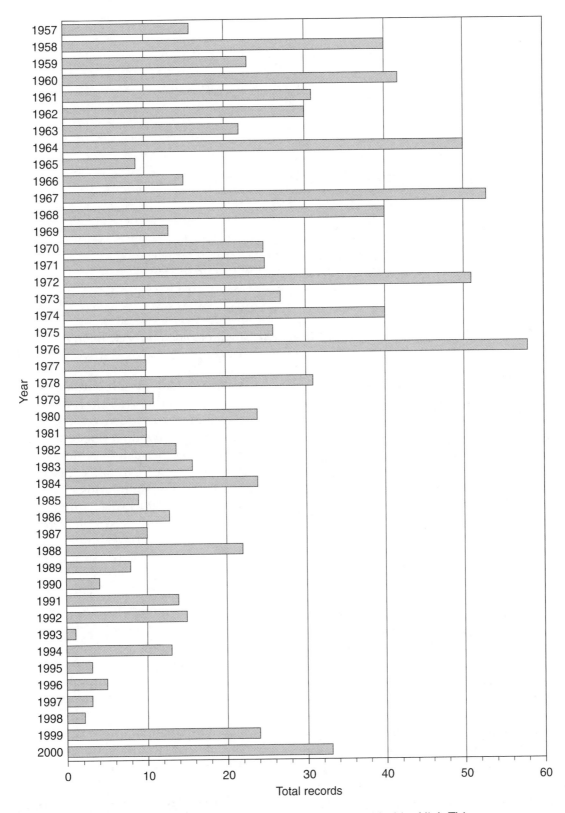

Figure 11.1 World long-course records, 1957–2000. Graph provided by Nick Thierry.

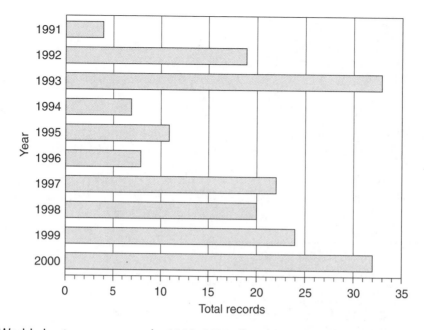

Figure 11.2 World short-course records, 1991–2000. Graph provided by Nick Thierry.

Champions of the Late 19th Century

It was remarkable that most of the great swimmers of the 19th century came from the inland towns of Lancashire. Their methods revolutionized the sport and resulted in a great increase in speed. For many years, the swimmers from the north of England were the fastest in the world. Much of the success of the Lancashire swimmers was due to the fact that teachers with proper credentials were employed to watch and guide the younger swimmers, and they carried out their duties in an efficient manner, with the results already described.

In the last 20 years of the 19th century, a succession of champion swimmers greatly reduced the times for the various racing distances. In the English Championships, the winning time for the 100-yard race was reduced by 15 seconds, the time for the 220-yard race was reduced by 35 seconds, the time for the 500-yard race was reduced by 62 seconds, and the time for the mile was reduced by 5 minutes. Particularly notable in this era were the champions J. Nuttall, J.H. Tyers, J.H. Derbyshire, and J.A. Jarvis. These men, in their individual eras, made a habit of retaining their championship titles year after year.

As an amateur, Joseph Nuttall was the 100-yard champion from 1886 to 1888 and the 220-yard champion from 1886 to 1888. Nuttall later entered the professional ranks, where he was recognized as the fastest professional swimmer of his time. All Nuttall's amateur records were exceeded by John Jarvis.

Jarvis was the 500-yard champion from 1898 to 1901, the half-mile champion from 1898 to 1901, and the one-mile champion from 1897 to 1902. He was champion of England and won championship races in France, Germany, Austria, and Italy, racing against the best-known and fastest swimmers in these countries and beating them in their own waters.

J.H. Tyers was the 100-yard champion from 1892 to 1897, the 220-yard champion from 1892 to 1897, the 440-yard champion from 1893 to 1896, the 500-yard champion from 1893 to 1896, the half-mile champion from 1893 to 1896, and the one-mile champion from 1893 to 1896. J.H. Derbyshire was the 100-yard champion from 1898 to 1901 and again in 1903 and 1904.

Competitive Swimming in the 20th Century

By the mid-20th century, swimming knowledge had spread worldwide, with the result

Matthew Webb, Swimming's First Popular Figure

Captain Matthew Webb was not a competitive swimmer, but he popularized swimming worldwide when he became the first person to swim the English Channel in 1875. Born at Irongate in Shropshire, Webb was 27 years old when he swam the Channel. Webb learned to swim at 7, and when on board the Conway training ship, saved the life of a comrade in danger of drowning. After leading a seafaring life for some years, he returned to England able to swim a good breaststroke, but he was not a fast swimmer. When he started for the Channel swim he was 5 feet 8 inches high, measured 43 inches around the chest, and weighed about 203 pounds.

that international champions could now be expected to come from almost any country. The rise of countries such as Romania, Yugoslavia, France, Brazil, Spain, Mexico, West Germany, Switzerland, and the Soviet Union showed that no one nation owned swimming expertise.

The dominant nations in 20th-century swimming were the United States, Australia, Japan, Hungary, and Holland. Other occasionally successful nations were Germany (up to 1939), the Soviet Union, Great Britain, Denmark, France, Sweden, West Germany, and South Africa.*

Three countries—Australia, the United States, and Japan—established a particularly fine tradition of success in international swimming, each rising to pre-eminence at various times during the 20th century. Although their programs were distinctly different, each country contributed to the growing concept of building a nation's swimming strength through a definite preconceived plan. It is appropriate to examine the contributions made in their time by each of these three countries.

Swimming in Australia

From the start of the first European settlements, swimming was a popular sport in Australia. The warm climate and numerous beaches, rivers, and waterways naturally attracted people to the water for recreation. But few knew how to swim and many drowned until swimming instruction became available and rock pools were built and other areas enclosed to provide safer facilities. With the passage of time came the first swimming races and the eventual forming of clubs and interclub competitions.

First Swimming Race in Australia

The first swimming race in Australia was held in Sydney Harbor (then called Sydney Bay) in the vicinity of Robinson's Baths alongside the Sydney Domain, in February 1846. The event was won by W. Redman, who swam the 440-yard race in 8 minutes, 43 seconds.

Bell's Life in Sydney and Sporting Review (1846) reported this historic event. The match was open to anyone in the colony, but only six swimmers, all subscribers to the local baths, competed: W. Redman Jr., Alister Maclean, J. Redman Sr., G. Thornton, a Mr. Green, and a Mr. Whitbread. The champion won a silver cup, valued at eight pounds, eight shillings, and the privilege of wearing a championship swimming belt for the next year.

At 7:00, the swimmers appeared stripped and wearing different swimming caps to distinguish one from the other. At 7:15, the race began. As described by *Bell's Life in Sydney and Sporting Review*, it was a well-swum race, "but especially the contest for the first and second place was most gallant." Redman Jr., had anointed himself with oil in preparation for the event, as the ancient Romans had. Due to the

---

* East Germany has been excluded from this list because it has been proven in German courts that throughout the 1970s and 1980s, the Olympic and World Championship successes of East German female swimmers were the result of performance-enhancing drugs administered by officials in charge of their state-controlled program.

cold and the rough waters of Sydney Bay, this probably gave him an advantage.

Maclean led for the first 220 yards, followed by Redman Jr., then Redman Sr. As he rounded the southern buoy, Maclean led by about a length, but as they rounded the northern buoy, Redman Jr. turned sharply and was able to close the gap and catch up to Maclean. Redman Jr. continued to swim strongly and eventually gained about 10 yards on Maclean, which is how they finished the race, "the struggle being most gallantly maintained by Mr. Maclean to the end of the very long distance, upwards of a quarter of a mile." Redman Sr. finished third. Thornton and Green finished together, but early in the race Thornton had taken time to assist Whitbread, "who suffered from the boisterous state of the Bay, and was exhausted, but was quickly picked up by one of the boats in attendance."

The final times were 8 minutes, 43 seconds for Redman Jr. and 8 minutes, 49 seconds for Maclean, "which, considering the state of the weather, was very excellent."

Early British Influence on Swimming in Australia

The early British influence on Australian swimming centers around two key individuals: Charles Steedman and Professor Fred Cavill.

Professor Fred Cavill, who emigrated to Australia in 1879, is generally credited with being the chief pioneer of Australian swimming. But it is little known that an equally famous figure in British swimming, Charles

Charles Steedman: Swimming's First Internationalist

Charles Steedman was born in London, England in 1830 and died in Victoria, Australia in 1901. He was swimming's first internationalist, champion of England and later champion of Victoria, Australia. For good measure, he wrote the world's first text on competitive swimming, published it in Melbourne, and later published it in London.

Steedman was an internationalist in the true sense of the word. When Steedman was champion, England was the world's leading swimming country. He took England's advanced knowledge of the sport to Australia and shared it with his new countrymen. Steedman's arrival in Australia caused considerable interest. At the age of 24, Steedman was already an accomplished, knowledgeable, and articulate man who passed on to local enthusiasts detailed accounts of swimming techniques in his native land. In January 1858, Steedman competed in the first World Swimming Championship in Captain Kenney's Ship Baths at St. Kilda, Melbourne. The race, held over 100 yards, was won by John Bennett of Sydney.

Steedman was not only a top professional swimmer, but almost as soon as he arrived, he earned a good living as a skilled pianoforte maker. Always seeking to advance himself, Steedman learned Latin and Greek and became a schoolmaster as well as a journalist.

In 1867, Steedman published *A Manual of Swimming*, the first important swimming book of the modern era. Unlike previous texts, Steedman's book was the first ever written on the sport of competitive swimming. The practical value of the book was enhanced by the fact that it was actually written with the authority of experience by one of the great competitive swimmers of the era. The book was later reprinted in 1873 in Steedman's native London at the price of three shillings and sixpence, quite a hefty sum in those days. It is safe to say that Charles Steedman was the first notable contributor to the development of competitive swimming as a recognized sport, and his seminal work set the stage for the beginning of the modern era of swimming later in the 19th century.

In recognition of his contribution to swimming, Charles Steedman was inducted into the International Swimming Hall of Fame in 2000, nearly 100 years after his death.

Steedman (1830–1901), the reigning English Champion emigrated to Australia in July 1854. With him, Steedman brought the Championship belt of England as proof of his eminent status.

Steedman settled in Melbourne, then a small provincial town of about 23,000 people. Sydney, on the other hand, was already a bustling city with a population of 100,000, so it is more than likely that Steedman's name was not immediately known to the growing number of swimming enthusiasts in Sydney. However, word eventually leaked out that Steedman, the Champion of England, the world's leading swimming nation at the time, was living in Melbourne. Not long after, Captain Kenney staged the First World Championship at St. Kilda, Melbourne, in January 1858 between Steedman and John Bennett, Sydney's leading swimmer. The race was over 100 yards. Bennett beat the veteran Steedman, who had swum his first race 15 years earlier in 1843.

Professor Fred Cavill (1839–1927) was born in London on July 16, 1839, and settled in Sydney in 1879 with his wife, four sons, and three daughters. (He later had two more sons.) Cavill learned to swim in the Serpentine in London at the age of 10, went to sea at 13, served in the Crimean War and Indian rebellion, and held silver and bronze medals from the Royal Humane Society and the Australian Humane Society. He first attempted to swim the English Channel in 1876, a feat he practically accomplished a year later, when he almost swam from France to England on August 20, 1877. However, 50 yards from the English shore, the boatman following Cavill refused to allow the boat to go any farther because of the strong tide flowing to the shore and because of the rocky nature of the coast (Thomas 1904).

On his arrival in Sydney, Cavill built a swimming bath at Rushcutters Bay in Sydney Harbor. He later built another pool at Lavender Bay, where he guaranteed to teach people to swim for one guinea. He moved yet again to open an elegant natatorium built on floats in Farm Cove near the Botanic Gardens, which became one of the wonders of the town (Clarkson 1990). Cavill retired at the age of 70 after a storm ripped the pool enclosure from its moorings and dashed it on the rocks. He died in 1927 at the age of 88 (Dawson 1987).

Professor Cavill's family were all remarkable swimmers. His sons Charles and Arthur (nicknamed Tums) swam across the entrance to San Francisco Harbor. His youngest son, Dick, won 18 Australian and 22 New South Wales titles, and was the first man to break 60 seconds for 100 yards. His son Percy won the 440-yard championship and 5-mile championship of the world in 1897. His son Sydney won the Australian 220-yard championship at the age of 16. Later Sydney was appointed swimming coach to the Olympic Club in San Francisco and with his brother Arthur, helped introduce the Australian crawl to America (Clarkson 1990).

Australia Challenges England

By the end of the 19th century, J.H. Derbyshire had established himself as the fastest swimmer in the world, having recorded a time of 1 minute, 2/5 of a second for the 100 yards. In 1899 after a three-month sea voyage, Freddie Lane, a wiry young Australian, competed in the English 220-yard championship and won, beating Derbyshire in 2 minutes, 38-1/5 seconds.

In May 1902, Lane was back in England with Dick Cavill and other Australian swimmers. Again they competed against Derbyshire, this time in the 100 yards. Lane beat Derbyshire and Cavill, becoming the first swimmer to cover 100 yards in 1 minute, a new world record.

Two weeks later, Cavill regained his form to reduce Lane's record to 58.8 seconds, a record that wasn't recognized because it was recorded in a handicap race. Later that year in Leicester, Lane officially became the first to break 1 minute for the 100 yards, with a time of 59.6 seconds. During their English tour, Cavill and Lane each won two national titles: Lane for 100 and 220 yards, Cavill for 440 and 880 yards. Cavill's crawl stroke was completely new to the English experts and captured the admiration of everyone present. Australian swimming had arrived on the world scene. (For further details of Cavill's stroke, see chapter 1.)

Australia at the Olympics

Australian swimmers such as Lane, Dick Cavill, Barney Kieran, Frank Beaurepaire, and Cecil Healy and women swimmers Fanny Durack and Mona Wylie were the prominent swimmers from the start of the 20th century to the beginning of World War I.

The 1920s saw Andrew Boy Charlton become an Australian national hero for his fighting spirit and fine sportsmanship in his famous duels with Johnny Weissmuller of the United States and Arne Borg of Sweden. Charlton won the 1,500-meter race in Paris in 1924, thus starting Australia's long tradition in this event.

At the 1932 Olympics in Los Angeles, Claire Dennis won Australia's only medal when she won the 200-meter breaststroke. For 16 years, Australian swimming went into a slump. In the first postwar Olympics in London, 1948, Judy Joy Davies, Nancy Lyons, and John Marshall won place medals. After the Olympics, Marshall went on to Yale University, where he trained under Bob Kiphuth. In 1951, in a never-before-seen spate of record breaking, Marshall broke every world mark from the 200-meter to the 1,500-meter freestyle. In 1952 John Davies, a butterfly-breaststroke swimmer and a student at Michigan University, won the only gold medal for Australia in the 200-meter breaststroke.

After training hard for several months in tropical Queensland, the Australians reestablished their long-lost supremacy before wildly cheering home crowds at the 1956 Melbourne Olympics. They won six individual gold medals, several minor placings, and two relay championships. Their success was attributed mainly to the pioneering use of interval training and the introduction of radically improved stroke techniques. (Refer to chapter 1 for more details.)

After any great success, maintaining the momentum can be difficult, especially after the Olympics have been staged in one's own country with all the accompanying public support. However, to the Australians' credit, they held a steady individual gold medal count at the next four sets of Olympic Games (Rome, Tokyo, Mexico City, and Munich) before what had become known as the Second Golden Age of Australian swimming suddenly collapsed, due largely to lack of depth. There were to be eight lean years before Australian swimming started the long climb back to pre-eminence on the world scene at Sydney (2000) and Fukuoka (2001).

The Olympic successes recorded by Australian swimmers are a remarkable achievement for a nation with a population of only 17 million. From 1900 to 2000, Australian swimmers have won 39 individual Olympic gold medals.

Swimming in America*

The Montreal Swimming Association organized the first competitive swimming meets in North America in 1876, and the New York Athletic Club organized the first meets in the United States one year later. The first municipal swimming pool in the United States was built in Brookline, Massachusetts in 1896, but an even older pool, the Detroit Natatorium, had existed since 1816; its dimensions were 16 feet by 33 feet.

The first YMCA swimming bath in the United States was built in Brooklyn, New York in 1885. It measured 14 feet by 45 feet. By 1909, when the YMCA officially launched its National Swimming Campaign, there were 293 pools in YMCAs. Around 1905, a swimming missionary named George Corson introduced mass swimming classes throughout eastern North America. Corson was a horticulture professor at the University of Toronto. A showman, publicist, and traveling teacher, Corson is generally credited with increasing the number of swimmers throughout the YMCA movement in eastern North America.

After a late start, American swimming enjoyed rapid progress from the beginning of the 20th century, mainly because of the elevation of the swimming coach's status from that of bath house attendant to that of professional teacher, the vast number of competitions, the continual improvement in swimming techniques and training methods, the institutional backing of secondary school and university competitions, and the use of administrative methods of the English ASA.

---

* Parts of this section were contributed by William "Buck" Dawson, First Executive Director, International Swimming Hall of Fame. Used by permission of Buck Dawson.

American Domination of World Swimming

America's eventual dominance of world swimming, highlighted by world records and Olympic performances (see table 11.1) of such all-time greats as John Weissmuller, Mark Spitz (seven gold medals at the 1972 Olympics), and many other illustrious American swimmers, began hesitantly with world records by Schaeffer (1899) and LeMoyne (1903) but really took off with Charles Daniels (1906) and the swimming of Duke Kahanamoku in the 1912 Olympics. The United States took charge at the 1920 Olympics and dominated in 1924 and 1928 but dipped to second, as the very young Japanese swimmers took over in 1932 and 1936. The United States resurfaced as number one in 1948 and 1952 but lost to the interval-training and shoulder-rolling Australians in 1956.

In the 1960s, the United States accumulated 80 individual medals at the three Olympic Games (Rome 1960, Tokyo 1964, and Mexico City 1968); other nations claimed the remaining 61 medals (Thierry 1972). At the Montreal Olympics in 1976, the U.S. men's team, under head coach James Counsilman, won 12 of 13 gold medals, the first time in Olympic swimming history that this had been accomplished.

At the Sydney Olympic Games in 2000, the U.S. Olympic team won a total of 97 medals; 38 medals were gold. The U.S. swimming team accounted for 34 percent of the total medals won and 37 percent of the gold medals. In the 32 swimming events, the U.S. team won 33 medals out of a potential 58 medal opportunities (an efficiency rating of 57 percent). The U.S. women's team took home 16 medals; the men's team 17. There were only seven events in which the U.S. team did not win a single medal: men's 200-meter freestyle (4th), men's 200-meter breaststroke (6th), men's 100-meter butterfly (4th), women's 400-meter individual medley (4th), women's 100-meter backstroke (6th), women's 200-meter backstroke (5th), and women's 200-meter freestyle (12th). (Data courtesy of N. Thierry.)

The lessons of American dominance largely have been misunderstood. U.S. success is due to the coaching free market that exists in America. The United States has the largest body of knowledgeable professional swimming coaches in the world, coaches who are highly motivated and dedicated to success. Other nations in the free world have missed the importance of this model and have centralized decision making while retaining tight control of national programs through appointed national coaches.

Over the years, through personal contacts and lecture clinic visits, American swimming coaches traveled overseas to make their experience and expertise available to all countries, irrespective of their forms of government or political affiliations. In particular, for more than a quarter century the American Swimming Coaches Association (ASCA) has provided

Table 11.1 U.S. Swimming Olympic Medals, 1972–2000

	Gold	Silver	Bronze	Total
1972 Munich	17	14	12	43
1976 Montreal	12	14	7	33
1980 Moscow*	N/A	N/A	N/A	N/A
1984 Los Angeles	20	12	1	33
1988 Seoul	8	6	4**	18
1992 Barcelona	11	9**	7	27
1996 Atlanta	13	12	2	27
2000 Sydney	14	8	11	33

* The United States did not compete at the 1980 Moscow Games to protest the Soviet invasion of Afghanistan.

** Additional medals were awarded as the result of ties.

Table provided by Nick Thierry.

leadership and coaching education in the United States and worldwide by conducting its well-attended annual world swim clinics and making membership open to coaches from all countries. In any given year, about 10 percent of the coaches attending the ASCA Annual World Clinic are not U.S. citizens. Similarly, in any given year, foreign membership of ASCA numbered about 350 coaches, mainly from Europe and undeveloped countries.

United States Swimming Programs

American competitive swimming was dominated first by the East Coast, then by Chicago and the Midwest, and finally by California. The Hawaiian influence was strong from 1911 to 1956. There is no longer one area that dominates United States swimming, however. Good coaching has spread nationwide and good programs spring up wherever good coaching exists.

Similarly, United States collegiate swimming, which started with a Yale, Pennsylvania, and Columbia meet in 1896, went through a long period—1924 to 1958—during which six universities dominated the scene: Navy, Northwestern, Rutgers, Michigan, Ohio State, and Yale. It is now becoming more balanced after recent dominance by Sunbelt schools. The total United States swimming picture was dominated by the urban, private-membership athletic clubs from 1875 to 1940 and by the colleges from 1936 to 1960.

High school swimming in the United States became a major development program, as did the YMCA and the Boys and Girls Clubs of America. More recently, community recreation swim clubs have played a big part in America's learn-to-swim program, which continues through to the structured high school and college programs and ultimately to USA Swimming (formerly AAU), the FINA-recognized governing body of American senior swimming.

Americans also originated age-group swimming, an exposure and developmental program begun in the 1950s through Carl Bauer at the Missouri Athletic Club in St. Louis and developed by Beth Kaufman in California. The impact of United States age-group swimming was so great in the 1960s that swimming became a kindergarten sport, with world-record holders as young as 12 years old and Olympic champions in their teens.

The development of age-group swimming was the biggest single factor in the tremendous growth of American swimming in the post–World War II years. Peter Daland, coach of the University of Southern California and one of

Charlotte "Eppy" Epstein (1885–1938)

Charlotte "Eppy" Epstein, the mother of American women's swimming, established women's swimming as a recognized sport in the United States and was responsible for its inclusion at the 1920 Antwerp Olympic Games. During her 22 years with the New York Women's Swimming Association (NYWSA), the club's swimmers set 51 world records and registered 31 National (USA) Champion relay teams. Within months of the NYWSA's establishment, Eppy persuaded the Amateur Athletic Union to permit women swimmers to register as athletes with the AAU for the first time.

By profession a court stenographer, Epstein led the United States lady swimmers to the 1920, 1924, and 1932 Olympiads. During this time, American female swimmers dominated the Games, and those considered her proteges were champions: Claire Galligan, Gertrude Ederle, Aileen Riggen, Helen Wainwright, and Eleanor Holm.

When Epstein was named assistant manager of the 1932 U.S. Women's Olympic Swim Team, she became the first woman to be appointed to such a position. Four years later, she was invited to coach the 1936 U.S. Women's Olympic Team in Berlin but declined and resigned from the U.S. Olympic Committee in protest against Nazi Germany's policies.

the prime movers in American swimming during the second half of the 20th century, told me that the first result of the new program showed up at the Melbourne Olympic Games in 1956, when Sylvia Ruuska, an age-group product, won the bronze medal in the 400-meter freestyle.

According to Daland, the first results of real depth from the new age-group program were at the Rome Olympics in 1960. The United States had seen a great upsurge of swimming, particularly in California. Daland coached at the University of Southern California, and at the Los Angeles Athletic Club (with co-coach Don Gambril), while George Haines at Santa Clara, developed the most successful homespun team of all time.

The Santa Clara swim club, coached by George Haines, achieved the remarkable tally of 43 national titles, 55 Olympians, and 51 Olympic medals (33 gold, 11 silver, and 7 bronze)—an achievement rivaled only by coach Mark Schubert during his 13-year tenure at Mission Viejo, California, where Schubert's swimmers won 44 national titles.

During the years 1957 to 1959, a number of age-groupers began to break world records. The age-group program spread across the United States, causing a great influx of young swimmers. The large increase in numbers was not without attendant difficulties, particularly in administration and coaching development. The swimming population of America multiplied about ten-fold between 1956 and 1964. What had been small meets became huge meets. For example, in southern California, a senior meet that at one time had 1 heat, sometimes 2, but rarely 3, soon came to have 10 or 12 heats, even with set-qualifying times.

Although Carl Bauer, Beth Kaufman, Peter Daland, and Dave Beaver are generally acknowledged as the pioneers of the age-group movement, its expansion largely resulted from development by the local swimming committees in Sunbelt states such as Texas, Florida, and California. It was promoted mainly by age-group parents, upper-middle class people who had taken over the leadership role in swimming administration.

American University Swimming

As the age-group youngsters grew up, an influx of swimmers entered American university swimming programs. It was not long before university swimming benefited from the dynamic age-group program that had taken shape beneath it. Soon, many hard-working former age-group swimmers were participating in the college ranks, causing a revolution in the size of college teams, the size of competitions, and the number of good swimmers.

Athletic scholarships were offered to induce swimmers to compete while pursuing their degrees. According to Daland (1984), athletic scholarships existed for 50 to 60 years but became more numerous in the 1950s and 1960s. In the mid-1970s, however, the financial crisis that developed in American colleges caused severe cutbacks. The National Collegiate Athletic Association (NCAA) removed 40 percent of the aid in nonrevenue sports. However, there always has been a high percentage of nonscholarship swimmers in American universities—a majority, in fact.

Collegiate swimming programs for women really grew when the federal government passed Title IX, which mandated all programs in schools, colleges, or universities that receive funds from the federal government have equal opportunity for women. Before Title IX, female swimmers tended to drop out of the sport earlier than male swimmers. But increased opportunities in athletic programs provide a strong incentive for women to remain longer in the sport.

In the years since Title IX was passed, however, the face of American college campuses has changed. Nationwide, there are now more female undergraduate students than male; on some campuses, the difference can be as much as 55 percent to 45 percent female to male population. Because one of the goals of Title IX was to make participation and scholarship levels approximate the relative percentages in the student population, athletic administrators have felt increasing pressure to cut programs and scholarships for male student-athletes to comply with Title IX. Since big-ticket men's sports such as football require many of the resources available (a typical Division I football program is allowed 85 scholarships, plus walk-ons), it has become exceedingly difficult to maintain balance between men's and women's athletic programs without dropping some of the less visible men's programs, such as swimming.

Although Title IX has caused great problems for male swimming programs at the collegiate level, it has provided huge opportunities on the women's side. This has contributed to the development of the dominant U.S. women's swimming program. The ratio of female to male swimmers overall in USA Swimming is 60 percent to 40 percent. Within a few years, two-thirds of American swimmers registered with USA Swimming could be female. This is indirectly related to Title IX; parents put their kids in sports that they perceive provide the greatest opportunities.

The current federal administration is likely to reexamine the way Title IX is administered. This may or may not impact male swimming programs. Several legislators, including Congressman Dennis Hastert (R-Illinois), a former wrestling coach, are leading the charge to make compliance to Title IX live up to the word of the legislation, changing the way it has been applied to provide more opportunities for women without sacrificing opportunities for men (Neuburger 2001).

The Professional Development of American Swimming Coaches*

Begun in 1985, the American Swimming Coaches Association certification program is a voluntary system designed to identify professionally prepared swimming coaches. By January of 2000, 6,050 coaches had applied for certification and over 5,200 had been granted certification.

The program grew steadily, with the upper-level coaches (3, 4, and 5) generally coming into the program first, as might be expected, followed by the newer coaches in subsequent years. The statistics are revealing. In 1985, over 74 percent of the coaches certified were level 3 or higher. By 1987, this percentage had dropped to 39 percent, and in 1988 and 1989, over 80 percent of the coaches certified were at levels 1 and 2. In 1999, the percentages were 64 percent at levels 1 and 2, 21 percent at level 3, 9 percent at level 4, and 6 percent at level 5.

This indicates that the program has received considerable acceptance by the coaching community. The ASCA certification program was accepted by every organized coaching group in the United States, beginning with National Interscholastic Coaches Association (NISCA) and followed by masters coaches, YMCA coaches, and college coaches' associations.

The Golden Era of Japanese Swimming

Swimming has been an organized sport in Japanese schools since 1603. Japanese interschool competitive swimming programs have continued to the present time (Oppenheim 1970).

From 1932 to 1936, Japan reigned supreme in world swimming, but after World War II—with the exception of great swimmers such as Furuhashi, Hashizume, Yamanaka, Taguchi, Tanaka, Suzuki, and a few others—Japan never regained its former depth in world swimming.

The dramatic rise of the Japanese to world supremacy at the Los Angeles Olympics in 1932 marked the first occasion that a single country had put into effect a definite national plan with the aim of achieving complete mastery. It also was the first time that the motion picture camera was used as a scientific device for improving swimming technique on a national scale. The Japanese made extensive motion film studies of leading American and European champions from above and below water. The films were then shown to schoolchildren throughout Japan to give them a visual idea of good technique.

These children were carefully nurtured in sound stroke technique from an early age. The American crawl was cleverly adapted to the

---

*"The Professional Development of American Swimming Coaches" was contributed by John Leonard, Executive Director, American Swimming Coaches Association. Used by permission of John Leonard.

shorter Japanese physique, but the Japanese crawl, as it came to be called, was not fundamentally different from the American style. The Japanese youngsters were taught well from an early age, and they trained harder than swimmers had ever done before. Good technique and strenuous training were consistently applied. The results of this first conscientious application of a national development plan were outstanding.

In the Amsterdam Olympics in 1928, the breaststroke swimmer Tsuruta was the only Japanese to win a title. His success inspired all of Japan. Four years later, Japan brought a team of young teenagers to the 1932 Los Angeles Olympic Games and shook the world of swimming, winning every event but the 400 meters, which was won by Clarence "Buster" Crabbe, an American.

The American team coach, Bob Kiphuth, was reportedly pleased by the fact that in practice, the 1932 American Olympic team had beaten the 800-meter relay record by over 15 seconds. This improvement was not enough to beat the Japanese team, which eclipsed the old relay record by more than 37 seconds to establish an undreamed-of mark (Cureton 1934). In all, the Japanese accumulated 86 points, while the Americans earned 33. Japanese swimmers won first and second in every race but one; in that race they placed third, fourth, and fifth. These results showed a Japanese team of unusual mass strength (Cureton 1934).

An amazing feature of the great Japanese rise to victory was that it happened without warning between the Games of 1928 and 1932. The Japanese success in the 1930s was the first example in competitive swimming of what can be achieved by careful planning and specialized training that works purposefully rather than hopefully toward a set goal. They didn't know it at the time, but the Japanese developed what would prove to be a basic recipe for national success in international sport.

The Development of Multilevel National Programs

Growth of the sport and the desire to excel led to the development of multilevel national programs and the employment of professional administrators, often university trained in sport leadership. Assisting these professionals were lay volunteers, prominent people in commerce, industry, and other professions. In more advanced countries, the better-organized lay volunteers contributed their expertise and guidance, supplanting the old part-time amateur hobbyist. In a sense, swimming administration was taken off the kitchen table and put into the board room.

In some countries, competitive swimming, like all sports, was organized and centrally controlled by the state. Elsewhere, governments directly involved in funding national programs tried to give an impression of remaining at arm's length, but often it was apparent that whoever paid the piper called the tune.

The Need for Motivators and Innovators

Many beginning coaches, unsure of what information to accept and what to discard, really didn't know how to start coaching. They came to expect more from science than science could provide. In the late 20th century, young coaches had grown up in the sport expecting that science would supply them with all the answers instead of trying to become more competent and self-sufficient by testing new ideas as part of their daily practical coaching.

As competitive swimming entered the 21st century, some penetrating questions were being asked. Had modern coaches been caught between two approaches, the pool-deck empirical and the scientific? Had modern coaches lost the ability to innovate? Did young coaches in particular rely too much on scientific research papers and not enough on developing an ability to innovate?

A trust in science does not imply the abandonment of hunch and intuition. On the contrary, the history of science itself is studded with cases of important discoveries made through chance, hunch, serendipity—even dreams. Most coaches who use their hunches well also seem to possess a high level of knowledge and understanding about their activities. So, the question is not when to apply science and when to rely on intuition but rather how to combine the two effectively.

William Wilson, Swimming's First Innovator

William Wilson was an important swimming pioneer, a skilled and lucid writer, a visionary, and an innovator. He was born in London on November 13, 1844, to Scottish parents and moved to Glasgow when he was a child. Had he been born 100 years later, there's little doubt that his thinking would still have been in the vanguard of swimming progress.

Wilson stressed the need for scientific study of swimming, holding that a successful swimming teacher ought to devote as much thought, application, hard work, and constant practice as instructors did in almost any branch of education or science. Wilson was a swimmer, a swimming instructor, and the sport's first regular newspaper journalist. He studied the sport carefully and concluded that swimming had undergone very little improvement "during its many years' practice." With great foresight, he announced that humans should be able to use their superior intellect to move through water at a much faster rate than they had so far attained.

Wilson had many firsts. He was the first to describe and illustrate the racing start and turn, the first in the literature to advocate an overarm recovery for the sidestroke, and the first to develop a life-saving drill. He created the idea of water polo. He pioneered land- and water-training methods. With the early shortage of swimming pools, he promoted year-round cold-water swimming in the sea.

In 1883, Wilson published *The Swimming Instructor*, one of the 19th century's three landmark books on swimming. Along with Charles Steedman's *A Manual of Swimming*, Wilson's work was considered a great advance on the literature of the time. Wilson, far ahead of his time, said that there was a need to invent and introduce some method, or methods, whereby the body would move through water faster than the present rate.

Wilson thought it was necessary to acknowledge our helplessness regarding swimming and consider how best to improve the present state of the art. His references to resistance versus propulsion, made nearly 120 years ago, still form the fundamental basis on which present-day discussions on stroke mechanics evolve. (Several times Wilson mentioned momentum, an aspect of human swimming propulsion that remains a much-neglected study.)

Chapter 12

Doping, Testing, and Modern Efforts to Gain an Edge

For most of 20 years, powerful East German females ruled women's swimming. Though suspected of taking performance-enhancing drugs and despite drug testing at the Olympics, not one positive result was recorded during these years.

The truth emerged after the fall of the East German state in 1989. Starting in the 1970s, the officials of the German Democratic Republic's elite state-controlled sports schools routinely gave performance-enhancing drugs to swimmers under the pretense that they were merely taking vitamins. In reality, they were ingesting the now notorious little blue pills (oral turinabol), a powerful performance-enhancing drug capable of producing damaging side effects.

Although athletes from West Germany, the United States, and Canada also used drugs, they did so of their own volition. What was specifically different about drug cheating in East Germany was that it was a state-ordered policy aimed at improving athletic performance with drugs (State Plan 14.25 of 1974), forged by a group of officials and doctors, including Dr. Ewald and Dr. Hoeppner, and implemented on a large scale. This fact, in itself, ensured that the plan was highly researched, controlled, and specialized.

Never before in the history of sport had such a depraved, cynical, and shameful act been systematically perpetrated on youngsters entrusted to the care of adults. At the bottom of it were qualified medical doctors, who had taken a professional oath to practice medicine and cause no intentional harm to those in their care.

Only after the East German state ceased to exist did the world learn that the long-held suspicions were true. The doping trials that began in Berlin in March 1998 revealed that the former East German sporting regime, under State Plan 14.25 of 1974, had made it a state policy to improve athletic performance through performance-enhancing drugs. There was no out-of-competition testing at that time, but when the story of the cheating East German regime finally emerged, it was understood that East German swimmers had either been given diuretic-masking agents before the Games started or that the steroids had naturally passed through their systems long before they came to the Olympics. The great coach-educators of the early 20th century could never have foreseen how their concepts of good sportsmanship and fair play would be trampled on in the interests of political ideology.

By taking anabolic steroids to increase muscle mass and strength, an athlete can undertake much higher levels of work than normally possible; of course, doing so starkly contrasts the old ideal of striving for success through honest effort. East Germany and other totalitarian countries, with their cold, impersonal, state systems of sport preparation, had no such traditions. For two decades, East German officials insisted they were winning fairly because of a superior system, but, in fact, they had not the slightest compunction about administering performance-enhancing drugs to athletes without the athletes' knowledge.

I will abstain from all intentional wrongdoing and harm, especially from abusing the bodies of man or woman.

From the Hippocratic Oath

The East German Doping Regime

The last decade of the 20th century produced incontrovertible proof of drug cheating by athletes under the East German regime. The discovery of secret police (Stasi) files confirmed that thousands of athletes, including swimmers, were involved in systematic state-controlled cheating between 1972 and 1989. The German Democratic Republic's much vaunted scientific sports program was spearheaded by doped female swimmers who swept the boards in Olympic, World, and European Championships. The Stasi files also revealed that Russia was involved in state-controlled doping in sport, as were most of the Eastern Bloc countries.

Most of the athletes given the drugs were under the age of 16 (some were as young as 10), and they had no idea what they were given. Younger athletes were not informed about the drugs or their consequences and were usually kept away from their parents to avoid the discovery of this interference with their children's well-being. Athletes over 18 had to sign an oath of secrecy.

The indelible fact is that for 20 years the performances of the East German swimmers resulted from the ingestion of performance-enhancing drugs, administered covertly by the officers of the state. For 20 years FINA, the international governing body of swimming, failed to catch the East Germans, who were experts at pretesting their athletes to ensure that they were clear before allowing them to compete. Out-of-competition testing was nonexistent at that time, and since testing was conducted only during competitions, not one East German tested positive.

The world records set by East German swimmers were allowed to remain in the FINA record books, and the athletes still have their Olympic medals. Neither FINA nor the IOC have seen fit to retroactively award medals and other honors to those dispossessed of what is rightfully theirs. A large section of the swimming world, particularly those who still cherish achievement by honest effort, still carry considerable resentment that these injustices have yet to be set right.

At the 2000 Olympics, the German Olympic Committee's media guide book included the results of GDR swimmers as part of Germany's Olympic history. This was done despite the fact that their judicial system prosecuted the former GDR officials responsible for state-sponsored cheating.

East German Doping Trials*

The historic East German doping trials began in March 1998, nearly nine years after the fall of the Berlin Wall, with the so-called "pilot trial" of doctors and swimming coaches from the former SC Dynamo Club (East Berlin). This was the first of a series of trials that would last until October 2, 2000, the statute of limitations. It is difficult to determine if they would ever have taken place without the relentless efforts of a Heidelberg molecular biologist Professor Dr. Werner Franke and his wife, Brigitte Berendonk. The first to uncover and publish much of the East German doping history, they also provided valuable documentation and support to investigating and prosecuting authorities, not to mention former athletes who had been doped.

A special division of the criminal police, the Central Investigations Office for Government and Reunification Crimes (ZERV), was charged with investigating doping crimes. Charges ranged from bodily harm to assisting in bodily harm, and in the complicated amalgamation of Eastern and West law, courts were obliged to operate with the milder form of punishment (East or West accordingly). The Dynamo trial saw a great deal of denial, and sometimes refusal, by former athletes to denounce their coaches and their personal achievements by admitting to doping. As the top East German officials came to trial, more victims came forward to testify, and at this point, they stopped being pariahs and found a greater degree of support from their respective communities.

Effects of Doping on Athletes

Women like Birgit Matz and Carola Beraktchjan, former swimmers for Berlin's Dynamo Club, testified against their coaches in 1998. Both have permanently deepened voices, and Matz has noticeable facial hair.

Rica Reinisch, a triple Olympic champion in 1980, has had five miscarriages and suffers

---

* Reprinted by permission of Karin Helmstaedt, a freelance journalist and author who followed the doping trials in Berlin. Reprinted by permission of *Swimnews*, July 2000.

Chronology of German Doping Trials and Verdicts

March 18, 1998. First trial of systematic doping in the former East Germany opens. Four swimming coaches and two doctors from Berlin's Dynamo Club are accused of bodily harm for distributing anabolic steroids to underage female swimmers.

August 18, 1998. Second trial of doping perpetrators opens in Berlin. Three swimming coaches from Berlin's TSC club—Klaus Klemenz, Peter Mattonet, and Bernd Christochowitz—and two doctors—Dr. Dorit Rösler and Dr. Ulrich Sünder—are charged with bodily harm.

August 24, 1998. TSC trial ends with all five defendants found guilty of bodily harm. Fines range from 7,000 to 27,000 DM (approximately $3,200 to $12,500 U.S.).

August 31, 1998. First verdicts handed down in the Dynamo trial. Former Olympic swimming coach Rolf Gläser confesses to charges and is fined 7,200 DM (approximately $3,300). Dr. Dieter Binus also confesses and is fined 9,000 DM (approximately $4,100).

(continued)

(continued)

September 14, 1998. Former Dynamo swim coach Volker Frischke is fined 5,000 DM (approximately $2,300). Shortly afterward, his colleague Dieter Lindemann, former coach of world record-holder Franziska van Almsick, gets off with 4,000 DM (approximately $1,800). Dieter Krause is fined 3,000 DM (approximately $1,400).

December 7, 1998. After 42 days of proceedings, a final verdict is handed down in the Dynamo trial. Dr. Bernd Pansold is fined 14,400 DM (approximately $6,700). His appeal is denied.

April 12, 1999. Dietrich Hannemann, former director of East Germany's Sports Medicine Services, receives a fine of 45,000 DM (approximately $20,900).

June 21, 1999. The first suspended prison sentence is handed down to a former doper. Dr. Dietbert Freiberg from Sports Medicine Services is given a six-month suspended sentence.

October 22, 1999. Horst Röder, former vice president of the East German Sports and Gymnastics Union (DTSB), gets a one-year suspended sentence.

November 1999. Uwe Neumann, former coach of triple Olympic champion Rica Reinisch, is fined 8,000 DM in Dresden (approximately $3,700).

December 22, 1999. Egon Müller, former general secretary of East Germany's swimming federation, and Wolfgang Richter and Jürgen Tanneberger, former men's and women's national team coaches, receive one-year suspended sentences and fines of 5,000 DM (approximately $2,300).

January 12, 2000. Dr. Lothar Kipke, 72, former Swimming Federation doctor, receives a suspended sentence of one year and three months, plus a fine of 7,500 DM (approximately $3,400), the heaviest sentence at this point.

March 26, 2000. Sport doctor Jochen Neubauer from Potsdam is fined 9,000 DM (approximately $4,100) and dismissed from his position as a physician at Potsdam's Olympic Training Centre, though he still has his position as team doctor for Tennis Borussia Football.

April 11, 2000. In the state of Thüringia, prosecutors wrap up all doping-related cases. Five doctors and one coach are fined 2,500 to 11,700 DM (approximately $1,100 to $5,400). Fifty-three investigations are officially closed. Also in April, swimming coach Bernd Henneberg is fined 5,000 DM (approximately $2,300) for his doping activities in the city of Halle.

April 13, 2000. In Leipzig court, Stefan Hetzer, former coach of East Germany's most successful swimmer ever, six-time Olympic gold medallist Kristin Otto, is charged with bodily harm and is fined 15,000 DM (approximately $7,000) after he admits to doping Otto and eight other swimmers.

July 18, 2000. Most significant doping trial comes to an end in Berlin. Manfred Ewald, former president of the DTSB and leader of the country's medals-at-any-price policy, is given a 22-month suspended jail term. Dr. Manfred Hoeppner, the doctor in charge of overseeing the system, gets 18 months, also suspended. Both are convicted of contributing to bodily harm in 20 cases through their leading roles in the doping system.

July 25, 2000. Council for Manfred Ewald announces it will appeal the Berlin court's decision to Germany's Federal Court of Justice in Leipzig. Victims' lawyer Michael Lehner will also appeal both senior officials' sentences.

Reprinted by permission of Karin Helmstaedt, a freelance journalist and author who followed the doping trials in Berlin, and by permission of *Swimnews*, July 2000.

from recurring ovarian cysts. Catherine Menschner, who received male hormones from the age of 10, suffers from permanent damage to her spine and reproductive organs.

Jutta Gottschalk, a former swimmer from Magdeburg, gave birth to a daughter who is blind in one eye. Her teammate Martina Gottschalt has a 15-year old son who was born with severe club feet.

Shot and discus throwers Brigitte Michel and Birgit Boese both had great difficulties conceiving; as a young woman wanting to get pregnant, Michel was told by a gynecologist she would have to give up sport because her reproductive organs were like those of a 10-year-old girl.

Perhaps the most grotesque story of all came from Andreas Krieger, formerly European champion shot-putter Heidi Krieger. She was so physically changed by the drugs she received that she finally underwent a sex change in 1997, suffering great emotional trauma and contemplating suicide along the way.

The Chinese Doping Problem

In 1992, as if from nowhere, the number of Chinese swimmers ranked in the top 25 world rankings soared from a plateau of less than 30 to 98. Furthermore, all but 4 of the 98 swimmers were female, and their improvement rate was much greater than could be expected as a result of normal growth and development.

This huge change led to a growing suspicion that Chinese swimmers were being doped.

Although the sudden upsurge in Chinese swimming was reminiscent of the 20 years of drug cheating by the former East German regime, some fair-minded people initially wanted to give the Chinese the benefit of the doubt. In the first edition of this book, I commented

> Chinese swimmers, competing in their first Olympics at Seoul, reached several finals and served notice that China could well achieve a rapid rise to world prominence even before the end of the 20th century (Colwin 1992, p. 182).

But no one could have guessed that in 1991, at the World Swimming Championships in Perth, the Chinese swimmers would come away with six medals—four gold, one silver, and one bronze—and that at the 1994 World Championships in Rome, the Chinese women would astound the world by winning 12 of the 16 gold medals at stake, setting five world records in the process (see table 12.1).

Not only because the Chinese girls came from nowhere to sweep these events, but also their incredible muscularity and other typical signs of steroid abuse caused immediate suspicion among experienced coaches from several countries, having the memory of 20 years of East German cheating still fresh in their minds. Moreover, several world-renowned endocrinologists concluded that Chinese female swimmers had been subjected to testosterone medication. Throughout the meet, simmering resentment grew to downright anger that

Table 12.1 Chinese Olympic and World Swimming Medals, 1988–2000

	Gold	Silver	Bronze	Total
1988 Seoul Olympic Games	0	3	1	4
1991 Perth World Championships	4	1	1	6
1992 Barcelona Olympic Games	4	5	0	9
1994 Rome World Championships	12	6	1	19
1996 Atlanta Olympic Games	1	3	2	6
1998 Perth World Championships	3	2	2	7
2000 Sydney Olympic Games	0	0	0	0

Data courtesy of Nick Thierry.

reached a flash point on the final day of the championships. Dave Johnson, the Canadian head coach, called a news conference at which he produced a petition signed by representatives from 18 countries urging FINA to introduce a more rigorous program of drug testing.

While the petition did not refer specifically to China, there was no mistaking the terse message it contained: the apparent reemergence of the extensive use of performance-enhancing drugs, especially in women's competition, constitutes the single greatest threat to the progress and integrity of the sport.

Subsequent events proved that the Chinese girls used a very sophisticated skin-applied (topical) testosterone derivative. But the Chinese continued to maintain that their dramatic improvement resulted from traditional Chinese medicine and the use of various Chinese herbs. They insisted that their swimmers were girls of strong peasant stock who descended from people accustomed to hard work, harder than any Westerner could ever have done, and this was why they were so successful. Western coaches were accused of being racist and jealous of Chinese success.

After the sudden, unbelievable performances of Chinese swimmers at the 1994 World Championships in Rome, the world of swimming was in turmoil. After 20 years of undetected East German doping, FINA's ability to identify and punish major drug offenders came to be strongly questioned, particularly among the major swimming nations. The thought of the sport enduring another long period of uninterrupted drug cheating caused a great deal of anger. A call went out to FINA to deal decisively with this new and very obvious drug threat to the sport.

Despite the dissimulating and evasive statements made by prominent Chinese coaches, the early suspicions about the Chinese swimming team were confirmed at the Asian Games in Hiroshima, October 1994, when seven Chinese swimmers—including Yang Aihua and Lu Binn, the world champions from the Rome World Championships earlier that same year—were tested soon after stepping off their plane. Caught by surprise, they had no time to use diuretics to mask the presence of steroids,

and their tests proved positive. At this point, the number of Chinese positive tests had reached a total of 11. The drug detected in Hiroshima was a relatively new and very powerful dehydrotestosterone (DHT), first seen in the pharmacopoeia in 1991 and 1992. The new DHT combined with any kind of base and thus could be used as a massage cream that was quickly absorbed through the skin.

In the wake of this startling news, the China Swimming Association (CSA) could not, or would not, give any explanation of the large number of positive tests accumulated by their swimmers, who, at the time, were far more than the rest of the world put together.

First FINA Delegation to China, March 2–6, 1995

On February 15, 1995, FINA appointed a delegation to visit China to investigate the background behind the many positive drug tests in 1994.

During this first meeting with the Chinese, Gunner Werner, secretary of FINA, to his credit, told the Chinese that 11 positive tests in 1994 was an unacceptably high number from any one country and that the purpose of the FINA visit was to investigate the background to these events.

Without going into all the specifics of the copious FINA reports, certain distinct conclusions resulted from the FINA investigation:

- Whereas the East German motivation for cheating had been to boost the so-called benefits of their political system, it would seem that money was the main motivation for Chinese swimmers and their coaches to cheat.
- CSA had suspended several coaches from domestic and international competition because of positive tests found in their swimmers.
- The FINA delegation was unable to find proof of systematic doping.
- The CSA promised to institute a number of measures and reforms, including out-of-competition doping tests.

Second FINA Delegation to China, February 1998

On January 8, 1998, a few days before the start of the World Championships in Perth, West Australia, customs officers at the Sydney airport discovered human growth hormone (HGH) in the baggage of Chinese swimmer Yuan Yuan, placed there by her coach Zhou Zhewen.

Six days later, it was announced that tests in Perth showed the presence of the diuretic-masking agent triamterine—a banned substance—in the urine samples of four Chinese swimmers, Wang Luna, Yi Zhang, Huijue Cai, and Wei Wang. (The swimmers were later each suspended from competition for two years, while three coaches associated with the swimmers—Zhi Cheng, Hiuqin Xu, and Zhi Cheng—were each suspended for three months.)

The world of swimming could not have imagined the vast media coverage resulting from these discoveries. The Australian media, from the most conservative to the tabloids, ran page after page on the developing story, usually on the front page and several inside pages as well. In Europe and much of Asia, the story was featured in big metropolitan newspapers. To the dismay of the organizers, the World Championships in Perth were becoming a fiasco even before the meet started. Never before had competitive swimming received so much publicity—most of it adverse. Following the worldwide media uproar, and concerned about the discovery of HGH at the Sydney airport, FINA immediately announced that they would send a second delegation to China to examine and study measures to eliminate doping.

A FINA delegation arrived in China the following month on February 16, 1998, and met with leading officials of the CSA, including the swimmers who had tested positive and their coaches. At the meeting, the CSA made a reassuring Eleven Points Declaration outlining in detail how it proposed to tackle the doping problem in Chinese swimming. The main points centered on increased testing, severe punishment for swimmers and coaches, improved antidoping regulations, registration of swimmers, limitation of cash awards, and several other positive steps.

Third FINA Delegation to China, December 1–4, 1999

FINA's third visit to China was held in Shanghai to meet with members of the Shanghai Swimming Association as well as the CSA.

On the positive side, more funding had ensured a great increase in the number of out-of-competition tests. As promised, CSA conducted exactly 600 tests in 1998 (162 in competition, 15 at the FINA World Cup, and 423 out of competition), with 4 positive (3 for DHT, 1 for testosterone/epitestosterone ratio). Each of the four swimmers who tested positive was suspended for four years, the FINA minimum. For the first 10 months of 1999, 646 tests were conducted (217 in competition, 429 out of competition), with no positives.

In its Eleven Points Declaration, the CSA assured FINA that it would ban for life any swimmer violating the rules against the use of steroids or similar substances. But it had not been able to do so, saying that it was difficult dealing with other groups, including coaches and public officials, who opposed a life ban. However, the CSA seemed to have been working with state authorities regarding criminal penalties for doping but without result.

Disappointing Progress

One of the main reasons for the FINA delegation's second visit to Beijing (February 1998) had been to hear and discuss the CSA's report on the incident at the Sydney airport before the 1998 World Championships. The third FINA delegation found the progress made by CSA since its second visit disappointing. The only attempt at investigating the incident had been the interrogation of the principals, who continued to deny knowledge of any wrongdoing.

Educational sessions had been held in Baoding (May 1998) and in Daqing (April 1999), at the time of the national championships in those cities, to discuss antidoping issues with swimmers, coaches, and team leaders, and translations of FINA's latest doping rules had been distributed by the CSA to all clubs.

The CSA had registered by computer all its approximately 1,200 elite swimmers, and the swimmers had signed a Letter of Guarantee pledging to follow the doping rules. Registered swimmers were to receive ID cards to assist their identification by FINA's sampling agents.

The CSA advised the delegation that it was testing blood drawn from swimmers, not to determine the presence of banned substances, but to see whether blood doping was occurring.

The CSA's promise that coaches of swimmers who test positive will be severely sanctioned seems to have been adhered to. The coach of the three swimmers who tested positive for DHT in November 1998 was suspended for four years and fined Y10,000, while the coach of the four swimmers who tested positive for a diuretic in Perth, January 1998, was suspended from coaching for eight years.

In addition, Chinese labor authorities prohibited the total withholding of prize money until after retirement. As a result, CSA now pays one-fifth of all prize money won to the swimmer within a year of competition and the remainder after four years but only if no doping offenses have occurred. The FINA delegation expressed understanding with this compromise but wanted to be told of changes as soon as implemented.

Regarding the CSA's stated intention to announce all sanctions immediately to the public, the delegation expressed concern that it had taken 10 months to advise FINA of the three DHT positives in November 1998.

Despite the CSA being able to register all of its 1,200 members, it was still experiencing difficulties in maintaining proper registration procedures throughout such a large country, a problem compounded by the fact that the great majority of Chinese swimmers were not registered members of CSA. This gives the CSA no authority over these swimmers when it comes to out-of-competition testing and other regulatory measures.

In particular there had been an incident in 1998 in which a FINA sampling agent had sought to test a Chinese swimmer who the CSA claimed was not registered with CSA, even though he was training with other CSA-registered swimmers in Shanghai. It appears that CSA only controls the elite swimmers in China, while the provincial swimming organizations such as the Shanghai Swimming Association registered the bulk of the grass-roots and open group level swimmers.

CSA was trying to develop a national registration system to cover all new swimmers developed in China and stated that it would employ a full-time person responsible for doping control. This person would communicate results and ensure that accurate identities of swimmers in the top 50 lists be communicated to the FINA office in Lausanne.

The Shanghai Swimming Association

The SSA has about 30,000 swimmers, many of whom are novices or just learning to swim. The better age-group swimmers number about 3,200, of whom it was estimated only 60 to 100 are registered. While the SSA seems to do the same kind of education and dissemination of antidoping information that the CSA does, it does not conduct out-of-competition testing.

During FINA's third visit to China, SSA representatives appeared exceedingly naive. They seemed quick to accept excuses by swimmers that positive doping tests were the result of ingesting food or food supplements, even when such explanations made no sense at all (e.g., that two swimmers tested positive for the diuretic triamterine after eating pig liver).

SSA representatives admitted the SSA lacked control over swimmers. Even when a swimmer was suspended for a doping violation, that swimmer could continue to train and receive a stipend from his or her club. However, such a swimmer did lose financial benefits in the way of prizes and sponsorships (Leonard 2000).

When asked why there was such a high incidence of positive doping tests in Shanghai, the answer was that more good swimmers lived in Shanghai than in other provinces so more testing occurred.

By the end of FINA's third visit to China in December 1999, it was clear that this policy toward China was meeting with mixed results. The FINA delegation did not recommend another visit by a similar FINA delegation. They believed that as much had been accomplished by such visits as could be hoped for and that FINA rather should assist those in responsible positions within the CSA to continue the fight against doping.

Positive Drug Tests by Swimmers by Country

1. China—38 total, with two swimmers caught twice

2. Russia/USSR—8 total, with one swimmer caught twice

3. United States, Great Britain—7

4. Spain—6

5. Austria, Australia—4

6. Belgium, Poland, Brazil, France—3

7. Canada, Germany, New Zealand, South Africa—2

8. Tunisia, Egypt, Argentina, Indonesia, Finland, Ukraine, Ireland, Mexico, Lithuania, Slovenia, Ecuador, Italy, Slovakia, Singapore—1

9. Excused (no sanction): Netherlands—one swimmer twice; Greece—1

10. Not counted: United States—1, swimmer retired

Reprinted by permission from *Swimming's Hall of Shame* by B.S. Rushall (2000).

FINA Extraordinary Congress on Doping, Hong Kong, March 31, 1999

The sole purpose of the FINA Extraordinary Congress on Doping was to improve the FINA doping rules. To this end, FINA appointed a working group of medical and legal personnel to rewrite the FINA doping rules.

According to Leonard (1999), the working group did an excellent job on the rewrite, and, combined with subsequent revisions, they provided a solid groundwork for taking the process even further. The current edition of the FINA Rule Book includes the new legislation.

Toward a Level Playing Field

During the past 30 years, the scourge of doping has reached a crisis point where the survival of our sport, as we once knew it, now lies in the balance. Many people are deeply concerned about the rampant doping in many countries. In wealthy populations, the use of anabolic steroids is rapidly becoming passé in favor of human growth hormone and EPO (erythropoietin). Although athletes are not yet being thoroughly tested for HGH and EPO, the growing consensus is that these powerful—and highly dangerous—drugs are now the prime choice of dishonest competitors and their handlers. In poorer countries, the less sophisticated drugs appear to be the more common choice. One can imagine the distracting effect on a clean swimmer about to start a race, wondering whether the ensuing competition will be against someone whose prowess is prompted by honest effort or by pill or needle.

The pioneers of our sport would have found it extremely difficult to understand the vastly changed character of competitive swimming as it exists today. They just would not have understood the biochemical manipulation of athletes and all the associated quarrels, debate, rhetoric, and legal loopholes that have beset the sport as a result. They wouldn't have begun to understand the problems associated with trying to keep the sport clean for those athletes who still believe in fair play, least of all the often unfounded suspicions that attend any athlete's pronounced and sudden improvement, whether by natural means or not. The sad fact is that today's sport is permeated with suspicion at almost any indication of sudden improvement, not to mention the odd occasion when swimmers glare at each other across the lanes at the end of a race and make personal comments that are more than innuendo.

There is a growing appreciation by the general swimming public that they have not been listening to the voices of crackpots, eccentrics,

The Future of Doping Control

In their article "The Future of Doping Control in Athletes," Birkeland and Hemmersbach (1999) state that sport cannot maintain its standards and reputation in society without methods to detect modern doping agents like peptide hormones. Such methods probably will rely on blood sample analysis. A secondary advantage of blood sampling is that DNA technology identifies the donor. However, sport organizations and society in general must answer legal and ethical questions before blood sampling becomes part of routine doping control.

When antidoping programs were first developed, anabolic steroids and stimulants were the most frequently used doping agents. These were easily detected in urine samples with gas chromatography and mass spectrometry. In recent years, many athletes have turned to other means to improve performance, including blood doping, erythropoietin, and human growth hormone, all of which are not easily detected in urine. Therefore, additional strategies must be developed, probably including the analysis of blood samples.

Nonautologic blood doping is an admixture of self and foreign red blood cells. Methods are available to detect this form of doping in blood tests.

Erythropoietin use can be detected by finding an elevated level of soluble transferrin receptor in serum. (Transferrin receptors are responsible for the transfer of iron and its transport protein into the cell.) Erythropoietin use also can be detected by an abnormal spectrum of erythropoietin isoforms, showing recombinant (synthetic) erythropoietin.

or people with a hidden self-serving agenda but to the voices of people, many of whom have given a lifetime of service to the sport and are deeply concerned. A great deal of attention focuses on methods of drug control, on how tests are conducted, even sham testing that denigrates the whole system, not to mention the fine line between target testing and random testing.

A new development prior to the start of the Sydney Olympics was the pretesting of national teams immediately prior to their departure to the Olympic Games.

In the last decade of the 20th century, the leaders of most national swimming federations were caught off guard by the sudden crisis caused by renewed drug cheating in swimming. However, for the first time in the history of swimming, coaches from around the world banded together to give international leadership to the sport. Memories of many talented swimmers, with world-beating potential, who were ousted by drugged East German swimmers continued to haunt and anger them. The World Swimming Coaches Association, the American Swimming Coaches Association, and the Australian Swimming Coaches Association led the way in rallying support for stringent penalties against cheating swimmers and their coaches, ranging from temporary suspension to outright expulsion.

Chapter 13

Looking Back, Looking Ahead

At the start of the 20th century, few swimmers did any training or had any idea what training meant. Nor had they any idea what constituted good stroke mechanics. A hundred years ago, the sport was in its infancy, and conditions were simple and primitive.

When Dick Cavill and Freddie Lane traveled from Australia to compete in the 1902 English championships—where they both broke the world record of 60-1/5 seconds for the 100-yard freestyle—their return sea voyage took over three months! Today's air travel takes a matter of hours. Modern swimmers constantly travel worldwide to compete on the World Cup circuit and other major meets. Their speed and technical efficiency would simply baffle the champions of yesteryear, and the intensity and extent of their training methods would be likewise unbelievable.

In many parts of the world, designing a beautiful and practical modern swimming stadium became an advanced art. Swimming pools designed for speed with wave-reducing lane markers significantly improved standards. The giant modern swimming stadiums—complete with thousands of comfortable theater-type seats banked tier upon tier high into the air; separate pools for diving and warm-ups; and all the

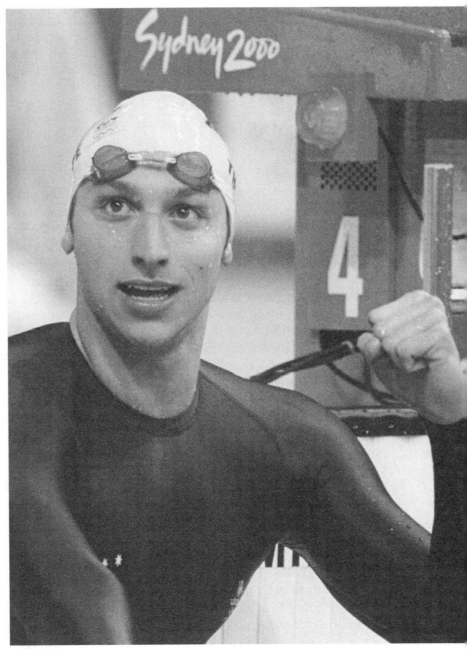

accoutrements of advanced technology, an environment totally dedicated to produce inspired swimming—would have left them awestruck. Rapid communications, television, and other mass media spread technical knowledge around the world and popularized swimming to the extent that by the mid-20th century countries with no previous record of success were producing world-class swimmers.

But contrasts do not end there. Today's male and female swimmers could easily beat the turn-of-the-century 100-yard freestyle record. In fact, even young children today are swimming faster than the champions of only a few decades ago!

Throughout the 20th century, psychological barriers continued to fall as swimmers gained in confidence and raised their levels of aspiration. Their coaches concentrated on reducing their swimmers' weaknesses rather than merely developing their strong points. Swimmers learned the importance of relaxation and concentration under pressure and were helped to this end through mastering various visualization techniques.

Supplementary land training was introduced early in the second decade of the 20th century by Yale coach Bob Kiphuth, who claimed that free exercises, pulley weights, and medicine ball work helped swimmers improve muscular strength and power quicker than equivalent time spent in the water. Kiphuth's exercises aimed to develop the big muscles of the trunk with special emphasis on the latissimus, pectoral, and teres major muscles as well as the long back muscles and those of the abdominal wall and legs. The exercises mainly were specific to swimming and involved the propulsive movements of arms and legs and the muscles that maintain good body position in the water. Workouts included rapid movements of the big muscle groups, which greatly stimulated circulation and respiration. To maintain swimmers' interest, Kiphuth varied the exercises. Kiphuth included stretching for the shoulder to enable an easy arm recovery and pelvic rolling, lower back flattening, and overhead arm stretching to achieve a streamlined body position in the racing dive and the glide following turns (Kiphuth 1942, 1950).

The successes of Olympic star Johnny Weissmuller in the 1920s were said to have motivated thousands to become swimmers, and the introduction of age-group swimming in the late 1940s saw an even greater increase in participants as the sport spread worldwide. The start of a formal age-group program in the United States led to similar programs in many other countries, causing a dramatic worldwide surge in participation. Competitive swimming annually attracted thousands of children generally too young to be recruited by other sports. Important incentives included fun, challenge, travel, athletic scholarships, and public recognition. Because of the youth of the participants, swimming became a family activity. Many parents gave valuable support by assisting with club administration.

Improvements in Stroke Mechanics

Imagine discovering a new swimming stroke faster than any other ever known. That's exactly what happened in Sydney, Australia, at the start of the 20th century. The crawl stroke, as it became known, was based on the powerful ocean stroke used by the Polynesians for over 1,000 years. The stroke quickly proved far superior to the retarding stop-start actions of the traditional English side-overarm stroke and the trudgen.

But the early crawl stroke was a difficult stroke to swim and bore little resemblance to the polished techniques of modern swimming. Few could use the stroke to complete the 100-yard racing distance. Poor arm-stroke mechanics and the lack of a breathing technique suited to the welter of rapidly spinning arms caused premature fatigue.

For the first half of the century, swimmers and coaches experimented with all kinds of different techniques. Only after decades of intense technical analysis and experimentation did the crawl stroke evolve into the facile and fluent racing stroke that is today a masterpiece of human ingenuity and adaptation. Even young children can swim it for miles, and they often do so as easily as they can walk.

And so it went also with the other strokes of swimming. Backstroke was first swum in competition in the form of an inverted breaststroke with a double overarm recovery. Around 1902, backstroke was first swum with an inverted reverse crawl action while using an inverted flutter kick. In 1912 the back crawl became an official event, and swimmers such as Harry Hebner and Adolph Kiefer were among the great pioneers of the stroke. Kiefer swam with a shallow straight-arm pull and a very low lateral straight-arm recovery.

The butterfly stroke was invented in 1933 by swimmer Henry Myers and subsequently improved by other outstanding swimmers. Originally the butterfly complied with the rules of breaststroke swimming as they existed. But in 1935, Jack Sieg, a University of Iowa swimmer, developed the skill of swimming on his side and beating his legs in unison similar to the action of a fish's tail.

[Sieg] tried the same leg action while swimming face down. Sieg synchronized his leg action with the butterfly arm action using two leg beats to each arm pull. Sieg showed the stroke's speed potential by swimming 100 yards in 60.2 seconds, but the dolphin kick was ruled illegal because the legs moved in the vertical plane (Armbruster 1942, p. 24).

Not until 1956 was the butterfly stroke allowed in Olympic competition, simply because the IOC refused to add new competitions to the Olympic program. Thus for 21 years, the world of swimming had a new stroke with great potential but with *no* event in which it could be legally swum—a sad reflection on FINA and the IOC.

For hundreds of years, breaststroke had been the traditional swimming stroke. When first swum in competition, the stroke was usually performed to a sedate and carefully timed rhythm of pull-kick-glide, using a wide arm-pull and kick. Today, of course, skilled swimmers try to keep their rhythm as continuous as possible.

For years, progress in breaststroke swimming was hindered by rulemakers ignorant of

Stroke Technicians and Innovators

Canadian coach Howard Firby (1924–1991) is regarded as one of the greatest stroke teachers ever. Like Counsilman, Firby was a World War II pilot. While Counsilman applied his knowledge of aerodynamics to the science of swimming, Firby applied his to the art of coaching. Firby coached Vancouver's Canadian Dolphins Club, where he produced a long line of great swimmers. As a full-time commercial artist, Firby used his drawing expertise to revolutionize the art of coaching swimming. His unique drawings and ability to illustrate the strokes from a variety of angles clearly showed how crawl swimmers and backstrokers naturally roll their bodies on the long axis, while butterfly and breaststroke swimmers rotate their bodies up and down on the short axis like airplanes taking off and landing. Firby illustrated his book *Howard Firby on Swimming* (1975) himself. The book became a classic and a collector's item. In the 1990s, Firby's writings and unique descriptive terminology have been frequently copied.

Walter Schlueter (1910–1987), U.S. Olympic and Pan American Games coach, was another great stroke technician and innovator of the 20th century. He originated the short-rest broken swim training method for learning the pace of a race. As coach of the Arizona Desert Rats in Phoenix (where he was popularly known as the "Pied Piper"), Schlueter developed many of the popular stroke drills still in vogue today. He later became technique coach to California's highly successful Mission Viejo team under coach Mark Schubert, where he is said to have done his finest work honing the strokes of dozens of America's best swimmers. Schubert said he had never seen a coach with so quick an eye for detecting the flaws in a swimmer's technique.

the basic nature of the stroke. Consequently the rules they set were easily circumvented by swimmers using deviations such as butterfly-breaststroke and prolonged underwater swimming. In order to prevent underwater swimming, the rules required that part of the head remain visible above the surface, but this stifled the natural flow of the stroke. Eventually progressive rules were made that permitted a swimmer to submerge for part of each stroke cycle, an improvement that resulted in a more fluent overall action.

Improvements in Training Methods

Most of the training methods used in swimming originated on the running track. At the turn of the century, track athletes were already experimenting with interval training, but this form of training was not adapted to competitive swimming until the mid-1950s. Before then, swimmers were preoccupied with perfecting techniques and had no idea how much stress the human body could endure.

In the 1960s, the work of coaches such as Forbes Carlile, Sherman Chavoor, Dr. James Counsilman, Peter Daland, Harry Gallagher, Don Gambril, George Haines, and Don Talbot showed how subtle variations of work-to-rest ratios could be applied to produce speed or endurance effects, or both. Training programs were set according to individual needs—training for short-, middle-, or long-distance events. These formats included ascending or descending series, reverse IMs, and endless other such permutations. As the century progressed, many other items were included in the typical seasonal training format, such as cyclic training, negative splits, pace training, and balancing distance per stroke with stroke rate.

Scientific Research

Scientific research assisted some programs despite a tendency to cause confusion through information overload and lack of simple communication. Most research, however, had little or no use in actual practice because its primary aim generally was not to help swimmers go faster. Where coach and scientist cooperated at training venue and competition site, however, more positive results were achieved; this approach gradually became common in several countries.

Most technical improvement resulted from practical coaches and talented athletes learning through trial and error. It became clear from past achievements that when the need was imperative, progress could not wait for the development of theory. More often than not, the search for theory was inspired by practical success.

Continuing improvements were implemented by coaches who were inspirational and innovative leaders and often natural practical psychologists. They encouraged their swimmers to believe that possibilities for improvement had no limits. This intrinsic quality—the striving by the human spirit to excel, to surpass previous achievements, and to seek new horizons—has been the most important factor in the remarkable progress of the sport.

After Counsilman's innovative work had revolutionized the technical approach to swimming and showed how science, *useful* science, could be beneficially applied, a spate of scientific papers followed from many sources. Novice coaches apparently were dazzled by the volume of scientific results and evidence placed before them. They didn't realize that most research is a progress report rather than a conclusion. Perhaps the classic quote of the 20th century on the subject of the information explosion came from a Canadian coach, Alain Lefebvre: "Years ago there was a desert of information. Now it is a jungle. The question is how to get through it" (Young 1990).

The Evolution of the Modern Swimming Stadium

The modern swimming stadium is a far cry from the first public bath halls and wash houses or even the first public swimming baths. Most pools were totally inadequate for competitive swimming, and some were so filthy and lacking in good hygiene that one observer commented that they were "better suited for ratting expeditions."

Top Swimmers of the 20th Century

The seven judges who compiled these rankings are all long-time students of the sport: Cecil Colwin; Peter Daland, historian and U.S. Olympic Coach; Buck Dawson, first director of the International Swimming Hall of Fame; Bob Duenkel, current director of the Hall; Bob Ingram, an editor of *Swimming World* and *Junior Swimmer* for 27 years; Craig Lord of *The London Times* and senior European correspondent of *Swimming World* and *Junior Swimmer*; and Dr. Phillip Whitten, editor in chief of *Swimming World* and *Junior Swimmer*. Among the selection criteria set by Dr. Phillip Whitten and used by the judges were

1. dominance;

2. number and quality of world records;

3. Olympic and other major titles, bearing in mind that the number of meets and the number of events at each meet has expanded greatly in the last few decades, and bearing in mind the impact of the two world wars, boycotts, and doping;

4. longevity in the sport;

5. longevity of the swimmer's records;

6. impact of the swimmer on the sport and on the wider society; and

7. other factors such as training conditions, overcoming various obstacles, etc.

Table 13.1   Top Male Swimmers of the 20th Century

Rank	Swimmer	Points	Rank	Swimmer	Points
1	Mark Spitz, USA (4)	172		Mike Barrowman, USA	60
2	Johnny Weissmuller, USA (3)	163	15	Arne Borg, SWE	56
3	Matt Biondi, USA	128	16	Mike Burton, USA	55
4	Murray Rose, AUS	123		Roland Mathes, GDR	55
5	Duke Kahanamoku, USA	116	18	Eric Rademacher, GER	44
6	Kieren Perkins, AUS	107	19	Ian Thorpe, AUS	41
7	Don Schollander, USA	103	20	Hironoshin Furuhashi, JPN	37
8	Alexander Popov, RUS	102	21	Tim Shaw, USA	34
9	Vladimir Salnikov, RUS	99	22	Tamas Darnyi, HUN	33
10	Adolph Kiefer, USA	86	23	Yoshiyuki Tsuruta, JPN	28
11	John Naber, USA	85	24	John Konrads, AUS	25
12	Michael Gross, GER	73		Denis Pankratov, RUS	25
13	Charlie Daniels, USA	60			

First-place votes are in parentheses.

Others receiving votes: Barney Kieran, AUS (24); Grant Hackett, AUS (24); Buster Crabbe, USA (23); John Hencken, USA (23); David Theile, AUS (19); Steve Clark, USA (17); Charlie Hickox, USA (16); Pablo Morales, USA (16); Andrew Charlton, AUS (12); Brian Goodell, USA (12); Alex Baumann, CAN (12); Fred Lane, AUS (12); Warren Kealoha, USA (11); David Wilkie, GBR (11); Gary Hall Sr., USA (11); Tom Jager, USA (11); Evgeni Sadovyi, RUS (11); Richard Cavill, AUS (11); Tedford Cann, USA (10); John Devitt, AUS (8); Jeff Rouse, USA (7); Jonty Skinner, RSA (7); Rowdy Gaines, USA (7); Walter Bathe, GER (6); Gunnar Larsson, SWE (5); Kevin Berry, AUS (4); George Hodgson, CAN (4); Jim Montgomery, USA (4); Henry Taylor, GBR (3); George Kojac, USA (2); Danyon Loader, NZ (1); Sir Frank Beaurepaire, AUS (1); Michael Wenden, AUS (1).

(continued)

(continued)

Table 13.2 Top Female Swimmers of the 20th Century

Rank	Swimmer	Points	Rank	Swimmer	Points
1	Dawn Fraser, AUS (4)	171	14	Sybil Bauer, USA	66
2	Janet Evans, USA	151	15	Penny Heyns, RSA	61
3	Tracy Caulkins, USA	145	16	Donna de Varona, USA (1)	58
4	Shane Gould, AUS	138	17	Ann Curtis, USA	51
5	Mary T. Meagher, USA (1)	137	18	Tracey Wickham, AUS	50
6	Debbie Meyer, USA	103	19	Karen Muir, RSA	43
7	Ragnhild Hveger, DEN (1)	91		Amy Van Dyken, USA	43
8	Shirley Babashoff, USA	80	21	Jenny Thompson, USA	41
9	Kristina Egerszegi, HUN	78	22	Hendrika Mastenbroek, NED	40
10	Claudia Kolb, USA	76	23	Galina Prozumenshikova, RUS	38
11	Helene Madison, USA	74	24	Fanny Durack, AUS	36
	Lorraine Crapp, AUS	74	25	Gertrude Ederle, USA	29
13	Ethelda Bleibtrey, USA	73			

First-place votes are in parentheses.

Others receiving votes: Sharon Stouder, USA (26); Martha Norelius, USA (25); Robyn Johnson, USA (24); Ada Kok, NED (24); Cor Kint, NED (22); Katherine Rawls, USA (20); Eleanor Holm, USA (17); Claudia Poll, CRC (16); Chris Von Saltza, USA (16); Franziska Van Almsick, GER (16); Melissa Belote, USA (14); Catie Ball, USA (13); Greta Andersen, DEN (11); Willemijntje den Ouden, NED (11); Cynthia Woodhead, USA (9); Karen Harup, DEN (9); Nancy Garapick, CAN (9); Summer Sanders, USA (9); Ilsa Konrads, AUS (9); Jan Henne, USA (7); Susie O'Neill, AUS (7); Katalin Szoke, HUN (7); Catherine Plewinski, FRA (3); Elaine Tanner, CAN (2); Maria Braun, NED (1).

The rankings of the top male and female swimmers of the 20th century first appeared in *Swimming World* and *Junior Swimmer*, December 1999, and are reprinted here by permission of the editor, Dr. Phillip Whitten, and the publisher, Sports Publications, Inc.

At the international level, it was a long time before competitions were held over standard distances. Some 28 years passed after the revival of the Olympic Games at Athens in 1896 before the Olympic swimming events were conducted in the 50-meter course we know today.

The modern swimming pool is designed for speed, with constant depth and overflow gutters to dampen turbulence. The early rope lane markers, supported by wooden or cork floats, gave way to continuous antiturbulence plastic lanes. For the first 60 years of the century, before electronic timing and judging systems, swimmers were timed by handheld watches and were subject to the vagaries of human error in timing and judging. Delays resulted at the end of each race while timekeepers and judges reported times and placings to the recorder, who then gave them to the official announcer.

Training Aids and Equipment

The introduction of the pace clock and the humble swimming goggle may well have been among the most important items of technical equipment introduced in the 20th century. The pace clock, for the first time, freed the coach from the need to carry a stopwatch. Swimmers were able to time themselves, and the use of the built-in time interval enabled each swimmer to work to a specific work-to-rest ratio. The swimming goggle protected the eyes from chemical irritation and contributed significantly to improved standards, as swimmers could increase distances swum in training.

The list of equipment and other training aids grew throughout the century. First, the wooden kickboard appeared (now replaced by a plastic one), then inflated tubes to raise the hips (now replaced by plastic pull buoys). Then came a whole array of new devices—big flippers, small flippers, racing flippers, monofins for dolphin kicking, fist gloves for improving feel of the water, resistance cords and surgical tubing of all types, friction-resistance exercisers such as the Exergenie, velocity meters, the isokinetic swim bench, Universal and Nautilus machines, pulley weight machines, free weights, and medicine balls.

Viewing windows that enabled underwater stroke analysis were at once a novelty and a valuable coaching aid. In the latter half of the 20th century, the former East German regime operated six swimming flumes, or specially designed tanks, in which tethered swimmers swam against a regulated flow of water to have their stroke techniques analyzed. In the 1990s, a whole new opportunity for learning opened up with the advent of the robotic underwater camcorder that can move around the pool while clearly recording everything swimmers do while racing.

Swimming Suits

Annette Kellermann, an early pioneer of women's swimming, complained bitterly about the voluminous water overcoats that threatened to drown early women swimmers. Then came the era of heavy woolen suits for both men and women, with shoulder straps and frontal skirts to preserve modesty. The evolution of the swimsuit was marked by sleeker and sleeker—and lighter—suits specially designed for racing. Gradually the skirts gave way to suits that were gradually, and even fashionably, scalloped away to reveal more and more of the lower torso, while remaining passably modest.

Natural Swimming Versus Equipment Swimming

Controversy arose with the advent of bizarre-looking, full-length body suits for racing, with long sleeves and leggings down to the ankles. The accompanying advertising encouraged swimmers to "swim out of your skin," then added the somewhat disconcerting comment that the "water won't even know you're there."

According to one manufacturer's advertising, the suit had gripper fabric to grip and feel the water and was designed to provide an optimal silhouette, to control the flow of water, and to reduce drag. In effect, the swimmer is encased in a racing shell that sloughs off water resistance, while the special grippers on the medial surfaces enable him or her to grip the water, much like using a swim paddle. In light of the apparent advantages afforded by the suit, it came as a surprise to many that on October 8, 1999, FINA ruled that the suits could be worn at international meets because FINA did not consider them a "device" (a device that aids swimming is clearly prohibited in their rules).

Many observers thought FINA had made a big mistake in approving the use of body suits, saying that the FINA bureau had ignored its own rule SW 10.7, namely that "No swimmer shall be permitted to use or *wear* any device that *may* aid his speed, buoyancy or endurance during a competition" (my italics) and, furthermore, that the "etc." in the examples of devices given therein, "gloves, flippers, fins, etc." should logically be taken to include *all* equipment or devices worn *around* the body.

The Natural Evolution Argument

The manufacturers argued that the long suits reflected progress into the space age and that such suits represented a natural progression from wool to cotton, silk, Nylon, and Lycra. This argument was not strictly accurate, as it overlooked the greatly increased amount of material used in the body suit.

Prior to the advent of the new suits, the amount of fabric used in manufacturing the traditional racing suit was limited to covering the torso within the confines of modesty, and it was reasonable and defensible to attempt to reduce drag in the choice and design of this limited amount of fabric. But many thought the swimsuit manufacturers had taken too much upon themselves in attempting to alter the concept of natural swimming by using high-tech fabrics that cover a large percentage of the body—that is, everything but the head, hands, and feet—and are designed to reduce natural skin-to-water drag and, as reported, perhaps even increase buoyancy and natural propulsive effort.

The suits were considered to be too expensive for what hitherto has been regarded as a popular sport within the reach of all. And, furthermore, even if they weren't performance enhancing and too expensive for the wider swimming population, more often than not, unless personally measured, they don't fit most swimmers properly. Contrary to the claims made by manufacturers, it's impossible to provide perfectly fitting suits for the wide variety of human body shapes, bearing in mind that shape is only partially related to height and weight. Poorly fitting suits purchased off the rack could actually prove to be performance retarding.

Interference With Natural Sensory Perception

Apart from legalistic arguments, there's no escaping the fact that wearing a full-length body suit changes the whole character of competitive swimming, from a natural sport, in which the human body interfaces directly with the water, into an implement sport, in which the body suit intervenes between the body and its natural contact with the water.

Under normal circumstances, human swimming movements are modified by sensory stimuli received from the skin, muscles, and joints, and these sensory impulses act at all times to guide muscular contractions. The sense of balance in the water and the pressure of the water against the sensory surfaces of the hands, legs, and other parts of the body must aid tremendously in regulating a smooth and effective stroke. The development of this sensitivity to the proprioceptive and afferent nerve currents is largely the difference between an expert and a mediocre swimmer.

Many swimmers and coaches protest that the body suit is an aberration and that if you can't feel the water on your body, then you're not really swimming. However, there may be one real plus to wearing a body suit. When worn as a practice suit, the suit in effect blinds the sensory nerve endings to the feel of the water. Thus, when the suit is taken off, the nerve endings overcompensate by becoming extra sensitive to the feel of the transient (moving) flow of the water on the limbs. When the swimmer reverts to swimming in a normal, traditional swimsuit, he or she finds that feel of the water has been almost miraculously enhanced.* The little exercise mentioned here seems to lend weight to the opinion that wearing a body suit is not a natural way of swimming because it takes away a swimmer's general feel of the water!

Speed Enhancing or Not

At this point, the jury is still out on whether the body suits actually aid performance, even when worn by great athletes receiving huge endorsement fees. So far, no tangible proof or guarantee exists that these new suits achieve anything new or spectacular in the way of increased performance that can definitely be attributed to scientific advances. Independently conducted, scientific hydrodynamic testing is needed to prove (1) that the suits really work and (2) that they are the worth the money. If the suits are proved to help performance, then surely they should be banned from competition. Conversely, if the suits do not improve performance, then what's the point of all the extra material and the extra financial cost to the swimmer?

At the Sydney Olympics, swimmers wore a variety of body suits made by different manufacturers. A few wore suits that covered the arms and legs entirely, while others reached to the knees only. Some swimmers still preferred to wear traditional style suits without sleeves or leggings. But even these suits are now made of a new material that appears to be water repellent and perhaps even designed to increase buoyancy.

---

* The physiological basis/explanation of these observations on increased skin sensitivity after wearing the body suit are based on scientific fact, especially in the work of Dr. A. Lee Dellon, in rehabilitating sensory perception after hand surgery. See chapter 6, page 116.

Some freestyle swimmers cut the sleeves off their body suits because they said the sleeves hampered the recovery of their arms from the water, a claim also made by some backstroke swimmers. Breaststroke swimmers preferred not to wear body suits at all, saying that the suits caused their legs to rise too high in the water, an awkward position that made an efficient kick difficult to perform. On the other hand, some butterfly swimmers felt an increase in buoyancy that they say made their strokes feel easier, if not faster. One of the world's greatest swimmers, Alexander Popov, Olympic 100-meter freestyle champion in 1992 and 1996, however, continued to swim in a standard pair of trunks, saying, "I like my own skin best," thus confirming the opinion of at least one hydrodynamacist. Time will tell whether the controversial suits will win general acceptance.

While these ultraexpensive suits may represent a bonanza in the form of increased profits for racing swim suit manufacturers, the cost of participation has increased by hundreds of dollars a year for thousands of swimmers around the world. This large expense instantly changes swimming from a popular sport, in which the price of equipment was minimal, into yet another high-tech sport. Swimming is now part of a general trend by manufacturers of most sports equipment to use the Olympic Games as a quadrennial showcase for their increasingly expensive products.

The FINA World Cup Circuit

As predicted in the first edition of this book (but not expected so soon), a new elite tier of swimmers has risen. Of these full-time professionals, two or three are already reputed to be millionaires—largely through corporate sponsorship and endorsement fees rather than through prize money at swim meets.

Between this group and the groups at the grass-roots levels, a large gap has been forged in the sport's organizational pyramid. In fact, the new structure closely resembles that of the former East German swimming regime, where the grass-roots level formed a convenient nursery from which the plums were picked for specialized training in centralized schools.

The FINA World Cup meets are held in different geographical zones—Europe, the Americas, the Far East (Asia), and Australia. The program of events is the same at each meet, and in recent years, all World Cup meets have been held in the short course, 25-meter course.

The amount of available prize money is minimal and not really comparable with that offered in most other professional sports. In fact, prize money amounts to far less than the average cost of traveling to meets on other continents. For example, a swimmer wanting to travel to every World Cup meet would probably face expenses totaling about $10,000.

The prize money and bonuses for breaking world records are still relatively small. The average prize money for winning a series is only $4,000. Many leading American swimmers say that they can earn more money staying at home and conducting clinics and camps than they can make on the World Cup circuit.

If a nation is hosting a World Cup meet, it is compulsory to send a minimum of four competitors to each of the other meets, and there is a financial penalty for failing to comply with this rule.

The big money is to be made through sponsorship by a big company, such as a communications firm or a swimwear manufacturer, or through bonuses from sponsors for breaking records. The earnings of most so-called professional swimmers are said to be merely at subsistence levels and cannot begin to be compared with those of millionaire basketball players, for example. The cream of the crop in swimming might make a few hundred thousand dollars, whereas an NFL football player recently signed a $55 million contract. Swimming is not in that league, and it probably never will be.

As far as FINA's annual World Cup circuit is concerned, spectator interest is not particularly keen, although there are notable exceptions at some venues. For example, the stands are always filled at Australian meets and sometimes also in Germany and Sweden, where TV coverage is particularly good and meets are often spectacularly staged, with attractive prizes offered. By contrast, in Hong Kong and Shanghai, World Cup meets are sparsely attended.

The overall impression is that interest in the World Cup seems to hold a greater attraction for European followers of the sport, probably because of the shorter traveling distances. Citing the meager prize money, the preponderance of 50-meter events, and that the meets are held in the short course, many people in North America and Australia question the need for a World Cup circuit. It appears the Australians attended mainly because they had a little extra funding available after staging the Olympics in their own country. On the other hand, although the leading swimmers do not always compete in the World Cup, some people believe that if the World Cup disappeared completely, media exposure and sponsorship for the sport would diminish.

Critics of the World Cup circuit are not slow to point out that not all the meets on the circuit can be said to be truly world-class meets, in which world-class swimmers compete against each other. Although some meets are billed as "World Cup Meets," the entry often consists mainly of local swimmers with few, if any, entries of world-class stature. Furthermore, world-class swimmers prefer long-course swimming, which they consider a better test of swimming ability, compared with short-course racing, which they view as more like gymnastic events consisting mainly of turning and a great deal of underwater kicking. These swimmers regard competing in the occasional short-course meet as a useful sharpening-up exercise in preparation for the more prestigious long-course competition. (A passing thought: even the Olympic Games would soon lose their luster if they were held every week. Rarity is what makes them so special.) According to Dennis Pursley, national team director of US Swimming, most of the 2000 Olympic swimming medalists were "very selective" in participating in the international competition circuit prior to the Olympics. Only 18 percent of the Olympic medalists had medaled in the Short Course World Championships (Pursley 2000).

A growing perception is that the World Cup circuit tends to attract a cluster of athletes, about a hundred in number, who tour the world like a little circus group. Although the federations fund their travel costs and the athletes get to keep whatever prize money they win, it is not unlikely that one day, the federations may not be able to afford this game, and they may have to ask themselves, "Is it really worth our while to spend thousands of dollars in travel on meets of inconsistent quality?"

The question also arises whether the lower levels of grass-roots competitors—the amateurs, for want of a better term—may not also be losing out somewhere along the line. Their subscription fees, in effect, are sponsoring the continuous overseas travel of a so-called elite tier of professionals.

History As It Happens

For at least two years before the Sydney Olympics, swimming enthusiasts around the world debated whether Kieren Perkins, the great Australian 1,500-meter swimmer and long-time world-record holder in the event, would successfully defend his Olympic title for the third time, this time against Grant Hackett, his countryman and a fast-rising star.

Finally, on September 23, 2000, the big day came. But there was one big snag. Although NBC, the official Olympic Games network, had broadcast a record 441 hours of Games coverage, not one second of it had been broadcast live. Because of the 15-hour time difference between Sydney and New York, NBC had decided to wait until prime time the following day before showing the hot-ticket sports, including swimming, track and field, and gymnastics.

But, as the exciting 1,500-meter duel between Kieren Perkins and Grant Hackett rapidly unfolded, a journalist on the *Sydney Morning Herald,* watching the event in the Olympic Stadium, made history by tapping out a live stroke-for-stroke report from his pool-side laptop direct to the Worldwide Web.

Sport Science and the Information Explosion

We have seen how the nature and character of competitive swimming changed over the last 100 years. But progress was slow and gradual, with the greatest improvements in swimming knowledge coming from imaginative coaches working with talented swimmers. Progressive

Professional Olympic Athletes

In the July 17, 2000, issue of the *Financial Post,* Paul Gaines reported that Mr. Pound, the vice president of the Olympic Committee, said that . . .

> . . . athletes indirectly get support. They don't have to pay their way to the Olympics or pay for their accommodation and food. And their federations get money for coaching and for qualifying competitions. They don't get money in their pocket, and I don't see that happening in the future.

However, already some of the world's leading swimmers and their agents are asking why the IOC should not share some of the billions of dollars of sponsorship and advertising money with the athletes, who have always performed at the Olympics free of charge. Times are changing, and it might not be long before the world's top swimmers and track athletes seek large fees for competing in the Olympics before billions of TV watchers around the world.

Even before the 2000 Sydney Olympics had ended, postmortems were being held in several countries, attempting to assess why their athletes had not done better than expected. Canada, a country that relies heavily on direct government funding, finished 24th overall in all sports, with only three gold medals. The immediate reaction, on national TV programs and in the printed media, was to call for more money to be thrown at the problem. The media compared funding and rewards offered in Canada (population 31 million) with those offered in Australia (population 19 million), a country that finished 4th overall in all sports with 15 gold medals (behind the United States, Russia, and China). Australia spent $280 million on Olympic sports compared to Canada's budget of $62 million (Deacon 2000).

All the political parties were immediately in favor of such a solution, especially with signs of a general election in the offing. However, others suggested that taxpayer money should no longer fund professional athletes without requesting that such funding be paid back eventually in the same manner as loans paid to university students learning a profession.

Another suggestion was that individual sports should be reorganized along the lines of the very popular sport of Formula One motor racing, with different multinational corporations instead of governments sponsoring their own national teams of leading professional swimmers, athletes, and gymnasts. Furthermore, an essential part of the contractual agreements between the parties concerned would include regular out-of-competition drug testing, with salary refund penalties and suspensions for those testing positive.

coaches accepted or rejected new ideas and methods and intuitively modified and developed them with the conscious goal of making swimmers faster. Thus, the world of swimming was offered an ever-expanding range and variety of inspiration for its future development.

Coaches and swimmers have been the greatest innovators and contributors to swimming knowledge, despite claims that may be made on behalf of formal scientific research. And it is important to note that when science did have an impact on swimming methods, the most significant contributions were made by scientists who were coaches, swimmers, or both. These intuitive coach-swimmer-scientists understood the needs of the sport, and thus their research was aimed at providing specific information essential to progress.

Increased quantities of scientific research and the information explosion were expected to intensify and accelerate the processes of change. Contrary to expectation, technical progress became trapped amid a great logjam of diverse junk information. The purpose and potential usefulness of this information was not always clear, but it was certainly not always aimed directly at solving practical problems.

Although science has acquired a rich heritage of ideas from coaches and swimmers from which to work, the specific problems that face the coaching practitioner have not always been fully recognized nor adequately addressed. And, although science has developed many ways of acquiring new knowledge and invented increasingly flexible and efficient instruments for using it, it is still far from being used in the most effective and practical manner.

For years, many swimming coaches have had an aversion to working with scientists, mainly because they perceived many scientists to be patronizing or condescending and generally more keen on acquiring academic credits than helping the sport to progress. Whether true or not, scientists often have been viewed as cold, emotionless people living in a remote world of their own.

While scientific literature must be clear on what the scientist means when describing a particular study, scientists may have built a barrier to understanding between themselves and laypersons by using esoteric scientific language instead of the simple everyday English that practical pool-deck coaches can readily understand and put into practice. These coaches prefer the easy-to-understand communication like that used by James "Doc" Counsilman in his heyday.

The Role of the Professional Swimming Coach

Although when it was inaugurated FINA had stipulated only who could and who could not compete as an amateur, the amateur laws were applied in such a way as to purposefully exclude paid coaches and instructors from official positions within the governing bodies of swimming. In fact, until recently, paid coaches were often treated in many countries as pariahs and lesser breeds without the law.

Professional coaches, as they were quaintly termed, were excluded from the governing bodies of the sport and from official coaching assignments with international teams, despite that much of the progress in the sport and the develop-

ment of leading swimmers was attributable to their efforts. It is to the credit of many of these coaches that throughout their careers, they often traveled to national and international meets at their own expense to assist their swimmers.

The history of swimming has shown time and again that the leadership of capable and inspired coaches, the people who possess the real practical knowledge of the sport, can help a country consistently produce elite swimming teams despite a mediocre or even self-serving administration at the helm. In some countries, discrimination against career coaches must have had a retarding effect on the development of swimming, especially when compared with the giant strides made in the United States, where career coaches were officially recognized as a welcome and integral part of the swimming organization. Particularly significant examples of these advances were the appointments of leading coaches Ray Essick and Don Talbot to the positions of executive director of United States Swimming, Inc., and executive director of Canadian Swimming, respectively.

The career of Terry Gathercole (1935-2001) is further evidence that the future of swimming depends on the coaches. Gathercole rose through the ranks, first as an Olympic swimmer and prolific world-record breaker then later as a successful national coach, president of the Australian Swim Coaches Association, and president of Australian Swimming during the 2000 Olympics. In addition to many other notable contributions to the sport, Gathercole played a leading role in the fight against performance enhancing drugs. Gathercole's career proved that professional coaches can make great contributions at all levels, suggesting that FINA's existing legislation should be changed to include professionals in every facet of its organization, not just as token members of certain commissions.

In any country, the future starts with the coaches—not administrators or scientists, but inspirational coaches working with talented swimmers. This is the first essential: the future starts on the pool deck. Only afterward come the administrators who plan the programs and the possible assistance that science can provide. The future of swimming depends on the coaches.

Appendix

A 400-Year Bibliography of the Historical Development of the Swimming Strokes

Grateful thanks are extended to Thomas K. Cureton, a pioneer of scientific research in swimming, for giving me permission to use as a framework for this bibliography the footnotes originally contained in Cureton's classic *How to Teach Swimming and Diving*, volumes 1 and 2 (1934).

These materials were then arranged in chronological order, and other titles were added. The materials shown in brackets following a number of the entries are the results of further research—including additions, verifications, revisions, and annotations—conducted by me in the records of the Library of Congress; the British Library Catalogue; the National Union Catalog; the Rare Books Division of the National Library of Canada; the Library of Parliament, Canada; and the North Carolina Collection of the University of North Carolina at Chapel Hill.

The bracketed notes point out items of information that might prove interesting to sport historians and scientists (and anyone else interested in swimming). Also, note that the bibliography covers the 400 years from 1531 to 1930. To be sure, modern definitive texts on swimming appear after these years, but the bibliography is meant to provide historical rather than state-of-the-art resources.

Elyot, Sir Thomas. 1531. *The boke named the governour.* London: Thomas Berthelet.

[This book on the training of gentlemen included a section on swimming. The popularity of the volume is evidenced in a string of subsequent editions in 1537, 1544, 1546, 1553, 1557, 1565, and 1580. Near the end of the 19th century, scholars began a set of reprints—1880, 1906, 1962, and 1970—with translations into German and Italian in the 1930s.]

Wynman, Nicolaus. 1538. *Colymbetes, sive de arte natandi dialogus et festivus et iucundus lectu.* (Dutch Copy). Ingolstadt, Bavaria: H. Steiner.

[Wynman's very early text experienced many reincarnations, including three Latin reprints in 1623, 1638, and 1644, and even an 1889 extract in a German publication titled *Heidelberg*.]

Magnus, Olaus. 1555. *Historia de gentibus septentrionalibus.* Rome: Magno Gotho.

[Magnus's *History of the Nordic Folk* told of swimming practices in Scandinavia among many other things. Magnus, Archbishop of Upsala, went into voluntary exile in Rome after the Swedish Reformation. In 1546 he represented Pope Paul III to the Council of Trent. The first complete Italian translation of his history appeared in 1565, some seven years after his death.]

Dygbeio (Digby), Everardo (Everard). 1587. *De arte natandi libri duo, quorum prior regulas ipsius artis, posterior vero praxin demonstrationemque continet.* London: (s.n.).

[Digby's *De arte natandi* was translated into French from Latin by Melchisedec Thevenot under the title *L'Art de nager* a century later. An interesting bibliography of Everard Digby, MA, fellow of St. John's college, Cambridge, can be found in the *Dictionary of National Bibliography*. He was a different person from Sir Everard Digby, who was not born until 1578 and was executed for his infamous role in Guy Fawkes' Gunpowder Plot of 1606. However, Mr. Digby, the swimming author, got into much trouble through his eccentric conduct, which included his "habit of blowing a hunting horn and hallooing in the college, most unseemly conduct for a clergyman" (Thomas 1904, page 177).]

Middleton, Christopher. 1595. *A short introduction for to learne to swimme gathered out of Master Digbie's booke of the art of swimming (trans.).* Translated into English for the better instruction of those who understand not the Latine tongue. With wooden cuts of persons swimming. London: (s.n.).

Percey, William. 1658. *The compleat swimmer, or The art of swimming.* London: J.C. for H. Fletcher. About 90 pages with preface.

Thevenot, Melchisedec. 1696. *L'art de nager.* Paris: T. Moette, rue de la Boucherie. Avec privilege du Roi.

[This was a direct translation of the Latin book *De Arte Natandi* (Digby 1587) and was published four years after Thevenot's death in 1692. In 1699, the book was translated back into English by an unknown translator and published in London by Dan Brown, D. Midurnter, T. Leigh, and Robert Knaplock. (Digby's work was translated three times, twice into English and once into French. The French edition was translated into Spanish and Italian.) Contrary to general opinion, Thevenot was not the orginator of the work but merely the translator.]

M'Iver, J. 1764. *The art of swimming, with advice for bathing* (Thevenot, trans.). London: John Lever.

Bernardi, de Oronzio. 1797. *Vollstandiger Lehrbegriff der Schwimmkunst, auf neue Versuche uber die spezifische Schwere des menschlichen Korpers gegrundet.* Weimar: (s.n.).

Muths, Guts. 1798. *Kleines lehrbuch der Schwimmkunst zum selbstunterrichte (Manual for self-instruction in the art of swimming).* Weimar: (s.n.).

Strutt, Joseph. 1801. *Glig-gamena angel-deod, or The sports and pastimes of the people of England.* London: White.

[This oft-quoted work gives only one page (p. 66) on swimming. This work outlasted three authors, five publishers, and the whole 19th century, with 10 editions spanning 1801 to 1903. Of course it dealt with more than swimming, but the swimming discussion provides some insight into this ancient island nation's perception of swimming.]

Bernardi, de Oronzio. 1807. *Arte de Nadar Compendiada del que Escribio en Italiano.* Madrid: (s.n.).

Frost, J. 1816. *Scientific swimming. A series of practical illustrations on an original and progressive plan, by which the art of swimming may be readily attained, with every advantage of power in the water; accompanied with 12 copper-plate engravings, comprising 26 appropriate figures.* London: Darton, Harvey and Darton, Gracechurch Street. 8 volumes, 12 plates.

[Frost, many years teacher of the art of swimming at Nottingham, sought to approach swimming scientifically. His *Scientific Swimming* was described as a series of scientific instructions that facilitated the attainment of the art of swimming.]

Frost, J. 1818. *The art of swimming.* New York: P.W. Gallaudet.

Clias, Peter H. 1825. *An elementary course of gymnastic exercises and a new and complete treatise on the art of swimming with the report made to the medical faculty of Paris on the subject* (4th ed.). London: Sherwood, Gilbert and Piper.

Mason, James, and Payne, A.M. 1839 and 1840. *Prize essays of the national, now the British society on the art of swimming.* London: (s.n.).

Howard, Sydney (pseudonym). 1849. *The science of swimming as taught and practiced in civilized and savage countries.* New York: Fowler and Wells.

Richardson, B.C. 1857. *Instructions on the art of swimming.* London: James Ridgeway.

Forrest, George (pseudonym for Rev. John George Wood). 1858. *A handbook of swimming and skating.* London: Routledge and Sons.

Forrest, George (pseudonym for Rev. John George Wood). 1863. *A handbook of swimming.* London: Routledge and Sons.

Steedman, Charles. 1867. *A manual of swimming, including bathing, plunging, diving, floating, scientific swimming, training, drowning and rescuing.* Melbourne, Australia: Henry Tolman Dwight.

[The illustrations are good and mark a distinct advance in the method of delineating the correct movements in swimming.]

Steedman, C. 1873. *A manual of swimming, including bathing, plunging, diving, floating, scientific swimming, training, drowning and rescuing* (English edition). London: Lockwood and Co.

[Steedman's book was first published in Melbourne in 1867 and again in London in 1873. Full references are given below, including the names of collections where copies of this rare book are housed.]

Steedman, Charles. *A manual of swimming, including bathing, plunging, diving, floating, scientific swimming, training, drowning and rescuing* by Charles Steedman

Melbourne: H.T. Dwight, 1867. vxi, 270 p. front, plates 16".

257687A. I. Swimming
NYPL December 14, 1924.
NS 0883329 NN RPB
New York Public Library
Brown University, Providence
The State Library of Victoria, Melbourne, Australia

Steedman, Charles. *A manual of swimming, including bathing, plunging, diving, floating, scientific swimming and training, with a chapter on drowning, rescuing, and resuscitation.* London, Lockwood and Co., 1873. xvl, 270 p. IX pl. (incl. front.) 16.5cm. 1. swimming

NS 0883330 CtY   PU   MdBP
Yale University
University of Pennsylvania
Peabody Institute, Baltimore
Henning Library, ISHOF, Fort Lauderdale

Thomas, Ralph. 1868. *A Bibliographical List of Works on Swimming.* London: s.n.

[Only 125 copies printed. This publication is of invaluable service to any student of swimming lore.]

Beadle. 1869. *Dime guide to swimming.* New York: (s.n.).

Wilson, William. 1876. *The swimming instructor.* Glasgow: (s.n.).

Wilson, W. 1883. *The swimming instructor.* London: Horace Cox, The Field Office 346, Strand, London.

[Wilson was also author of *Swimming and Diving, and How to Save Life, The Bather's Manual,* etc. Swimming as a science, training, the teaching of swimming, and the rescue of life from drowning are the principal matters dealt with. The records and championship performances to date are included.]

Andrews, Capt. W.D. 1889. *Swimming and Life-saving.* Toronto: s.n.

[Much of the work was written after blindness had come upon the author and is largely of an autobiographical character. 136 pages. Numerous illustrations.]

Sinclair, A., and Henry, W. 1893. *Swimming.* London: Longmans, Green.

[By 1912, this volume was in its seventh impression, with four new editions and three reprinted editions. Sinclair and Henry were honorary secretaries of the Royal Life-Saving Society, and Henry was one of the founders of FINA, the international governing body of swimming.]

Riley, Tom. 1903. *Swimming.* New York: (s.n.).

Douglas, W.G. 1903. *How to swim.* New York: American Sports.

Sterrett, James H. 1903. *How to swim.* New York: American Sports.

[As well as covering the by-now standard topics of swimming with various strokes, diving, and floating, Sterrett's book contains a chapter on modern life-saving and one for women and girl swimmers. Sterrett was known as "The Father of American Swimming."]

Thomas, Ralph. 1904. *Swimming.* London: Sampson Low, Marston.

[The nonspecific title hides the uniqueness of Thomas's book—a bibliography of swimming books in English, German, French, and other European languages. The book also discusses swimming and resuscitation and includes a history of swimming and biographies of persons important in the field. Under the pseudonym of Hamst Olphar, Thomas also wrote *The Handbook of Fictitious Names* (1868).]

Fountain, P. 1904. *The swimming powers of animals.* London: (s.n.).

Daniels, C.M., Johnson, H., and Sinclair, A. 1907. *How to swim and save life* (Spalding's Athletic Library, no. 21). London: British Sports.

Sinclair, Archibald. 1909. *Swimming.* London: Routledge and Son.

Sachs, Frank. 1912. *The complete swimmer.* London: Methuen.

Daniels, C.M. 1919. *Speed swimming.* New York: American Sports.

Handley, Louis de B. 1920. *Swimming and watermanship.* New York: MacMillan.

Bachrach, William. 1924. *The outline of swimming.* Chicago: Author.

Handley, Louis de B. 1927. *Swimming for women.* New York: American Sports.

Sullivan, Frank. 1927. *The science of swimming.* New York: American Sports.

Cureton, T.K. 1929. *Outline of Pageant. Evolution of swimming.* Philadelphia: P. Blakison's Son.

Handley, Louis de B., and Howcroft, W.J. 1929. *Crawl-stroke swimming.* London: E.J. Larby.

Weissmuller, John, and Bush, Clarence. 1930. *Swimming the American crawl.* Boston: Houghton.

References

Absaliamov, T. 1984. Controlling the training of top level swimmers. In J.L. Cramer (ed.) *How to develop Olympic level swimmers*. Finland: International Sports Media.

Anderson, O. 1999. A critical survey of the latest thinking about the ins and outs of training. *Peak Performance* 126:1-4.

Armbruster, D.A. 1942. *Competitive swimming and diving*. St. Louis: Mosby.

Bachrach, W. 1924. *The outline of swimming*. Chicago: Author.

Baldwin, K.M. 2000. Research in the exercise sciences: Where do we go from here? *Journal of Applied Physiology* 88:332-336.

Banister, E.W., Morton, R.H., and Clarke, J.R. 1997. Clinical dose-response effects of exercise. In J.M. Steinacker and S.A. Ward (eds.) *The physiology and pathophysiology of exercise tolerance*. New York: Plenum. 297-309.

Bannister, R. 1955. *First four minutes*. London: Putnam.

Bell's Life in Sydney and Sporting Review. 1846. First swimming race in Australia 3:32.

Bergen, P. 1985. Executing a year training program. In T. Welsh (ed.) *American Swimming Coaches Association world clinic yearbook 1985*. Fort Lauderdale, FL: American Swimming Coaches Association. 195-204.

Berger, J. 1982. Die zyklische Gestaltung des Trainings prozesses unter besonderer Beruecksichtigung der Periodiserung des Trainingsjahres (The cyclic establishment of the training process in special consideration of a cyclic subdivision of the training year). *Medizin und Sport* 22:282-286.

Birkeland, Kare I., and Hemmersbach, Peter. 1999. The future of doping control in athletes. *Sports Medicine* 28(1):25-33.

Bompa, T.O. 1983. *Theory and methodology of training: The key to athletic performance*. Dubuque, IA: Kendall Hunt.

Bompa, T.O. 1985. *Theory and methodology of training*. Dubuque, IA: Kendall Hunt.

Brasch, T. 1970. *How did sports begin? A look at the origins of man at play*. New York: David McKay.

Brouha, L. 1945. Speficite de l'entrainement au travail musculaire. *Revue Canadienne Biologie* 4:144.

Byrd, W. 1928. *A journey to the Land of Eden and other papers*. Edited by Mark van Doren. New York: Macy-Masius.

Capelli, C., Pendergast, D.R., and Termin, B. 1998. Energetics of swimming at maximal speeds in humans. *European Journal of Applied Physiology* 78:385-393.

Carlile, F. 1956. The use of post-exercise heart rate counts in the prediction of maximum performance and assessing the progress of the swimmer in training. Report of the World Congress on Physical Education. Melbourne: W.J. Barr. 102-104.

Carlile, F. 1963. *Forbes Carlile on swimming*. London: Pelham.

Carlile, F. 1971. Where do we go from here? American Swimming Coaches Association's first world clinic, Montreal, 1971. *Swimming Technique* 8(4):98-100, 119.

Carlile, F. 1976. The philosophy of speed through endurance. *International Swimmer* 12(7):7-12.

Chapman, R.F., Stray-Gundersen, J., and Levine, B.J. 1998. Individual variation in response to altitude training. *Journal of Applied Physiology* 85:1448-1456.

Chavoor, S. 1967. Sherm Chavoor speaks out on training. *Swimming World* 8(10):5.

Clarkson, A. 1990. *Lanes of gold*. Sydney, Australia: Lester-Townsend.

Collins, G. 1934. *The new magic of swimming*. London: William Heinemann.

Colwin, C. 1969. *Cecil Colwin on swimming*. London: Pelham Books.

Colwin, C. 1984a. Fluid dynamics: Vortex circulation in swimming propulsion. In T.F. Welsh (ed.) *American Swimming Coaches Association world clinic yearbook 1984*. Fort Lauderdale, FL: American Swimming Coaches Association. 38-46.

Colwin, C. 1984b. Kinetic streamlining and the phenomenon of prolonged momentum in the crawl swimming stroke. *Swim Canada* 11(1):12-15.

Colwin, C. 1984c. Tethered swimming. *Swim Canada* 11(3):20-21.

Colwin, C. 1985a. Essential fluid dynamics of swimming propulsion. *American Swimming Coaches Association Magazine* 4:22-27.

Colwin, C. 1985b. Practical application of flow analysis as a coaching tool. *American Swimming Coaches Association Magazine* 5:5-8.

Colwin, C. 1987. Coaching the "feel of the water." In T.F. Welsh (ed.), *American Swimming Coaches Association world clinic yearbook 1987*. Fort Lauderdale, FL: American Swimming Coaches Association. 87-98.

Colwin, C. 1992. *Swimming into the 21st century*. Champaign, IL: Leisure Press.

Colwin, C. 1998. The wave action breaststroke. *Swimming Technique* 25(2):12.

Colwin, C. 1999. *Swimming dynamics: Winning techniques and strategies.* Chicago: Contemporary Press.

Colwin, C. 2000. From Red Army Team to Californian golden boy. *Swimnews* 27(7):20-21.

Costill, D.I. 1987. Building a better mousetrap. *Swimming Technique* 24(3):34-36.

Cottrell, L. (ed.). 1960. *The concise encyclopaedia of archaeology.* London: Hutchinson.

Counsilman, J.E. 1967. Problems: "Dirt" in interval training. *Swimming Technique* 3(4):112-113.

Counsilman, J.E. 1968. *The science of swimming.* Englewood Cliffs, NJ: Prentice Hall.

Counsilman, J.E. 1969. The role of sculling movements in the arm pull. *Swimming World* 10(12):6-7, 43.

Counsilman, J.E. 1971. The application of Bernoulli's principle to human propulsion in water. In L. Lewillie and J.P. Clarys (eds.) *Proceedings: First international symposium on biomechanics in swimming, waterpolo and diving.* Bruxelles: Universite Libre de Bruxelles Laboratoire de l'effort. 59-71.

Counsilman, J.E. 1975. Hypoxic and other methods of training evaluated. *Swimming Technique* 12(1):19-26.

Counsilman, J.E. 1977. *Competitive swimming manual.* Bloomington, IN: Author.

Counsilman, J.E. 1979. Biokinetics, the ultimate exercise. In R.M. Ousley (ed.) *American Swimming Coaches Association world clinic yearbook 1979.* Fort Lauderdale, FL: American Swimming Coaches Association. 29-36.

Counsilman, J.E. 1980. Hand acceleration patterns in swimming strokes. Big Ten Biomechanics Conference. Bloomington: Indiana University.

Counsilman, J.E. 1986. Strength training, sprint training and speed assisted training for sprint swimmers. In *Swim 86 yearbook.* Brisbane: Australian Swimming, Inc. and Australian Swimming Coaches Association. 1-16.

Counsilman, J.E., and Brown, R.M. 1970. The role of lift in propelling the swimmer. In J.M. Cooper (ed.) *Selected topics on biomechanics: Proceedings of the C.I.C. symposium on biomechanics.* Chicago: Athletic Institute. 179-188.

Counsilman, B.E., and Counsilman, J.E. 1991. The residual effects of training. *Journal of Swimming Research* 7:5-12.

Counsilman, B.E., and Counsilman, J.E. 1993. Problems with the physiological classification of endurance loads. *American Swimming Magazine* Dec.-Jan.:4-20.

Counsilman, J.E., and Wasilak, J.M. 1982. The importance of hand speed and acceleration in swimming the crawl stroke. *Swimming Technique* 18(1):22-26.

Coyle, E.F., Hemmert, M.K., and Coggan, A.R. 1986. Effects of detraining on cardiovascular responses to exercise: Role of blood volume. *Journal of Applied Physiology* 60:95-99.

Craig, A.B., and Pendergast, D.R. 1979. Relationships of stroke rate, distance per stroke, and velocity in competitive swimming. *Medicine and Science in Sports* 11:278-283.

Craig, A.B., Skeehan, P.L., Pawelczyk, J.A., and Boomer, W.L. 1985. Velocity, stroke rate and distance per stroke during elite swimming competition. *Medicine and Science in Sports and Exercise* 17(6):625-634.

Cureton, T.K. 1934. *How to teach swimming and diving* (vol. 1). New York: Association Press.

Curry, I. 1975. Stroke length, stroke frequency and performance. *Swimming Technique* 12(3):88, 91.

Cutmore, M. 1985. *The pocket watch handbook.* New York: Arco Publishing.

Daland, P. 1984. Personal communication. June 12.

Dalton, D. 1899. *How to swim.* New York: G.P. Putnam.

Daniels, C.M. 1919. *Speed swimming.* New York: American Sports.

Dawson B. 1987. *Weissmuller to Spitz.* Fort Lauderdale, FL: International Swimming Hall of Fame.

Deacon, J. 2000. Upsets down under. *Maclean's* 113(40):35.

Dellon, A., Curtis, R., and Edgerton, M. 1974. Re-education of sensation in the hand after nerve surgery and repair. *Plastic Reconstruction Surgery* 53:297-305.

Digby [Dygbeio], E. 1587. *De arte natandi libri duo, quorum prior regulas ipsius artis, posterior vero praxin demonstrationemque continet.* London: (s.n.).

East, D.E. 1970. Swimming: An analysis of stroke frequency, stroke length and performance. *New Zealand Journal of Health, Physical Education and Recreation* 3:6-27.

Ellis, W. 1831. *Hawaiian surfing in the 1820s: Polynesian researches* (volume 3). London: Fisher, Son, and Jackson.

Elyot, T. 1531. *The boke named the governour.* London: Thomas Berthelet.

Faith, H.D. 1912. The over-arm side stroke. Quoted in *The complete swimmer* by F. Sachs. London: Metheun. 140.

Finney, B., and Houston, J.D. 1996. *Surfing: A history of the ancient Hawaiian sport.* Rohnert Park, CA: Pomegranate Artbooks.

Firby, H. 1975. *Howard Firby on swimming.* London: Pelham Books.

Forsyth, S. 1939. *A quick way to better swimming.* (s.l): Sundial Press.

Foster, C. 1998. Monitoring training in athletes with reference to overtraining syndrome. *Medical Science in Sports and Exercise* 30:1164-1168.

Fricker, P.A., McDonald, W.A., Gleeson, M.G., Flanagan, A., Pyne, D.B., and Clancy, R.L. 2000. A clinical snapshot: Do elite swimmers experience more upper respiratory illness than non-athletes? *Journal of Clinical Exercise Physiology* 2(3):155-158.

Gaines, P. 2000. Olympic advertising going for the gold. *Financial Post* July 17.

Gerschler, Rosskamm, and Reindell. 1964. Das Interval Training [Interval Training]. Congress on running. Duisberg: Deutscher Leichtatletiek. March.

Gleeson, M., McDonald, W.A., Pyne, D.B., Cripps, A.W., and Francis, J.L. et al. 1999. Salivary IgA levels and infection risk in elite swimmers. *Medicine and Science in Sports and Exercise* 31:67-73.

Handley, L. de B. 1918. *Swimming and watermanship*. New York: Macmillan.

Handley, L. de B. 1928. *Swimming for women*. New York: American Sports Publishing.

Harre, D. 1982. *Principles of sports training*. Berlin: Sport Verlag. 58.

Hay, J.G., Guimaraes, A.C.S., and Grimston, S.K. 1983. A quantitative look at swimming biomechanics. *Swimming Technique* 20(2):11-17.

Helmstaedt, K. 2000a. German drug trials: The story told in court defies imagination. *Swimnews* No. 259, 27(6):20.

Helmstaedt, K. 2000b. Two men who distorted the course of sporting history. *Swimnews* No. 259, 27(6):21.

Holmer, G. 1972. Development in running. *Track Technique* 50:1584-1585.

Hooper, S.L., Mackinnon, L.T., Howard, A., Gordon, R.D., and Bachmann A.W. 1995. Markers for monitoring overtraining and recovery. *Medicine and Science in Sports and Exercise* 27:106-112.

Horwill, F. 1982. Gerschler: The innovator. He was 30 years ahead of his time. *Athletics Weekly* 36(38):33.

Howard, S. 1849. *The science of swimming as taught and practiced in civilized and savage countries*. New York: (s.n.).

Jochums, D. 1982. The dissident's view of distance freestyle training. In R.M. Ousley (ed.) *American Swimming Coaches Association world clinic yearbook 1982*. Fort Lauderdale, FL: American Swimming Coaches Association. 139-151.

Johnson, R. 1978. Organizing a season program. In R.M. Ousley (ed.) *American Swimming Coaches Association world clinic yearbook 1978*. Fort Lauderdale, FL: American Swimming Coaches Association. 129-143.

Johnson, R. 1982. Tempo awareness training. In R.M. Ousley (ed.) *American Swimming Coaches Association world clinic yearbook 1982*. Fort Lauderdale, FL: American Swimming Coaches Association. 39-54.

Karamcheti, K. 1966. *Principles of ideal-fluid aerodynamics*. New York: Wiley.

Keast, D., and Morton, A.R. 1992. Long-term exercise and immune function. In R.R. Watson and M. Eisinger (eds.) *Exercise and disease*. Boca Raton: CRC Press.

Kellermann, A. 1918. *How to swim*. New York: George H. Doran Company.

Kindermann, W. 1978. Regeneration und trainings Prozess in den Ausdauer—Sportarten aus medizinischer Sicht. *Leistungsport* 4:354-357.

King, James. 1778. First description of surfing. (unedited log). In J.C. Beaglehole (ed.) The voyage of the Resolution and the Discovery, 1776-1780, vols. 1 and 2, 1967. Cambridge: Hakluyt Society.

Kiphuth, R.J.H. 1942. *Swimming*. New York: Barnes.

Kiphuth, R.J.H. 1950. *How to be fit*. London: Nicholas Kaye.

Kiphuth, R.J.H., and Burke, H.M. 1951. *Basic swimming*. New Haven, CT: Yale University Press.

Koshkin, I. 1985. The system and methods of Vladimir Salnikov's development, 1980-1984. In T. Welsh (ed.) *American Swimming Coaches Association world clinic yearbook 1983*. Fort Lauderdale, FL: American Swimming Coaches Association. 5-8.

Lanchester, F.W. 1907. *Aerodynamics: Constituting the first volume of a complete work on aerial flight*. London: Constable.

Lavoie, J-M., and Montpetit, R.R. 1986. Applied physiology of swimming. *Sports Medicine* 3:165-189.

Leonard, J. 1999. FINA Extraordinary Congress on Doping, Hong Kong, March 31. *ASCA Newsletter* 2000(8):22.

Leonard, J. 2000. FINA's third visit to China. *ASCA Newsletter* 2000(2):2, 4.

Lighthill, M.J. 1973. On the Weis-Fogh mechanism of lift generation. *Journal of Fluid Dynamics* 60(pt. 1):1-17.

Lilienthal, O. 1889. *Der Vogelflug als Grundlage der Fliegekunst*. Berlin: Ouldenberg.

London, J. 1911. *The cruise of the Snark*. New York: Macmillan.

London Times. 1844. The "Flying Gull" and "Tobacco." April 22.

London Times. 1847. Report on Whitechapel baths. May 12.

London Times. 1899. Championship of 1899. September 18.

London Times. 1899. County of London long-distance professional championship. September 18.

London Times. 1899. Ulph annual challenge cup competition for amateurs held in the sea at Yarmouth. September 18.

Long Beach Daily Telegram. 1922. Duke Kahanamoku, famous swimming champion gives exhibition on surf board. July 31.

Maglischo, E.W. 1982. *Swimming faster*. Palo Alto, CA: Mayfield.

Maglischo, E.W. 1983. A three-dimensional cinematographical analysis of competitive swimming strokes. In R.M. Ousley (ed.) *American Swimming Coaches Association world clinic yearbook 1983*. Fort Lauderdale, FL: American Swimming Coaches Association. 1-14.

Maglischo, E.W. 1985. Constructing workouts with energy system considerations. In T. Welsh (ed.) *American Swimming Coaches Association world clinic yearbook 1985.* Fort Lauderdale, FL: American Swimming Coaches Association. 56-62.

Magnus, O. 1555. *Historia de gentibus septentrionalibus Romae* [History of the northern people] Rome: Magno Gotho.

Mason, B.R., and Fowlie, J.K. 1997. Competition analysis for high performance swimming. Australian-Ocean Swimming Professionals Convention. Broadbeach, QLD. 65-70.

Matveyev, L. 1981. *Fundamentals of sports training.* Moscow: Progress Publishers. 55-58.

Morehouse, L.E., and Miller, A.T. 1971. *Physiology of exercise.* St. Louis: Mosby.

Mujika, I., Busso, T., Lacoste, L., Barale, F., and Geyssant, A. et al. 1996. Modeled responses to training and taper in competitive swimmers. *Medical Science in Sports and Exercise* 28:251-258.

Murray, J., and Karpovich, P.V. 1956. *Weight training in athletics.* Englewood Cliffs, NJ: Prentice Hall. 141-144.

Muths, G. 1798. *Kleines lehrbuch der Schwimmkunst zum selbstunterrichte (Manual for self-instruction in the art of swimming).* Weimar: (s.n.).

Nemecek, S. 2000. Who were the first Americans? *Scientific American* 283(3):80-87.

Neuburger, D. 2001. Personal communication. March 15.

Oppenheim, F. 1970. *The history of swimming.* North Hollywood, CA: Swimming World.

Pai, Y-C., Hay, J.G., and Wilson, B.D. 1984. Stroking techniques of elite swimmers. *Journal of Sports Science* 2(3):225-239.

Pursley, D. 2000. Observations from the 2000 Olympic games. *American Swimmer* 2000(6):16.

Pyne, D.B. 1998. Performance and physiological changes in elite swimmers during altitude training. *Coaching and Sports Science Journal* 3:42-48.

Pyne, D.B. 1999a. Endurance training: How much huff and puff? *Swimming Technique* 35:16-20.

Pyne, D.B. 1999b. Physiological testing of elite Australian swimmers. In F. Fu (ed.) *Aquatic Sports Medicine in the New Century.* Hong Kong: Association of Sports Medicine and Sports Science. 109-126.

Pyne, D.B., and Gleeson, M. 1998. Effects of intensive exercise training on immunity in athletes. *International Journal of Sports Medicine* 19:S183-S194.

Pyne, D.B., Gleeson, M., McDonald, W.A., Perry, C., Clancy, R.L., and Fricker, P.A. 2000. Training strategies to maintain immunocompetence in athletes. *International Journal of Sports Medicine* 21(suppl. 1):S51-S60.

Pyne, D.B., Maw, G.J., and Goldsmith, W.M. 2000. Protocols for the physiological assessment of swimmers. In C. Gore (ed.) *Physiological tests for the elite athlete.* Champaign, IL: Human Kinetics. 372-382.

Pyne, D.B., McDonald, W.A., Gleeson, M., Flanagan, A., Clancy, R.L., and Fricker, P.A. 2001. Mucosal immunity, illness and competition performance in swimmers. *Medicine and Science in Sports and Exercise* 33(3):348-353.

Pyne, D.B., and Telford, R.D. 1988. Classification of training sessions. *Excel* 5(2):9-12.

Pyne, D.B., and Telford, R.D. 1989. Classification of swimming training sessions by blood lactate and heart rate responses. *American Swimming Coaches Association Magazine* February:7-9.

Rajki, B. 1956. *The technique of competitive swimming.* Budapest: Covina.

Reichel, A. 1897. Swimming in two movements and its superiority over the Pfuel and D'Argy methods with three. In Myers *Konversations-lexicon* (vol. 15). Leipzig: (s.n.). 16.

Rowbottom, D.G., Keast, D., and Morton, A.R. 1998. Monitoring and preventing of overreaching and overtraining in endurance athletes. In R.B. Kreider, A.C. Fry, and M.L. O'Toole (eds.) *Overtraining in sport.* Champaign, IL: Human Kinetics. 47-66.

Rushall, B.S. 2000. *Swimming's hall of shame.* Spring Valley, CA: Sports Science Associates.

Sachs, F. 1912. *The complete swimmer.* London: Methuen.

Schleihauf, R.E. 1974. A biomechanical analysis of freestyle. *Swimming Technique* 11(3):89-96.

Schleihauf, R.E. 1977. Swimming propulsion: A hydrodynamic analysis. In R. Ousley (ed.) *American Swimming Coaches Association world clinic yearbook 1977.* Fort Lauderdale, FL: American Swimming Coaches Association. 49-81.

Schleihauf, R.E. 1979. A hydrodynamic analysis of swimming propulsion. In J. Terauds and E.W. Bedingfield (eds.) *International symposium of biomechanics. Volume 8: Swimming III.* Baltimore: University Park Press. 70-109.

Schleusing, G., Rebentisch, J., and Schippel, C. 1964. Research on endurance and interval training. *Medicine and sport* (books I and II). Berlin: Verlag Volk and Gesundheit, V.E.B.

Selye, H. 1956. *The stress of life.* New York: McGraw-Hill.

Sharp, R.L., and Costill, D.L. 1989. Shaving a little time. *Swimming Technique* 26(3):10-13.

Sinclair, A., and Henry, W. 1885. *The badminton book of swimming.* London: Longmans, Green, and Co.

Sinclair, A., and Henry, W. 1903. *Swimming.* London: Longmans, Green, and Co.

Stampfl, F. 1955. *Franz Stampfl on running.* London: Jenkins.

Steedman, C. 1867. *A manual of swimming, including bathing, plunging, diving, floating, scientific swimming, training, drowning and rescuing.* Melbourne, Australia: (s.n.).

Steinacker, J.M., Lormes, W., Lehmann, M., and Alternburg, D. 1998. Training of rowers before world championships. *Medical Science and Sports Medicine* 30:1158-1163.

Stix, G., and Fischetti, M. 2000. Game theory. *Scientific American* 11(3):6-9.

Stray-Gundersen, J., and Levine, B.D. 1999. "Living high and training low" can improve sea level performance in endurance athletes. *British Journal of Sports Medicine* 33:150-151.

Sullivan, F.J. 1928. *The science of swimming*. New York: American Sports Publishing.

Thevenot, M. 1696. *L'art de nager*. Paris: T. Moette.

Thevenot, M. 1699. *The art of swimming*. London: D. Brown, D. Midurnter, T. Leigh, and R. Knaplock.

Thierry, N. 1972. The world scene. *Swimming Technique* 9(1):2-3, 10.

Thierry, N. 1981. The breaststroke saga. *AIPS Bulletin* 10(1):2.

Thomas, R. 1904. *Swimming*. London: Sampson Low, Marston.

Thornton, N. 1979. The Berkeley program. In R.M. Ousley (ed.) *American Swimming Coaches Association world clinic yearbook 1979*. Fort Lauderdale, FL: American Swimming Coaches Association. 1-15.

Thornton, N. 1987. A few thoughts on training, or a closer look at the path U.S. swimming seems to be currently following. *American Swimming Coaches Association Magazine* Jan.-Feb.:11-14.

Thrum, T.G. (ed.). 1896. Hawaiian surf riding. From *Thrums Hawaiian annual 1896*. 106-113.

Troup, J.P. 1999. The physiology and biomechanics of competitive swimming. *Aquatic Sports Injuries and Rehabilitation* 18:267-285.

Twain, M. 1872. *Roughing it*. Chicago: F.G. Gilman.

Ungerechts, B.E. 1983. A comparison of the movements of the rear parts of dolphins and butterfly-swimmers. In A.P. Hollander, P. Huijing, and G. de Groot (eds.) *International series on sports sciences. Volume 14: Biomechanics and medicine in swimming*. Champaign, IL: Human Kinetics. 215-221.

van Aaken, E., and Berben, D. 1971. Speed through endurance. *Swimming Technique* January: 108-113.

van Dam, C.P. 1988. In wind and water. *The Sciences* 28(1):37-39.

Vogel, S. 1998. *Cats' paws and catapults: Mechanical worlds of nature and people*. New York: Norton. 224-225.

Watson, R.P. 1873. Memoirs. *Encyclopedia Britannica* 22:772.

Weis-Fogh, T. 1973. Quick estimates of flight fitness in hovering animals including novel mechanisms for lift propulsion. *Journal of Experimental Biology* 59(1):169-230.

Weissmuller, J. 1930. *Swimming the American crawl*. London: Putnam.

Wilson, W. 1883. *The swimming instructor*. London: Horace.

Wynman, N. 1538. *Colymbetes, sive de arte natandi et festivus et iucundus lectu* (Dutch Copy). Ingolstadt, Bavaria: (s.n.).

Young, P. 1990. Education is the key. *Swim Canada* 17(1):6-7.

Index

About the Author

Cecil M. Colwin is a legend among swimming coaches. He has had a distinguished international coaching career in which he developed Olympic medalists, world-record holders, and national champions. Colwin is also acknowledged as one of the swimming world's most influential coach educators and historians. His indelible mark on the sport spans from pioneering swim training in South Africa to coaching South African national and international competitors. Colwin is acknowledged as a dynamic lecture-room and pool-deck clinician with a gift for vivid imagery and the ability to analyze and simplify complex techniques.

A former national technical director of Canadian swimming, Colwin was instrumental in researching, designing, and implementing Canadian Swimming's National Plan for the 1976 Montreal Olympic Games as well as the Canadian National Apprenticeship Program for training coaches in all sports. Colwin has also designed and conducted coaching certification courses for Level III coaches in the United States and Australia. In 1985 and 1986, he received the American Swimming Coaches Association's (ASCA) certificate of excellence for outstanding coaching achievement in the

United States. In 1993 he was inducted into the International Swimming Hall of Fame. In 2002 Colwin was awarded the Paragon Award.

Colwin has authored hundreds of articles, papers, and books on competitive swimming, and he continues to serve as a consultant to administrators, coaches, and swimmers worldwide. He is a regular contributor to several swimming magazines, including *Swimnews, Swimming World, Swimming Technique,* and *The American Swimmer.* Known as one of the swimming world's most inspirational lecturers, he has addressed the World Swimming Coaches' Conference on several occasions and has given hundreds of lectures and clinic presentations worldwide. Since 1995 Colwin has served as a member of the World Swimming Coaches' Association's Anti-Doping Committee. He is also the founder of Cecil Colwin's International Swim Camps, a leading stroke clinic and training experience for swimmers and coaches from many countries.

Colwin and his wife, Margaret, live in Ottawa, Ontario, where he pursues a variety of interests including portrait painting, videography, cartooning, reading, weight training, and listening to music.